Sentencing Handbook

Related titles available from Law Society Publishing include:

Criminal Defence: Good Practice in the Criminal Courts (3rd Edition)
Roger Ede and Anthony Edwards

Criminal Procedure Rules: A Guide to the Key Changes (2nd Edition)
Andrew Keogh

Fixed Fees in the Criminal Courts: A Survival Guide
Anthony Edwards

Prison Law: A Practical Guide
Margaret Obi

Road Traffic Offences Handbook
Kenneth Carr, Frank Lockhart and Patrick Musters

All books from Law Society Publishing can be ordered from all good bookshops or direct (telephone 0870 850 1422, email **lawsociety@prolog.uk.com** or visit our online shop at **www.lawsociety.org.uk/bookshop**).

SENTENCING HANDBOOK

Sentencing Guidelines in the Criminal Courts

Anthony Edwards and Joanne Savage

The Law Society

Whilst all reasonable care has been taken in the preparation of this
publication, neither the publisher nor the authors can accept any
responsibility for any loss occasioned to any person acting or
refraining from action as a result of relying upon its contents.

The views expressed in this publication should be taken as those of
the authors only unless it is specifically indicated that the Law Society
has given its endorsement.

The authors have asserted the right under the Copyright, Designs
and Patents Act 1988, to be identified as authors of this work.

Crown copyright material in the Appendices is reproduced with the
permission of the Controller of Her Majesty's Stationery Office.

Published in 2009 by the Law Society
113 Chancery Lane, London WC2A 1PL

Typeset by J&L Composition Ltd, Scarborough, North Yorkshire
Printed by TJ International, Padstow, Cornwall

FSC
Mixed Sources
Product group from well-managed
forests and other controlled sources
Cert no. SGS-COC-2482
www.fsc.org
© 1996 Forest Stewardship Council

The paper used for the text pages of this book is FSC certified.
FSC (The Forest Stewardship Council) is an international network
to promote responsible management of the world's forests.

Contents

CONTENTS

Preface

Sentencing is a critical stage of the criminal justice process. It cannot be left until the last moment and full preparations must be made even when a not guilty plea has been entered, lest there be a conviction.

This book is intended as a practical manual for the preparation of cases for sentencing whether as litigator, in terms of collecting relevant evidence, or as an advocate who will present the case at court. Prosecutors must be as aware as defence lawyers of sentencing issues so that courts are made aware of the powers that the Crown considers to be relevant or appropriate, and apply the often complex law correctly.

Discussion of the forthcoming changes to the sentencing framework for youths (under 18) is provided at **Chapter 8**.

The Magistrates' Court Sentencing Guidelines published by the Sentencing Guidelines Council in 2008, which are an essential tool for practitioners operating in that jurisdiction, are reproduced in full at **Appendix 16** and on the accompanying CD.

To restrict the length of this guide and for ease of use it applies only to offences committed on or after 5 April 2005. For earlier offences reference should be made to more detailed texts.

Introduction

Since 2004, the Sentencing Guidelines Council (SGC) has, through a series of guidelines relating to sentencing principles and specific offences, provided guidance, the aim of which is to encourage greater consistency in relation to the approach to sentencing. The SGC has identified (and reinforced through inclusion in all of its guidelines) the following eight stages in the sentencing process, the approach to which it describes as fluid and requiring the structured exercise of discretion:

(a) identification of dangerous offenders;
(b) identification of the appropriate starting point;
(c) consideration of relevant aggravating factors, both general and those specific to the type of offence;
(d) consideration of mitigating factors and personal (offender) mitigation;
(e) application of a reduction for a guilty plea;
(f) consideration of ancillary orders;
(g) application of the totality principle; and
(h) giving of reasons.

As a result of the steady stream of legislation relating to sentencing, it is more important than ever for advocates to be prepared for sentencing from the outset of a case. Representations as to the allocation of an either-way offence have to be made at an early stage and require consideration of aspects of sentencing such as the powers available to the courts on conviction and starting point recommendations in offence guidelines. A new allocation procedure, which for the first time will allow a court to know of an offender's criminal history before deciding where an either-way offence should be tried and will also permit an offender to seek an indication of sentence prior to deciding whether to elect trial in the Crown Court, is likely to be introduced in 2009. Generally, prosecution and defence advocates have a duty to assist the court in relation to the law and guidelines relevant to sentencing in a particular case (see comments of the Lord Chief Justice in *R* v. *Cain* [2006] EWCA Crim 3233). On conviction, advocates must be ready to influence the court as regards thresholds for particular sentences and the possible content of any sentence under consideration. These duties will arise, from 6 April 2009, under Part 37.10(3) of the Criminal Procedure Rules.

For practitioners, the approach to sentencing may be summarised in this way:

1. Consider the relevant sentencing law: that is, sentencing powers including maximum penalties, obligatory sentences and relevant guidelines.
2. Against that background, consider the seriousness of the particular offence looking at the starting points as well as aggravating and mitigating factors that may influence movement within the appropriate sentencing range.
3. Consider the personal circumstances of the defendant.
4. Identify the appropriate level of any guilty plea discount using the SGC guideline.
5. Identify potential outcomes, in terms of both primary and secondary sentencing.

A form for the collection of relevant information appears at **Appendix 4**.

Advocates should be particularly aware of the date of each offence as sentencing powers vary substantially depending on the date the offence was committed (*R* v. *Bao* [2008] Crim LR 234), and the age of the offender, particularly at the threshold for being sentenced as a youth or an adult. In addition, guidelines published by the SGC relating to principles of sentencing, individual offences and allocation decisions are effective from dates specified in the forewords. Once a guideline has been issued it will be the exception to refer to earlier case law (*R* v. *Tongue and Doyle* [2007] EWCA Crim 561), although the Court of Appeal will continue to give guidance which may be of relevance as regards offences.

A list of definitive guidelines and other guidance published by the SGC appears at **Appendix 1**. The Magistrates' Court Sentencing Guidelines (MCSG) inclusive of the first two updates (issued July and December 2008) appears at **Appendix 16**. All guidelines are available at **www.sentencing-guidelines. gov.uk** and as at 5 January 2009 on the CD attached.

The law is stated as at January 2009 in relation to offences committed on or after 5 April 2005 when the Criminal Justice Act 2003 sentencing framework was implemented. The text includes references to provisions likely to be brought into force in 2009 highlighted by a line above and below.

Table of cases

Table of statutes

Table of statutory instruments

Abbreviations

ABD	application for benefit deduction
AEO	attachment of earnings order
ASBO	anti-social behaviour order
CA 2003	Courts Act 2003
CDA 1998	Crime and Disorder Act 1998
CEMA 1979	Customs and Excise Management Act 1979
CJA 1977	Criminal Justice Act 1977
CJA 1982	Criminal Justice Act 1982
CJA 1988	Criminal Justice Act 1988
CJA 1991	Criminal Justice Act 1991
CJA 2003	Criminal Justice Act 2003
CJIA 2008	Criminal Justice and Immigration Act 2008
CYPA 1933	Children and Young Persons Act 1933
CYPA 1963	Children and Young Persons Act 1963
DTO	detention and training order
ISSP	Intensive Supervision and Surveillance Programme
MCA 1980	Magistrates' Courts Act 1980
MCSG	Magistrates' Court Sentencing Guidelines
MHA 1983	Mental Health Act 1983
MHA 2007	Mental Health Act 2007
PCC(S)A 2000	Powers of Criminal Courts (Sentencing) Act 2000
POCA 2002	Proceeds of Crime Act 2002
RTOA 1988	Road Traffic Offenders Act 1988
RWI	relevant weekly income
SGC	Sentencing Guidelines Council
SOA 2003	Sexual Offences Act 2003
TIC	[offence] taken into consideration
UKBA 2007	UK Borders Act 2007

CHAPTER 1

Purposes and principles of sentencing

1.1 STATUTORY PURPOSES

For offenders aged 18 and over, Parliament has provided that there are five purposes (or objectives) of sentencing to which courts must have regard:

(a) the punishment of offenders,
(b) the reduction of crime (including its reduction by deterrence),
(c) the reform and rehabilitation of offenders,
(d) the protection of the public, and
(e) the making of reparation by offenders to persons affected by their offences.
Criminal Justice Act (CJA) 2003, s.142(1)

No priority is given to any one objective and they will all be relevant but to a greater or lesser extent depending on the individual circumstances of the case.

In relation to 'the reduction of crime' the Sentencing Guidelines Council (SGC) has given particular guidance in the context of the prevalence of an offence (see guideline *Overarching Principles: Seriousness*, paras.1.38–1.39). It states that the seriousness of an individual case should be judged on its own dimensions of harm and culpability, while making it clear that it is legitimate for the overall approach to sentencing levels for particular offences to be guided by their cumulative effect (collective social harm). However, the guideline continues by advising that it would be wrong to further penalise individual offenders by increasing sentence length for committing an individual offence of that type.

In relation to prevalence issues, exceptional local or national circumstances may arise that should influence sentencing levels in the light of the harm being caused to a community or more widely. The guideline stresses the importance of evidence from an external source being available to justify a finding that a particular crime is prevalent in an area and that there is a compelling need to treat the offence more seriously (*R v. Oosthuizen* [2005] EWCA Crim 1978). See the note to the Magistrates' Court Sentencing Guidelines (MCSG), 'Sentencing for possession of a weapon – knife crime',

1

issued on 1 August 2008 (**Appendix 17**) following the decision in *R* v. *Povey; R* v. *Bleazard and others* [2008] EWCA Crim 1261 which considered the prevalence of knife crime.

1.2 SENTENCING THRESHOLDS

For defence lawyers the prescribed sentencing thresholds provide an opportunity for significant advocacy to persuade a court to the best outcome for the client. Such representations will always need to be realistic and made with knowledge of the relevant law and available sentences.

Custody

The court must not pass a custodial sentence unless it is of the opinion that the offence, or the combination of the offence and one or more offences associated with it, was so serious that neither a fine alone nor a community sentence can be justified for the offence (CJA 2003, s.152(2)).

In applying the threshold test, the SGC has provided guidance in relation to factors relevant to the test and the approach to imposing custodial sentences. Emphasis is placed on the intention of the threshold test being to reserve prison as a punishment for the most serious offences. The SGC has reiterated in its guidelines that passing the custody threshold does *not* mean that a custodial sentence should be deemed inevitable. It is still possible to avoid custody, where the offender's personal mitigation so merits, or where there is a suitable intervention in the community that provides sufficient restriction (by way of punishment) while addressing the rehabilitation of the offender so as to prevent future crime.

The approach to the imposition of a custodial sentence under the CJA 2003 legislative framework is:

1. Has the custody threshold been passed?
2. If it has, is it unavoidable that a custodial sentence be imposed?
3. If so, can that sentence be suspended?
   (Sentencers should be confident that they would have imposed a custodial sentence if the power to suspend had not been available.)
4. If sentence cannot be suspended, impose a sentence that takes immediate effect for a term commensurate with the seriousness of the offence.

Community sentences

A court must not pass a community sentence on an offender unless it is of the opinion that the offence, or the combination of the offence and one or more offences associated with it, was serious enough to warrant such a sentence (CJA 2003, s.148(1)).

Additionally, the threshold for a community sentence can be crossed even though the seriousness criterion is not met, where an offender aged 16 or over has, on three or more previous occasions since reaching that age, received sentences consisting only of a fine. In such cases a community sentence may be imposed (if it is in the interests of justice) despite the fact that the seriousness of the current offence (and others associated with it) might not warrant such a sentence (CJA 2003, s.151).

The SGC has made it clear that sentencers should consider all of the disposals available (within or below the threshold passed) at the time of sentence before reaching the provisional decision to impose a community sentence, so that, even where the threshold for a community sentence has been passed, a financial penalty or discharge may still be an appropriate penalty.

In addition CJA 2003, s.148(5) provides that:

The fact that by virtue of any provision of this section –

(a)   a community sentence may be passed in relation to an offence; or
(b)   particular restrictions on liberty may be imposed by a community order or youth rehabilitation order,

does not require a court to pass such a sentence or to impose those restrictions.

Having assessed the seriousness of an individual offence, sentencers must consult the sentencing guidelines for an offence of that type for guidance on the factors that are likely to indicate whether a custodial sentence or other disposal is most likely to be appropriate.

Factors vary too widely between offences for it to be possible to identify exactly where the thresholds for community and custodial sentences lie. However, SGC guidelines for individual offences provide more detailed guidance on what features within that offence point to a custodial or non-custodial sentence, and also deal with issues such as sentence length, the appropriate level of and requirements for inclusion in a community sentence, and the use of appropriate ancillary orders.

1.3   PRINCIPLES OF SENTENCING

Factual basis – *Newton* hearing

A defendant must be sentenced on the defence version of the facts unless the Crown proves a more serious version to the criminal standard (the *Newton* principle (*R* v. *Newton* (1983) 77 Cr App R(S) 13)).

The defence is required to indicate to the Crown that its version of events is not accepted. This should be done in writing (*R* v. *Tolera* [1999] 1 Cr App R 29). These rules apply from 6 April 2009, repeated in Part 37.10(5) of the Criminal Procedure Rules. It is often desirable that there is a written basis of plea. This may move a case to a lower sentencing bracket within a guideline and may be particularly important if there is a later breach of any sentence imposed.

Specimen charges

A defendant can only be sentenced for offences of which he has been convicted or which he has asked to be taken into consideration (TIC) (*R* v. *Kidd; R* v. *Canavan; R* v. *Shaw* [1998] 1 Cr App R 79; *R* v. *Tovey; R* v. *Smith* [2005] EWCA Crim 530 and on TICs see **p.9**).

A court may not, for sentencing purposes, treat charges that fall into those categories as being specimens of others, though the number of proved or admitted offences and the length of time over which they are committed will affect the sentence imposed. In addition, if the Crown chooses not to charge a particular offence the offender cannot be sentenced as if convicted of it (*R* v. *Davies* [1998] 1 Cr App R(S) 380; *R* v. *O'Callaghan* [2005] EWCA Crim 317) though the court may take account of all facts relevant to the offence charged (*R* v. *Nottingham Crown Court* ex p *DPP* [1996] 1 Cr App R(S) 283). See, for instance, the definitive guideline, *Assaults and Other Offences Against the Person*, p.4, para.11.

Expectation

Courts must observe the 'expectation' principle.

If a court gives an indication of the sentence it intends to impose, it must not later increase that penalty if the defendant has done all that was asked of him and has committed no new offence. Otherwise, the defendant would be left with a justified sense of grievance. This principle underlies the law on deferred sentences (see **Chapter 4**) but is of general application.

The basic principle is stated in *R* v. *Gillam* (1980) 2 Cr App R(S) 267. This applies not only to express statements of intention (which an advocate should seek in appropriate cases) but also to implied statements, so that where a court orders reports but wishes to hold open the option of imprisonment, it must expressly do so; similarly where a magistrates' court wishes to maintain the right to commit to the Crown Court for sentence (*R* v. *Feltham JJ* ex p *Rees* [2001] Crim LR 47; cf. *R* v. *Southampton Magistrates' Court* ex p *Sansome* [1998] Crim LR 595). In *R* v. *Isleworth Crown Court* ex p *Irvin* (1992) 156 JP 453, a magistrates' court, having accepted jurisdiction, ordered reports and on their receipt a differently constituted tribunal committed the case for sentence. The Divisional Court held that the expectation principle bound the

Crown Court as well as the lower court. The most extreme application of the principle has been in *R* v. *Chamberlain* [1995] Crim LR 85 where reports were ordered, holding open all options, but at a later hearing a specific report was requested without such a proviso. That was held to limit the sentencing court, on receipt of a positive report, to a non-custodial sentence.

An indication that the court considers that it has sufficient sentencing power brings the principle into operation and prevents a committal for sentence (*R* v. *Nottingham Magistrates' Court* ex p *Davidson* [2000] 1 Cr App R(S) 167). It is therefore particularly important that advocates take a careful note of the words used by the court when adjourning a case or ordering reports and in the magistrates' court it is good practice to confirm the indication to the court in writing. A letter to a client confirming the words may provide the necessary evidence (*R* v. *Sheffield Magistrates' Court* ex p *Ojo* (2000) 164 JPN 665).

There are two exceptions to the expectation principle:

1. **Dangerous offenders**
   Care is needed in giving an indication of a particular outcome that would avoid the proper imposition of a sentence upon a dangerous offender (*R* v. *Kulah* [2007] EWCA Crim 1701; *R* v. *Seddon* [2007] EWCA Crim 3022 and see the SGC's *Dangerous Offenders: Guide for Sentencers and Practitioners*).

2. **Attorney General references**
   Notwithstanding a clear indication given by a Crown Court judge, it does not (unless the Crown was party to it) bind the Attorney General who may apply for leave to appeal on the basis that a sentence is unduly lenient in cases where that remedy is available (see **Appendix 2**). A defendant is deemed to know of the Attorney General's rights when receiving the initial indication. It is important that lawyers advise carefully in such cases.

Totality

Courts must observe the 'totality' principle (recognised by CJA 2003, s.166(3); see the MCSG, p.147 (**Appendix 16, pp.318–319**).

When imposing sentences for more than one offence it is necessary for the court to apply this principle before finalising the sentence to ensure that the totality of the sentence imposed is not disproportionate to the overall seriousness of the offences proved and taken into consideration. If an adjustment is required this can be done either by lessening each sentence that is consecutive to another or by making some part of the sentence concurrent.

Proportionality

Courts must observe the 'proportionality' principle.

Where more than one defendant is to be sentenced, the court must ensure that the sentence of one defendant is not disproportionate to that of another (*R* v. *Church* (1985) 7 Cr App R(S) 370; *R* v. *Sykes* (1980) 2 Cr App R(S) 173; *R* v. *Frankson* [1996] 2 Cr App R(S) 366). However, the principle is not applied by the courts when, because one defendant appears to have been treated leniently, another can have no real feeling of injustice (*R* v. *Tate* [2006] EWCA Crim 2373).

1.4   OVERARCHING PRINCIPLES

The SGC is able to give general guidance as regards sentencing, and has published 'overarching' principles guidelines dealing with:

- seriousness;
- domestic violence; and
- assaults on children.

Seriousness

The seriousness guideline (see *Overarching Principles: Seriousness*) has been drawn upon in later parts of this book with regard to assessing seriousness and the thresholds for sentences.

Domestic violence

See the MCSG, p.177 (**Appendix 16, pp.348–9**).

As there is no offence of 'domestic violence' and conduct that might amount to domestic violence could fall within a variety of statutory provisions, the guideline *Overarching Principles: Domestic Violence* uses the CPS definition:

> Any incident of threatening behaviour, violence or abuse [psychological, physical, sexual, financial, emotional] between adults who are or have been intimate partners or family members, regardless of gender or sexuality.

The guideline emphasises that an offence is no less serious because it is committed in a domestic context, and may be *more* serious as aggravating factors are more likely to be present. It reviews the aggravating and mitigating factors of particular relevance to offences committed in a domestic context, and considers the extent to which the wishes of the victim (as regards a relationship being permitted to continue), and when the interests of any children, may be taken into account.

Where the custody threshold is only just crossed, the guideline suggests that a court will wish to consider whether a suspended sentence or community order, including a requirement to attend a domestic violence programme may be a better option. This will only be appropriate when there is no pattern of abuse, the offender seriously intends to reform and there is a real prospect of rehabilitation.

Assaults on children

The guideline *Overarching Principles: Assaults on Children and Cruelty to a Child* sets out additional relevant principles for sentencing where the victim of an assault was a child. In such cases, this guideline should be read in conjunction with the Assaults and Other Offences Against the Person guideline which details starting points and sentencing ranges for various offences of violence.

The guideline provides that a presumption that an assault against a child will normally merit a custodial sentence will not always be appropriate, but in all cases where the offender is an adult, the fact that the victim is a child is likely to aggravate the seriousness of the offence.

Aggravating and mitigating circumstances are identified, including issues surrounding chastisement where the charge is assault occasioning actual bodily harm. Other relevant factors are considered as regards the position where the sentence may have an adverse effect upon the victim or where the offender has sole or primary caring responsibilities.

Out of court disposal

See the MCSG, p.188 (informal warnings, cannabis warnings and simple cautions) (**Appendix 16, p.359**), p.189 (conditional cautions) (**Appendix 16, p.359**) and p.189 (penalty notices) (**Appendix 16, p.360**).

Many criminal offences are now dealt with by out of court disposals. The Magistrates' Court Sentencing Guidelines confirm the following principles:

- The existence of such an outcome does not increase the seriousness of a later offence and must not be treated as an aggravating factor.
- The existence of such an outcome may influence the court's assessment of the offender's suitability for a particular sentence.

Sentencing for offences aggravated by issues relating to race, religion, disability or sexual orientation

For magistrates' court cases see the MCSG, p.178 (**Appendix 16, p.349**).

Sections 29–32 of the Crime and Disorder Act (CDA) 1998 make increased maximum sentences available for certain racially or religiously aggravated offences. A court should not treat an offence as racially or religiously aggravated if there was an acquittal for the aggravated offence (*R* v. *McGillivray* [2005] EWCA Crim 604) or if the Crown could have charged such an offence and chose not to do so (*R* v. *O'Callaghan* [2005] EWCA Crim 317). When sentencing any offence where such aggravation is found to be present, the following approach should be followed. This applies both to the specific racially or religiously aggravated offences under CDA 1998 and to offences that are regarded as aggravated under CJA 2003, s.145 or s.146.

- Sentencers should first determine the appropriate sentence, leaving aside the element of aggravation related to race, religion, disability or sexual orientation but taking into account all other aggravating or mitigating factors.
- The sentence should then be increased to take account of the aggravation related to race, religion, disability or sexual orientation.
- The increase may mean that a more onerous penalty of the same type is appropriate, or that the threshold for a more severe type of sentence is passed.

Refer to *R* v. *Kelly; R* v. *Donnelly* [2001] EWCA Crim 170 in which the court considered the approach to sentencing in cases involving racial or religious aggravation.

The extent to which the sentence is increased will depend on the seriousness of the aggravation. The following factors could be taken as indicating a high level of aggravation.

- Offender's intention:

    - the element of aggravation based on race, religion, disability or sexual orientation was planned;
    - the offence was part of a pattern of offending by the offender;
    - the offender was a member of, or was associated with, a group promoting hostility based on race, religion, disability or sexual orientation;
    - the incident was deliberately set up to be offensive or humiliating to the victim or to the group of which the victim is a member.

- Impact on the victim or others:

    - the offence was committed in the victim's home;
    - the victim was providing a service to the public;
    - the timing or location of the offence was calculated to maximise the harm or distress it caused;
    - the expressions of hostility were repeated or prolonged;
    - the offence caused fear and distress throughout a local community or more widely;
    - the offence caused particular distress to the victim and/or the victim's family.

- At the lower end of the scale, the aggravation may be regarded as less serious if:
  - it was limited in scope or duration;
  - the offence was not motivated by hostility on the basis of race, religion, disability or sexual orientation, and the element of hostility or abuse was minor or incidental.

Offences taken into consideration (TIC)

In assessing seriousness a court will have regard to matters that a defendant asks it to take into account (*R* v. *Miles* [2006] EWCA Crim 256).

Such matters can also have an impact on:

- compensation (see **pp.38–40**);
- assessment of criminal lifestyle for confiscation.

They may also prevent diversion from prosecution.

CHAPTER 2

The sentencing process

2.1 THE USE OF GUIDELINES

The sentencing process is outlined in the **Introduction** and is repeated in each definitive guideline. Its importance was emphasised in *R* v. *Larcombe* [2008] EWCA Crim 2310 when the Court of Appeal stated as follows:

> 13. The expected approach is for the court to identify the description which most nearly matches the particular facts of the offence. This will identify a starting point from which the sentencer can depart to reflect aggravating or mitigating factors affecting the seriousness of the offence. The particular circumstances may make it appropriate that the provisional sentence falls outside the range, including previous convictions. Then the court will take account of personal mitigation, together with any plea of guilty.

It must be noted that all guidelines are prepared on the basis of the following two assumptions.

1. **That the offender has been convicted after a trial.**
   In the majority of cases this is not in fact the case and the court must allow a discount for guilty plea, either by reducing the sentence within the range or by using a less severe sentence.
2. **That the offender is a 'first-time' offender.**
   This phrase identifies an offender who does not have a conviction for a relevant offence. What is 'relevant' will vary depending on the facts of an individual case. A conviction for dishonesty is unlikely to be relevant to an offence of violence; a public order conviction may be. Different guidelines may define 'first-time' offender differently. In the guideline *Breach of an Anti-Social Behaviour Order* a 'first-time' offender is one who has no conviction for breach of an anti-social behaviour order. Even where an offender has relevant convictions, the guideline still sets the parameter against which the relevant decisions are made.

In sentencing, care should be taken to use the appropriate guideline and not just to refer to the particular offence charged. Where an offence ought to be sentenced as a lesser or different offence that guideline should be used (see for example the definitive guideline, *Assaults and Other Offences Against the Person*, p.14: Note 4 on offences under the Offences Against the Person Act 1861, s.20; and p.16: Note 3 on offences under the 1861 Act, s.47). The court should consider how the offence is best characterised.

2.2 ASSESSING SERIOUSNESS

Introduction

The SGC has issued a definitive guideline – *Overarching Principles: Seriousness* – to which every court must have regard (in accordance with CJA 2003, s.170(7)). The guideline is concerned only with defendants aged 18 years or over but aspects are applicable to young offenders also.

A court must start the sentencing process by considering the seriousness of the offence, as the sentence ultimately imposed must be commensurate with seriousness. This is the critical stage in the decision-making process. Prosecutors will wish to concentrate particularly on this stage to ensure that all relevant factors are put before the court (the information that should be provided by prosecutors in all Crown Court cases and in complex magistrates' court cases appears at **Appendix 3**). The defence advocate will need to be prepared to put factors relevant to seriousness into context and to guide the court further in making its assessment.

The assessment of offence seriousness:

- determines which of the sentencing thresholds has been crossed;
- indicates whether a custodial, community or other sentence is the most appropriate;
- is the key factor in deciding the length of a custodial sentence, the onerousness of requirements to be incorporated in a community sentence and the amount of any fine imposed.

Culpability and harm

Seriousness is determined by two concepts:

- the *culpability* of the offender in committing the offence; and
- the *harm* caused, intended to be caused or which might foreseeably have been caused (CJA 2003, s.143).

11

Culpability

The primary indicator for sentencing is culpability. Harm must always be judged in the light of the level of culpability of the offender in an individual case, as shown by factors such as the motive of the offender and whether the offence was planned or spontaneous.

There are four levels of criminal culpability, where the offender:

(a) has the *intention* to cause harm, with the highest culpability when an offence is planned. The worse the harm intended, the greater the seriousness;

(b) is *reckless* as to whether harm is caused. That is where the offender appreciates that at least some harm would be caused but proceeds giving no thought to the consequences even though the extent of the risk would be obvious to most people;

(c) has *knowledge* of the specific risks entailed by their actions even though they do not intend to cause the harm that results;

(d) is guilty of *negligence*.

Even with strict liability offences, where no culpability need be proved for the purposes of obtaining a conviction, the degree of culpability is still important when deciding sentence. The extent to which recklessness, knowledge or negligence are involved in a particular offence will vary.

When using offence guidelines published by the SGC, it is important to be aware that those which have starting points that do not specify a particular level of culpability are based on the highest level of culpability.

Harm

Harm includes harm caused as well as the risk of harm. It can derive from three categories, as described in the guideline *Overarching Principles: Seriousness*:

To Individual Victims

1.9 The types of harm caused or risked by different types of criminal activity are diverse and victims may suffer physical injury, sexual violation, financial loss, damage to health or psychological distress. There are gradations of harm within all of these categories.

1.10 The nature of harm will depend on personal characteristics and circumstances of the victim and the court's assessment of harm will be an effective and important way of taking into consideration the impact of a particular crime on the victim.

1.11 In some cases no actual harm may have resulted and the court will be concerned with assessing the relative dangerousness of the offender's conduct; it will consider the likelihood of harm occurring and the gravity of the harm that could have resulted.

To the Community

1.12 Some offences cause harm to the community at large (instead of or as well as to an individual victim) and may include economic loss, harm to public health, or interference with the administration of justice.

Other Types of Harm

1.13 There are other types of harm that are more difficult to define or categorise. For example, cruelty to animals certainly causes significant harm to the animal but there may also be a human victim who also suffers psychological distress and/or financial loss.

Imbalance between culpability and harm

Guidance is provided by the SGC in relation to assessing seriousness where there is an imbalance between culpability and harm (*Overarching Principles: Seriousness*, para.1.16). Sometimes the harm that actually results from an offence is greater than the harm intended by the offender. In other circumstances, the offender's culpability may be at a higher level than the harm resulting from the offence.

The guideline states (para.1.17) that culpability will be greater if:

- an offender deliberately causes more harm than is necessary for the commission of the offence, or
- where an offender targets a vulnerable victim (because of their old age or youth, disability or by virtue of the job they do).

Further, if unusually serious harm results, that was not intended by and was outside the control of the offender, the offender's culpability will be 'significantly influenced by the extent to which that harm could have been foreseen' (para.1.18).

2.3 AGGRAVATING AND MITIGATING FACTORS

The assessment of seriousness provides a starting point for sentence. It is then necessary to adjust the sentence by reason of aggravating or mitigating factors and to balance these against each other. The SGC has published guidance as regards factors of general application, including statutory factors, and for all individual offences identifies factors of specific relevance. This guidance does not 'weight' the factors and discretion is left with the court to determine the effect on sentence of individual and collective factors present in a case.

13

Aggravating factors

Offence guidelines will normally include a list of aggravating features which, if present in an individual instance of the offence, would indicate either a higher than usual level of culpability on the part of the offender, or a greater than usual degree of harm caused by the offence (or sometimes both). Advocates should be prepared to deal with all such factors, putting them into context and minimising or maximising them as appropriate in order to influence the court's determination of the weight to attach to them.

The lists below from the SGC guideline *Overarching Principles: Seriousness* (which are not exhaustive and not in any order of priority) bring together the most important aggravating features with potential application to more than one offence or class of offences. The factors starred with an asterisk are statutory aggravating factors in force at the date the guideline came into effect (4 April 2005).

The following points should be noted:

(a)   The lists include some factors (such as the vulnerability of victims or abuse of trust) that are integral features of certain offences; in such cases, the presence of the aggravating factor is already reflected in the penalty for the offence and the court cannot use them as justification for increasing the sentence further.

(b)   Care needs to be taken by the court to avoid 'double counting' where two or more of the factors listed describe the same feature on an offence.

(c)   A previous conviction will be treated as an aggravating factor if the court considers that it may reasonably be so treated having regard in particular to the nature and relevance of the offence and the time that has elapsed since the conviction (CJA 2003, s.143(2)).

Factors indicating higher culpability

- Offence committed while on bail for other offences.*
- Failure to respond to previous sentences.
- Offence was racially or religiously aggravated.*
- Offence motivated by, or demonstrating, hostility to the victim based on his or her sexual orientation (or presumed sexual orientation).
- Offence motivated by, or demonstrating, hostility based on the victim's disability (or presumed disability).
- Previous conviction(s), particularly where a pattern of repeat offending is disclosed.*
- Planning of an offence.
- An intention to commit more serious harm than actually resulted from the offence.
- Offenders operating in groups or gangs.

- 'Professional' offending.
- Commission of the offence for financial gain (where this is not inherent in the offence itself).
- High level of profit from the offence.
- An attempt to conceal or dispose of evidence.
- Failure to respond to warnings or concerns expressed by others about the offender's behaviour.
- Offence committed while on licence.
- Offence motivated by hostility towards a minority group, or a member or members of it.
- Deliberate targeting of vulnerable victim(s).
- Commission of an offence while under the influence of alcohol or drugs.
- Use of a weapon to frighten or injure victim.
- Deliberate and gratuitous violence or damage to property, over and above what is needed to carry out the offence.
- Abuse of power.
- Abuse of a position of trust.

Factors indicating a more than usually serious degree of harm

- Multiple victims.
- An especially serious physical or psychological effect on the victim, even if unintended.
- A sustained assault or repeated assaults on the same victim.
- Victim is particularly vulnerable.
- Location of the offence (for example, in an isolated place).
- Offence is committed against those working in the public sector or providing a service to the public.
- Presence of others, e.g. relatives, especially children or partner of the victim.
- Additional degradation of the victim (e.g. taking photographs of a victim as part of a sexual offence).
- In property offences, high value (including sentimental value) of property to the victim, or substantial consequential loss (e.g. where the theft of equipment causes serious disruption to a victim's life or business).

Mitigating factors

The SGC has identified a few factors of general application that may indicate that an offender's culpability is unusually low, or that the harm caused by an offence is less than usually serious. As for aggravating factors, individual offence guidelines will identify other offence-specific factors that advocates should be prepared to draw to the attention of the court.

Factors indicating significantly lower culpability

- A greater degree of provocation than normally expected.
- Mental illness or disability.
- Youth or age, where it affects the responsibility of the individual defendant.
- The fact that the offender played only a minor role in the offence.

Personal mitigation

Having formed an initial assessment of seriousness, adjusted for aggravating and mitigating factors, the court should consider offender or personal mitigation. The court must take into account any matters that in its opinion are relevant in mitigation of sentence (CJA 2003, s.166(1)).

Remorse, often best evidenced by regret expressed at the investigative stage, requires consideration of a discount additional to any resulting from an early guilty plea, especially if made in admissions to the police in interview.

The potential for elements of personal mitigation to influence outcome should not be underestimated. In a case that on its facts has passed a sentencing threshold, personal mitigation may enable the court to draw back and impose a sentence of a different type.

The SGC has not listed 'general' matters, but in offence guidelines does detail aspects of personal mitigation that might be of relevance as well as those that should not be taken into account. It is suggested that relevant considerations include:

- personal characteristics of the defendant;
- circumstances preceding the offence;
- effect of sentence on others;
- additional hardships that will follow conviction;
- conduct after the offence may be particularly pertinent;
- factors arising from conduct of proceedings.

A form for the collection of these data is at **Appendix 5**. Where financial information is required relevant data may be collected on the form at **Appendix 6**.

The Prison Reform Trust has published research on personal mitigation (J. Jacobson and M. Hough, *Mitigation: The Role of Personal Factors in Sentencing*, Prison Reform Trust, 2007). This identifies personal factors going to sentence under five heads:

- immediate circumstances of the offence;
- defendant's wider circumstances at the time of the offence;
- defendant's response to the offence and prosecution;
- factors relating to the defendant's past;
- factors relating to the defendant's present and future.

Examples of matters that might fall into the respective categories can be found in a form for collecting information at **Appendix 7**.

2.4 REDUCTION IN SENTENCE FOR A GUILTY PLEA

In any case where a guilty plea is or may be entered, particular attention must be paid to the discount that will be available for such a plea. It is critical that clients are made aware of this issue throughout a case, but particularly at the earliest stage as that is the opportunity to ensure that the largest discount possible is available.

CJA 2003, s.144 provides:

(1) In determining what sentence to pass on an offender who has pleaded guilty to an offence in proceedings before that or another court, a court must take into account –

   (a) the stage in the proceedings for the offence at which the offender indicated his intention to plead guilty, and
   (b) the circumstances in which this indication was given.

This provision is based on common law principles and has since been subject to specific guidance from the SGC (see guideline *Reduction in Sentence for a Guilty Plea* (revised July 2007)).

When given, the discount for guilty plea results in a sentence that is less than that commensurate with seriousness. The justification for the principle is that a guilty plea avoids the need for a trial (thus enabling other cases to be disposed of more expeditiously), shortens the gap between charge and sentence, saves considerable cost, and, in the case of an early plea, saves victims and witnesses from the concern about having to give evidence. It derives from the need for the effective administration of justice and not as an aspect of mitigation (*Reduction in Sentence for a Guilty Plea*, para.2.2).

Important points to note include:

- the discount cannot be denied because the court considers the maximum available sentence to be inadequate (ibid., para.5.6), as it is separate from all issues of mitigation or of aggravation;
- when appropriate the reduction of a sentence for a genuine expression of remorse, or for assisting the prosecuting authorities, or the change in a sentence because of TICs, must be made *before* the discount is applied (ibid., paras.2.4 and 2.5);
- the discount should be applied only to the punitive aspect of a sentence and not to orders for rehabilitation or ancillary orders (ibid., para.2.6).

Critically, the discount for a guilty plea may itself take a case down through a sentencing threshold (ibid., para.2.3 and *R* v. *Seed; R* v. *Stark* [2007] EWCA Crim 254).

17

The discount is applied on a sliding scale depending on the stage in the proceedings at which a formal indication of a willingness to admit guilt is given (*Reduction in Sentence for a Guilty Plea*, para.4.30). Levels of reduction are recommended by the SGC as shown below (ibid., paras.4.2 and 4.3), but a court should follow the recommendations unless it is able to set out reasons for applying a different proportionate reduction.

Table 2.1 Recommended levels of reduction

In each category, there is a presumption that the recommended reduction will be given unless there are good reasons for a lower amount

First reasonable opportunity	After a trial date is set	Door of the court/after trial has begun
Recommended 1/3	Recommended 1/4	Recommended 1/10

The guideline stresses that the largest recommended reduction will not normally be given unless the offender indicated willingness to admit guilty at the 'first reasonable opportunity', a point that will vary from case to case. Thereafter, the guideline provides:

- the reduction will normally be less than one-third where the admission of guilt comes later than the first reasonable opportunity;
- it will be appropriate to give some reduction where the plea of guilty comes very late;
- if after a guilty plea the offender's version of the circumstances of the offence is rejected at a *Newton* hearing, this should be taken into account in determining the level of reduction;
- a late guilty plea should attract very little, if any, discount if the not guilty plea was entered and maintained for tactical reasons (ibid., para.4.3).

The 'first reasonable opportunity' will vary with a wide range of factors in any individual case. Examples are given in Annex 1 to the guideline (see below). However, they are not exclusive. The late availability of critical medical evidence (*R* v. *R* [2007] EWCA Crim 1874) and an acceptance of the facts but a genuine issue on whether they amount to a crime could also qualify (*R* v. *Scammell* [2001] EWCA Crim 1631). 'Over-cautious' legal advice should not result in a loss of discount (*R* v. *Eastwood* [2002] EWCA Crim 155). Annex 1 to the guideline provides as follows:

(a) the first reasonable opportunity may be the first time that a defendant appears before the court and has the opportunity to plead guilty;

(b) but the court may consider that it would be reasonable to have expected an indication of willingness even earlier, perhaps whilst under interview.
Note: For a) and b) to apply, the Court will need to be satisfied that the defendant (and any legal adviser) would have had sufficient information about the allegations

(c) where an offence triable either way is committed to the Crown Court for trial and the defendant pleads guilty at the first hearing in that Court, the reduction will be less than if there had been an indication of a guilty plea given to the magistrates' court (recommended reduction of one third) but more than if the plea had been entered after a trial date had been set (recommended reduction of one quarter), and is likely to be in the region of 30%;

(d) where an offence is triable only on indictment; it may well be that the first reasonable opportunity would have been during the police station stage; where that is not the case, the first reasonable opportunity is likely to be at the first hearing in the Crown Court;

(e) where a defendant is convicted after pleading guilty to an alternative (lesser) charge to that to which he/she had originally pleaded not guilty, the extent of any reduction will be determined by the stage at which the defendant first formally indicated to the court willingness to plead guilty to the lesser charge, and the reason why that lesser charge was proceeded with in preference to the original charge.

Special circumstances

The guideline outlines special circumstances in relation to how the reduction principle applies in certain cases.

Obligatory sentences

By virtue of CJA 2003, s.144(2) the reduction for a guilty plea is limited to 20 per cent where there are obligatory minimum sentences for burglary or Class A drug trafficking. No discount may be given for offences referred to in the Firearms Act 1968, s.51A (Powers of Criminal Courts (Sentencing) Act (PCC(S)A) 2000, ss.111 and 112).

Dangerous offenders who are made subject to life sentences or imprisonment or detention for public protection are subject to a minimum term. That term should reflect any discount for a guilty plea (*Reduction in Sentence for a Guilty Plea*, para.5.1). Where an extended sentence is imposed, the discount for a guilty plea may be applied, but not so as to reduce a sentence below 12 months' immediate custody (see below **p.36**).

Young offenders

Sentences of detention and training have to be of specific lengths (see **Chapter 8**) and should reflect any discount for a guilty plea, but the application of the proportionate discount will be to the nearest available sentence.

A detention and training order of 24 months may be imposed on an offender aged under 18 if the offence is one which would, but for the plea, have attracted a sentence of long-term detention in excess of 24 months under PCC(S)A 2000, s.91 (*Reduction in Sentence for a Guilty Plea*, para.5.9).

Overwhelming prosecution case

While there is a presumption in favour of the full reduction being given where a plea has been indicated at the first reasonable opportunity, the fact that the prosecution case is overwhelming without relying on admissions from the defendant may justify departure from the guideline, though reasons should be given. A recommended reduction of 20 per cent is likely to be appropriate where the guilty plea was indicated at the first reasonable opportunity (ibid., paras.5.2–5.5).

Summary-only offences

Reduction in Sentence for a Guilty Plea, para.5.7 provides:

> When the total sentence for both or all of the offences is limited to 6 months imprisonment, a court may determine to impose consecutive sentences which, even allowing for a reduction for a guilty plea where appropriate on each offence, would still result in the imposition of the maximum sentence available. In such circumstances, in order to achieve the purpose for which the reduction principle has been established, some modest allowance should normally be given against the total sentence for the entry of a guilty plea.

Either-way offences

A magistrates' court may impose a sentence of imprisonment of six months for a single either-way offence where that offence would have attracted a greater sentence if it had been committed to the Crown Court.

Murder

Parliament has set starting points (CJA 2003, Sched.21) (based on the circumstances of the killing) which a court will apply when it fixes the minimum term and has further prescribed that, having identified the appropriate starting point, the court must then consider whether to increase or reduce the term in the light of aggravating or mitigating factors, some of which are listed in statute.

Legislation specifically provides that the obligation to have regard to any guilty plea applies to the fixing of the minimum term, by making the same statutory provisions that apply to other offences apply to murder (*Reduction in Sentence for a Guilty Plea*, para.6.3). However, the reduction for a guilty plea will have double the effect on time to be served in custody when compared with a determinate sentence.

The SGC guideline provides that the approach to determining the level of reduction for a guilty plea is different, and is as follows (para.6.6):

1. Where a Court determines that there should be a whole life minimum term, there will be no reduction for a guilty plea.
2. In other circumstances:

    (a) the Court will weigh carefully the overall length of the minimum term taking into account other reductions for which the offender may be eligible so as to avoid a combination leading to an inappropriately short sentence;
    (b) where it is appropriate to reduce the minimum term having regard to a plea of guilty, the reduction will not exceed one sixth and will never exceed 5 years;
    (c) the sliding scale will apply so that, where it is appropriate to reduce the minimum term on account of a guilty plea, the recommended reduction (one sixth or five years whichever is the less) is only available where there has been an indication of willingness to plead guilty at the first reasonable opportunity, with a recommended 5% for a late guilty plea;
    (d) the Court should then review the sentence to ensure that the minimum term accurately reflects the seriousness of the offence taking account of the statutory starting point, all aggravating and mitigating factors and any guilty plea entered.

Other indeterminate sentences

The court must determine what the equivalent determinate sentence (see **Chapter 3**) would have been. The calculation of any reduction for guilty plea is therefore on the normal principles for such determinate sentences (*Reduction in Sentence for a Guilty Plea*, para.7.3).

2.5 ALLOCATION OF CASES

The allocation of cases where the offence is triable either way between the magistrates' courts and the Crown Court is provided for by the Magistrates' Courts Act (MCA) 1980.

Adult offenders

In relation to adult offenders, an indication of plea is sought to begin the process.

* If a guilty plea is indicated, the court will either proceed towards sentencing, or commit the case to the Crown Court for sentence.

- If the offender indicates a not guilty plea or gives no plea indication, the court undertakes the mode of trial procedure under MCA 1980, s.19.

The mode of trial procedure currently provides that the court shall consider which is the most suitable venue for the case to be tried having regard to the following matters:

- representations by the parties;
- the nature of the case;
- whether the circumstances make the offence one of a serious character;
- whether the punishment(s) that the magistrates' court has power to impose would be adequate; and
- any other circumstances that appear to make it more suitable for the case to be tried one way rather than the other.

However, the procedure and relevant legislative provisions have been revised by CJA 2003 and further amended by the Criminal Justice and Immigration Act 2008. It is expected that the new allocation procedure will come into force in 2009.

MCA 1980, s.19 (as amended) provides that:

- the Crown shall be given the opportunity to inform the court of the defendant's previous convictions; and
- the Crown and defence shall be given the opportunity to make representations as to which court is more suitable to try the case.

The court shall then consider whether its sentencing powers would be adequate having regard to any allocation guideline issued by the SGC.

The allocation guideline is likely to provide that the primary test is the adequacy of the sentencing powers of the magistrates' court, but that court should start with a *general presumption* towards trial in the magistrates' court. The court should have regard to the Magistrates' Court Sentencing Guidelines and the principles regarding assessment of offence seriousness in *Overarching Principles: Seriousness* and other relevant guidelines.

The court must work on the prosecution's version of the facts, so that mitigation is irrelevant and no allowances made for a potential subsequent guilty plea.

The court will be presented with details of an offender's criminal history and thus will be better informed in terms of assessing the seriousness of the offence. If all or some of the previous convictions are judged to be relevant, they will increase the seriousness of the offence.

Further offences to be taken into consideration (TICs) and issues of dangerousness are not relevant at this stage and will be considered following conviction in the magistrates' court when committal for sentence can be contemplated.

Another new aspect of the procedure is the ability of an offender to seek an 'indication of sentence' before deciding whether to elect trial in the Crown Court. The indication is limited to whether or not a custodial or non-custodial sentence would be the likely outcome if the case remained in the magistrates' court. The court should assess the type of sentence realistically possible in the light of the facts as presented by the prosecution (subject to defence representations as to accuracy) with the additional element of the discount for a guilty plea (normally of one-quarter in these circumstances as this stage is beyond the first reasonable opportunity).The key elements of the basis of plea should be recorded in writing. The information provided will include personal mitigation only if it has influenced the facts of the case or is actively agreed by the Crown.

If an indication is given, and the offender then accepts summary trial and pleads guilty immediately, the indication will be binding.

Youth offenders

See also **Chapter 8**.

Youths aged under 18 may be *committed* to the Crown Court under MCA 1980, s.24 and *sent* under the dangerous offender provisions.

Youths convicted of specified offences may also be committed for sentence (MCA 1980, s.3C).

Section 24 provides that the case should be committed if:

- the offence is homicide or the defendant is 16 or 17 and the minimum sentence provisions of the Firearms Act 1968, s.51A(1) would be satisfied;
- the offence is a grave crime and the court considers that sentencing under PCC(S)A) 2000, s.91 should be possible;
- the youth is charged jointly with an adult and the court considers it necessary in the interests of justice for them to be tried together.

The normal rule in relation to grave crimes is that jurisdiction should only be declined if a sentence of more than two years would be required (*R (on the application of W)* v. *Southampton Youth Court* [2002] EWHC 1640 Admin).

When brought into force, provisions of CJA 2003 amend the youth court allocation procedure (see MCA 1980, ss.24(1), 24A, 24B as amended; CDA 1998, ss.51 and 51A; note that CDA 1998, ss.51C and 51D continue to allow prosecuting authorities to transfer certain cases to the Crown Court).

Allegations of homicide, and of offences (in relation to those aged 16 and 17) subject to the Firearms Act 1968, s.51A will be sent to the Crown Court.

In relation to all other matters the defence will be invited to indicate a plea. On a guilty plea (or conviction) the court will be able to commit for sentence if:

- the offence is a grave crime (see **Chapter 8**) and the court considers that sentencing under PCC(S)A 2000, s.91 should be possible; or
- the offence is a specified offence and the case may require the use of the dangerous offender provisions.

If there is no indication, or a not guilty plea is indicated, the court will proceed to trial unless the youth is jointly charged with an adult and the court considers it necessary in the interests of justice for them to be tried together. In that eventuality the youth will be sent for trial.

In relation to joint charges, the SGC allocation guideline is likely to provide that any presumption in favour of sending the youth to the Crown Court to be tried jointly with an adult who is being sent must be balanced with the general presumption that young offenders should be dealt with in a youth court. In determining which is the appropriate court, examples of factors that should be considered when deciding whether to separate the youth and adult defendants include:

- the young age of the offender, particularly where the age gap between the adult and youth offender is substantial;
- the immaturity and intellect of the youth;
- the relative culpability of the youth compared with the adult and whether or not the role played by the youth was minor;
- lack of previous convictions on the part of the youth compared with the adult offender;
- whether the trial of the adult and youth can be severed without inconvenience to witnesses or injustice to the case as a whole.

In relation to the dangerous offender provisions relevant to youths, specified offences must be sent to the Crown Court if it appears to the court that the criteria for the imposition of detention for life, detention for public protection, or an extended sentence would be met (CDA 1998, s.51 and CJA 2003, ss.226 and 228). Given the precondition in the case of youths that were a determinate sentence to be imposed it would have to be of at least four years there will be few of these cases and they will normally be identified under the grave crimes procedure. In *R (on the application of Crown Prosecution Service)* v. *South East Surrey Youth Court* [2005] EWHC 2929, the court indicated that the policy of the legislature is that those under 18 should, wherever possible, be tried in the youth court and there was a need to be particularly rigorous before finding that the criteria for dangerous offender sentencing have been met. This is unlikely to be possible until full pre-sentence reports are available following conviction. There is no need for the court to decline jurisdiction at an early stage as there is a specific power following conviction to commit for sentence.

2.6 INDICATIONS OF SENTENCE

In *R* v. *Goodyear* [2005] EWCA Crim 888, the Court of Appeal laid down rules on the right of advocates to seek an indication of sentence from the judge in the Crown Court (for the statutory provisions in CJA 2003 in relation to sentence indications within the allocation procedure in magistrates' courts, see **2.5**). The key points are as follows:

- The indication must be at the request of the defendant who must instruct the advocate in writing to obtain one – the plea and case management hearing is the best time for an indication to be given and seven days' notice of the request for an indication should be given in more complex cases.

- An indication if given is binding provided there is a plea within a reasonable time, but it cannot be 'banked'.
- An indication can only be given if the facts are agreed by the Crown, defence and judge.
- The judge may indicate the maximum sentence appropriate if a plea of guilty is entered – the plea must remain voluntary.
- If a trial does takes place, no reference may be made on conviction to issues arising at the indication hearing.

The greatest control on the use of the *Goodyear* procedure is that, as long as the prosecution does no more than agree the facts, the Attorney General can seek leave, in prescribed cases (see **Appendix 2**), to review any sentence imposed as being unduly lenient.

A judge may always refuse to give an indication and may be well advised to do so when a specified or serious specified offence is alleged. In *R* v. *Kulah* [2007] EWCA Crim 1701 it was suggested that an indication could not prevent the imposition of an obligatory dangerous offender sentence (while it could limit the minimum term before the case can be considered by the Parole Board as to the sentence to be served) but the case is in doubt as all such sentences are now discretionary.

CHAPTER 3

Obligatory sentences and dangerous offenders

3.1 OBLIGATORY SENTENCES

Murder

If a defendant is convicted of a murder committed on or after December 2003, not only is the court required to impose a life sentence but it must also comply with statutory requirements as to the minimum term to be served before the Parole Board may consider release (CJA 2003, s.269).

Minimum terms

The minimum term must be appropriate, taking into account:

- the seriousness of the offence in accordance with CJA 2003, Sched.21; and
- the effect of any direction that would have been given in relation to time on remand under CJA 2003, s.240 if the court had imposed a determinate term.

CJA 2003, Sched.21, paras.4–11 provide as follows:

Starting points

4   (1)   If –

(a)   the court considers that the seriousness of the offence (or the combination of the offence and one or more offences associated with it) is exceptionally high, and

(b)   the offender was aged 21 or over when he committed the offence,

the appropriate starting point is a whole life order.

(2)   Cases that would normally fall within sub-paragraph (1)(a) include –

(a)   the murder of two or more persons, where each murder involves any of the following –

(i)   a substantial degree of premeditation or planning,

(ii)   the abduction of the victim, or

(iii)   sexual or sadistic conduct,

    (b)   the murder of a child if involving the abduction of the child or sexual or sadistic motivation;

    (c)   a murder done for the purpose of advancing a political, religious or ideological cause; or

    (d)   a murder by an offender previously convicted of murder.

5   (1)   If –

    (a)   the case does not fall within paragraph 4(1) but the court considers that the seriousness of the offence (or the combination of the offence and one or more offences associated with it) is particularly high, and

    (b)   the offender was aged 18 or over when he committed the offence,

    the appropriate starting point, in determining the minimum term, is 30 years.

    (2)   Cases that (if not falling within paragraph 4(1)) would normally fall within sub-paragraph (1)(a) include –

    (a)   the murder of a police officer or prison officer in the course of his duty,

    (b)   a murder involving the use of a firearm or explosive,

    (c)   a murder done for gain (such as a murder done in the course of furtherance of robbery or burglary, done for payment or done in the expectation of gain as a result of the death),

    (d)   a murder intended to obstruct or interfere with the course of justice,

    (e)   a murder involving sexual or sadistic conduct,

    (f)   the murder of two or more persons,

    (g)   a murder that is racially or religiously aggravated or aggravated by sexual orientation, or

    (h)   a murder falling within paragraph 4(2) committed by an offender who was aged under 21 when he committed the offence.

6   If the offender was aged 18 or over when he committed the offence and the case does not fall within paragraph 4(1) or 5(1), the appropriate starting point, in determining the minimum term, is 15 years.

7   If the offender was aged under 18 when he committed the offence, the appropriate starting point, in determining the minimum term, is 12 years.

Aggravating and mitigating factors

8   Having chosen a starting point, the court should take into account any aggravating or mitigating factors, to the extent that it has not allowed for them in its choice of starting point.

9   Detailed consideration of aggravating or mitigating factors may result in a minimum term of any length (whatever the starting point), or in the making of a whole life order.

10   Aggravating factors (additional to those mentioned in paragraph 4(2) and 5(2)) that may be relevant to the offence of murder include:

    (a)   a significant degree of planning or premeditation,

    (b)   the fact that the victim was particularly vulnerable because of age or disability,

    (c)   mental or physical suffering inflicted on the victim before death,

    (d)   the abuse of a position of trust,

(e)   the use of duress or threats against another person to facilitate the commission of the offence,

(f)   the fact that the victim was providing a public service or performing a public duty, and

(g)   concealment, destruction or dismemberment of the body.

11   Mitigating factors that may be relevant to the offence of murder include –

(a)   an intention to cause serious bodily harm rather than to kill,

(b)   lack of premeditation,

(c)   the fact that the offender suffered from any mental disorder or mental disability which (although not falling within section 2(1) of the Homicide Act 1957 (c.11)), lowered his degree of culpability,

(d)   the fact that the offender was provoked (for example, by prolonged stress) in a way not amounting to a defence of provocation,

(e)   the fact that the offender acted to any extent in self-defence,

(f)   a belief by the offender that the murder was an act of mercy, and

(g)   the age of the offender.

Relevant previous convictions and other statutory aggravating factors apply. The unlawful possession of a weapon is a relevant factor (*R* v. *Richardson* [2005] EWCA Crim 1408).

The statutory criteria and these lists are not exclusive (*R* v. *Peters; R* v. *Palmer; R* v. *Campbell* [2005] EWCA Crim 605; *R* v. *Height; R* v. *Anderson* [2008] EWCA Crim 2500). A discount for a guilty plea must still be given (see **pp.20–21**).

Firearms offences

Minimum sentences are required under two statutory provisions in relation to offences involving defined firearms, committed by a defendant who was at least 16 years old at the date of the offence, unless the court can find exceptional circumstances. In these cases there can be no discount for a guilty plea (*R* v. *Jordan* [2004] EWCA Crim 3291). The relevant offences are set out in **Appendix 8**.

Firearms Act 1968, s.51A

For those who are 16 but under 18 at the date of conviction the minimum sentence is three years' detention. For those of 18 and over the minimum sentence is five years' detention or imprisonment.

Violent Crime Reduction Act 2006, ss.28 and 29

For those who are 18 or over at the date of conviction for an offence under the Violent Crime Reduction Act, s.28, the minimum sentence is five years' detention or imprisonment (s.29).

Exceptional circumstances

The minimum sentence *need not* be imposed if the court is of the opinion that there are 'exceptional circumstances' relating to the offence or the offender.

The minimum sentence *should not* be imposed if it is arbitrary and disproportionate (*R* v. *Rehman* [2005] EWCA Crim 2056). In this respect, it has been found that mental illness not requiring a hospital admission did not qualify (*R* v. *McEneaney* [2005] EWCA Crim 431), nor did keeping a weapon following an earlier attack (*R* v. *Blackall* [2005] EWCA Crim 1128). However, disability and old age (over 65) might do so. Individual factors, not themselves exceptional, may in total be sufficient to amount to exceptional circumstances (*R* v. *Edwards* [2006] EWCA Crim 2833).

Domestic burglary (PCC(S)A 2000, s.111)

A minimum sentence of three years is required for a defendant who is aged 18 or over on the date of conviction when he is:

(a) convicted of domestic burglary; and
(b) at the date of the commission of that offence he has already been convicted on two separate occasions (at whatever age) of domestic burglary committed after 30 November 1999 (attempted burglary is not a qualifying offence – *R* v. *Maguire* [2002] EWCA Crim 2689).

Note: It is essential to check both the dates of the relevant offences as well as the dates of conviction.

Class A drug trafficking (PCC(S)A 2000, s.110)

A minimum sentence of seven years is required for a defendant who is aged 18 or over on the date of conviction when he is:

(a) convicted of Class A drug trafficking; and
(b) at the date of the conviction of that offence he has already been convicted on two separate occasions (at whatever age) of Class A drug trafficking.

Class A drug trafficking includes, in relation to Class A drugs, the following offences:

1. An offence under any of the following provisions of the Misuse of Drugs Act 1971:

    (a) s.4(2) or (3) (unlawful production or supply of controlled drugs);
    (b) s.5(3) (possession of controlled drug with intent to supply);
    (c) s.8 (permitting certain activities relating to controlled drugs);
    (d) s.20 (assisting in or inducting the commission outside the UK of an offence punishable under a corresponding law).

2. An offence under any of the following provisions of the Customs and Excise Management Act 1979 if it is committed in connection with a prohibition or restriction on importation or exportation which has effect by virtue of the Misuse of Drugs Act 1971, s.3:

    (a) s.50(2) or (3) (improper importation of goods);
    (b) s.68(2) (exploration of prohibited or restricted goods);
    (c) s.170 (fraudulent evasion).

3. An offence under either of the following provisions of the Criminal Justice (International Co-operation) Act 1990:

    (a) s.12 (manufacture or supply of a substance for the time being specified in Sched.2 to that Act);
    (b) s.19 (using a ship for illicit traffic in controlled drugs);

    or an offence of attempting, conspiring, or inciting another person, to commit any such offence.

Note: It is essential to check both the dates of the relevant offences as well as the dates of conviction.

In relation to both domestic burglary and class A drug trafficking the court *need not* impose the minimum sentence if it is of the opinion that there are particular circumstances which relate to the offence or to the offender that would make it unjust in all the circumstances. A significant time lapse between offences could make the obligatory sentence unjust (*R* v. *McDonagh* [2005] EWCA Crim 2568), as might the fact that earlier supply was of his own drugs to feed his own habit (*R* v. *Turner* [2005] EWCA Crim 2363). The facts of the earlier case could not make the present sentence unjust but the basis of plea to the current matter might do so (*R* v. *Pearce* [2004] Crim LR 961). A legitimate expectation of a drugs referral followed by a positive report could make the minimum sentence unjust (*R* v. *Gibson* [2004] EWCA Crim 593).

3.2   DANGEROUS OFFENDERS

The following pages describe the law as it applies to those sentenced on or after 14 July 2008, whatever the date of the offence.

If the defendant is convicted of a specified or serious specified offence, and the additional statutory criteria are met, the court has the ability to impose an extended sentence or in addition, for serious offences, imprisonment or detention for public protection, or a life sentence.

Additional or extended penalties

These sentences provide additional protection for the public in relation to offenders convicted of:

- *specified offences* – the violent and sexual offences set out in CJA 2003, Sched.15 (listed in **Appendix 9**);
- *serious specified offences* – specified offences that for an adult carry a maximum penalty of 10 years' imprisonment or more on conviction (listed in **Appendix 10**).

The SGC has published a guide (*Dangerous Offenders: Guide for Sentencers and Practitioners*) to the use of these sentences which has been revised and updated to include the changes made by the Criminal Justice and Immigration Act 2008 and guidance that has emerged from the Court of Appeal. The law is summarised in the diagrams from that guide reproduced below (**Figures 3.1** and **3.2**).

Availability of penalties

The statutory criteria limit the availability of these penalties and there is a two-stage test.

- For adults the sentences are only available if either:
    - the offender has a previous conviction for an offence listed in CJA 2003, Sched.15A (see **Appendix 11**); or
    - the offence warrants a determinate sentence of four years (a minimum term of two years). That determinate sentence may, however, reflect the seriousness of the totality of the offending conduct and so be based on the totality of consecutive sentences, which would individually be under four years (*Attorney General's Reference (No.55 of 2008)*; sub nom. *R* v. *C* [2008] EWCA Crim 2790).
- For youths the sentences are only available if the second criterion is met.

31

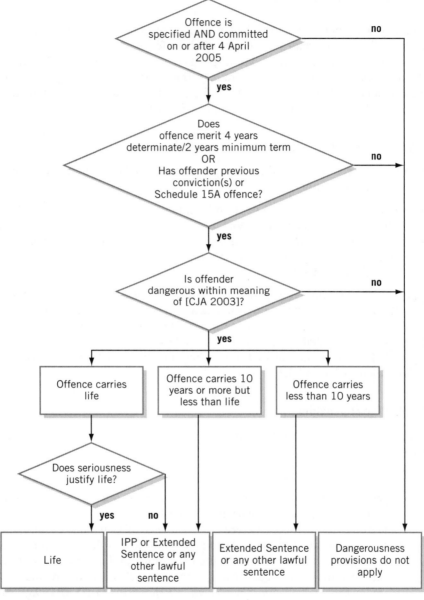

Figure 3.1   Dangerous offender provisions flow chart – adults

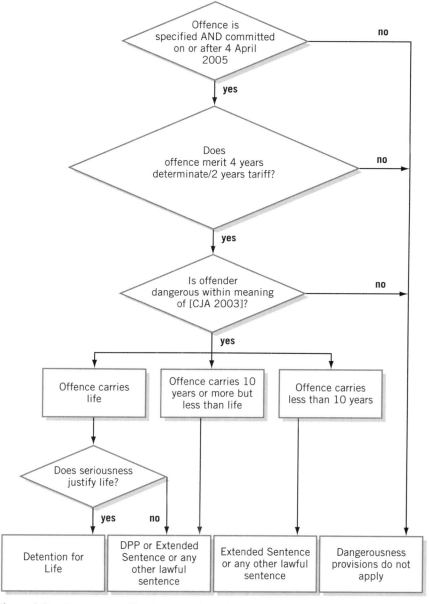

Figure 3.2 Dangerous offender provisions flow chart – youths

Significant risk

Where the availability criteria is met, in addition the court must be of the opinion that there is a significant risk to members of the public of serious harm occasioned by the commission of a further specified offence. In *R* v. *Lang* [2005] EWCA Crim 2864, the court emphasised that this requires the court to consider:

- **Is there a significant risk of a further specified offence?**
  The court will consider all relevant evidence and there need be no similar previous convictions (*R* v. *Green* [2007] EWCA Crim 2172) or any convictions at all if other material satisfies the court as to the risk (*R* v. *Johnson* [2006] EWCA Crim 2486).
- **Is there a significant risk of serious harm to a member of the public?**
  This can be to a single person such as the member of a family.

In assessing significant risk it should be noted that 'significant' is a higher threshold than mere possibility of occurrence, and it can be taken to mean 'noteworthy, of considerable . . . importance'.

When assessing the risk of further offences being committed, the court should take into account the nature and circumstances of the current offence, the offender's history of offending (including kind of offence, its circumstances, sentence passed, whether offending demonstrates any pattern), social and economic factors in relation to the offender (including accommodation, employability, education, associates, relationships, and drug and alcohol abuse), and the offender's thinking/attitude towards offending and supervision and emotional state. Such information most readily, though not exclusively, should come from antecedents (the detail of which must be provided by the prosecution) and pre-sentence probation and medical reports. In relation to such reports the court will be guided, but not bound, by any assessment of risk, but if departure from any such assessment is contemplated, both counsel should be given the opportunity of addressing the point.

When assessing the risk of serious harm, the court must guard against assuming that there is a significant risk of serious harm merely because the foreseen specified offence is serious; a pre-sentence report (and, in the small number of cases where the circumstances of the current offence or the history of the offender suggest mental abnormality, a medical report) should usually be obtained before any sentence is passed which is based on significant risk of serious harm.

Where the foreseen specified offence is not serious, there will be comparatively few cases in which a risk of serious harm will properly be regarded as significant; repetitive violent or sexual offending at a relatively low level without serious harm does not of itself give rise to a significant risk of serious harm in the future (there may in such cases be some risk of future victims being more adversely affected than past victims but this, of itself, does not give rise to significant risk of serious harm).

In relation to young offenders, it is still necessary to bear in mind that, within a shorter time than adults, they may change and develop (which might, together with their level of maturity, be highly pertinent when assessing what their future conduct may be and whether it may give rise to a significant risk of serious harm).

With particularly young offenders, an indeterminate sentence may be inappropriate even where a serious offence has been committed and there is a significant risk of serious harm from further offences.

Even when these criteria are met the court is not obliged to impose a dangerous offender sentence.

Sentences for public protection

The court is entitled to and should have in mind all the alternative and cumulative methods of providing the necessary public protection. Sexual offences prevention orders (see below **p.86**) with appropriate conditions could be attached to a determinate or extended sentence in order for the overall sentencing package to provide appropriate protection.

Imprisonment for public protection is concerned with further risks and public protection. The sentence is directed not in the past but to the future. Courts should ensure that longer than appropriate sentences are not imposed in order to allow a dangerous offender sentence (*Attorney General's Reference (No.55 of 2008)*; sub nom. *R* v. *C* [2008] EWCA Crim 2790).

Sentences of imprisonment or detention for public protection are indeterminate sentences and are only available on conviction for a serious specified offence.

When imposing detention or imprisonment for public protection, the court must fix a minimum term before which the case cannot be reviewed by the Parole Board. This is the same procedure as when a life sentence is imposed. The court must decide what the appropriate determinate sentence would be, halve it, and deduct any time spent on remand. A discount for a guilty plea is given when fixing the notional determinate term.

Extended sentences

An extended sentence is a custodial sentence which is then followed by an extended period of licence (the extension period).

Adult defendants without a Sched.15A conviction and youths

The custodial element must be a minimum of four years. If the guilty plea discount would take the sentence for such a defendant below four years the sentence ceases to be available.

Adult defendants with a Sched.15A conviction

If the defendant does have a relevant conviction:

- the custodial element cannot be reduced below 12 months – credit must be given for a guilty plea subject to that minimum;
- the extension period must not exceed five years for violent offences or eight years for sexual offences;
- the total of the custodial element and extension period cannot exceed the maximum for the offence.

CHAPTER 4

Available primary sentences

4.1 SUMMARY

Table 4.1 Available sentences for offenders aged 18 or over

Sentence/Order	Legislative reference	Magistrates' Court Sentencing Guidelines page nos. [Appendix 16]
Absolute discharge	PCC(S)A 2000, ss.12–15	
Conditional discharge	PCC(S)A 2000, ss.12–15	
Compensation order	PCC(S)A 2000, ss.130–134	p.165 [**p.335**]
Fine	MCA 1980, s.32	p.148 [**p.318**]
Deferred sentences	PCC(S)A 2000, s.1	p.176 [**p.347**]
Community sentence	CJA 2003, ss.177–180, ss.199–223	p.160 [**p.331**]
Imprisonment:	PCC(S)A 2000 and CJA 2003	p.163 [**p.333**]
Immediate		
Suspended		
Short local detention	MCA 1980, s.135	
Detention in young offender institution (under 21-year-olds)	PCC(S)A 2000, ss.76–84, ss.96–98	

4.2 DISCHARGE: ABSOLUTE AND CONDITIONAL

Where the court considers that punishment is inexpedient or inappropriate (because of the nature of the offence or character of the offender) it may make an order discharging the offender:

- absolutely; or
- subject to the condition that no other offence is committed during such period as the court determines, not exceeding three years.

A discharge is not a conviction.

Before making a conditional discharge, the court is required to explain to the offender in ordinary language that if a further offence is committed during the period of the order, they will be liable to be sentenced for the original offence. The standard court pronouncement emphasises that this would be in addition to any penalty imposed for the new offence.

Availability

The obvious benefit of a conditional discharge is that it provides a means of controlling future behaviour and preventing further offending, and may be appropriate:

- where an offence is 'trivial' and/or a first conviction; or
- where an offender is already subject to a sentence or sentences and a further immediate additional penalty would be inappropriate.

A conditional discharge may *not* be imposed for breach of an anti-social behaviour order or breach of a sexual offences prevention order, or within two years of a final warning given while the offender was under 18 unless in each case there are exceptional circumstances.

Interaction with other sentences/orders

Note that:

- a fine may not be imposed in addition to an order of discharge;
- a deprivation order cannot be made where a discharge is imposed.

4.3   COMPENSATION ORDER

For guidance in relation to making orders in magistrates' courts see the MCSG, p.165 (**Appendix 16, p.335**).

A compensation order can be imposed as a sentence in its own right or as an ancillary order. If imposed as a penalty the rehabilitation period is five years; if as an ancillary order, the rehabilitation period depends on the primary sentence imposed. The willingness to pay compensation may show remorse and so provide mitigation.

An order *must be considered* in any case where injury to a person, or loss or damage results from an offence, and must be ordered wherever possible. Loss can include financial loss, such as the cost of repairs, loss of earnings, medical expenses or a sum for pain and suffering from an injury assessed in light of relevant factors and medical evidence. In determining whether or not to make an order, the court may have regard to the availability of financial recompense from other sources, such as the Criminal Injuries Compensation Scheme.

Reasons must be given if a court decides not to order compensation.

A compensation order can be made in relation to any offence before the court or any admitted offence being taken into consideration (TIC). Note that:

- in a magistrates' court, an order is limited to a maximum of £5,000 for each offence charged;
- an order in relation to a TIC is limited by the maximum for the offence(s) of which the offender has been convicted.

In determining the amount of an order, the court should have regard to:

- any evidence and representations made by the offender and/or prosecutor (PCC(S)A 2000, s.130(4)); and
- the offender's means (PCC(S)A 2000, s.130(11)).

An advocate must satisfy himself as to the accuracy of the information provided (*R* v. *Roberts* (1987) 9 Cr App R(S) 275).

The SGC has emphasised that compensation should benefit, not inflict further harm on, the victim. Any financial recompense from the offender has potential to cause distress. A victim may or may not want compensation from the offender and assumptions should not be made; the victim's views should be obtained whenever possible. If the victim does not want compensation this should be respected. See the SGC guidance in the definitive guidelines, *Sexual Offences Act 2003* and *Assaults and Other Offences Against the Person*.

Where information or evidence as to the full extent of the victim's loss is not available or is difficult to ascertain, an order should be made for an amount that represents the likely or agreed loss. The court should not undertake complicated investigations (*R* v. *Briscoe* (1994) 15 Cr App R(S) 699).

Where injury, loss or damage arises from the presence of a motor vehicle on a road, a compensation order may be made only if:

- the damage arises from an offence under the Theft Act 1968 (*R* v. *Crutchley* (1994) 15 Cr App R(S) 627; *R* v. *Tyce* (1994) 15 Cr App R(S) 415); or
- the offender was uninsured and the Motor Insurers' Bureau will not cover the loss (excess of £300 applies) (PCC(S)A 2000, s.130(6)).

The court will form a preliminary view of the appropriate level of compensation using available guidance, such as the charts in the MCSG, pp. 166–167 (**Appendix 16, pp.337–8**).

The court must have regard to the means of the offender as far as they are known, and reflect this in the amount of the compensation ordered and the term over which it should be paid.

Compensation takes priority over any other financial order imposed and the victim surcharge where an offender's means are limited. It should normally be payable within 12 months or up to three years in exceptional circumstances.

4.4   FINE

For magistrates' courts see the MCSG, p.148 (**Appendix 16**, **p.318**).

Statutory limits

In relation to the majority of criminal offences, statutory limits for financial penalties are prescribed. In relation to the powers available to magistrates' courts, fines are usually expressed as 'levels' and the maxima provided by CJA 1982, s.36 are given in **Table 4.2**.

Table 4.2 Maximum fine levels

Level 1	£200
Level 2	£500
Level 3	£1,000
Level 4	£2,500
Level 5	£5,000

Some offences carry much higher prescribed maximum fines, such as some offences under health and safety legislation. In the Crown Court, the maximum financial penalty is an unlimited fine (CJA 1977, s.32(1)).

General approach

Ultimately, the amount of a fine must reflect the seriousness of the offence (CJA 2003, s.164(2)). A court is required to take into account the financial circumstances of the offender and this may have the effect of increasing or reducing the fine (CJA 2003, s.164(1) and (4)). In relation to the offender's means to pay, the order of priority for financial orders is:

(a)   compensation;
(b)   surcharge;
(c)   fine; and
(d)   costs.

The court must order the offender to pay a surcharge of £15 (the victim surcharge) whenever it imposes a fine for an offence committed after 1 April 2007 (CJA 2003, ss.161A and 161B).

In the case of a corporation the court must take account of its financial circumstances so far as they are known. In the event of safety issues arising, a fine should reflect the degree of fault and the consequences of the corporation's failure so as to raise appropriate concern on the part of shareholders and act as a deterrent (*R* v. *Balfour Beatty Rail Infrastructure Services Ltd* [2006] EWCA Crim 1586). At the time of writing a definitive guideline on corporate manslaughter and health and safety offences resulting in death is in the course of preparation.

Assessment of fines

A detailed approach to the assessment of fines, aimed at encouraging consistency of approach and equal impact on offenders who have different financial circumstances, is included in the revised MCSG. Key parts of that scheme are summarised below. In order to obtain a fair outcome for clients, advocates should ensure that the best financial information is made available to the court given the need to establish the appropriate 'relevant weekly income' (RWI) sum (see the financial questionnaire in **Appendix 6**) and be in a position to influence the level of the fine imposed having regard to relevant offence guidelines.

There are essentially four stages for a court to consider:

1. Identify the seriousness of the offence by fixing a percentage of RWI.
2. Identify the RWI.
3. Apply an appropriate guilty plea discount.
4. Consider enforcement.

Summary: assessment

The following is a summary of the approach to the assessment of fines as contained in the MCSG.

Table 4.3 Assessment of fines

	Range	Starting point
Band A	25%–75%	50%
Band B	75%–125%	100%
Band C	125%–175%	150%
Band D	200%–300%	250%
Band E	300%–500%	400%

Identifying the seriousness of an offence

A series of fine 'bands' is established; each band has a starting point and range. The seriousness of an offence determines the appropriate band in an individual case *and* the position of the offence within the range for that band. The percentages are of the RWI, which is determined as set out below.

- Bands A–C are used generally for the offences contained in the MCSG.
- Bands D and E are for use in those cases where an offence might otherwise merit a community order or custodial sentence. Where a court decides not to impose such sentences, an appropriate sentence may instead be a fine, using Band D where the case crossed the threshold for a community sentence and Band E where a custodial sentence might have been imposed.

Identifying the RWI

The court must first make a determination in relation to an offender's financial circumstances to establish their RWI figure.

- Where an offender is in receipt of income from employment or is self-employed and their income is more than £100 per week after tax and national insurance contributions (or equivalent), the RWI is actual income.
- Where an offender's only source of income is state benefit (excluding supplementary benefits such as tax credits, housing, child and council tax benefits) or their income from employment/self-employment is less than £100 per week after tax and national insurance contributions (or equivalent), the RWI is deemed to be £100.
- Where an offender has not provided information/sufficient reliable information the court is entitled to make such determination as it thinks fit as regards financial circumstances (CJA 2003, s.164(5)). Where there is no information, the RWI is assumed to be £350. A court can remit a fine in whole or in part if information is provided subsequently (CJA 2003, s.165(2)).
- Where an offender has no income, the court is not obliged to fix RWI using the above guidance and may impose a fine that it considers reasonable to reflect the seriousness of the offence and lack of means. The power to impose one day's detention may be appropriate in such cases.

Having determined the appropriate fine band and position of the offence within the range for that band, the court will take into account information about the offender's wider financial circumstances, which may have the effect of increasing or reducing the amount of the fine. Relevant information will include the following:

- Out of ordinary expenses – reasonable living expenses have been reflected in the proportions of the RWI in the bands. Out of the ordinary expenses may be relevant to the amount of the fine only where they will substantially reduce ability to pay such that the offender would suffer undue hardship if required to pay a fine based on the standard approach.
- Unusually low outgoings – a fine may be adjusted to reflect living expenses that are substantially lower than normally expected.
- Savings – the fact that an offender has savings should normally be relevant to terms of payment of a fine rather than the amount of the fine. However, where an offender has little/no income but substantial savings, the amount of a fine may be adjusted to reflect this.
- Income of the household – where an offender's household has more than one source of income, a fine should normally be based on the income of the offender alone. However, if their part of the income is very small or the offender is dependent on the income of another, the court may have regard to income and assets that will be available to pay any fine imposed.
- Potential earning capacity – the amount of a fine may be adjusted to reflect an offender's potential earning capacity, such as where the offender is to start a new job shortly after a period of unemployment.
- High income offenders – the court may adjust a fine where a fine based on the RWI of a high earning offender would be disproportionate to the seriousness of the offence. A fine should not normally exceed three-quarters of the maximum fine.

Guilty plea discount

The fine must be reduced to reflect a guilty plea.

Collection and enforcement of fines

The expectation is that the fine imposed will be payable in full on the day that it is imposed. Part payment will be considered where the fine cannot be paid in full immediately. An offender must request 'time to pay' and the court may agree to periodic payments. A fine should normally be payable within 12 months.

The Courts Act (CA) 2003 defines the scheme for the collection of fines with stronger enforcement powers for courts and administrators. At the imposition stage the court must consider the following options for collecting a financial order:

(a) Collection order – this must be made in every case in which a fine or compensation order is made unless this would be impracticable or inappropriate (CA 2003, Sched.5, para.12). The order must set out the sum due and the terms of payment, including whether an order is made to deduct payments from earnings or benefits.

(b) Attachment of earnings/application for benefit deductions – where a compensation order is made or the offender is an existing defaulter the court must make an attachment of earnings order (AEO) or application for benefit deductions (ABD) unless it would be impracticable or inappropriate to do so (CA 2003, Sched.5, para.7A and para.8). In other cases such orders can be made with the consent of the offender (CA 2003, Sched.5, para. 9).

Immediate custody for non-payment of a fine may only be imposed (MCA 1980, s.82) if the offender:

- appears to have sufficient means to pay immediately; or
- is unlikely to remain long enough at a fixed address to allow for enforcement; or
- is simultaneously sentenced or already serving a custodial sentence.

In the Crown Court a fine may be imposed in place of or in addition to any other sentence except a discharge unless an obligatory sentence applies. When imposing a fine the Crown Court must fix a default term of imprisonment for the total fine imposed. The maximum default terms are set out in **Appendix 12**.

4.5 DEFERRED SENTENCES

A court can defer passing sentence for up to six months to enable the sentencing court to have regard to the offender's conduct post conviction (PCC(S)A 2000, s.1 as amended by CJA 2003). In most cases, sentence may only be deferred once (PCC(S)A 2000, s.1(4) as amended by CJA 2003). In order to defer sentence:

- the court must consider that deferring sentence is in the interests of justice; and
- the offender must consent.

In order to make the ability to defer sentence purposeful the court is able to prescribe requirements (including the making of reparation for the offence) to be fulfilled during the period of deferment (PCC(S)A 2000, s.1(3)(b) as amended by CJA 2003). The offender must undertake to comply with these requirements.

The SGC guideline, *New Sentences: Criminal Justice Act 2003* provides guidance on the use of deferred sentences (pp.14–15, paras.1.2.1–1.2.9). It suggests that the decision to defer should be predominantly for cases at the custody or community sentence threshold where the sentencer considers that the offender successfully complying with conditions and requirements would justify a different (lesser) sentence at the end of the period.

Deferring sentence provides an opportunity for an offender to have some influence as to the sentence passed:

(a) it tests the commitment of the offender not to re-offend;
(b) it gives the offender an opportunity to do something where progress can be shown within a short period;
(c) it provides the offender with an opportunity to behave or refrain from behaving in a particular way that will be relevant to sentence (*New Sentences: Criminal Justice Act 2003,* para.1.2.6).

A court may impose any conditions during the period of deferment that it considers appropriate (PCC(S)A 2000, s.1(3)(b)). These could be specific requirements as set out in the provisions for community sentences (CJA 2003, s.177), a residence condition or requirements that are drawn more widely (PCC(S)A 2000, s.1A(1)).

The requirements set must be specific and measurable so that the offender knows exactly what is required (and has a reasonable expectation of being able to comply) and the court can properly assess compliance. The court is able to appoint the probation service or other responsible person to oversee the offender's conduct during this period and prepare a report for the court at the end of the deferment period.

In the interests of clarity for the offender and sentencing court, a precise indication should be given and recorded as to the type of sentence that the court would be minded to impose if it had not decided to defer. The offender must also fully understand the consequences of failure to comply with the requirements imposed: the offender can be called back to court and dealt with before the end of the deferment period, and if a new offence is committed during the deferral period the court may have power to sentence for the original offence and the new offence immediately.

If the offender has substantially conformed or attempted to conform with the proper expectation of the deferring court, an immediate custodial sentence should not be passed (*R* v. *George* (1984) 79 Cr App R 26). The sentence should therefore only be used when, on compliance, a lesser sentence can be justified (*Attorney General's Reference (No.101 of 2006)*; sub nom. *R* v. *P* [2006] EWCA Crim 3335).

4.6 COMMUNITY SENTENCES

Requirements

A community order can contain one or more of a total of 12 requirements depending on the seriousness of the offence. Guidance in relation to the community order has been published by the SGC in its guideline *New Sentences: Criminal Justice Act 2003*. The powers on breach of the community order are different from those previously available for the separate community sentences.

Availability of community sentences was amended from 14 July 2008 by the Criminal Justice and Immigration Act (CJIA) 2008. The power to make community orders is restricted to imprisonable offences unless the offender comes within the 'persistent offender' category (see below). Where an offence is imprisonable only in the Crown Court, a magistrates' court will not be able to impose a community sentence.

Duration

A community order must not last more than three years from the date of imposition, by which time all of the requirements imposed must have been complied with.

Where two or more different requirements are imposed, the court may impose an earlier date or dates in relation to compliance with any one or more of them (CJA 2003, s.177(5)).

Thresholds

A community sentence may only be imposed if one of two thresholds is passed: one is a threshold based upon the seriousness of the offence and the other relates to persistent offenders who have previously been dealt with by way of fines.

Seriousness criterion

CJA 2003, s.148(1) provides that:

> A court must not pass a community sentence on an offender unless it is of the opinion that the offence, or the combination of the offence and one or more offences associated with it, was serious enough to warrant such a sentence.

All of the available disposals should be considered by the court up to and within the threshold, as even if this threshold has been passed advocates should be prepared to try to persuade the court that a fine or discharge may represent an appropriate penalty (*New Sentences: Criminal Justice Act 2003*, para.1.1.9). CJA 2003, s.148(5) provides that a court is not required to impose a community sentence in cases merely because the threshold is passed (in relation to offenders sentenced on or after 14 July 2008 as inserted by CJIA 2008, s.10). In making such representations, emphasis can helpfully be attached to the potential inappropriateness of interventions with a low risk offender, which can increase the risk of re-offending rather than decrease it, and to improvements in enforcement of financial penalties which make them a more viable sentence in a wider range of cases (see *New Sentences: Criminal Justice Act 2003*, p.5).

The guideline reminds sentencers always to be mindful of the possibility of breach when passing sentence. The seriousness of the offence should be reflected in setting sufficiently demanding requirements as part of a community sentence, but there is 'little value in imposing requirements that would "set an offender up to fail" and almost inevitably lead to sanctions for a breach' (*New Sentences: Criminal Justice Act 2003*, para.1.1.13).

Persistent offender criterion

In relation to offenders aged 16 or over who have on three or more previous occasions been sentenced by way of a fine only, a community order may be imposed on a persistent offender instead of a fine if the court considers that, having regard to all the circumstances, it would be in the interests of justice to make such an order (CJA 2003, s.151(1) and (2)). This criterion can apply where a court does not regard the current offence, or the combination of the current offence and one or more offences associated with it, as being serious enough to warrant a community sentence under the seriousness threshold.

Available requirements

In determining the appropriate community sentence the court must have regard to three basic requirements:

1. Suitability – the particular requirement or requirements forming part of the community order must be such as, in the opinion of the court, is, or taken together are, the most suitable for the offender.
2. Proportionality – the restrictions on liberty imposed by the order must be such as, in the opinion of the court, are commensurate with the seriousness of the offence, or the combination of the offence and one or more offences associated with it (CJA 2003, s.148(2)(a) and (b)).
3. Compatibility – before making a community order imposing two or more different requirements falling within CJA 2003, s.177(1), the court must consider whether, in the circumstances of the case, the requirements are compatible with each other (CJA 2003, s.177(6)). In addition the court should seek to avoid conflict with the offender's religious belief and the times they are at work or in education (CJA 2003, s.217).

The seriousness of the offence is the critical consideration in determining the appropriate type and level of restriction of liberty requirements.

A community sentence may comprise any one or more of the requirements as given in **Table 4.4** (CJA 2003, s.177(1)).

47

Table 4.4 Requirements for community sentence

Type of requirement	Relevant sentencing purposes*	Limits
Unpaid work requirement (CJA 2003, s.199)	Punishment/Reparation/ Rehabilitation	Minimum 40 hrs Maximum 300 hrs
Activity requirement (CJA 2003, s.201)	Punishment/Reparation/ Rehabilitation/Protection	Maximum 60 days
Programme requirement (CJA 2003, s.202)	Reparation/Protection	
Prohibited activity requirement (CJA 2003, s.203)	Punishment	
Curfew requirement (CJA 2003, s.204)	Punishment	Maximum 6 months of between 2 and 12 hours each day
Exclusion requirement (CJA 2003, s.205)	Punishment	Maximum 2 years
Residence requirement (CJA 2003, s.206)	Rehabilitation/Protection	
Mental health treatment requirement (CJA 2003, s.207)	Rehabilitation	Consent required
Drug rehabilitation requirement (CJA 2003, s.209)	Rehabilitation	Minimum 6 months for drug treatment or testing Consent required
Alcohol treatment requirement (CJA 2003, s.212)	Rehabilitation	Minimum 6 months Consent required
Supervision requirement (CJA 2003, s.213)	Rehabilitation	
Attendance centre requirement (CJA 2003, s.214)	Punishment	Minimum 12 hours Maximum 36 hours Maximum 3 hours per day
NB: only for offenders under 25 years of age		

Probation Bench Handbook: A Guide to the Work of the National Probation Service for Judges (Ministry of Justice, 2nd edn 2007).

Electronic monitoring

When the court makes an order imposing a curfew requirement or an exclusion requirement the court must also impose an electronic monitoring requirement unless consent cannot be obtained from a third party whose co-operation will make it practical; or monitoring is not available in the area; or in the particular circumstances it is inappropriate to do so. A court may impose an electronic monitoring requirement (with the same exceptions) when it imposes any other requirement (CJA 2003, s.177).

Approach

Range of sentences

There is considerable flexibility within the range of requirements available for community sentences and advocates should assist the court as to factors relevant to a client's suitability for and ability to comply with requirements under consideration.

The court will have a pre-sentence report of one form or another before it which will be based on an indication from the court of the relevant sentencing range (see below) and the purpose(s) of sentencing that it is seeking to fulfil.

The *New Sentences: Criminal Justice Act 2003* guideline provides useful guidance on the principles and practicalities of determining the type and level of requirements that may be imposed. The following are the key considerations:

- The sentence must be commensurate with the seriousness of an offence – courts will properly consider those factors that heighten the risk of the offender committing further offences or causing further harm with a view to lessening that risk.
- There is no single guiding principle, but the seriousness of the offence that has been committed is the most important factor.
- Three sentencing ranges (low, medium and high) within the community sentence band are identified, though flexibility exists to allow for variation to take account of an offender's suitability, etc.:
  - the lowest range of community sentence is for those offenders whose offence was relatively minor within the community sentence band and would include persistent petty offenders whose offences only merit a community sentence by virtue of failing to respond to the previous imposition of fines;
  - the top range is for those offenders who have only just fallen short of a custodial sentence and for those who have passed the threshold but for whom a community sentence is deemed appropriate;

- it is not intended that an offender necessarily progress from one range to the next on subsequent sentencing occasions. The decision as to the appropriate range each time is based upon the seriousness of the new offence(s).

The *New Sentences: Criminal Justice Act 2003* guideline provides (p.9):

The decision on the nature and severity of the requirements to be included in a community sentence should be guided by:

(i)   the assessment of offence seriousness (LOW, MEDIUM OR HIGH);
(ii)   the purpose(s) of sentencing the court wishes to achieve;
(iii) the risk of the offender re-offending;
(iv) the ability of the offender to comply, and
(v)   the availability of requirements in the local area.

The resulting restriction on liberty must be a proportionate response to the offence that was committed.

1.1.24 Below we set out a non-exhaustive description of examples of require-ments that might be appropriate in the three sentencing ranges. These examples focus on punishment in the community, although it is recognised that not all packages will necessarily need to include a punitive requirement. There will clearly be other requirements of a rehabilitative nature, such as a treatment requirement or an accredited programme, which may be appropriate depending on the specific needs of the offender and assessment of suitability. Given the intensity of such interventions, it is expected that these would normally only be appropriate at medium and high levels of seriousness, and where assessed as having a medium or high risk of re-offending. In addition, when passing sentence in any one of the three ranges, the court should consider whether a rehabilitative intervention such as a programme requirement, or a restorative justice intervention might be suitable as an additional or alternative part of the sentence.

Low

1.1.25 For offences only just crossing the community sentence threshold (such as persistent petty offending, some public order offences, some thefts from shops, or interference with a motor vehicle, where the seriousness of the offence or the nature of the offender's record means that a discharge or fine is inappropriate).

1.1.26 Suitable requirements might include:

- 40 to 80 hours of unpaid work or
- a curfew requirement within the lowest range (e.g. up to 12 hours per day for a few weeks) or
- an exclusion requirement (where the circumstances of the case mean that this would be an appropriate disposal without electronic monitoring) lasting a few months or
- a prohibited activity requirement or
- an attendance centre requirement (where available).

1.1.27 Since the restriction on liberty must be commensurate with the seriousness of the offence, particular care needs to be taken with this band to ensure that this obligation is complied with. In most cases, only one requirement will be appropriate and the length may be curtailed if additional requirements are necessary.

Medium

1.1.28   For offences that obviously fall within the community sentence band such as handling stolen goods worth less than £1000 acquired for resale or somewhat more valuable goods acquired for the handler's own use, some cases of burglary in commercial premises, some caes of taking a motor vehicle without consent, or some cases of obtaining property by deception.

1.1.29   Suitable requirements might include:

- a greater number (e.g. 80 to 150) of hours of unpaid work or
- an activity requirement in the middle range (20 to 30 days) or
- a curfew requirement within the middle range (e.g. up to 12 hours for 2–3 months) or
- an exclusion requirement lasting in the region of 6 months or
- a prohibited activity requirement.

1.1.30   Since the restriction on liberty must be commensurate with the seriousness of the offence, particular care needs to be taken with this band to ensure that this obligation is complied with.

High

1.1.31   For offences that only just fall below the custody threshold or where the custody threshold is crossed but a community sentence is more appropriate in all the circumstances, for example some cases displaying the features of a standard domestic burglary committed by a first-time offender.

1.1.32   More intensive sentences which combine two or more requirements may be appropriate at this level. Suitable requirements might include an unpaid work order of between 150 and 300 hours; an activity requirement up to the maximum 60 days; an exclusion order lasting in the region of 12 months; a curfew requirement of up to 12 hours a day for 4–6 months.

Persistent offenders

When dealing with a persistent offender it is 'the persistence of the offending behaviour rather than the seriousness of the offences being committed' that must be addressed. The court should impose requirements such that 'the restriction on liberty is proportionate to the seriousness of the offending, to reflect the fact that the offences, of themselves, are not sufficiently serious to merit a community sentence' (*New Sentences: Criminal Justice Act 2003*, p.7).

The effect of time on remand

Credit for time spent on remand (in custody or equivalent status) should be given in all cases. When announcing sentence the court should make it clear whether or not such credit has been given (bearing in mind that there will be no automatic reduction in sentence). If such credit is *not* to be given the court should explain its reasons, i.e. it considers that it is not justified, would not be practical, or would not be in the best interests of the offender (*New Sentences: Criminal Justice Act 2003*, p.12).

If an offender has already served the maximum sentence on remand the court cannot impose a conditional discharge (*R* v. *Lynch* [2007] EWCA Crim 2624) or a community order (*R* v. *Hemmings* [2007] EWCA Crim 2413).

4.7   CUSTODIAL SENTENCES

Principles applying to custodial sentences

A number of conditions have to be satisfied in relation to the imposition of custodial sentences:

- the offender is legally represented (or had the opportunity to be) (MCA 1980, s.31) unless he has previously been sentenced to an immediate custodial term;
- the custody threshold criteria are met (CJA 2003, s.152(1) and (3) and see **Chapter 1**);
- a pre-sentence report has been obtained and considered, or the court has determined that it is unnecessary to obtain one (CJA 2003, s.156(3));
- if the offender is, or appears to be, mentally disordered, the court must obtain a medical report unless it determines that it is unnecessary to do so (CJA 2003, s.157(1) and (3));
- the length of the custodial sentence must be commensurate with the seriousness of the offence(s) (CJA 2003, s.153(2));
- time spent by the offender on remand in custody (or on bail with a qualifying curfew condition) for an offence (and any related offence) must count towards the sentence as time served (subject to limited exceptions (CJA 2003, s.240)) (for remands on or after 3 November 2008, see CJA 2003, s.240A). A curfew condition qualifies if it imposes an electronically monitored curfew for not less than nine hours in any day. Half of the time subject to such a curfew counts towards the custodial term unless rules provide otherwise or it would be just in all the circumstances to rule otherwise;
- the court must give reasons for and explain the effect of the sentence to the offender (CJA 2003, s.174).

Approach to imposition of custodial sentences

Guidance regarding the threshold test and the general approach to imposition of custodial sentences has been given by the SGC (in its guideline *Overarching Principles: Seriousness*) and can be summarised as follows:

1. The statutory threshold test is intended to ensure that custodial sentences are used as punishment for the most serious offences.
2. Even where the threshold for a custodial sentence is passed, such a sentence is not inevitable.
3. The court should consider the following:

   (a) Has the custody threshold been passed?
   (b) If so, is a custodial sentence unavoidable?
   (c) If so, does the sentence need to take effect immediately or can it be suspended?
   (d) What is the shortest term commensurate with the seriousness of the offence?

Custodial sentences of less than 12 months

Other than where the custodial sentence for an offence is fixed by law, or the offender is sentenced as a dangerous offender, the following points apply:

- The minimum term of imprisonment that can be imposed by a magistrates' court is five days (MCA 1980, s.132).
- Unless and until the CJA 2003 framework for custodial sentences is implemented in full, the maximum term of imprisonment that can be imposed in a magistrates' court for a single offence is six months (PCC(S)A 2000, s.78).
- Consecutive terms can be imposed by a magistrates' court in respect of two or more offences sentenced on the same occasion, to a maximum of 12 months if both offences are either-way offences or six months in other circumstances (MCA 1980, s.133).
- The offender will be released unconditionally having served half of the term (CJA 1991, s.33).
- Commission of a further imprisonable offence after release but before the end of the sentence will render the offender liable to return to prison to serve the whole or part of the unexpired term (PCC(S)A 2000, s.116), and any custodial sentence for the new offence can be ordered to run consecutively.

Custodial sentences of 12 months or more

Where a custodial sentence is of longer than 12 months:

- The length of the sentence must be commensurate with the seriousness of the offence.
- If the offender is not sentenced as a dangerous offender they will be entitled to be released from custody after completing half of the sentence (CJA 2003, ss.244–246).

- The whole of the second half of the sentence will be subject to licence requirements. Such requirements will be set shortly before release by the Secretary of State (as prescribed by order (CJA 2003, s.250)) and continue to the end of the sentence. A court may make recommendations at the sentencing stage on the content of those requirements, which are not binding on the Secretary of State (CJA 2003, s.238(1)). See guideline *New Sentences: Criminal Justice Act 2003*, paras.2.1.11–2.1.14, for further guidance.
- Breach of the post-release requirements at any stage will result in the offender being returned to custody.
- When announcing sentence, the court should explain the way in which the sentence has been calculated, how it will be served and the implications of non-compliance with licence requirements (with reference to the *Consolidated Criminal Practice Direction* [2002] 2 Cr App R 35, Annex C).

Key considerations

General matters that ought to be considered in relation to imposition of custodial sentences include:

- Care should be taken before imposing a custodial sentence on offenders of previous good character, particularly if it was positive good character.
- There should be a particular reluctance to impose a custodial sentence for the first time and care should be taken because of the risk of contamination (*R* v. *Seed; R* v. *Stark* [2007] EWCA Crim 254).
- It is appropriate for the court to take account of family responsibilities.
- Imprisonment of a sole carer is harsh on children where there is lack of violence and of any individual suffering loss (*R* v. *Mills* [2002] EWCA Crim 26; *R* v. *Kefford* [2002] EWCA Crim 519).
- Short prison sentences give little chance for positive action.
- The overcrowded prison regime is likely to be more punitive and the length of the sentence should reflect this.
- If custody is necessary it should be for the shortest time.
- Custody should not be imposed unless the threshold had been passed – a heavy fine could often be an adequate and appropriate penalty. A fine should be used in preference to imprisonment for offenders who gain steady employment and are unlikely to prey on the public again (*R* v. *Baldwin* [2002] EWCA Crim 2647).
- Even if the threshold had been passed personal mitigation and/or a guilty plea may justify a lesser penalty. A clean record is important personal mitigation.

Consecutive sentences

Consecutive sentences should not be imposed for offences that arise out of the same incident unless there are exceptional circumstances. However, consecutive sentences are common where violence has been used to resist arrest or the offence involves possession of a firearm or the offender is in breach of a non-custodial sentence. The totality principle must always be applied.

Time on remand

An order must be sought if time on remand or on bail with a qualifying curfew condition (*R* v. *Baldwin* [2002] EWCA Crim 2647) is to count towards a sentence. However, the court must direct that time served on remand shall count towards a custodial sentence except where an order provides otherwise (where the offender is already serving a sentence and not on licence; or if a sentence is consecutive and the day has already been allowed to count against the earlier sentence (Remand in Custody (Effect of Concurrent and Consecutive Sentences of Imprisonment) Rules 2005 (SI 2005/2054)) or it would be just in all the circumstances not to give a direction (CJA 2003, s.240). In relation to a qualifying bail condition see the Remand on Bail (Disapplication of Credit Period) Rules 2008 (SI 2008/2793). A curfew will not count if it is already part of a sentence. In addition, the time may be *dis*allowed if it is just in all the circumstances to do so – perhaps because of regular breaches of the order (CJA 2003, s.240A). A denial of the offence whilst on remand cannot justify time being disallowed. It only affects discount for a guilty plea (*R* v. *Vaughan* [2008] EWCA Crim 1613).

Offenders aged 18 but under 21

If an offender aged 18 but under 21, on the date of conviction, is sentenced to a custodial sentence, except for dangerous offenders and those receiving custody for life, the sentence is one of detention in a young offender institution (until the Criminal Justice and Courts Services Act 2000, s.61 is brought into effect and abolishes this penalty). Note that:

- the minimum term is 21 days;
- the maximum is the maximum available for the offence; and
- a sentence may be suspended if committed on or after 4 April 2005.

Suspended sentences of imprisonment

A suspended sentence is a sentence of imprisonment, which means that the custody threshold must have been passed and the length of the term must be the shortest that is commensurate with the seriousness of the offence.

Duration

The legislation as currently enacted (by the Criminal Justice Act 2003 (Sentencing) (Transitory Provisions) Order 2005, SI 2005/643) provides that a court which passes a custodial sentence of at least 14 days and not more than 12 months if imposed by the Crown Court, or six months if imposed in a magistrates' court, may suspend it for between six months and two years (the operational period). The guidance provides that 'A prison sentence that is suspended should be for the same term that would have applied if the offender were being sentenced to immediate custody' (*New Sentences: Criminal Justice Act 2003*, para.2.2.1). In addition:

> The operational period of a suspended sentence should reflect the length of the sentence being suspended. As an approximate guide, an operational period of up to 12 months might normally be appropriate for a suspended sentence of up to 6 months and an operational period of up to 18 months might normally be appropriate for a suspended sentence of up to 12 months.
> *New Sentences: Criminal Justice Act 2003*, para.2.2.13

Requirements

The court must impose one or more requirements for the offender to undertake in the community during the operational period. The power to suspend does not arise unless at least one requirement is imposed (*R* v. *Lees-Wolfenden* [2006] EWCA Crim 3068). The requirements are identical to those available for a community sentence. However:

> In order to ensure that the overall terms of the sentence are commensurate with the seriousness of the offence, it is likely that the requirements to be undertaken during the supervision period would be less onerous than if a community sentence had been imposed.
> *New Sentences: Criminal Justice Act 2003*, para. 2.2.14

The period during which the offender undertakes community requirements under the supervision of a responsible officer (the supervision period) may be shorter than the operational period.

The court may periodically review the progress of the offender in complying with the requirements and the reviews will be informed by a report from the responsible officer.

CHAPTER 5

Available ancillary sentencing powers

The ancillary sentencing powers considered in this section are classified in two groups as shown in **Table 5.1**.

Table 5.1 Ancillary sentencing powers

	Magistrates' Court Sentencing Guidelines page nos* [Appendix 16]
(1) Orders relating to property	
Confiscation	169 [**p.342**]
Compensation	165–167 [**pp.335–339**]
Costs	175 [**p.346**]
Property deprivation	169 [**p.342**]
Forfeiture	172 [**pp.344–345**]
Restitution	173 [**pp.345–346**]
(2) Orders relating to future conduct	
Anti-social behaviour order	168 [**p.339**]
Deportation	
Companies Act disqualification	171 [**p.343**]
Disqualification from driving	171 and 184–186 [**p.343** and **pp.355–359**]
Disqualification from working with children	
Drinking banning order	172 [**pp.343–344**]
Exclusion from licensed premises	
Financial reporting order	
Football banning order	172 [**p.344**]
Restraining order	173 [**p.346**]
Serious crime prevention order	
Sexual offences prevention order	174 [**p.346**]
Sexual offence notification on conviction	
Travel restriction order	

* The Magistrates' Court Sentencing Guidelines also contain information about: the deprivation of ownership and disqualification from ownership of animals (p.170) (**Appendix 16, p.342**); binding over orders (p.169) (**Appendix 16, p.341**); and forfeiture and suspension of liquor licences (p.172) (**Appendix 16, p.345**).

Each order is considered under such of the following headings as are relevant:

- statutory basis;
- preconditions;
- effect;
- limitations;
- the position of third parties;
- duration;
- evidential issues;
- penalty on breach;
- definitions; and
- guidance.

5.1 ORDERS RELATING TO PROPERTY

Confiscation

Statutory basis

Proceeds of Crime Act (POCA) 2002, Pt 2.

Preconditions

The court must proceed with a view to a confiscation order if the prosecution invites it to do so or the court believes it is appropriate to do so, unless the court believes that the victim has initiated civil proceedings or intends to do so, when it has a discretion (POCA 2002, s.6).

Requirements

The offender must have been convicted in the Crown Court or committed for sentence under PCC(S)A 2000, ss.3, 4 or 6 or POCA 2002, s.70 giving magistrates' courts power to commit so that a confiscation order may be made. See **Figure 5.1**.

Effects (POCA 2002, ss.6–8)

IF THE OFFENDER HAS A 'CRIMINAL LIFESTYLE'

The court must decide whether the defendant has benefited from his general criminal conduct, whenever it took place.

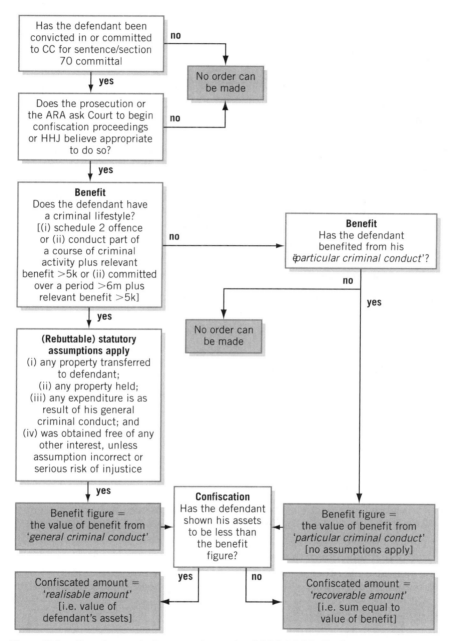

Figure 5.1   Requirements for an order under POCA 2002, Pt 2
Reproduced with the kind permission of Andrew Langdon QC and James Bennett of
Guildhall Chambers

The court must make any of the assumptions (POCA 2002, s.10) required unless the assumption is shown to be incorrect or there would be a risk of serious injustice if the assumptions were made.

The assumptions are:

- that any property transferred to the defendant within the period of six years ending on the day on which proceedings were started against the defendant was obtained by him as a result of his general criminal conduct;
- that any property held by the defendant at any date after the date of conviction was obtained by him as a result of his general criminal conduct;
- that any expenditure incurred by the defendant within a period of six years ending with the date on which the proceedings were first started against him was met from property obtained by him as a result of his general criminal conduct;
- that any property obtained or assumed to have been obtained by the defendant was free of any other interests in the property.

The court should avoid double counting both the acquisition and sale values of the same asset. The higher of the two should be used (*R* v. *Scragg* [2006] EWCA Crim 2916).

IF THE OFFENDER DOES NOT HAVE A 'CRIMINAL LIFESTYLE'

The court must decide whether the defendant has benefited from his particular criminal conduct.

AVAILABLE ASSETS

The court must make an order for the value of the defendant's benefit so ascertained (see further **p.62**) unless:

- the victim has started or intended to start civil proceedings when the court may make the order for such amount up to the value of the benefit as it believes is just;
- the defendant proves that the available amount is less than the benefit in which case the order is for a nominal sum or the available amount.

COURT MUST FIX A DEFAULT TERM

This is in accordance with the table which appears at **Appendix 12**.

The confiscation order cannot be taken into account when deciding the appropriate sentence for the offence where the sentence is not a financial order (POCA 2002, s.13), and financial orders cannot be made while confiscation remains outstanding.

Evidential issues

The burden of proof both for the Crown and the defence is the civil standard.

Penalty on breach

The court may appoint the Director of the Serious Organised Crime Agency as the enforcement authority or an enforcement receiver. If the Director has been appointed as the enforcement authority, all issues over enforcement are dealt with in the Crown Court. In other circumstances they are dealt with in a magistrates' court.

Definitions

CRIMINAL LIFESTYLE

A person has a criminal lifestyle (POCA 2002, s.75) if:

(a) he is convicted of an offence listed in POCA 2002, Sched.2 (see **Appendix 13**); or
(b) the offence constitutes 'conduct forming part of a course of criminal activity' (POCA 2002, s.75(2)(b)); or
(c) the offence was committed over a period of at least six months and the offender has benefited from the conduct to at least £5,000.

CONDUCT FORMING PART OF A COURSE OF CRIMINAL ACTIVITY

Conduct is included if either:

(a) the defendant has been convicted in the same proceedings of at least four offences, he has benefited from at least four offences, and his 'relevant benefit' is at least £5,000; or
(b) the defendant has been convicted on at least two separate occasions during the period of six years ending with the day when the proceedings for the present offence were started, and has benefited from the offences in respect of which he was convicted on both of those occasions, and the 'relevant benefit' amounts to at least £5,000. The latest offence must have been committed on or after 24 March 2003 but it is not necessary that the two earlier offences should have been.

THE AVAILABLE AMOUNT (POCA 2002, S.9)

This is the value of the defendant's property (after allowing for any charge) added to the value of all relevant gifts.

The House of Lords has conducted a basic analysis of the law, identifying the three stages through which every enquiry must proceed (*R* v. *May* [2008] UKHL 28; *Jennings* v. *Crown Prosecution Service* [2008] UKHL 29; and *R* v. *Green* [2008] UKHL 30):

1. Has the defendant benefited from the relevant criminal conduct?
2. If so, what is the value of the benefit he has so obtained?
3. What part of that sum is recoverable by way of realisable assets?

The key issue is to identify the property obtained. Where co-defendants have jointly received the criminal property, each is liable for the full value subject to their realisable assets. It is otherwise for a conspiracy (see *R* v. *Allpress* [2009] EWCA Crim 8). However, mere couriers or custodians or very minor contributors, rewarded by a specific fee and having no interest in the property or proceeds of sale, are unlikely to be found to have obtained the property.

A defendant ordinarily obtains property if in law he owns it, solely or jointly, which implies a power of disposition or control. 'Obtains' means that the defendant should have contributed to a non-trivial extent to the getting of the property.

These decisions clarify the law although every case will depend on its own facts. The clarification is important because, once an application is made, a court cannot refuse to make a confiscation order (*R* v. *Hockey* [2007] EWCA Crim 1577).

The 'benefit' for confiscation purposes is not the profit from a transaction but the turnover of the relevant business. The rules on avoiding serious injustice apply only to the making of the statutory assumptions and not to the making of the order itself (*R* v. *Neuberg* [2007] EWCA Crim 1994).

Great care is required when advising an offender on issues going to confiscation and the repayment of moneys improperly obtained which can be a major head of mitigation. In *R* v. *Farquhar* [2008] EWCA Crim 806, the defendant obtained £26,000 in benefits dishonestly but repaid the total amount due. It was held that in confiscation proceedings the court will be required to make an order for the total amount obtained (regardless of the fact that it had been repaid), unless either there were insufficient realisable assets or there was an abuse (e.g. an indication by the Crown that no confiscation order would be sought). For abuse see *R* v. *Mahmood; R* v. *Shahin* [2005] EWCA Crim 2168.

This aspect received further consideration by the Court of Appeal in *R* v. *Morgan; R* v. *Bygrave* [2008] EWCA Crim 1323. The court recognised the public interest in encouraging the voluntary repayment of moneys improperly obtained. It held that it would be oppressive to require double payment in the following circumstances:

- the defendant's crimes are all offences causing loss to identifiable losers; and
- the defendant's benefit is limited to those crimes; and
- there are no civil proceedings; and
- the loss has been repaid or the full amount is immediately available for payment.

In such circumstances an application for a confiscation order would be an abuse. However, it would not be oppressive in circumstances where:

- the defendant has received additional profit from the crime; or
- the statutory assumptions identify an additional benefit; or
- repayment is uncertain.

Compensation

See **Chapter 4 (p.38)**.

Prosecution costs

Statutory basis

Prosecution of Offences Act 1985, s.18.

Preconditions

There must be a conviction, or dismissal, by the Crown Court of an appeal.

Effect

The court may order the payment of such costs to the prosecutor as it considers to be just and reasonable.

Limitations

1. The amount must be specified in the order.
2. The court must be satisfied that the offender has the means to pay the costs ordered or will have them within a reasonable time (*R* v. *Maher* [1983] QB 784). The defence must provide evidence of means to avoid adverse inferences (*R* v. *Northallerton Magistrates' Court* ex p *Dove* [2000] 1 Cr App R(S) 136).

Penalty on breach

The Crown Court may enlarge beyond 12 months the enforcement powers of the magistrates' court.

Guidance

When the offender is sentenced to immediate custody, an order should not normally be made unless he has the means to pay or good prospects of employment on release. An order should not be made only because the offender refused to consent to summary trial (*R* v. *Mountain* (1979) 68 Cr App R(S) 41). A guilty plea is a relevant factor in deciding whether to make an order but does not make an order inappropriate. Time may be allowed for payment. Costs may include investigation costs (*Neville* v. *Gardner Merchant Ltd* (1983) 5 Cr App R(S) 349). An order for costs should not be grossly disproportionate to a fine imposed (*R* v. *Northallerton Magistrates' Court* ex p *Dove* [2000] 1 Cr App R(S) 136).

Defence costs (when the defence is publicly funded)

Statutory basis

Access to Justice Act 1999 and Criminal Defence Service (Recovery of Defence Costs Orders) Regulations 2001 (SI 2001/856) (as amended).

Preconditions

The magistrates' court has no jurisdiction to order against the defendant the payment of defence costs.

The Crown Court has no jurisdiction to order defence costs against the defendant following a committal for sentence.

In other circumstances the Crown Court may make an order (Criminal Defence Service (Recovery of Defence Costs Orders) Regulations 2001 (SI 2001/856), reg.3 as amended). There are rules for disregarding certain capital sums and the prescribed income (Criminal Defence Service (Recovery of Defence Costs Orders) Regulations 2001 (SI 2001/856), reg.9(2) as amended). Those on passported benefits are exempt.

Property deprivation

Statutory basis

PCC(S)A 2000, s.143.

Preconditions

The court may make an order depriving the offender of his rights in property if he has used or was intending to use it to commit or facilitate the commission of an offence or of property of which he was unlawfully in possession.

Limitations

1. The property must have been lawfully seized from the offender or been in his possession or control when apprehended for the offence or when process was issued.
2. The order may not relate to land or buildings.
3. In making an order the court must have regard to the value of the property and must normally have evidence of the value of the property concerned. It is considered part of the total sentence so that the totality principle applies (*R* v. *Highbury Corner Magistrates' Court* ex p *Di Matteo* (1991) 92 Cr App R 263). The penalty must be commensurate with the offence.

Definitions

1. Facilitation: the commission of an offence includes the taking of any steps after it has been committed for the purpose of disposing of any property to which it relates or of avoiding apprehension or detection.
2. A vehicle shall be regarded as used for the purpose of committing an offence if the conviction is for:

   (a) an imprisonable offence under the Road Traffic Act 1988 including excess alcohol offences and failure to stop and report;
   (b) manslaughter or wanton and dangerous driving.

Guidance

The court may order the proceeds of a sale of the property subject to the order to be paid to a victim of the offence if the court would have made a compensation order but the offender had insufficient means (*R* v. *Highbury Corner Magistrates' Court* ex p *Di Matteo* (1991) 92 Cr App R 263). These are powers routinely used to forfeit offensive weapons, bladed articles and firearms.

Forfeiture

Statutory basis

Misuse of Drugs Act 1971 and other statutory provisions including the Terrorism Act 2000, s.23 as amended by the Counter-Terrorism Act 2008. There are other specific provisions for forfeiture, e.g. the Knives Act 1997, s.6.

Preconditions

The offender must be convicted of a drug trafficking offence or an offence under the Misuse of Drugs Act 1971, or under the Terrorism Act 2000, ss.13–18.

Effect

The court may make the order in relation to anything shown to its satisfaction to relate to the offence (drugs) or which the offender knew or had reasonable cause to suspect might be used for the purposes of terrorism.

Limitations

Forfeiture does not apply to intangible property or land or buildings or to the proceeds of offences or to property that facilitates future offences.

Third party rights

Anyone claiming to be an owner of the property or otherwise interested in it must be allowed to show cause why the order should not be made.

Restitution

Statutory basis

PCC(S)A 2000, s.148.

Preconditions

The court may make an order if:

(a) goods have been stolen; and
(b) the offender has been convicted of any offence with reference to the theft; and
(c) all relevant facts are admitted or established in evidence (no new investigation is possible).

Effect

The offender will be required:

(a)   to restore the goods to any person entitled to recover them; or

(b)   to pay to the owner a sum not exceeding the value of the stolen goods, out of money taken from the possession of the offender on arrest.

Position of third party

1.   A person entitled to recover goods may seek an order for the transfer or delivery to them of any other goods which directly or indirectly represent the stolen goods.

2.   Any third party in possession of the stolen goods may be ordered to release them. They may be ordered to be paid money taken from the possession of the offender on his apprehension if bought or lent by them in good faith.

Penalty on breach

Breach is a contempt of court.

5.2   ORDERS RELATING TO FUTURE CONDUCT

Anti-social behaviour order (ASBO)

Statutory basis

CDA 1998, s.1C.

Preconditions

The court may make an order if:

(a)   an offender is convicted of an offence; and

(b)   the court considers that the offender has acted in a manner that caused or was likely to cause harassment, alarm or distress to one or more persons not of the same household as himself; and

(c)   the order is necessary to protect persons in any place in England and Wales from further acts by the offender which are likely to cause harassment, alarm or distress to one or more persons not of the same household as himself.

Effect

The offender is prohibited from doing anything described in the order.

Duration

The minimum term is two years (for at least one part of the order), otherwise for a specified period or indefinite.

Penalty on breach

Breach of the order is an either-way offence carrying five years' imprisonment on indictment.

Guidance

The SGC has published guidance on the sentencing for breach of an anti-social behaviour order. The guideline also summarises the principles that are relevant to the making of an ASBO as derived from the Court of Appeal authorities (see Annex A to the definitive guideline *Breach of an Anti-Social Behaviour Order*), as follows:

1. Proceedings for the imposition of an ASBO are civil in nature, so that hearsay evidence is admissible, but a court must be satisfied to a criminal standard that the individual has acted in the anti-social manner alleged.
2. The test of 'necessity' requires the exercise of judgement or evaluation; it does not require proof beyond reasonable doubt that the order is 'necessary'.
3. It is particularly important that the findings of fact giving rise to the making of the order are recorded by the court.
4. As the ASBO is a preventative order it is unlawful to use it as a punishment; so, when sentencing an offender, a court must not allow itself to be diverted into making an ASBO as an alternative or additional sanction.
5. The police have powers to arrest an individual for any criminal offence, and the court should not impose an order which prohibits the subject from committing an offence if it will not add significantly to the existing powers of the police to protect others from anti-social behaviour by the subject. An order must not prohibit a criminal offence merely to increase the sentence range available for that offence.
6. The terms of the order made must be precise and capable of being understood by the subject. ['A Guide for the Judiciary' produced by the JSB (third edition published January 2007, supplement published January 2008) provides a list of examples of prohibitions that the higher courts have found to be too wide or poorly drafted; www.jsboard.co.uk]. Where the subject is aged under 18, it is important for both the subject and the parent or guardian to confirm their understanding of the order and its terms. The prohibitions must be enforceable in the sense that they should allow a breach to be readily identified and capable of being proved.
7. An order should not impose a 'standard list' of prohibitions, but should identify and prohibit the particular type of anti-social behaviour that gives

rise to the necessity of an ASBO. Each separate prohibition must be necessary to protect persons from anti-social behaviour by the subject, and each order must be specifically fashioned to deal with the individual concerned.

8. The order must be proportionate to the legitimate aim pursued and commensurate with the risk guarded against. The court should avoid making compliance very difficult through the imposition of numerous prohibitions, and those that will cause great disruption to the subject should be considered with particular care. It is advisable to make an order for a specific period; when considering the duration of an order imposed on a youth, the potential for the subject to mature may be a relevant factor.

9. Not all prohibitions set out in an ASBO have to run for the full term of the ASBO itself. The test must always be what is necessary to deal with the particular anti-social behaviour of the offender and what is proportionate in the circumstances. At least one of the prohibitions must last for the duration of the order but not all are required to last for the 2 years that is the minimum length of an order. The court can vary the terms of an order at any time upon application by the subject (or the applicant in the case of an order made upon application).

10. When making an order upon conviction, the court has the power to suspend its terms until the offender has been released from a custodial sentence. However, where a custodial sentence of 12 months or more is imposed and the offender is liable to be released on licence and thus subject to recall, an order will not generally be necessary. There might be cases where geographical restraints could supplement licence conditions.

11. Other considerations:

    (i) Where an ASBO is imposed on a subject aged 10–17, the court must consider whether a **parenting order** would be desirable in the interests of preventing repetition of the anti-social behaviour [Crime and Disorder Act 1998, s.8. The Anti-social Behaviour Act 2003 [ASBA] now provides for a court to impose stand-alone Parenting Orders, if it is satisfied that the child has engaged in criminal or anti-social behaviour. The ASBA also provides for certain agencies to enter into Parenting Contracts which, as an alternative to legal action, have much in common with the non-statutory Acceptable Behaviour Contracts]. Such an order *must* be made where the offender is aged under 16 and the condition is met, but is discretionary where the offender is aged 16 or 17.

    (ii) Where a magistrates' court imposes a stand-alone ASBO it must also consider whether an **individual support order** (ISO) would be desirable to tackle the underlying causes of the behaviour [Crime and Disorder Act 1998, s.1AA].

    (iii) In the case of an adult the court may make an **intervention order** if the underlying causes of the anti-social behaviour are drug-related and appropriate treatment is available [Crime and Disorder Act 1998, s.1G].

12. Interim orders:
    Where a decision to impose an order (either upon application or conviction) is pending the court may make an interim order if it considers it just to do so [Crime and Disorder Act 1998, s.1D]. The court must balance the seriousness of the behaviour and the urgency with which it is necessary to take steps to control it, with the likely impact of an interim order upon the potential subject [*Leeds Magistrates' Court, ex parte Kenny; Secretary of State for Constitutional Affairs and another, ex parte M* [2004] EWCA Civ 312].

Evidence relevant to the making of an ASBO which was not relevant at trial, may be introduced following conviction (CDA 1998, s.1C(3A) and (3B)), but notice should be given of hearsay evidence (*R* v. *W; R* v. *F* [2006] EWCA Crim 686).

Special measures are available for witnesses (CDA 1998, s.11H).

Automatic deportation

Statutory provision for automatic deportation is contained in the UK Borders Act (UKBA) 2007, s.32.

A 'foreign criminal', that is a non-British citizen convicted in the UK of an offence, must be deported if:

- he is sentenced to imprisonment for a 'serious' offence as prescribed under the Nationality, Immigration and Asylum Act 2002, s.72(4)(a) (this provision is not yet in force); or
- he is sentenced for any offence to 12 months or more.

The deportation is deemed in these circumstances to be conducive to the public good.

However these provisions do not apply where there is an 'exception' (UKBA 2007, s.33) (in which case a discretion to deport remains), and the provisions are subject to the Immigration Act 1971, ss.7 and 8 (Commonwealth citizens, Irish citizens, crew and other exemptions).

UKBA 2007, s.33(2)–(6A) lists the exceptions as follows:

(2) Exception 1 is where removal of the foreign criminal in pursuance of the deportation order would breach –

    (a) a person's Convention rights, or

    (b) the United Kingdom's obligations under the Refugee Convention.

(3) Exception 2 is where the Secretary of Stage thinks that the foreign criminal was under the age of 18 on the date of conviction.

(4) Exception 3 is where the removal of the foreign criminal from the United Kingdom in pursuance of a deportation order would breach rights of the foreign criminal under the Community treaties.

(5) Exception 4 is where the foreign criminal –

    (a) is the subject of a certificate under section 2 or 70 of the Extradition Act 2003,

    (b) is in custody pursuant to arrest under section 5 of that Act,

    (c) is the subject of a provisional warrant under section 73 of that Act,

    (d) is the subject of an authority to proceed under section 7 of the Extradition Act 1989 or an order under paragraph 4(2) of Schedule 1 to that Act, or

    (e) is the subject of a provisional warrant under section 8 of that Act or of a warrant under paragraph 5(1)(b) of Schedule 1 to that Act.

(6) Exception 5 is where any of the following has effect in respect of the foreign criminal –

(a) a hospital order or guardianship order under section 37 of the Mental Health Act 1983,

(b) a hospital direction under section 45A of that Act,

(c) a transfer direction under section 47 of that Act, [. . .]

(6A) Exception 6 is where the Secretary of State thinks the application of section 32(4) and (5) would contravene the United Kingdom's obligations under the Council of Europe Convention on Action against Trafficking in Human Beings (done at Warsaw on 16th May 2005).

Appeals lie under the Nationality, Immigration and Asylum Act 2002 and not to the criminal courts. It is in that jurisdiction that human rights issues may be raised.

Recommendations for deportation

Statutory provision

Immigration Act 1971, s.6 and Sched.3.

Effect

If a non-British citizen of 17 or over is convicted of an imprisonable offence the court may recommend deportation in those cases where deportation is not automatic.

Notice in writing of the power should be given but a failure to do so does not invalidate an order and an adjournment may be ordered (*R* v. *Abdi* [2007] EWCA Crim 1913).

The power does not apply to Irish and Commonwealth citizens provided specific conditions are met (Immigration Act 1971, ss.7 and 8). EU citizens are entitled to the protection of the EC Treaty (see Directive 2004/38/EC on the right of citizens of the Union and their family members to move and reside freely within the territory of the Member States and *R* v. *Carmona* [2006] EWCA Crim 508) and the court must not make a recommendation unless it is satisfied that the offender's continued presence in the UK involves a genuine and sufficiently serious threat (*R* v. *Bouchereau* [1978] QB 732).

The court is concerned with future behaviour but its judgment may be influenced by what has happened in the past. A recommendation for deportation, not being a final disposal, does not engage rights under the European Convention on Human Rights which should be left to the Home Secretary and the Asylum and Immigration Tribunal at the appropriate time. The primary issue is whether the continued presence of the offender was a detriment to the UK/contrary to the public interest (*R* v. *Carmona* [2006] EWCA Crim 508, and note the effect for EU citizens of Directive 2004/38/EC on 'expulsion decisions').

A distinction is to be drawn between those who enter the country fraudulently and those who entered unlawfully who were convicted of an offence unconnected with their status (*R* v. *Benabbas* [2005] EWCA Crim 2113). The court is not concerned with conditions in the offender's country of origin. That is a matter for the Home Office and the Asylum and Immigration Tribunal (*R* v. *Carmona* [2006] EWCA Crim 508).

If a recommendation is made the offender will remain in detention unless the court orders his release.

Disqualification of company directors

Statutory basis

Company Directors Disqualification Act 1986, s.2.

Preconditions

The court may make an order if:

(a)   the offender is convicted of an indictable offence;
(b)   the offence was committed in connection with the promotion, formation, management or liquidation of a company or with the receivership of the company's property.

Duration

Disqualification may be for such a term as the court considers appropriate, subject to 15 years' maximum in the Crown Court and a five-year maximum term in the magistrates' court.

Guidance

The offence may relate to the internal management or to the general conduct of the business of the company (*R* v. *Corbin* (1984) 6 Cr App R(S) 17). The discretion to disqualify is entirely general.

Disqualification from driving

Disqualification from driving will be considered under four headings:

- general power;
- discretionary powers linked to motor vehicles;
- obligatory disqualification; and
- totting up.

Note: If the court disqualifies it does not award penalty points.

Disqualification from driving – general power

Statutory basis

PCC(S)A 2000, s.146.

Preconditions

This is a primary sentencing power and may be used as the penalty for any offence whether or not connected with the use of a motor vehicle and whether or not the offender holds a driving licence. It may also be used as an ancillary order where the sentence is fixed by law or subject to a mandatory custodial sentence. The sentence is available as part of the overall punitive element of a sentence (*R* v. *Sofekun* [2008] EWCA Crim 2035).

Disqualification following a custodial sentence should not inhibit rehabilitation unless there is a bad driving record (*R* v. *Lee* [1971] RTR 30; *R* v. *Thomas (K)* (1984) 78 Cr App R 55).

Disqualification from driving – discretionary power linked to motor vehicles

Statutory basis

PCC(S)A 2000, s.147; Road Traffic Offenders Act (RTOA) 1988, s.34 and Sched.2.

Preconditions

PCC(S)A 2000, S.147

This Crown Court power arises where a vehicle has been used in connection with a crime following conviction on indictment or committal for sentence. The offence must carry at least two years' imprisonment or involve an assault.

The court may disqualify (but not endorse) on conviction for:

(a)   stealing or attempting to steal a motor vehicle;
(b)   taking a motor vehicle without consent or being carried; or
(c)   going equipped to steal a motor vehicle.

This provision is largely redundant because of the general power to disqualify in PCC(S)A 2000, s.146.

RTOA 1988, S.34

The court may also disqualify on conviction of any offence carrying an obligatory endorsement.

Effect

The court may disqualify for such period as it considers appropriate.

Disqualification from driving – obligatory disqualification

Statutory basis

RTOA 1988, s.34.

Precondition

The court must disqualify for the following offences unless there are special reasons for not doing so or for disqualifying for a shorter period:

(a)   causing death by dangerous driving;
(b)   dangerous driving;
(c)   causing death by careless driving while under the influence of drink or drugs;
(d)   causing death by careless or inconsiderate driving;
(e)   causing death by driving while unlicensed, disqualified or uninsured;
(f)   driving or attempting to drive while unfit;
(g)   driving or attempting to drive with excess alcohol;
(h)   failing to provide a specimen for analysis (driving or attempting to drive);
(i)   racing or speed trials;
(j)   manslaughter;
(k)   aggravated vehicle taking;
(l)   furious driving (Offences Against the Person Act 1861, s.35);
(m)   using a vehicle in a dangerous condition within three years of a like conviction.

Duration

The minimum terms are as follows but the length is otherwise in the discretion of the court. If the court finds no special reasons, it must disqualify for at least 12 months, unless:

(a)   the defendant is convicted of manslaughter, causing death by dangerous driving, or causing death by careless driving while under the influence of drink or drugs – minimum two years; or
(b)   the defendant has been twice disqualified for 56 days or more in the three years before the commission of the present offence – minimum two years; or
(c)   the defendant has been convicted of an excess alcohol offence and has been convicted of an excess alcohol offence within the last 10 years – minimum three years.

The court may disqualify the offender for any period longer than the minimum. In relation to the four causing death by driving offences the SGC has advised the duration of the order should allow for the length of any custodial sentence imposed in order to ensure that the disqualification has the desired impact (*Causing Death by Driving*, p.7, para.31).

Requirement to take a basic or extended driving test

The court must order the offender to take an extended driving test if the conviction is for:

(a) manslaughter;
(b) causing death by dangerous driving;
(c) causing death by careless driving when affected by alcohol;
(d) dangerous driving.

The court may require the offender to take a further driving test in other cases carrying obligatory disqualification.

Penalty on breach

Driving while disqualified is a summary offence carrying six months' imprisonment or a level 5 fine.

Guidance

The onus is on the offender to establish special reasons in order to avoid a disqualification; the relevant facts must be established on the balance of probabilities. A special reason is an extenuating circumstance directly relating to the circumstances of the offence. Matters related to the effect of disqualification on the personal circumstances of the offender cannot constitute special reasons for this purpose.

If the court finds that special reasons exist, it is not obliged to disqualify the defendant, but may do so in the exercise of its discretion. If the court finds that special reasons exist and does not disqualify, the court must award penalty points (within the range of 3 to 11) and follow the penalty points procedure, unless special reasons prevail again (RTOA 1988, s.44).

Disqualification from driving – totting up

Statutory basis

RTOA 1988, s.35.

Preconditions

Totting up applies if the total number of points endorsed on an offender's licence reaches 12 or more when the points endorsed for the current offence(s) are added to any others endorsed on the offender's licence. Points are ignored if:

(a)   they relate to offences committed more than three years before the date of the commission of the current offence(s); or

(b)   the points were awarded before a disqualification imposed on an earlier totting up.

The key is to look three years before and three years after the date of the current offence and add together penalty points for those not more than three years apart from one another (RTOA 1988, s.29).

A totting up disqualification need not be imposed if the court finds there were grounds for mitigating the normal consequences of the conviction.

Duration

The normal minimum period is six months. If there are previous disqualifications to be taken into account, the minimum period of disqualification may be 12 months or two years.

Guidance

The offender must establish 'mitigating circumstances', normally by calling evidence.

The following matters may not constitute grounds for mitigating the normal consequences of conviction:

(a)   circumstances alleged to make the offence or any of the offences not a serious one;

(b)   hardship, other than exceptional hardship;

(c)   any circumstances that have been taken into account as mitigating grounds within the last three years.

The fact that the offender has been sentenced to custody on this occasion may constitute a mitigating ground in an appropriate case.

If the court finds that there are mitigating grounds, the court may either disqualify for a shorter period than would otherwise be required, or refrain from disqualifying at all.

If the court does not disqualify, it should order the licence to be endorsed with the appropriate penalty points unless there are special reasons for not doing so. The offender may be ordered to take a further driving test.

If the defendant does not establish mitigating grounds, the court must disqualify for at least the relevant minimum period; there is no maximum period.

Disqualification from working with children

Statutory basis

Criminal Justice and Courts Services Act 2000, ss.26–31.

Note: These provisions are repealed by the Safeguarding Vulnerable Groups Act 2006 from a day to be appointed. That Act introduces a barring scheme which is not dependent on an order of the court.

Drinking banning order

Statutory basis

Violent Crime Reduction Act 2006, s.6, when brought into force.

Preconditions

The court must consider making an order if:

(a) the offender is aged 16 or over;
(b) the offender has engaged in criminal or disorderly conduct while under the influence of alcohol;
(c) the court considers that the order is necessary to protect other persons from further criminal or disorderly conduct while under the influence of alcohol.

Effect

The offender is prohibited from doing things directed in the order including such prohibition as the court considers necessary on the offender entering licensed or other premises where alcohol is available.

Limitations

An order cannot prohibit the offender from access to a place where he resides or where he is required to attend for work or employment or education or medical treatment or by statute or court order.

Duration

Different prohibitions may last for different times within these parameters. The period can be halved on completion of an approved course. Note that:

• the minimum term is six months;
• the maximum term is two years.

Evidential issues

Evidence that is not admissible in the main proceedings may be introduced by prosecution or defence.

Penalty on breach

Breach of the order is a summary-only offence punishable with a maximum level 4 fine.

Exclusion order (licensed premises)

Statutory basis

Licensed Premises (Exclusion of Certain Persons) Act 1980, s.1.

Preconditions

The court may make an order if the offender is convicted of an offence committed on licensed premises, in the course of which he resorts or threatens to resort to violence.

Effect

The offender is excluded from named premises (whether or not the offence was committed there) without the express consent of the licensee or his servant or agent.

Duration

Note that:

- the minimum term is three months; and
- the maximum term is two years.

Penalty on breach

Breach of the order is a summary-only offence punishable with one month's imprisonment and/or a level 3 fine.

Note that the Violent Crime Reduction Act 2006 contains power to repeal this provision.

Financial reporting order

Statutory basis

Serious Organised Crime and Police Act 2005, s.76 (such an order is a sentence that may be subject to an appeal to the Court of Appeal – *R* v. *Adams* [2008] EWCA Crim 914).

Preconditions

A court may make an order when:

(a) the offender is convicted of a relevant offence;
(b) the court is satisfied that the risk of the offender committing another such offence is sufficiently high to justify making the order.

It is particularly suitable for fraudsters who are likely to continue to commit financial crime.

Effect

The offender must make a report to a specified person of such particulars of his financial affairs as are specified at the end of the specified periods.

Penalty on breach

A failure to report is a summary offence carrying six months' imprisonment.

Duration

The order will be for the period specified subject to the following maxima:

- magistrates' court sentence: five years;
- sentence of life imprisonment: 20 years;
- otherwise 15 years.

Definition

A relevant offence is:

- obtaining by deception (Theft Act 1968, s.15);
- obtaining a money transfer by deception (Theft Act 1968, s.15A);
- obtaining a pecuniary advantage by deception (Theft Act 1968, s.17);
- procuring a valuable security by deception (Theft Act 1968, s.20(2));
- obtaining services by deception (Theft Act 1978, s.1);
- evasion of liability by deception (Theft Act 1978, s.2);
- any offence specified in POCA 2002, Sched.2;
- fraud (Fraud Act 2006, s.1);
- obtaining services dishonestly (Fraud Act 2006, s.11);
- conspiracy to defraud;
- false accounting (Theft Act 1968, s.17);
- bribery (common law);
- corruption of public bodies (Public Bodies Corrupt Practices Act 1889, s.1);

- bribes obtained by or given to agents (Prevention of Corruption Act 1906, s.1);
- assisting another to retain the benefit of criminal conduct (CJA 1988, s.93A);
- acquisition, possession or use of proceeds of criminal conduct (CJA 1988, s.93B);
- concealing or transferring proceeds of criminal conduct (CJA 1988, s.93C);
- concealing or transferring proceeds of drug trafficking (Drug Trafficking Act 1994, s.49);
- assisting another person to retain the benefit of drug trafficking (Drug Trafficking Act 1994, s.50);
- acquisition, possession or use of proceeds of drug trafficking (Drug Trafficking Act 1994, s.51);
- fundraising for purposes of terrorism (Terrorism Act 2000, s.15);
- use and possession of money, etc. for purposes of terrorism (Terrorism Act 2000, s.16);
- funding arrangements for purposes of terrorism (Terrorism Act 2000, s.17);
- money laundering in connection with terrorism (Terrorism Act 2000, s.18);
- acquisition, use and possession of criminal property (POCA 2002, s.329);
- cheating in relation to the public revenue;
- fraudulent evasion of duty (Customs and Excise Management Act 1979, s.170);
- VAT offences (Value Added Tax Act 1994, s.72);
- fraudulent evasion of income tax (Finance Act 2000, s.144);
- tax credit fraud (Tax Credits Act 2002, s.35);
- attempting, conspiring in or inciting the commission of, or aiding, abetting, counselling or procuring or any of these offences.

Football banning orders

Statutory basis

Football Spectators Act 1989, s.14A.

Preconditions

The court must make an order if:

(a)   an offender is convicted of a relevant offence; and
(b)   the court is satisfied that there are reasonable grounds to believe that a banning order would help to prevent violence or disorder at or in connection with any regulated football matches.

Effect

The effects of the order are:

(a)   to prohibit the offender from attending a regulated football match in England and Wales; and

(b)   to require the offender to report when required at a police station when regulated football matches are played outside England and Wales;

(c)   to require the offender to surrender his passport in connection with matches played outside England and Wales unless there are exceptional circumstances.

Other conditions may also be imposed.

Duration

If a custodial sentence is imposed the order may be for a minimum of six years and a maximum of 10. If another sentence is imposed the duration is a minimum of three years and a maximum of five.

Guidance

Proceedings may be adjourned after the offender is otherwise sentenced and both Crown and defence may introduce further evidence not relevant to the original charge although there is no requirement for repetition or propensity (*R* v. *Hughes* [2005] EWCA Crim 2537). Deterrence is a proper consideration even when the incident was an isolated act (*R (on the application of White)* v. *Blackfriars Crown Court* [2008] EWHC 510). An offence can relate to football matches on a journey away from the game (*DPP* v. *Beaumont* [2008] EWHC 523).

Penalty on breach

Breach of the order is a summary offence carrying six months' imprisonment and/or a fine up to level 5.

Definitions

REGULATED FOOTBALL MATCH

A regulated football match is an association football match in which one or both of the participating teams represents a club which is for the time being a member (whether a full or associate member) of the Football League, the Football Association Premier League or the Football Conference, or represents a club from outside England and Wales, or represents a country or territory; and which is played at a sports ground which is designated by order under the Safety of Sports Grounds Act 1975, s.1(1) or registered with the Football League or the Football Association Premier League as the home ground of a club which is a member of the Football League or the Football Association Premier League at the time the match is played; or is played in the Football Association Cup (other than in a preliminary or qualifying round).

RELEVANT OFFENCES

Relevant offences are as follows:

(a) any offence under the Football Spectators Act 1989, ss.2(1), 5(7), 14J(1) or 21C(2);

(b) any offence under the Sporting Events (Control of Alcohol, etc.) Act 1985, ss.2 or 2A (alcohol, containers and fireworks) committed by the accused at any regulated football match or while entering or trying to enter the ground;

(c) any offence under the Public Order Act 1986, s.5 (harassment, alarm or distress) or any provision of Pt III of that Act (racial hatred) committed during a period relevant to a regulated football match at any premises while the accused was at, or was entering or leaving or trying to enter or leave the premises;

(d) any offence involving the use or threat of violence by the accused towards another person committed during a period relevant to a regulated football match at any premises while the accused was at, or was entering or leaving or trying to enter or leave, the premises;

(e) any offence involving the use or threat of violence towards property committed during a period relevant to a regulated football match at any premises while the accused was at, or was entering or leaving or trying to enter or leave, the premises;

(f) any offence involving the use, carrying or possession of an offensive weapon or a firearm committed during a period relevant to a regulated football match at any premises while the accused was at, or was entering or leaving or trying to enter or leave, the premises;

(g) any offence under the Licensing Act 1872, s.12 (persons found drunk in public places, etc.) of being found drunk in a highway or other public place committed while the accused was on a journey to or from a regulated football match in respect of which the court makes a declaration of relevance;

(h) any offence under the Criminal Justice Act 1967, s.91(1) (disorderly behaviour while drunk in a public place) committed in a highway or other public place while the accused was on a journey to or from a regulated football match in respect of which the court makes a declaration of relevance;

(i) any offence under the Sporting Events (Control of Alcohol, etc.) Act 1985, s.1 (alcohol on coaches or trains to or from sporting events) committed while the accused was on a journey to or from a regulated football match in respect of which the court makes a declaration of relevance;

(j) any offence under the Public Order Act 1986, s.4A or s.5 (harassment, alarm or distress) or any provision of Pt III of that Act (racial hatred) committed while the accused was on a journey to or from a regulated football match in respect of which the court makes a declaration of relevance;

(k) any offence under the Road Traffic Act 1988, ss.4 or 5 (driving, etc. when under the influence of drink or drugs or with an alcohol concentration above the prescribed limit) committed while the accused was on a journey to or from a regulated football match in respect of which the court makes a declaration of relevance;

(l) any offence involving the use or threat of violence by the accused towards another person committed while one or each of them was on a journey to or from a regulated football match in respect of which the court makes a declaration of relevance;

(m) any offence involving the use or threat of violence towards property committed while the accused was on a journey to or from a regulated football match in respect of which the court makes a declaration of relevance;

(n) any offence involving the use, carrying or possession of an offensive weapon or a firearm committed while the accused was on a journey to or from a regulated football match in respect of which the court makes a declaration of relevance;

(o) any offence under the Football (Offences) Act 1991;

(p) any other offence under the Public Order Act 1986, s.5 (harassment, alarm or distress) or any provision of Pt III of that Act (racial hatred) which was committed during a period relevant to a regulated football match in respect of which the court makes a declaration that the offence related to that match or to that match and any other football match which took place during that period;

(q) any other offence involving the use or threat of violence by the accused towards another person which was committed during a period relevant to a regulated football match in respect of which the court makes a declaration that the offence related to that match or to that match and any other football match which took place during that period;

(r) any other offence involving the use or threat of violence towards property which was committed during a period relevant to a regulated football match in respect of which the court makes a declaration that the offence related to that match or to that match and any other football match which took place during that period;

(s)   any other offence involving the use, carrying or possession of an offen-
       sive weapon which was committed during a period relevant to a regu-
       lated football match in respect of which the court makes a declaration
       that the offence related to that match or to that match and any other
       football mach which took place during that period;
(t)   any offence under the Criminal Justice and Public Order Act 1994, s.166
       (sale of tickets by unauthorised persons) which relates to tickets for a
       football match.

The period relevant to a football match is the period beginning two hours
before the start of the match, or the advertised start or the time when spectators are first admitted to the premises, whichever is the earliest, and ending
one hour after the end of the match. In relation to certain offences, the period
extends from 24 hours before to 24 hours after the match.

   The court may not make a declaration of relevance unless the prosecutor
gave notice to the defendant five days before the first day of the trial that it
was proposed to show that the offence related to football matches, unless the
offender consents to waive the requirement or the court is satisfied that the
interests of justice do not require more notice to be given.

Restraining order

Statutory basis

Protection from Harassment Act 1997, s.14A.

Preconditions

The court may make an order on conviction of an offence contrary to the
Protection from Harassment Act 1997, s.2 or s.4.

Effect

The defendant is prohibited from doing anything described in the order for
the purpose of protecting the victim or any other person named from further
conduct that amounts to harassment or will cause a fear of violence.

Duration

The order may be for a specified term or until further order.

Penalty on breach

Breach of the order is an either-way offence carrying the penalty of five years'
custody on indictment.

Serious crime prevention orders

Statutory basis

Serious Crime Act 2007, s.1.

Preconditions

This is a civil order but is available in the Crown Court where a person aged 18 or over is convicted of a 'serious offence' or has been so convicted in the magistrates' court and committed for sentence.

Effect

The court may impose such restrictions or requirements as it considers appropriate to protect the public by preventing, restricting or disrupting involvement by the person in serious crime (examples of orders appear in the Serious Crime Act 2007, s.5). An order may not require a person to produce excluded material under the Police and Criminal Evidence Act 1984 or any privileged material or oral answers or confidential material without the consent of the person enjoying that confidence.

Conditions

An application must be made by the Crown.

The court may make an order if it has reasonable grounds to believe that the order would protect the public by preventing, restricting or disrupting involvement by the person in serious crime.

Duration

An order may last a maximum of five years. Different parts may last for different times.

Position of third parties

The court must allow third parties to make representations if an order would have a significant adverse effect.

Evidence

Additional evidence not admissible in criminal proceedings may be led.

Penalty on breach

Breach of the order is an either-way offence with five years' imprisonment on indictment.

Definitions

A 'serious offence' is defined as one listed in the Serious Crime Act 2007, Sched.1 or any offence which the court considers to be sufficiently serious to be treated as if it were specified in the Schedule (s.2(2)).

Sexual offences prevention order

Statutory basis

Sexual Offences Act (SOA) 2003, s.104.

Preconditions

A court may make an order if:

(a)   an offender is convicted (or found to be under a disability and to have done the act of which he is charged; or found not guilty by reason of insanity) of an offence in SOA 2003, Sched.3 or Sched.5; and

(b)   the court is satisfied that it is necessary to do so to protect the public or any particular members of the public from serious sexual harm.

Effect

The defendant is prohibited from doing anything described in the order.

Duration

The minimum term is five years. Otherwise the order may be for a fixed term or until further notice.

Definitions

Serious sexual harm is serious physical or psychological harm caused by the defendant committing an offence in SOA 2003, Sched.3 (SOA 2003, s.106(3)) (see **Appendix 14** for Sched.3 and **Appendix 15** for Sched.5).

Penalty on breach

Breach of the order is an either-way offence carrying five years' custody on indictment.

Guidance

The fact that the court does not impose a dangerous offender sentence does not preclude a sexual offences prevention order (*R* v. *Rampley* [2006] EWCA Crim 2203) and the existence of such an order may make a penalty as a dangerous offender less likely to be required (*R* v. *Terrell* [2007] EWCA Crim 3079).

Sexual offence notification on conviction

Note: This is not a penalty imposed by the criminal courts but the automatic outcome of certain convictions. However, for offenders under 18 the court may make a direction that the notification obligations are to be those of the person having parental responsibility (SOA 2003, s.89).

Statutory basis

SOA 2003, ss.80–92.

Preconditions

The requirements to notify apply on conviction of offences in SOA 2003, Sched.3 (see **Appendix 14**) (or on a finding of not guilty by reason of insanity, or that the offender is under a disability but has done the act or on the imposition of a caution).

Duration

The periods during which the offender is liable to the notification requirements are as shown in **Table 5.2**.

Effect

The information to be notified is:

(a)   date of birth;
(b)   national insurance number;
(c)   names;
(d)   home address (SOA 2003, s.83).

Table 5.2 Duration of notification requirements

Offender	Period
A person who, in respect of the offence, is or has been sentenced to imprisonment for life or for a term of 30 months or more	An indefinite period beginning with the date of conviction (the relevant date)
A person who, in respect of the offence or finding, is or has been admitted to a hospital subject to a restriction order	An indefinite period beginning with that date
A person who, in respect of the offence, is or has been sentenced to imprisonment for a term of more than 6 months but less than 30 months	10 years beginning with that date
A person who, in respect of the offence, is or has been sentenced to imprisonment for a term of 6 months or less	7 years beginning with that date
A person who, in respect of the offence or finding, is or has been admitted to a hospital without being subject to a restriction order	7 years beginning with that date
A person who has been cautioned	2 years beginning with that date
A person in whose case an order for conditional discharge is made in respect of the offence	The period of conditional discharge
A person who receives a detention and training order*	If the custodial element exceeds 12 months, period is 5 years beginning with the date of conviction** If the custodial element is 12 months or less, period is 3½ years beginning with the date of conviction**
A person of any other description	5 years beginning with the date of conviction

Note: In relation to those under 18 at the date of conviction the above periods are halved.
* This is not part of the statutory provisions but is the effect of the interpretation of those provisions by the Court of Appeal in *R* v. *Slocombe* [2005] EWCA Crim 2997.
** In assessing the length of the sentence for these purposes consecutive terms are aggregated.

The requirements are:

(a) to notify within three days; and

(b) to re-notify at least once in each year.

There must also be notification within three days of changes in name or address or a stay of seven days (or two or more stays totalling seven days in any 12-month period) away from the home address.

Penalty on breach

Failure to comply with notification requirements is an either-way offence carrying five years' custody on indictment.

Travel restriction order

Statutory basis

Criminal Justice and Police Act 2001, s.33.

Preconditions

The court must make an order, unless it determines that it is not appropriate to do so, on conviction of an offender for a drug trafficking offence for which it imposes a custodial sentence of four years or more.

Effect

The order prohibits the offender from leaving the United Kingdom. The court may require the delivery of any UK passport.

Duration

The minimum terms for an order are as follows:

- two years if the custodial sentence is four years;
- four years if the sentence is more than four but less than 10 years;
- five years if the sentence exceeds 10 years.

Guidance

The restriction order must be proportionate and fair and prevent or reduce the risk of offending. Relevant considerations include:

- the public interest in preventing re-offending;
- age;

- previous/personal mitigation;
- risk of re-offending;
- family contacts;
- employment considerations, ability to work;
- the nature and scale of the operation (*R* v. *Mee* [2004] EWCA Crim 629).

Definitions

A drug trafficking offence is:

(a)   an offence under the Misuse of Drugs Act 1971, s.4(2) or (3) (production and supply of controlled drugs);

(b)   an offence under the Misuse of Drugs Act 1971, s.20 (assisting in or inducing commission outside the UK of an offence punishable under a corresponding law);

(c)   an offence under:

(i)   the Customs and Excise Management Act (CEMA) 1979, s.50(2) or (3) (improper importation);

(ii)   CEMA 1979, s.68(2) (exportation); or

(iii) CEMA 1979, s.170 (fraudulent evasion), in connection with a prohibition or restriction on importation or exportation having effect by virtue of the Misuse of Drugs Act 1971, s.3;

(d)   an offence under the Criminal Law Act 1977, s.1 of conspiracy to commit any of the offences in paragraphs (1) to (c) above;

(e)   an offence under the Criminal Attempts Act 1981, s.1 of attempting to commit any of those offences; and

(f)   an offence under the Misuse of Drugs Act 1971, s.19 or at common law of inciting another person to commit any of those offences.

Penalty on breach

Leaving the UK in breach of a restriction order is an either-way offence carrying five years' imprisonment.

CHAPTER 6

Mental health orders

6.1 INTRODUCTION

Impact on obligatory sentence

The imposition of any mental health disposal other than as part of a community order overrides the normal rules on obligatory sentences in relation to firearms offences, burglary and drug trafficking.

Definitions

The Mental Health Act (MHA) 2007 came into force on 3 November 2008. 'Mental disorder' means any disorder or disability of the mind (MHA 2007, s.1).

A person with learning difficulties shall not be considered by reason of that difficulty to be mentally disordered unless the disability is associated with abnormally aggressive or seriously irresponsible behaviour (MHA 2007, s.2).

Dependence on alcohol or drugs is not a disability of the mind (MHA 2007, s.3), though their effect may lead to such disability.

6.2 HOSPITAL ORDER WITHOUT CONVICTION

Under MHA 1983, s.37(3) if a magistrates' court would have power to make a hospital order on conviction, it may instead make an order on finding that the defendant did the act or made the omission.

Under the Criminal Procedure (Insanity) Act 1964, s.5 in the Crown Court, when a defendant is found unfit to plead but then held to have done the act or made the omission charged against him, or not guilty by reason of insanity, the court shall make in respect of him a hospital order, or a supervision order or an order for absolute discharge.

6.3 INTERIM ORDERS

Remand to hospital for psychiatric reports

Statutory provision

MHA 1983, s.35.

Effect

Power is given to magistrates' courts and the Crown Court to remand an accused to hospital for the preparation of a report on his mental condition.

The power may be exercised by a magistrates' court in relation to a person who has been convicted of an offence punishable on summary conviction with imprisonment, or one who is charged with such an offence and the court is satisfied that he did the act or made the omission charged or he has consented to the exercise of the power.

The same power on the same evidence may be exercised by the Crown Court in relation to any person awaiting trial at that court or post conviction for an imprisonable offence. A Crown Court may remand the defendant to a specified hospital for a report on his mental condition at any stage before he is sentenced for an imprisonable offence, including before trial.

Preconditions

The court must be satisfied on the written or oral report of a single approved clinician that there is reason to suspect that the defendant is suffering from a mental disorder. The court must be of the opinion that it would be impractical for a report to be made if he were remanded on bail.

The power may be used for a person awaiting trial for but not convicted of murder.

The court must be satisfied that arrangements have been made for admission to hospital within seven days.

The individual remands may be for 28 days to a maximum of 12 weeks.

Remand to hospital for psychiatric treatment

Statutory provision

MHA 1983, s.36.

Effect

The Crown Court may remand an accused charged with facing an imprisonable offence to hospital for treatment before trial or sentence. If used before trial the power may enable the defendant to undertake a full trial rather than be treated as unfit to plead.

Preconditions

This is a Crown Court power. It is not available for a defendant awaiting trial for murder. The case must not be suitable for bail.

The court must be satisfied on the written or oral evidence of two approved clinicians that the defendant is suffering from mental disorder of a nature or degree which makes it appropriate for him to be detained in hospital for treatment and that appropriate medical treatment is available.

Individual remands may be for 28 days to a maximum of 12 weeks. The remands may be terminated at any stage.

Interim hospital orders

Statutory provision

MHA 1983, s.38.

Effect

An order authorises the admission and detention of a convicted offender to a hospital for treatment for a trial period to assess their response to treatment and their suitability for a hospital order.

Preconditions

The court must be satisfied on the written or oral evidence of two approved clinicians that the defendant is suffering from mental disorder and that there is reason to suppose that the mental disorder is such that it may be appropriate for a hospital order to be made.

The offence must be imprisonable.

A hospital place must be available at the hospital at which one of the approved clinicians is based within 28 days.

The order may not exceed 12 weeks in the first instance. It may be continued 28 days at a time for up to 12 months in total.

6.4 AVAILABLE SENTENCES

Community order with a mental health treatment requirement

Statutory provisions

CJA 2003, ss.207–208.

Nature of the order

A community order may contain, with the consent of the defendant, a requirement that the offender submit to treatment under the direction of a qualified medical practitioner or chartered psychologist with a view to the improvement of his mental condition.

Procedure

The court must be satisfied on the evidence of a registered medical practitioner that the mental condition of the offender is such as to require and be susceptible to treatment but does not warrant detention under a hospital order or a guardianship order and that arrangements for the offender's treatment have been or can be made.

Guardianship order

Statutory provision

MHA 1983, s.37.

Nature of the order

A guardianship order places the offender in the guardianship of the local authority.

Preconditions

The defendant must be at least 16 years old and convicted of an imprisonable offence.

The court must be satisfied on the written or oral evidence of two approved clinicians that the defendant is suffering from a mental disorder of such a nature or degree as to warrant the defendant's reception into guardianship.

An order shall not be made unless the court is satisfied that the local authority or another person concerned is willing to receive the defendant with guardianship. Information may be sought by the court in accordance with MHA 1983, s.39A.

Hospital order

Statutory provision

MHA 1983, s.37.

Nature of the order

An order authorises admission to and detention in hospital.

Preconditions

The court must be satisfied on the written or oral evidence of two approved clinicians that the defendant is convicted of an imprisonable offence, and is suffering from a mental disorder of such a nature or degree as to make it appropriate for him to be detained in a hospital for medical treatment.

An order shall not be made unless the court is of the opinion, having regard to all the circumstances, including the nature of the offence and the character and antecedents of the defendant, and to other means of dealing with him, that the hospital order is the most suitable means of dealing with the case.

The court must be satisfied that arrangements have been made for admission to a hospital within 28 days of the order.

Guidance

The court may request any regional health authority to furnish such information as the authority has or can reasonably obtain with respect to hospitals in the region or elsewhere (MHA 1983, s.39).

Restriction order

Statutory provision

MHA 1983, s.41.

Nature of the order

The order restricts the offender's discharge from hospital (the restrictions appear at MHA 1983, s.41(3)).

Preconditions

The court must have made a hospital order.

It must appear to the court to be necessary to protect a member of the public from serious harm having regard to the nature of the offence, the antecedents of the offender and the risk of his committing further offences.

An order may not be made unless at least one of the approved clinicians whose evidence has been taken into account has given oral evidence.

Guidance

Only a Crown Court may impose a restriction order but the magistrates' court may commit to the Crown Court for this purpose (MHA 1983, s.43 which includes summary-only offences as long as they are imprisonable). A restriction order is normally made without a limit of time.

Hospital and limitation direction

Statutory provisions

MHA 1983, ss.45A and 45B.

Effect

When imposing a sentence of imprisonment the Crown Court may make a hospital and limitation direction directing the defendant's detention in hospital. Should the defendant be released from hospital the prison sentence continues to take effect. If the prison sentence has expired the defendant will continue in hospital as an unrestricted patient. The order must be accompanied by a restriction order.

Preconditions

This is a Crown Court power. The court must be satisfied on the evidence of two approved clinicians (one of whom must give oral evidence) that:

- the offender is suffering from mental disorder;
- the disorder is of a nature or degree which makes it appropriate for the defendant to be detained in a hospital for medical treatment and that appropriate medical treatment is available to him;
- the defendant will be admitted to the hospital within 28 days.

CHAPTER 7

Breach proceedings and offences

7.1 INTRODUCTION

This chapter covers proceedings for breach or non-compliance with any of the following:

- conditional discharge;
- fine;
- community order;
- suspended sentence of imprisonment;
- protective order;
- anti-social behaviour order.

The relevant SGC guidelines are:

- *New Sentences: Criminal Justice Act 2003*;
- *Breach of a Protective Order*;
- *Breach of an Anti-Social Behaviour Order*;
- Magistrates' Court Sentencing Guidelines (MCSG).

7.2 BREACH OF CONDITIONAL DISCHARGE

Statutory provision

The power to deal with a breach of a conditional discharge arises when the offender is convicted of an offence committed during the period of the discharge (PCC(S)A 2000, s.13).

Procedure

Breach of a Crown Court order must be dealt with by committal for sentence to that court.

Either the Crown Court or a magistrates' court may deal with breach of a discharge imposed by a magistrates' court, but within magistrates' court powers.

Power

The court may sentence the offender as if just convicted of the original offence, but with powers appropriate to the offender's current age.

7.3 FINE: NON-PAYMENT OF

See the MCSG, pp.156–159 (**Appendix 16, pp.328–331**).

Statutory provisions

MCA 1980, ss.75–96A; CA 2003, s.97 and Scheds.5 and 6.

Power

Where an offender defaults on a collection order made when the fine was imposed, and is not already subject to an attachment of earnings order (AEO) or an application for deductions from benefits (ABD), unless impracticable or inappropriate, a fines officer *must* make an AEO or ABD (CA 2003, Sched.5, para.26). If this is not possible, a fines officer must either issue a 'further steps' notice advising that further enforcement action is intended or refer the case to court (CA 2003, Sched.5, para.37).

Options available to the *fines officer* include:

- making an AEO or ABD;
- issuing a distress warrant;
- registering the sum; or
- taking enforcement action in the High Court or county court.

Options available to the *court* include (CA 2003, Sched.5, para.39):

- varying the terms;
- taking any of the steps available to a fines officer;
- increasing the fine by up to 50 per cent where there is culpable neglect or wilful refusal to pay (CA 2003, Sched.5, para.42A); or
- discharge of the collection order and exercise of standard enforcement powers (as detailed below).

In cases where a collection order is not made or which is referred to a court by a fines officer, or an offender appeals against a further steps notice, the powers normally available to a court are:

1. **Remission:** If it thinks just to do so having regard to a change of circumstances since the date of conviction, the court can remit a fine (MCA 1980, s.85). A fine imposed in the absence of details of means may also be remitted (CJA 2003, s.165).

2. **Imprisonment in default:** If, after a means enquiry, the court is satisfied that the defaulter has the means to pay immediately, and the offence for which the fine was imposed was imprisonable, the defaulter can be committed to prison (MCA 1980, s.82(4)(a)). In other cases, if after a means enquiry the court is satisfied that default is due to wilful refusal or culpable neglect and all other methods have been considered or tried and were inappropriate or unsuccessful, the court can commit the defaulter (MCA 1980, s.82(4)(b)).

The period of commitment must be the shortest that is likely to succeed in obtaining payment. Committal can be suspended on condition that regular payments are made.

Maximum periods (as prescribed in MCA 1980, Sched.4) are as shown in **Table 7.1**.

Table 7.1 Maximum periods of imprisonment for non-payment of fines

Amount of fine	Period of imprisonment
An amount not exceeding £200	7 days
An amount exceeding £200 but not exceeding £500	14 days
An amount exceeding £500 but not exceeding £1,000	28 days
An amount exceeding £1,000 but not exceeding £2,500	45 days
An amount exceeding £2,500 but not exceeding £5,000	3 months
An amount exceeding £5,000 but not exceeding £10,000	6 months
An amount exceeding £10,000	12 months

3. **Detention in court precincts or police station:** Detention for a specified period up to 8 pm on the day on which the order is made is available as a sentence in its own right or as an order in respect of an unpaid fine (as an alternative to remission) (MCA 1980, s.135). The court is not required to conduct a means enquiry.

4. **Warrant for detention in a police station:** A warrant authorising detention of a defaulter overnight in a police station may be issued by a court (MCA 1980, s.136). Release must be at 8 am the following day.

The court may commit to prison for non-payment if:

- the defendant is already serving a custodial sentence (MCA 1980, s.82(3));
- a means enquiry establishes an immediate ability to pay in relation to an imprisonable offence (MCA 1980, s.82(4));
- at a means enquiry the court is satisfied (MCA 1980, s.82(4)) that:
  - the default is due to wilful refusal or culpable neglect; *and*
  - it has considered or tried all other methods of enforcement and concluded that they are inappropriate or unsuccessful.

Other methods include a money payment supervision order (MCA 1980, s.88), an AEO, an ABD, a distress warrant, an attendance centre order (for offenders under the age of 25 and where available) (PCC(S)A 2000, s.60), and enforcement proceedings in the High Court or county court. Discharge by unpaid work is another option but is only available in certain areas.

7.4 BREACH OF A COMMUNITY ORDER

See also the MCSG, p.43, (**Appendix 16, p.207**).

Statutory provision

CJA 2003, Sched.8.

Preconditions

Where an offender fails without reasonable excuse to comply with one or more requirements of a community order, the 'responsible officer' (CJA 2003, Sched.8, paras.5–6) can either give a warning or initiate breach proceedings.

Where the offender fails to comply without reasonable excuse for the second time within a 12-month period, the responsible officer must initiate proceedings.

Power

When proceedings are brought, the court must (CJA 2003, Sched.8, paras.9–10) either:

(a) increase the severity of the existing sentence (i.e. impose more rigorous conditions including requirements aimed at enforcement, such as a curfew or supervision requirement); or

(b) revoke the existing sentence and proceed as though sentencing for the original offence.

The court must take account of the circumstances of the breach of the order (CJA 2003, Sched.8, para.9(2)), which will inevitably have an impact on the court's response.

The guideline *New Sentences: Criminal Justice Act 2003* elaborates, as follows:

1.1.43 In certain circumstances (where an offender has wilfully and persistently failed to comply with an order made in respect of an offence that is not itself punishable by imprisonment), the court can **impose a maximum of 51 weeks custody** [Criminal Justice Act 2003, Sched.8, para.9(1)(c) with limitations to current sentencing powers until custody plus is brought in].

1.1.44 When increasing the onerousness of requirements, the court must consider the impact on the offender's ability to comply and the possibility of precipitating a custodial sentence for further breach. For that reason, and particularly where the breach occurs towards the end of the sentence, the court should take account of compliance to date and may consider that extending the supervision or operational periods will be more sensible; in other cases it might choose to add punitive or rehabilitative requirements instead. In making these changes the court must be mindful of the legislative restrictions on the overall length of community sentences and on the supervision and operational periods allowed for each type of requirement.

1.1.45 The court dealing with breach of a community sentence should have as its primary objective ensuring that the requirements of the sentence are finished, and this is important if the court is to have regard to the statutory purposes of sentencing. A court that imposes a custodial sentence for breach without giving adequate consideration to alternatives is in danger of imposing a sentence that is not commensurate with the seriousness of the original offence and is solely a punishment for breach. This risks undermining the purposes it has identified as being important. Nonetheless, courts will need to be vigilant to ensure that there is a realistic prospect of the purposes of the order being achieved.

1.1.46 A court sentencing for breach must take account of the extent to which the offender has complied with the requirements of the community order, the reasons for breach and the point at which the breach has occurred. Where a breach takes place towards the end of the operational period and the court is satisfied that the offender's appearance before the court is likely to be sufficient in itself to ensure figure compliance, then given that it is not open to the court to make no order, an approach that the court might wish to adopt could be to re-sentence in a way that enables the original order to be completed properly – for example, a differently constructed community sentence that aims to secure compliance with the purposes of the original sentence.

1.1.47 If the court decides to increase the onerousness of an order, it must give careful consideration, with advice from the Probation Service, to the offender's ability to comply. [. . .]

Custody should be the last resort, reserved for those cases of deliberate and repeated breach where all reasonable efforts to ensure that the offender complies have failed.

In the absence of a discretion to the contrary only the Crown Court may deal with an order *originally* made at that level; a magistrates' court may commit a breach case to the Crown Court if the order was made at the higher level (CJA 2003, Sched.8, paras.8, 9(b)). If the order breached was made by a magistrates' court, committal to the Crown Court for sentence is not possible (*R* v. *Andrews* [2006] EWCA Crim 2228).

An offence does not become more serious by reason of breach of the order. If an offender spent time in custody on remand before receiving a community order and custody is imposed for the breach, an order under CJA 2003, s.240 should be made for the time served (*R* v. *Stickley* [2007] EWCA Crim 3184).

7.5 BREACH OF A SUSPENDED SENTENCE ORDER

See also the MCSG, pp.163–164 (**Appendix 16, pp.334–335**).

Statutory provision

CJA 2003, Sched.12.

Preconditions

A breach occurs if there is either:

- a failure without reasonable cause to comply with a requirement attached to the sentence during the supervision period; or
- the commission of an offence during the operational period of the original sentence.

The procedural steps for breach of a requirement attached to an order are the same as for breach of a community order.

Limitations

A magistrates' court may normally only deal with breach of an order imposed by a magistrates' court. Breach of a Crown Court suspended sentence order should be committed to that court so that it may issue process. The Crown Court can deal with all breaches.

Power

The court must order the sentence (CJA 2003, Sched.12, para.8(2) and (3)) to take effect with the original terms unaltered, or to take effect but with the term reduced.

However, the court may, if either of those outcomes is unjust in all the circumstances:

- impose more onerous community requirements; or
- extend either the supervision period or the operational period (CJA 2003, s.189(3) and (4)).

There is a *presumption* that the suspended sentence will be activated either in full or in part, unless the court takes the view that this would, in all the circumstances, be unjust. In considering whether it is unjust the court must consider all circumstances including as relevant the extent to which there has been compliance with the requirements attached and the facts of the subsequent case (CJA 2003, Sched.12, para.8(3) and (4)). If the court is persuaded not to activate the prison sentence, it must state its reasons (CJA 2003, Sched.12, para.8(3)).

It is expected that any activated suspended sentence will be consecutive to the custodial sentence imposed for any new offence. If time was spent on remand prior to the imposition of the suspended sentence an application should be made under CJA 2003, s.240.

7.6   BREACH OF A PROTECTIVE ORDER

Statutory provisions

Protection from Harassment Act 1997, s.5(5) and Family Law Act 1996, s.42A (not yet in force).

The maximum penalty is five years in custody.

Power

A definitive guideline was published by the SGC (*Breach of a Protective Order*, which came into force on 18 December 2006) in relation to breach of restraining orders (Protection from Harassment Act 1997, s.5(5)) and of non-molestation orders (Family Law Act 1996, s.42A(1) not yet in force). The guideline sets out the principles that relate to dealing with beach of such orders including:

- When sentencing for breach of an order the court's main aim should be to ensure that the offender will comply with that order where that is realistic (*Breach of a Protective Order*, para.3.4).
- In all cases the order will have been made to protect an individual from harm. The court's principal objective in response to a breach should be to ensure compliance with the order and that the order achieves the protection that it was intended to achieve (*Breach of a Protective Order*, para.3.3).
- A court must assess the level of risk posed by the offender. If the offender requires treatment or help for mental health or other issues, willingness to accept such treatment or help may influence sentence (*Breach of a Protective Order*, section E).
- The nature of the original conduct is relevant in so far as it allows the court to judge the level of harm caused to the victim by the breach and the extent to which that harm was intended by the offender (*Breach of a Protective Order*, para.3.5) However, sentence is for the breach alone (*Breach of a Protective Order*, para.3.7) and not the original conduct.
- When the conduct also amounts to a substantive offence this will often be charged. However, the principles of totality apply (*Breach of a Protective Order*, para.2.1).
- Where the nature of the breach is particularly serious but has not been dealt with by a separate offence being charged the risk posed by the

103

offender and the nature of the breach will be particularly significant in determining the response (*Breach of a Protective Order*, section E1(b)).

- Where an order was made in civil proceedings and was made to cause the defendant to modify behaviour rather than to imply that the conduct was especially serious, a custodial sentence is likely to be disproportionate if there are no threats or violence involved (*Breach of a Protective Order*, section E1(g)).

- Where a breach might result in a short custodial sentence but the court is satisfied that the defendant genuinely intends to reform his or her behaviour and there is a real prospect of rehabilitation the court may impose a sentence that will allow that, such as a suspended sentence or community order with appropriate requirements (*Breach of a Protective Order*, section E1(h)).

The guideline summary is as shown below.

Where the conduct is particularly serious, it would normally be charged as a separate offence. These starting points are based on the premise that the activity has either been prosecuted separately as an offence or is not of a character sufficient to justify prosecution of it as an offence in its own right.

Nature of activity	Starting points
Breach (whether one or more) involving significant physical violence and significant physical or psychological harm to the victim	**Custodial Sentence** More than 12 months The length of the custodial sentence imposed will depend on the nature and seriousness of the breach(es)
More than one breach involving some violence and/or significant physical or psychological harm to the victim	26–39 weeks custody [Medium/High Custody Plus order] **
Single breach involving some violence and/or significant physical or psychological harm to the victim	13–26 weeks custody [Low/Medium Custody Plus order] **
	Non-Custodial Sentence
More than one breach involving no/minimal contact or some direct contact	MEDIUM range community order
Single breach involving no/minimal direct contact	LOW range community order
Additional aggravating factors	**Additional mitigating factors**
1. Victim is particularly vulnerable. 2. Impact on children. 3. A proven history of violence or threats by the offender.	1. Breach occurred after a long period of compliance. 2. Victim initiated contact.

4. Using contact arrangements with a child to instigate an offence.
5. Victim is forced to leave home.
6. Offence is a further breach, following earlier breach proceedings.
7. Offender has a history of disobedience to court orders.
8. Breach was committed immediately or shortly after the order was made.

** When the relevant provisions of the Criminal Justice Act 2003 are in force.

7.7 BREACH OF AN ANTI-SOCIAL BEHAVIOUR ORDER (ASBO)

Statutory provision

Crime and Disorder Act 1998, s.1(10). The maximum penalty is five years in custody.

Power

A definitive guideline published by the SGC, *Breach of an Anti-Social Behaviour Order*, came into force on 5 January 2009. It includes principles and considerations relevant to the sentencing of both adult and young offenders. Those applying to adults are summarised below (and the aspects relating to youths can be found in **Chapter 8**):

• The main aim of sentencing for breach of a court order is to achieve the purpose of the order. Therefore the sentence for beach of an ASBO should primarily reflect the harassment, alarm or distress involved. The fact that it constituted breach of a court order is a secondary consideration (*Breach of an Anti-Social Behaviour Order*, para.7).
• The original conduct that led to the making of an order is a relevant consideration in so far as it indicates the level of harm caused and whether this was intended (*Breach of an Anti-Social Behaviour Order*, para.14).
• Breach of an interim order or a final order is equally serious (*Breach of an Anti-Social Behaviour Order*, para.18).
• Where the conduct involved in a breach of an order amounts to an offence this will often be charged. However, the principles of totality apply (*Breach of an Anti-Social Behaviour Order*, paras.22–24).
• As with all guidelines produced by the SGC, the starting points and range for adult offenders are for a 'first-time offender' who pleaded not guilty. However, in relation to breach of an ASBO a 'first-time offender' is one who has not previously breached an ASBO (*Breach of an Anti-Social Behaviour Order*, Factors to take into consideration, para.1).

- The suggested starting points are based on the assumption that the offender had the highest level of culpability (*Breach of an Anti-Social Behaviour Order*, Factors to take into consideration, para.3).

An ASBO may be breached in a very wide range of circumstances. The examples given below are intended to illustrate, rather than provide comprehensive definitions of, the levels of seriousness.

- Highest level of seriousness – breach at this level of seriousness will involve the use of violence, significant threats or intimidation or the targeting of individuals or groups of people in a manner that leads to a fear of violence.
- Middle level of seriousness – examples may include lesser degrees of threats or intimidation, the use of seriously abusive language, or causing more than minor damage to property.
- Lowest level of seriousness – in the absence of intimidation or the causing of fear of violence, breaches involving being drunk or begging may be at this level, as may prohibited use of public transport or entry into a prohibited area, where there is no evidence that harassment, alarm or distress was caused or intended (*Breach of an Anti-Social Behaviour Order*, Factors to take into consideration, para.2).

The guideline summary is as shown below.

Where the conduct amounting to a breach also constitutes a separate offence, that offence would normally be charged separately. These sentencing ranges are based on the premise that such conduct has either been prosecuted separately as an offence or is not of a character sufficient to justify prosecution of it as an offence in its own right.

Nature of failure & harm	Starting point	Sentencing range
Serious harassment, alarm or distress has been caused or where such harm was intended	26 weeks custody	Custody threshold – 2 years custody
Lesser degree of harassment, alarm or distress, where such harm was intended, or where it would have been likely if the offender had not been apprehended	6 weeks custody	Community Order (MEDIUM) – 26 weeks custody
No harassment, alarm or distress was actually caused by the breach and where none was intended by the offender	Community Order (LOW)	Fine Band B – Community Order (MEDIUM)

Aggravating factors	Mitigating factors
1. Offender has a history of disobedience to court orders. 2. Breach was committed immediately or shortly after the order was made. 3. Breach was committed subsequent to earlier breach proceedings arising from the same order. 4. Targeting of a person the order was made to protect or a witness in the original proceedings.	1. Breach occurred after a long period of compliance. 2. The prohibition(s) breached was not fully understood, especially where an interim order was made without notice.

CHAPTER 8

The sentencing of youths (under 18)

8.1 OVERVIEW

The sentencing of offenders who are under 18 requires particular attention. CDA 1998 created a new approach to dealing with young offenders and established a new sentencing framework for those convicted of criminal offences. That has since been developed and CJIA 2008 contains significant changes to the sentencing regime which are expected to come into force in October 2009. References to those changes are highlighted throughout this chapter with a line above and below.

The sentencing process for young offenders is much the same as for adults. The court should first determine the seriousness of the offence as described in **Chapter 2**. This will fix the most serious penalty that could be imposed and will determine whether the offence has crossed the necessary threshold for a community or custodial sentence. In the same way as for adults, even where a threshold has been crossed, the court is not required to impose that particular type of sentence (CJA 2003, s.148(5)).

The types of sentence available for sentencing youths differ from those for adults and their availability depends on the offender's age. The sentence imposed must be determined in the light of the overriding obligation to treat prevention of offending as the primary aim of sentencing (CDA 1998, s.37).

8.2 PROCEDURAL MATTERS

Committal to the Crown Court

There is an overarching presumption that offenders aged under 18 should be tried summarily. This restricts the availability and length of custodial sentences and ensures that trial in the Crown Court is reserved for the most serious cases. There is no general power to commit a young offender to the Crown Court for sentence. However, in certain circumstances cases should be tried or sentenced in the Crown Court.

Homicide

An offence of homicide (murder, manslaughter and other prescribed offences) should be committed to the Crown Court for trial (MCA 1980, s.24(1)). In the case of murder, the sentence is detention during Her Majesty's pleasure (PCC(S)A 2000, s.90).

Grave crimes (PCC(S)A 2000, s.91)

Long-term detention under PCC(S)A 2000, s.91 is available for those aged between 10 and 17 where there is a conviction on indictment for a grave crime.

An offence may be a grave crime and come within s.91 where the maximum sentence for an adult is 14 years' or more imprisonment, together with the following offences:

- sexual assault (SOA 2003, s.3);
- child sex offences by children and young persons (SOA 2003, s.13);
- sexual activity with a child family member (SOA 2003, s.25);
- inciting a family member to engage in sexual activity (SOA 2003, s.26);
- prohibited weapons offences under the Firearms Act 1968, s.5(1)(a), (ab), (aba), (ac), (ad), (af), (c) or (1A)(a), where the offender was aged 16 or over and the minimum three-year sentence applies (unless the Crown Court finds exceptional circumstances).

This general power to commit a young offender to the Crown Court for trial should be used rarely and only where there is a 'real possibility' of a sentence of long-term detention being imposed on conviction (*R (on the application of the Crown Prosecution Service)* v. *Redbridge Youth Court* [2005] EWHC 1390).

Where a grave crime is committed to the Crown Court, only if it is of the opinion that no other disposal would be suitable may it impose a sentence of long-term detention (PCC(S)A 2000, s.91(3)). There is power, seldom used, to impose a sentence that is shorter than two years.

Dangerous offenders (CJA 2003, ss.224–236, as amended by CJIA 2008)

A sentence under the dangerous offender provisions (for a fuller description see **Chapter 3**) can only be imposed in the Crown Court. The legal provisions relating to the sentencing of youths as dangerous offenders provide for a decision relating to 'dangerousness' to be taken either before or after conviction. The criteria are stringent and changes made by CJIA 2008 are likely to further restrict use of these sentences for young offenders.

The provisions relate to *specified offences* (**Appendix 9**) (listed violent and sexual offences) and *serious offences* (**Appendix 10**) (specified offences which carry a maximum penalty of 10 years' imprisonment or more in the case of adult offenders).

Following conviction of an offender for a specified or serious offence, the court must be satisfied that there is a significant risk both of the offender committing a further specified offence *and* of serious harm to members of the public arising from such an offence. In addition, were a determinate sentence to be imposed it would be for a term of at least four years.

Even where the criteria are met, the court retains discretion in relation to imposing a sentence under the dangerous offender provisions or another available sentence.

- Where a young offender is convicted of a *serious offence*, the sentences available are:

  - detention for life under PCC(S)A 2000, s.91; or
  - detention for public protection – unlike for adults, the sentence must always have a notional minimum term of two years.

- Where the offender is convicted of a *specified offence* (including a serious offence), the court may impose an extended sentence – unlike for adults, the appropriate custodial sentence must be at least four years.

When provisions of the Criminal Justice Act 2003 as amended are brought into force, introducing plea before venue to the youth court, there will be power to commit for sentence those admitting grave crimes (see **Appendix 10**).

Remittal to another court for sentence

A youth court dealing with a youth from another area may remit the case for sentence to the youth court for the place where the defendant habitually resides (PCC(S)A 2000, s.8).

A youth court may also remit a youth who becomes 18 to an adult court to be dealt with, but this will not affect the sentences available (PCC(S)A 2000, s.9).

Where a youth appears before an adult magistrates' court, that court must remit to a youth court (PCC(S)A 2000, s.8) for sentence unless it is planning to impose one of the following:

- an absolute or conditional discharge;
- a parental bind over;
- a referral order; or
- a fine, as limited by the age of the offender.

A Crown Court dealing with a youth has available all the powers of a youth court except in relation to making a referral order. However, it should remit for sentence to a youth court unless the judge is satisfied that it would be undesirable to do so (PCC(S)A 2000, s.8 and for guidance see *R* v. *Lewis* (1984) 6 Cr App R(S) 44).

8.3   THE SIGNIFICANCE OF AGE

The relevant age for sentencing purposes is normally the age at the date of conviction: that is, the date that a guilty plea was entered or the offender was convicted after a trial.

There are however, exceptions to this rule:

- in proceedings for breach of conditional discharge or of community rehabilitation orders, community punishment orders, community punishment and rehabilitation orders, curfew orders, drug abstinence orders, drug treatment and testing orders, and exclusion orders when the order is revoked, the relevant age is that on the day of appearance before the sentencing court;
- in relation to the obligatory minimum sentence provisions in the Firearms Act 1968, s.51A, it is the age at the date of the offence that is material.

However, the court should always have regard to the offender's age at the date of the offence. The starting point is the sentence that the defendant would have been likely to receive had they been sentenced at that date (PCC(S)A 2000, ss.91 and 164(1); CJA 2003, s.305(2); *R* v. *Ghafoor* [2002] EWCA Crim 1857).

The age of an offender is that which it appears to the court to be. Where the age is in doubt or disputed the court should adjourn and obtain further evidence.

8.4   GENERAL PRINCIPLES AND SENTENCING FRAMEWORK

The following summary of the sentencing framework and principles relating to young offenders is drawn from the SGC guideline *Breach of an Anti-Social Behaviour Order* (published December 2008, in force from 5 January 2009; see Annex D):

1. The principal aim of the youth justice system is to prevent offending by children and young persons [Crime and Disorder Act 1998, s.37].
2. Under domestic law, the court must have regard to the welfare of the child or young person when imposing sentence [Children and Young Persons Act 1933, s.44. In *R (A)* v *Leeds Magistrates' Court* [2004] EWHC Admin 554 the High Court held that where the person against whom the order is sought is a child, the child's best interests are a primary consideration but so are the interests of the public.]. In accordance with obligations under international convictions and treaties, the best interests of the child must be a

primary consideration [United Nations Standard Minimum Rules for the Administration of Juvenile Justice ('The Beijing Rules'), adopted by General Assembly resolution 40/33 of 29/11/1985; (www.orchr.org). See also United Nations Convention on the Rights of the child, Article 3; www2.orchr.org/English/law/crc/htm]. A sentence designed to prevent re-offending also helps to promote the welfare of the young offender.

3.   Restorative justice is an important underlying principle in all youth justice disposals, from referral and reparation orders to action plan and supervision orders [YJB, *A guide to the role of youth offending teams in dealing with anti-social behaviour* (2006); www.yjb.gov.uk]; as well as reducing the harm done, it can also help prevent re-offending.

4.   Where a young offender pleads guilty and is being sentenced for the first time, the court must impose a **referral order** unless either it considers the offence to be of such a nature that an absolute discharge or hospital order is appropriate or it considers the offence to be so serious that only a custodial sentence is appropriate [Powers of Criminal Courts (Sentencing) Act 2000, s.16. When in force, the Criminal Justice and Immigration Act 2008 will widen the circumstances in which a referral order can be made, to include where the offender has been bound over previously, or where the offender has one conviction in respect of which a referral order was not imposed].

- Such an order refers the offender to a youth offender panel, and the court may (or 'shall' in the case of a child aged under 16) require at least one parent or guardian to attend the panel meetings unless this would be unreasonable [Powers of Criminal Courts (Sentencing) Act 2000, s.20].
- Panel meetings are intended to result in a youth offender contract, which is aimed at repairing the harm caused by the offence and addressing the causes of the offending behaviour (including requirements such as unpaid work in the community).
- The terms of the 'contract' are determined by the panel, but the court must specify the period for which it is to have effect (between 3 and 12 months), which will depend on the seriousness of the breach.
- If the offender does not agree to the contract, fails to abide by its terms, or re-offends while it is in force, the case is returned to the youth court to be re-sentenced.

5.   If the offender has previous convictions or has been found guilty after a trial the court has the following options:

- absolute discharge
- reparation order
- fine
- community order
- detention and training order

6.   A **reparation order** requires a young offender to make reparation to the victim(s) of the offence, and before making such an order the court will obtain the views of anyone so affected [Powers of Criminal Courts (Sentencing) Act 2000, s.73]. In the case of breach of an ASBO, there will often be no identifiable victim, but the legislation provides for reparation to be made to the community at large. This work must last no longer than 24 hours and be completed within 3 months.

7.   The court may impose a fine of up to £250 for offenders aged between 10 and 14, and up to £1,000 for those aged 15–17. Where the offender is under 16,

the court must order that the fine is paid by the offender's parent unless that would be unreasonable; in the case of an offender aged 16 or 17, the court has discretion to do so.

8. Where a community sentence is imposed, it may consist of one or more of five **youth community orders** set out in section 147(2) of the Criminal Justice Act 2003 [when in force, the Criminal Justice and Immigration Act 2008 will replace these with the Youth Rehabilitation Order, a generic community order for youths]. These are:

- a **curfew order** – order to remain at a specified place for a designated period for a maximum of 6 months, or 3 months for those under 16
- an **exclusion order** – available for offenders aged under 16, prohibits the offender from entering a specified place for a maximum of 3 months.
- an **attendance centre order** – attendance at a designated place for a total of 12–36 hours (maximum 24 hours for offenders under 16)
- an **action plan order** – a short (3 months) but intensive period of super-vision, intended to be individually tailored by means of a series of requirements
- a **supervision order** – can impose a wide range of requirements and last for up to 3 years. A supervision order may also involve participation in the Intensive Supervision and Surveillance Programme (ISSP). Introduced in 2001, ISSP is the most rigorous non-custodial interven-tion available for young offenders, and offers the court an alternative to a short DTO.

9. Additionally, where the offender is 16 or 17, the court may impose a **community rehabilitation order** (which may require participation in the ISSP), a **community punishment order**, or a **community rehabilitation and punishment order** (combining both) [Powers of Criminal Courts (Sentencing) Act 2000, ss.41, 46 and 51 respectively. These orders will be replaced by a generic community order, the Youth Rehabilitation Order, when the relevant provi-sions in the Criminal Justice and Immigration Act 2008 are in force]. A community rehabilitation order lasts between six months and three years, and may involve reparation and/or programmes to address the offending behaviour. A community punishment order involves unpaid community work for a total of 40–240 hours.

10. Where a custodial sentence is imposed in the youth court, it must be a **Detention and Training Order (DTO)**, which can only be for 4, 6, 8, 10, 12, 18 or 24 months. Where the offender is aged 10 or 11, no custodial sentence is available in the youth court. Where the offender is aged between 12 and 14, a custodial sentence may be imposed only if the child is a 'persistent offender' [Powers of Criminal Courts (Sentencing) Act 2000, s.100].

CJIA 2008 introduces into CJA 2003 a single statutory provision as to the issues to which the court dealing with those under 18 must have regard (CJA 2003, s.142A, introduced by CJIA 2008, s.9).

Section 142A provides that the court must have regard to the principal aim of the youth justice system (which is to prevent offending or re-offending by persons aged under 18 (CDA 1998, s.37(1)), the welfare of the offender (in accordance with the Children and Young Persons Act (CYPA) 1933, s.44), and the purposes of sentencing which are:

- the punishment of offenders;
- the reform and rehabilitation of offenders;
- the protection of the public; and
- the making of reparation by offenders to persons affected by their offences.

As for adult offenders, no order of priority is given to the purposes of sentencing.

There are exceptions and s.142A does not apply:

- to an offence the sentence for which is fixed by law;
- to an offence the sentence for which falls to be imposed under the Firearms Act 1968, s.51A(2) (minimum sentence for certain firearms offences), the Violent Crime Reduction Act 2006, s.29(6) (minimum sentences in certain cases of using someone to mind a weapon), or CJA 2003, s.226(2) (detention for life for certain dangerous offenders);
- in relation to the making under MHA 1983, Pt 3 of a hospital order (with or without a restriction order), an interim hospital order, a hospital direction or a limitation direction.

8.5 AVAILABLE DISPOSALS AND SENTENCES FOR OFFENDERS UNDER 18

Binding over

This is an order whereby the court seeks to preserve the future peace and can be used following conviction, discontinuance or acquittal. A youth may consent to a binding over order and it would appear that an attendance centre order is available on breach (PCC(S)A 2000, s.60) even though imprisonment is not available (PCC(S)A 2000, s.89).

Sentencing options

Different sentencing options are available depending on the age of a young offender (see discussion of significance of age above).

An offender convicted at any age of a murder committed when the offender was under 18 must be sentenced to detention during Her Majesty's pleasure.

Table 8.1 sets out the sentences available until the implementation of the Criminal Justice and Immigration Act 2008.

Referral order (PCC(S)A 2000, Pt III)

A youth court dealing with a young offender convicted for the first time (of an imprisonable offence) following a guilty plea may only impose a referral order, an absolute discharge, a hospital order or a custodial sentence.

Table 8.1 Disposals and sentences for offenders under 18

Age	10	11	12	13	14	15	16	17
Referral order	X	X	X	X	X	X	X	X
Discharge	X	X	X	X	X	X	X	X
Fine	X	X	X	X	X	X	X	X
Compensation	X	X	X	X	X	X	X	X
Reparation order	X	X	X	X	X	X	X	X
Deferred sentence	X	X	X	X	X	X	X	X
Community threshold								
Exclusion order	X	X	X	X	X	X	X	X
Curfew order	X	X	X	X	X	X	X	X
Action plan order	X	X	X	X	X	X	X	X
Supervision order	X	X	X	X	X	X	X	X
Attendance order	X	X	X	X	X	X	X	X
Community rehabilitation order							X	X
Community punishment order							X	X
Community punishment and rehabilitation order						X	X	
Drug treatment and testing order							X	X
Youth rehabilitation order	X	X	X	X	X	X	X	X
Including supervision and surveillance or fostering	AB	AB	AB	AB	AB	A	A	A
Custodial threshold								
Detention and training			C	C	C	X	X	X
s.91 detention	X	X	X	X	X	X	X	X
Extended sentence	X	X	X	X	X	X	X	X
Detention for public protection	X	X	X	X	X	X	X	X
Detention for life								
Hospital order	X	X	X	X	X	X	X	X
Guardianship order							X	X
Restriction order	X	X	X	X	X	X	X	X

A. Offence imprisonable and but for this order custodial sentence appropriate.
B. Must be persistent offender.
C. Available for those aged 12, 13 or 14 deemed to be a persistent offender.

The court *must* make a referral order where *compulsory* referral conditions (PCC(S)A 2000, s.17(1)) exist, namely:

- guilty plea to all offences that are being sentenced together;
- no previous convictions;
- no previous order to be bound over; and
- all offences are imprisonable.

A court *may* make an order where *discretionary* referral conditions (PCC(S)A 2000, s.17(2) and (1A)) are present, either:

- the offender has been convicted of at least two offences, has pleaded guilty to at least one and not guilty to at least one, and has no previous convictions or orders to be bound over; or
- the compulsory referral conditions would be met except that one of the offences is non-imprisonable.

Prior to implementation of CJIA 2008, a 'conviction' included a bind over and conditional discharge. Section 35 of CJIA 2008 was implemented on 27 April 2009 meaning that these disposals will not now count as convictions (CJIA 2008, s.35).

Implementation of provisions in CJIA 2008 extends the circumstances in which a referral order can be made, to enable it to be used more widely and with greater flexibility. Those circumstances include where an offender has one previous conviction in relation to which a referral order was not made, or in exceptional circumstances where the offender has one or more previous convictions and has had one previous referral order (PCC(S)A 2000, s.17(2B) as inserted by CJIA 2008, s.35).

If a referral order is made, the offender is required to attend meetings, for a defined period, of a youth offender panel. A contract is drawn up and agreed between the offender and panel, which specifies activities and actions designed to prevent re-offending, such as reparation, unpaid work, attendance at school and limiting contact with particular persons.

In deciding the length of the referral the court shall have regard to the seriousness of the offence and offender mitigation. It is suggested that contracts of the lengths as set out in **Table 8.2** would be suitable, based on an offender aged 16–17 who pleaded guilty.

Table 8.2 Referral orders: contract lengths for offenders aged 16–17

Level of seriousness	Length
Low	3–4 months
Medium	5–7 months
High	8–9 months

The length of a contract should be shorter for younger offenders.

Contracts of 10–12 months should be reserved for the most serious crimes, where the discretionary criteria are met and there are mixed pleas, where the guilty plea was entered at a late stage or where further offences have been committed.

If the offender fails to comply with the order, the panel may refer them back to court and they may be re-sentenced.

If an offender subject to a referral order is convicted of another offence, either before or after the order is made, the court may either:

- in exceptional circumstances (PCC(S)A 2000, Sched.1, para.12), extend the compliance period of the existing order (though the period should not exceed 12 months in total); or
- unless an absolute discharge is imposed for the new offence, revoke the order and re-sentence.

Implementation of CJIA 2008, ss.36 and 37 on 27 April 2009 gives an additional power to the youth offender panel to refer an offender back to court with a view to revocation on the grounds of good progress, or to extending the period of the order (PCC(S)A 2000, ss.27A and 27B as inserted by CJIA 2008, ss.36 and 37).

Discharges

Absolute and conditional discharges are available as for adults.

However, a conditional discharge cannot be imposed following conviction of a first-time young offender who has pleaded guilty to an imprisonable offence (PCC(S)A 2000, s.19).

A conditional discharge may not be imposed if, within the two years prior to the commission of the offence, an offender has been given a formal warning by the police, unless there are exceptional circumstances relating to the offences or the offender (CDA 1998, s.56(4)(b)).

Fines

A fine cannot be imposed following conviction of a first-time young offender who has pleaded guilty to an imprisonable offence.

A fine may be imposed for any offence. However, there are maxima that apply depending on the age of the offender: an offender under the age of 14 may not be fined more than £250, and an offender aged 14–17 may not be fined more than £1,000.

The power to impose an alternative of one-day detention in default on the day of sentence is *not* available in relation to a fine imposed on a young offender.

A parent or guardian shall be ordered to pay the fine if the youth is under 16, and may be ordered to do so if the youth is 16 or 17 (PCC(S)A 2000, s.137) unless the parent or guardian cannot be found or it would be unreasonable having regard to all the circumstances of the case.

Compensation order

A compensation order must be considered in any case where personal injury, loss or damage resulted from an offence (PCC(S)A 2000, s.130), either as a sentence in its own right or as an ancillary order.

If an order is made, a parent or guardian shall be ordered to pay if the youth is under 16, and may be ordered to do so if the youth is 16 or 17 (PCC(S)A 2000, s.137), unless the parent or guardian cannot be found or it would be unreasonable having regard to all the circumstances of the case.

Reparation order (PCC(S)A 2000, s.73)

This is available for offenders aged 10 to 17. The maximum duration for an order is 24 hours. The requirements are to make reparation to a specified person or persons, or to the community at large.

This is not a community sentence. It may be combined with a fine, restitution order, compensation order or a supervision order without additional requirements.

The restrictions on liberty involved must be commensurate with seriousness.

The reparation must be completed within three months of the order. A report is required. The offender's consent is not required.

Youth community order (PCC(S)A 2000, s.70)

The offence must be 'serious enough' for such an order to be imposed, and the normal restrictions on making such an order apply. The order must be the most suitable for the offender.

The available options for inclusion in a youth community order are as follows:

- all ages:

    - curfew order;
    - exclusion order;
    - attendance centre order;
    - supervision order;
    - action plan order;

- additionally, for offenders aged 16–17:

    - community rehabilitation order;
    - community punishment order;
    - community punishment and rehabilitation order;
    - drug treatment and testing order.

Curfew order (PCC(S)A 2000, ss.37–40)

Curfew orders are available for offenders aged 10–17. The maximum duration for offenders aged 10–15 is three months; for offenders aged 16–17, it is six months.

The order specifies the period each day when the offender must not leave the specified place(s). It may be linked to a supervision order, and electronic monitoring is available.

Reports are not essential but the court must consider information about the place specified and attitude of persons likely to be affected.

Exclusion order (PCC(S)A 2000, ss.63–66)

Exclusion orders are available for offenders aged 10–17. The maximum duration for offenders aged 10–15 is three months; for offenders aged 16–17, it is 24 months.

The order is available in notified areas. It prohibits entry to specified places(s) for a specified period, and electronic monitoring is available.

Reports are desirable.

Attendance centre order (PCC(S)A 2000, ss.60–62)

Attendance centre orders are available for offenders aged 10 to 16-plus. The maximum duration for offenders aged 10–13 is 12 hours (unless excessive); for offenders aged 10–16 it is 24 hours (if 12 hours is inadequate); and for offenders aged 16-plus it is 36 hours.

A centre must be available for the relevant age group and gender of the offender, and reasonably accessible having regard to the offender's age and means of access available and any other circumstances.

Reports are required.

Action plan order (CYPA 1963, s.29(1))

Action plan orders are available for offenders aged 10–17. Duration is three months.

The order secures the offender's rehabilitation or prevents the commission of further offences. It can require any of the following:

- participation in activities specified, at the time(s) specified;
- presentation of themselves to a specified person at a place(s) and at a time(s) specified;
- attendance at an attendance centre;
- staying away from specified place(s);
- compliance with educational arrangements;

- making reparation;
- undergoing drug treatment and testing;
- attendance at any review fixed by the court.

Reports are required.

An action plan order may not be linked to:

- another action plan;
- custody;
- community rehabilitation;
- community punishment and rehabilitation;
- attendance centre order;
- supervision order;
- referral order.

Supervision order (PCC(S)A 2000, s.63 and Sched.6)

Supervision orders can be imposed in relation to offenders aged 10–17 and offenders who attain 18 during the proceedings (CYPA 1963, s.29(1)).

Duration is for a maximum of three years, commensurate with the seriousness of the offence(s).

The court may impose such requirements as it considers appropriate, and supplementary requirements to enable the supervisor to fulfil their duty to advise, assist and befriend, including prescribed provisions to confirm address and receive visits and participate in specified activities.

This order is very flexible and can provide suitable requirements for a case that is just serious enough up to the most serious, and allows extended periods of supervision when required.

Additional requirements may include:

- to live at a particular place, with a named person (residence as specified);
- a residence requirement, to live in local authority accommodation for a period not exceeding six months. This order is only available if:

  - there has been consultation with the authority;
  - there has been a previous supervision order which includes a requirement;
  - there has been failure to comply with a requirement or a further offence that was due to a significant degree to the circumstances in which the supervised person was living;
  - it will assist rehabilitation;

- to live with a local authority foster parent for a period up to 12 months (available in designated areas only). The order is only available if:

     – the offence is so serious that custody would normally be appropriate;
     – the behaviour constituting the offence was due to a significant extent to the circumstances in which the offender was living;
     – it will assist in rehabilitation.

It is limited to 12 months but may be varied later up to 18 months;

- requirements of the supervisor or court to attend a specified place at specified times, to take part in specified activities (including Intensive Supervision and Surveillance Programme (ISSP)) or refrain from taking part in specified activities, or to make reparation to specified persons or the community at large;
- to attend school or comply with other arrangements for the offender's education;
- to submit to drug treatment and testing (available in designated areas only);
- to receive treatment for a mental condition.

Community rehabilitation order (PCC(S)A 2000, s.41)

Community rehabilitation orders are available for offenders aged 16–17. There is a minimum duration of six months, maximum three years.

Requirements may be imposed where supervision is desirable to secure the offender's rehabilitation, or protect the public from harm from the offender, or prevent commission by him of further offences. The order requires the offender to keep in touch with a responsible officer.

Additional requirements can include:

- residence;
- participation in activities (for up to 60 days, except in relation to sex offenders);
- attendance at rehabilitation;
- sex offender requirement;
- curfew requirement (two to 12 hours per day);
- treatment for mental condition;
- treatment for drugs or alcohol dependency.

Consent is required for the last two requirements.

Community punishment order (PCC(S)A 2000, s.46)

Community punishment orders are available for offenders aged 16–17. There is a minimum duration of 40 hours, maximum 240 hours.

The order requires the offender to perform unpaid work within 12 months.

Community punishment and rehabilitation order (PCC(S)A 2000, s.51)

Community punishment and rehabilitation orders are available for offenders aged 16–17.

The minimum rehabilitation period is 12 months, minimum punishment 40 hours; maximum rehabilitation period is three years, maximum punishment 100 hours.

Requirements are as for community punishment orders and community rehabilitation orders.

Drug treatment and testing order (PCC(S)A 2000, s.52)

Drug treatment and testing orders are available for offenders aged 16–17. The minimum duration is six months, maximum is three years.

The order may be made if the offender is dependent on or has a propensity to misuse drugs and his dependency or propensity is such as requires, and may be susceptible to, treatment. Consent is required.

The court must order periodic reviews.

The following sentences will be available after implementation of CJIA 2008.

Youth rehabilitation order

A new community order is introduced by CJIA 2008, s.1 and Sched.1. Where an offence crosses the 'serious enough' threshold, the court may, but is not obliged to, impose a youth rehabilitation order.

The order will not be available for a first-time offender who has pleaded guilty to an imprisonable offence as they must be made subject to a referral order.

The rehabilitation order will balance the seriousness of the offence, the risk of harm from further offending and the needs of the young person.

Such an order may contain any of the following requirements:

(a) activity requirement;
(b) supervision requirement;
(c) unpaid work requirement (where the offender is aged 16 or 17 at the time of the conviction);
(d) programme requirement;
(e) attendance centre requirement;
(f) prohibited activity requirement;
(g) curfew requirement;
(h) exclusion requirement;
(i) residence requirement (where the offender is aged 16–17);
(j) local authority residence requirement;
(k) mental health requirement;
(l) drug treatment requirement;
(m) drug testing requirement;
(n) intoxicating substance requirement;

(o) electronic monitoring requirement;
(p) education requirement;
(q) intensive supervision and surveillance;
(r) fostering.

Note that a youth rehabilitation order *may* impose an electronic monitoring requirement and *must* do so if it imposes a curfew or an exclusion requirement unless in the particular requirement circumstances it considers it inappropriate to do so because a third party will not co-operate, or it is not possible to do so.

A youth rehabilitation order may be combined with intensive supervision and surveillance, or with fostering if:

(a) the court is dealing with the offender for an offence which is punishable with imprisonment;
(b) the court is of the opinion that the offending was so serious that, but for these provisions a custodial sentence would be appropriate; and
(c) if the offender was aged under 15 at the time of conviction, the court is of the opinion that the offender is a persistent offender.

All of these requirements are described in **Table 8.3**.

The requirements of an order must be completed no more than three years from the date on which the order comes into effect (CJIA 2008, Sched.1, para.32(1)). Some requirements have inherent time limits, such as unpaid work (must be completed within 12 months), curfew (must not apply for more than six months) and exclusion (must not apply for more than three months).

The court must have information about the offender's family circumstances and the effect of the order on those circumstances. So far as is practicable, requirements should not conflict with each other, or the offender's religious beliefs, working or education requirements (CJIA 2008, Sched.1, para.5), and should be compatible with each other.

Table 8.3 Youth rehabilitation order requirements

Requirement	CJIA 2008, Sched.1	Duration	Effect
Activity	Paras.6–8	Maximum 90 days An order for intensive supervision and surveillance may increase to 180 days	To attend, participate and comply with directions including a 'residential exercise'.
Supervision	Para.9		Attend appointment.
Unpaid work	Para.10	40–240 hours	16- and 17-year-olds only; perform unpaid work, complete within 12 months.
Programme	Para.11		Participate in systematic set of activities including to reside at a designated place. Must be recommended and available.

Table 8.3 Continued

Requirement	CJIA 2008, Sched.1	Duration	Effect
Attendance centre	Para.12	Age under 14: not more than 12 hours Age 14–15: 12–24 hours Age 16–17: 12–36 hours Sessions not to exceed 3 hours	To attend the attendance centre, engage and follow instructions as directed for the required hours.
Prohibited activity	Para.13		Refrain from participating in activities as specified (including a provision banning firearms).
Curfew	Para.14	Between 2 and 12 hours a day, for maximum of 6 months	Remain at specified location. Court must consider information about the place and attitude of people likely to be affected. Electronic monitoring requirement must be made unless inappropriate or unavailable.
Exclusion	Para.15	Not exceeding 3 months	Prohibition from entering specified place(s) during a specified period.
Residence	Para.16		Offenders aged 16 and over at date of conviction. To reside with a specified individual or at a specified place.
Local authority residence	Para.17	Maximum of 6 months, or until 18 if sooner	To reside in accommodation provided by the local authority and/or not to reside with a specified person. Available only if court satisfied that the circumstances in which the offender was living was a significant factor in the offence, and the requirement will assist the offender's rehabilitation.

Table 8.3 Continued

Requirement	CJIA 2008, Sched.1	Duration	Effect
Mental health treatment	Paras.20, 21		To submit to treatment (residential or non-residential) to improve the offender's mental condition. There must be evidence that the condition requires treatment but does not warrant a hospital or guardianship order. The court must be satisfied that arrangements have or can be made. The offender must be willing to comply.
Drug treatment	Para.22		Provides for residential or non-residential treatment to reduce or eliminate dependency on (or propensity to misuse) controlled drugs. It must be recommended, and the dependency must be susceptible to treatment. The offender must consent.
Drug testing	Para.23		Operate alongside a drug treatment requirement. During a treatment period, to provide samples as directed. Offender's consent required.
Intoxicating substance treatment	Para.24		To submit to treatment with a view to reduction or elimination of dependency on or propensity to misuse intoxicating substances. Must be recommended to the court. Dependency must be susceptible to treatment and the offender's consent given.
Education	Para.25		To comply with approved education arrangements. Suitable arrangements must exist

Table 8.3 Continued

Requirement	CJIA 2008, Sched.1	Duration	Effect
			and the requirement must be necessary to secure good conduct or to prevent further offences.
Electronic monitoring	Para.26	Cannot extend beyond compulsory school age	To secure compliance with other requirements. Arrangements must be in place and provision available to monitor as proposed.
Intensive supervision and surveillance	Para.3		Offender must be 15 or over, or a persistent offender if under 15.
			Offence must be imprisonable and but for inclusion of this or fostering requirement a custodial sentence would be appropriate. Also available on non-compliance with an order for pre-sentence drug testing. Other requirements may be included.
Fostering	Para.4	Maximum of 12 months or until attains 18 if sooner	Offender must be 15 or over, or a persistent offender if under 15.
			Offence must be imprisonable and but for inclusion of this or intensive requirement a custodial sentence would be appropriate. The circumstances in which a young person was living must have been a significant factor in the offence and fostering would assist rehabilitation. To reside for the specified period with a local authority foster parent. Supervisions requirement must also be made.

Once these provisions are in force the courts will not be able to make:

- curfew orders;
- exclusion orders;
- attendance centre orders;
- supervision orders;
- action plan orders.

Custodial sentences

In relation to offenders under the age of 18, custodial sentences may only be imposed if the custody threshold is passed and in the following circumstances:

(a) if the dangerousness provisions apply following the commission of a specified or serious specified offence (see **Chapter 3**);
(b) if a 'grave crime' is committed;
(c) if a detention and training order is available;
(d) if the offender is convicted of murder, when the sentence is detention during Her Majesty's pleasure.

Detention and training orders (DTOs)

The availability of a detention and training order depends on the age of the offender at the date of conviction. The order is not available for offenders aged 10–11; it *is* available for offenders aged 12–14 but only if the offender is a 'persistent offender'; and it is generally available for offenders aged 15–17.

There is no statutory definition of persistent offender. Each case turns on its own facts but the court may take account of cautions (*R* v. *AD (A Juvenile)* [2000] Crim LR 867), and offences occurring very close to each other (*R* v. *S (A Juvenile)* [2000] Crim LR 613; *R* v. *C (A Juvenile) (Persistent Offender)* [2001] 1 Cr App R(S) 120), but may disregard offences of a different type (*R* v. *D (Jamie) (A Juvenile)* (2001) 165 JP 1).

A young person who attains 18 between conviction and sentence may also receive a DTO because of the provisions of CYPA 1963, s.29(1) (*A* v. *DPP* [2002] EWHC 403 (Admin)).

Duration: the order may be for specified periods of 4, 6, 8, 10, 12, 18 and 24 months.

The length of a custodial sentence must be commensurate with the seriousness of the offence. It follows that if an offence does not carry or, on the facts, does not merit a sentence of four months, a DTO may not be made. The issue must be considered having regard to the sentence discounted for any guilty plea.

As the maximum length of a DTO is 24 months, a DTO may significantly exceed the normal maximum sentence for a magistrates' court (*C (A Child)*

v. *DPP* [2001] EWHC Admin 453). However, the sentence cannot exceed the maximum available for the offence. DTO sentences may in appropriate cases be made consecutive to each other, but the aggregate (including for summary-only offences) may not exceed 24 months. A discount for a guilty plea should be given even if the prosecution could have preferred an allegation of grave crime but chose not to do so.

Time spent in custody on remand (or in police detention, local authority secure accommodation or hospital under MHA 1983) in connection with the offence must be taken into account by the court when fixing the length of the sentence, but does not have to be reflected in a specific or precise way (*R* v. *Fieldhouse; R* v. *Watts* [2000] Crim LR 1020).

8.6 BREACH PROCEEDINGS

The general principles apply, as to which to see **Chapter 7**.

Table 8.4 Summary of breach provisions

Order	Provisions dealing with breach	Powers available to the court
Referral order	PCC(S)A 2000, Sched.1	Referral back – the court must be satisfied that the youth offending panel was entitled to make any finding of fact and exercised its discretion reasonably. The court must have regard to circumstances of referral back and extent of compliance with the order and may: • allow the order to continue; • revoke the order and re-sentence. [Not yet in force: under CJIA 2008 the court may on application revoke or extend a youth offender contract (CJIA 2008, ss.36, 37).]

Attendance centre order	PCC(S)A 2000, Sched.5	For failure to attend or breach of rules, the court may:
		• without prejudice to the order continuing:
		  – take no action; or
		  – fine up to £250 (under 14) or £1,000;
		• revoke the order and re-sentence.

Table 8.4 Continued

Order	Provisions dealing with breach	Powers available to the court
		On application of offender or officer, the order can be discharged and court may re-sentence.
Supervision order	PCC(S)A 2000, Sched.7	For failure to comply with requirements, the court may: • take no action; • vary the requirement; • impose a fine up to £250 (under 14) or £1,000; • make a curfew order (if not already subject to one); • make an attendance centre order; or • revoke the order and re-sentence. On application of offender or officer, the order can be revoked or amended to insert or remove a provision.

Reparation and action plan orders	PCC(S)A 2000, Sched.8	For failure to comply with requirements, the court may:
		
		• without prejudice to the order continuing:
		  – take no action;
		  – fine up to £250 (under 14) or £1,000;
		  – make a curfew order;
		  – make an attendance centre order;
		• revoke the order and re-sentence.

Curfew order Exclusion order Community rehabilitation order Community punishment order Community punishment and rehabilitation order Drug treatment and testing order	PCC(S)A 2000, Sched.3	For failure to comply with requirements, the court may: • take no action; • impose a fine not exceeding £1,000; • impose a community service order if over 16 (if the existing order is a community punishment order, the total of both orders must not exceed 240 hours); • if the relevant order is a community rehabilitation order or a community punishment and rehabilitation order, impose an attendance centre order in addition; • revoke the order and re-sentence.

Table 8.4 Continued

Order	Provisions dealing with breach	Powers available to the court
Detention and training supervision	PCC(S)A 2000, s.104	For failure to comply with requirements, the court may: • take no action; • fine up to £250 (under 14) or £1,000; • order detention for up to 3 months or for the remainder of the DTO sentence, whichever is shorter.
[Not yet in force] Youth rehabilitation order	CJIA 2008, Sched.2	At referral back to court after 2nd or 3rd failures to comply with requirements or to keep appointments/co-operate, the court may: • impose a fine of up to £250 (if under 14) or up to £1,000, which enables the order to continue; • amend the order to add or substitute requirements [If there was no unpaid work in the original order a minimum of 20 hours may be imposed on breach. The court may also impose an extended activity requirement or a fostering requirement if not already imposed. If fostering already required the period may be extended to 18 months.]; • revoke the order and re-sentence. When re-sentencing: • if there has been a wilful and persistent failure to comply in relation to an imprisonable offence, the court may impose an intensive supervision and surveillance order; • if the order has intensive supervision and surveillance, a custodial sentence may be imposed even though it is not normally available.

8.7 ORDERS IN RELATION TO PARENTS AND GUARDIANS

Binding over (PCC(S)A 2000, s.150)

The court shall make the following orders on conviction of a child or young person under 16, and may do so in relation to offenders aged 16–17 (if having regard to all the circumstances of the case the court considers it desirable in the interests of preventing the commission by the young offender of further offences), with the consent of the parent or guardian:

(a)   a bind over to take proper care of and exercise control over the offender;
(b)   a bind over to ensure that the offender complies with the requirements of a community sentence.

The court may require a recognisance of up to £1,000, taking into account available means information. Consent is required but a fine of up to £1,000 may be levied on refusal.

The bind over may be for a period of three years or up to the 18th birthday of the offender, whichever is the shorter period.

The power to bind over is not available if a referral order is made.

Parenting order (CDA 1998, s.8)

Where a person under the age of 18 is convicted of an offence (and in other circumstances), and the court considers that an order would be desirable in the interests of preventing re-offending (or other behaviour), it may make a parenting order in relation to a parent or guardian (or person convicted of an offence under the Education Act 1996) of the young person.

Where the offender is aged 16 or under, if the court is satisfied that an order is desirable, there is a presumption in favour of the order being made, and reasons must be given if it is not (CDA 1998, s.9).

A parenting order requires the parent or guardian, for a period not exceeding 12 months:

• to comply with requirements specified in the order that the court considers desirable in the interests of preventing repetition of behaviour or the commission of a further offence; and
• to attend for counselling or guidance sessions (for a concurrent period of up to three months) as specified by the responsible officer.

Before making an order the court should obtain and consider information about the offender's family circumstances and likely effect of an order.

Failure to comply with requirements in the order or directions of the responsible officer is punishable with a fine up to £1,000.

APPENDIX 1

Sentencing Guidelines Council: Definitive Guidelines and other guidance

	Definitive guidelines	Effective from
1.	Assault and Other Offences Against the Person	3 March 2008
2.	Breach of Anti-Social Behaviour Order	5 January 2009
3.	Breach of Protective Order	18 December 2006
4.	Causing Death by Driving	4 August 2008
5.	Fail to Surrender to Bail	10 December 2007
6.	Magistrates' Court Sentencing Guidelines (including update 1, 15 July 2008 and update 2, 9 December 2008)	4 August 2008
7.	Magistrates' Court Sentencing Guidelines, Sentencing for possession of a weapon – knife crime (additional note)	4 August 2008
8.	Manslaughter by Reason of Provocation	28 November 2005
9.	New Sentences: Criminal Justice Act 2003	4 April 2005
10.	Overarching Principles: Assaults on Children and Cruelty to a Child	3 March 2008
11.	Overarching Principles: Domestic Violence	18 December 2006
12.	Overarching Principles: Seriousness	4 April 2005
13.	Reduction in Sentence for a Guilty Plea (Revised)	23 July 2007
14.	Robbery	1 August 2006
15.	Sexual Offences Act 2003	14 May 2007
16.	Theft and Burglary (non-dwelling)	5 January 2009
	Guidance	
17.	Dangerous Offenders: Guide for Sentencers and Practitioners (Version 2)	July 2008

Offences allowing an Attorney General's review of unduly lenient sentences

All indictable only offences and in addition offences listed in Sched.1 to the Criminal Justice Act 1988 (Reviews of Sentencing) Order 2006 (SI 2006/1116), which lists the offences for which the Attorney General may seek a review as follows.

1. Any case tried on indictment –

    (a) following a notice of transfer given under section 4 of the Criminal Justice Act 1987 (notices of transfer and designated authorities) by an authority designated for that purpose under subsection (2) of that section; or

    (b) in which one or more of the counts in respect of which sentence is passed relates to a charge which was dismissed under section 6(1) of the Criminal Justice Act 1987 (applications for dismissal) and on which further proceedings were brought by means of preferment of a voluntary bill of indictment.

2. Any case in which sentence is passed on a person for one of the following offences:

    (a) an offence under section 16 of the Offences against the Person Act 1861 (threats to kill);

    (b) an offence under section 5(1) of the Criminal Law Amendment Act 1885 (defilement of a girl between 14 and 17);

    (c) an offence under section 1 of the Children and Young Persons Act 1933 (cruelty to persons under 16) or section 20 of the Children and Young Persons Act (Northern Ireland) 1968 (cruelty to persons under 16);

    (d) an offence under section 6 of the Sexual Offences Act 1956 (unlawful sexual intercourse with a girl under 16), section 14 or 15 of that Act (indecent assault on a woman or on a man), section 52 of the Offences against the Person Act 1861 (indecent assault upon a female), or Article 21 of the Criminal Justice (Northern Ireland) Order 2003 (indecent assault on a male);

    (e) an offence under section 1 of the Indecency with Children Act 1960 or section 22 of the Children and Young Persons Act (Northern Ireland) 1968 (indecent conduct with a child);

    (f) an offence under section 4(2) or (3) (production or supply of a controlled drug), section 5(3) (possession of a controlled drug with intent to supply) or section 6(2) (cultivation of cannabis plant) of the Misuse of Drugs Act 1971;

    (g) an offence under section 54 of the Criminal Law Act 1977 or Article 9 of the Criminal Justice (Northern Ireland) Order 1980 (inciting a girl under 16 to have incestuous sexual intercourse);

(h)   an offence under section 50(2) or (3), section 68(2) or section 170(1) or (2) of the Customs and Excise Management Act 1979, insofar as those offences are in connection with a prohibition or restriction on importation or exportation of either:

   (i)   a controlled drug within the meaning of section 2 of the Misuse of Drugs Act 1971, such prohibition or restriction having effect by virtue of section 3 of that Act; or

   (ii) an article prohibited by virtue of section 42 of the Customs Consolidation Act 1876 but only insofar as it relates to or depicts a person under the age of 16;

(i)   offences under sections 29 to 32 of the Crime and Disorder Act 1998 (racially or religiously aggravated assaults; racially or religiously aggravated criminal damage; racially or religiously aggravated public offences; racially or religiously aggravated harassment etc).

3.   To the extent that Part IV of the Criminal Justice Act 1988 does not apply by virtue of section 35(3)(b)(i), any case in which sentence is passed on a person for an offence under one of the following sections of the Sexual Offences Act 2003:

(a)   section 3 (sexual assault);
(b)   section 4 (causing a person to engage in sexual activity without consent);
(c)   section 7 (sexual assault of a child under 13);
(d)   section 8 (causing or inciting a child under 13 to engage in sexual activity);
(e)   section 9 (sexual activity with a child);
(f)   section 10 (causing or inciting a child to engage in sexual activity);
(g)   section 11 (engaging in sexual activity in the presence of a child);
(h)   section 12 (causing a child to watch a sexual act);
(i)   section 14 (arranging or facilitating commission of a child sex offence);
(j)   section 15 (meeting a child following sexual grooming etc);
(k)   section 25 (sexual activity with a child family member);
(l)   section 47 (paying for sexual services of a child);
(m)   section 48 (causing or inciting child prostitution or pornography);
(n)   section 49 (controlling a child prostitute or a child involved in pornography);
(o)   section 50 (arranging or facilitating child prostitution or pornography);
(p)   section 52 (causing or inciting prostitution for gain);
(q)   section 57 (trafficking into the UK for sexual exploitation);
(r)   section 58 (trafficking within the UK for sexual exploitation);
(s)   section 59 (trafficking out of the UK for sexual exploitation);
(t)   section 61 (administering a substance with intent).

4.   Any case in which sentence is passed on a person for attempting to commit or inciting the commission of an offence set out in paragraph 2(a) to (h) or paragraph 3.

APPENDIX 3

Addendum to the Attorney General's guidelines on the acceptance of pleas and the prosecutor's role in the sentencing exercise

1. In all cases before the Crown Court, and in cases before the magistrates' court where the issues are complex or there is scope for misunderstanding, the prosecution must commit to writing the aggravating and mitigating factors that will form the opening of the prosecution case as well any statutory limitations on sentencing. The prosecution will address, where relevant, the factors outlined at B4 [B4 can be found at **www.attorneygeneral.gov.uk/attachments/acceptance_of_pleas_guidance.doc**] including the matters set out in the next sub-paragraph.

2. The matters to be dealt with are:
    *   the aggravating and mitigating factors of the offence (not personal mitigation);
    *   any statutory provisions relevant to the offender and the offence under consideration so that the judge is made aware of any statutory limitations on sentencing;
    *   any relevant sentencing Guidelines and guideline cases;
    *   identifying any victim personal statement or other information available to the prosecution advocate as to the impact of the offence on the victim;
    *   where appropriate, any evidence of the impact of the offending on a community;
    *   an indication, where applicable, of an intention to apply for any ancillary orders, such as anti-social behaviour orders and confiscation orders, and so far as possible, indicating the nature of the order to be sought.

Form: Structure for presenting mitigation

1. **Offence**	
Facts	
Basis of plea/conviction	
Starting point	
Aggravating factors	
Mitigating factors	
2. **Offender**	
Personal information/characteristics	
Personal mitigation factors	
Issues	
3. **Guilty plea discount**	
Appropriate?	
Stage plea entered	
Guideline recommendation	
4. **Outcome**	
Primary sentence sought/recommended	
Relevant secondary/ancillary	
Sentencing powers and options	
Totality	

Form: Personal mitigation: data collection

a.	Personal characteristics of the defendant	
	Date of birth	
	Age at date of offence	
	Age at conviction	
	Level of maturity	
	Character: referees	
	Conduct including positive good conduct	
	Previous convictions	
	Defendant's mental health	
	Physical health	
	Educational and other achievements	
	Employment/training history	
	Disadvantage/trauma	
b.	Circumstances preceding the offence	
	Spontaneity	
	Level of intent	
	Family circumstances	
	Provocation	
	Pressure from others	
	Stress	
	Financial difficulties	
c.	Effect of sentences on others	
d.	Additional hardships from conviction	
	Illness	
	Job	

e. **Conduct after offence**	

Remorse
    Compensation
    Information and assistance to authorities[1]
    Plea
    Addressing problems	

f. **Factors arising from conduct of proceedings**	

Delay in bringing or concluding the proceedings
    Time in custody on remand
    Consistency with co-defendants	

[1] See in particular *R* v. *P; R* v. *Blackburn* [2007] EWCA Crim 2290.

Form: Information on financial resources: data collection

In every case the following financial information should be obtained

❑ Weekly   ❑ Fortnightly   ❑ Monthly

National Insurance Number

Income details	Outgoings	Other information
If you are employed Employer's name Employer's address Postcode _____ Employer's telephone number _____ Occupation (state if self-employed) _____ Net pay £_____ (take home pay)	**Essentials and accommodation** Rent, mortgage or lodgings £_____ Council tax £_____ Food £_____ Clothing £_____ Insurance £_____ Child maintenance £_____ **Travel and regular bills** Travel expenses and vehicle	Number of dependent children _____ Ages _____ Total savings £_____ Partner's income including benefits £_____ Number of adults in your home _____ Other relevant information
Any other income £_____ **If you are NOT employed** State since when _____ **If you receive benefits** Job seeker's allowance £_____ Income support Pension credit £_____ Tax credit £_____	fuel/public transport £_____ Vehicle insurance and tax £_____ Vehicle loan £_____ Utility bills £_____ (gas, water, electricity, etc.) £_____ Telephone subscription (licence, satellite, etc.) £____	

Other credits £ _____ (housing, child, etc.) **Total income £ _____**	**Other** Leisure e.g. drinking and smoking £_____ County court orders and other fines £_____ Loan repayments £_____ Catalogues £_____ Credit card repayments **Total outgoings £ _____**	

Form: Potential personal mitigating factors: data collection[1]

Category 2: **Immediate circumstances of the offence**	
Spontaneous offence	
Low level of recklessness/unintentional	
Provocation	
Acted under pressure from others	
Category 3: **Wider circumstances at time of offence**	
Offended in response to pressing need	
Vulnerability to the influence of others	
Social/intellectual limitations	
Youth/immaturity	
Offence linked to (treatable) psychiatric problems	
Under severe stress at time of offence	
Category 4: **Responses to the offence and prosecution**	
Remorse/acknowledgement of offence	
Efforts at reparation	
Co-operation with authorities	
Court processes have been stressful/ long-running	
Has spent time in custody (on remand)	
Has been addressing problems since arrest	
Supportive attitude of victim	
Consistency with co-defendants	

[1] Adapted from Table 2.1 of Jacobson and Hough, *Mitigation: The Role of Personal Factors in Sentencing* (Prison Reform Trust, 2007) with kind permission of the authors and the Prison Reform Trust. Category 1 relates to factors relevant to the criminal act rather than factors personal to the defendant.

Category 5: Defendant's past	
Good character; or limited previous offending	
Positive responses to previous sentences	
Has led a productive/worthwhile life	
Disadvantaged/disrupted background	
Traumatic life events	
General improvement in behaviour	
Category 6: Defendant's present and future	
Unlikely to re-offend/cause harm	
Can address/is addressing problems (e.g. drug, alcohol problems)	
Psychiatric problems are being/can be treated	
Has family responsibilities	
Has support from family/partner	
Currently in work/training/studying or has prospects of work/training/studies	
Physical; illness or disability	
Old age	

Firearms Act 1968: minimum sentences

The relevant offences for the purposes of the minimum sentence provisions are listed in section 51A(1) and (1A) of the Firearms Act 1968 as set out below; for completeness the offences referred to under s.5(1) and 5(1A) are also given.

51A Minimum sentence for certain offences under s. 5

(1) This section applies where –

  (a) an individual is convicted of –

    (i) an offence under section 5(1)(a), (ab), (aba), (ac), (ad), (ae), (af) or (c) of this Act,
    (ii) an offence under section 5(1A)(a) of this Act, or
    (iii) an offence under any of the provisions of this Act listed in subsection (1A) in respect of a firearm or ammunition specified in section 5(1)(a), (ab), (aba), (ac), (ad), (ae), (af) or (c) or section 5(1A)(a) of this Act, and

  (b) the offence was committed after the commencement of this section and at a time when he was aged 16 or over.

(1A) The provisions are –

  (a) section 16 (possession of firearm with intent to injure);
  (b) section 16A (possession of firearm with intent to cause fear of violence);
  (c) section 17 (use of firearm to resist arrest);
  (d) section 18 (carrying firearm with criminal intent);
  (e) section 19 (carrying a firearm in a public place);
  (f) section 20(1) (trespassing in a building with firearm).

Section 5(1)(a)–(af) and (c) and (1A)(a) provides as follows.

5 Weapons subject to general prohibition.

(1) A person commits an offence if, without the authority of the Secretary of State or the Scottish Ministers (by virtue of provision made under section 63 of the Scotland Act 1998), he has in his possession, or purchases or acquires, or manufactures, sells or transfers –

  (a) any firearm which is so designed or adapted that two or more missiles can be successively discharged without repeated pressure on the trigger;

(ab) any self-loading or pump-action rifled gun other than one which is chambered for .22 rim-fire cartridges;

(aba) any firearm which either has a barrel less than 30 centimetres in length or is less than 60 centimetres in length overall, other than an air weapon, a muzzle-loading gun or a firearm designed as signalling apparatus;

(ac) any self-loading or pump-action smooth-bore gun which is not an air weapon or chambered for .22 rim-fire cartridges and either has a barrel less than 24 inches in length or is less than 40 inches in length overall;

(ad) any smooth-bore revolver gun other than one which is chambered for 9mm. rim-fire cartridges or a muzzle-loading gun;

(ae) any rocket launcher, or any mortar, for projecting a stabilised missile, other than a launcher or mortar designed for line-throwing or pyrotechnic purposes or as signalling apparatus;

(af) any air rifle, air gun or air pistol which uses, or is designed or adapted for use with, a self-contained gas cartridge system; [. . .]

(c) any cartridge with a bullet designed to explode on or immediately before impact, any ammunition containing or designed or adapted to contain any such noxious thing as is mentioned in paragraph (b) above and, if capable of being used with a firearm of any description, any grenade, bomb (or other like missile), or rocket or shell designed to explode as aforesaid.

(1A) Subject to section 5A of this Act, a person commits an offence if, without the authority of the Secretary of State or the Scottish Ministers (by virtue of provision made under section 63 of the Scotland Act 1998), he has in his possession, or purchases or acquires, or sells or transfers –

(a) any firearm which is disguised as another object; [. . .]

Dangerous offenders: Criminal Justice Act 2003, Schedule 15

SPECIFIED OFFENCES FOR PURPOSES OF CHAPTER 5 OF PART 12

Section 224

Part 1

Specified Violent Offences

1   Manslaughter.
2   Kidnapping.
3   False imprisonment.
4   An offence under section 4 of the Offences against the Person Act 1861 (c 100) (soliciting murder).
5   An offence under section 16 of that Act (threats to kill).
6   An offence under section 18 of that Act (wounding with intent to cause grievous bodily harm).
7   An offence under section 20 of that Act (malicious wounding).
8   An offence under section 21 of that Act (attempting to choke, suffocate or strangle in order to commit or assist in committing an indictable offence).
9   An offence under section 22 of that Act (using chloroform etc to commit or assist in the committing of any indictable offence).
10   An offence under section 23 of that Act (maliciously administering poison etc so as to endanger life or inflict grievous bodily harm).
11   An offence under section 27 of that Act (abandoning children).
12   An offence under section 28 of that Act (causing bodily injury by explosives).
13   An offence under section 29 of that Act (using explosives etc with intent to do grievous bodily harm).
14   An offence under section 30 of that Act (placing explosives with intent to do bodily injury).
15   An offence under section 31 of that Act (setting spring guns etc with intent to do grievous bodily harm).
16   An offence under section 32 of that Act (endangering the safety of railway passengers).
17   An offence under section 35 of that Act (injuring persons by furious driving).
18   An offence under section 37 of that Act (assaulting officer preserving wreck).
19   An offence under section 38 of that Act (assault with intent to resist arrest).
20   An offence under section 47 of that Act (assault occasioning actual bodily harm).
21   An offence under section 2 of the Explosive Substances Act 1883 (c 3) (causing explosion likely to endanger life or property).

22 An offence under section 3 of that Act (attempt to cause explosion, or making or keeping explosive with intent to endanger life or property).

23 An offence under section 1 of the Infant Life (Preservation) Act 1929 (c 34) (child destruction).

24 An offence under section 1 of the Children and Young Persons Act 1933 (c 12) (cruelty to children).

25 An offence under section 1 of the Infanticide Act 1938 (c 36) (infanticide).

26 An offence under section 16 of the Firearms Act 1968 (c 27) (possession of firearm with intent to endanger life).

27 An offence under section 16A of that Act (possession of firearm with intent to cause fear of violence).

28 An offence under section 17(1) of that Act (use of firearm to resist arrest).

29 An offence under section 17(2) of that Act (possession of firearm at time of committing or being arrested for offence specified in Schedule 1 to that Act).

30 An offence under section 18 of that Act (carrying a firearm with criminal intent).

31 An offence under section 8 of the Theft Act 1968 (c 60) (robbery or assault with intent to rob).

32 An offence under section 9 of that Act of burglary with intent to –
   (a) inflict grievous bodily harm on a person, or
   (b) do unlawful damage to a building or anything in it.

33 An offence under section 10 of that Act (aggravated burglary).

34 An offence under section 12A of that Act (aggravated vehicle-taking) involving an accident which caused the death of any person.

35 An offence of arson under section 1 of the Criminal Damage Act 1971 (c 48).

36 An offence under section 1(2) of that Act (destroying or damaging property) other than an offence of arson.

37 An offence under section 1 of the Taking of Hostages Act 1982 (c 28) (hostage-taking).

38 An offence under section 1 of the Aviation Security Act 1982 (c 36) (hijacking).

39 An offence under section 2 of that Act (destroying, damaging or endangering safety of aircraft).

40 An offence under section 3 of that Act (other acts endangering or likely to endanger safety of aircraft).

41 An offence under section 4 of that Act (offences in relation to certain dangerous articles).

42 An offence under section 127 of the Mental Health Act 1983 (c 20) (ill-treatment of patients).

43 An offence under section 1 of the Prohibition of Female Circumcision Act 1985 (c 38) (prohibition of female circumcision).

44 An offence under section 1 of the Public Order Act 1986 (c 64) (riot).

45 An offence under section 2 of that Act (violent disorder).

46 An offence under section 3 of that Act (affray).

47 An offence under section 134 of the Criminal Justice Act 1988 (c 33) (torture).

48 An offence under section 1 of the Road Traffic Act 1988 (c 52) (causing death by dangerous driving).

49 An offence under section 3A of that Act (causing death by careless driving when under influence of drink or drugs).

50 An offence under section 1 of the Aviation and Maritime Security Act 1990 (c 31) (endangering safety at aerodromes).

51 An offence under section 9 of that Act (hijacking of ships).

52 An offence under section 10 of that Act (seizing or exercising control of fixed platforms).

53 An offence under section 11 of that Act (destroying fixed platforms or endangering their safety).

54 An offence under section 12 of that Act (other acts endangering or likely to endanger safe navigation).

55 An offence under section 13 of that Act (offences involving threats).

56 An offence under Part II of the Channel Tunnel (Security) Order 1994 (SI 1994/570) (offences relating to Channel Tunnel trains and the tunnel system).

57 An offence under section 4 of the Protection from Harassment Act 1997 (c 40) (putting people in fear of violence).

58 An offence under section 29 of the Crime and Disorder Act 1998 (c 37) (racially or religiously aggravated assaults).

59 An offence falling within section 31(1)(a) or (b) of that Act (racially or religiously aggravated offences under section 4 or 4A of the Public Order Act 1986 (c 64)).

60 An offence under section 51 or 52 of the International Criminal Court Act 2001 (c 17) (genocide, crimes against humanity, war crimes and related offences), other than one involving murder.

61 An offence under section 1 of the Female Genital Mutilation Act 2003 (c 31) (female genital mutilation).

62 An offence under section 2 of that Act (assisting a girl to mutilate her own genitalia).

63 An offence under section 3 of that Act (assisting a non-UK person to mutilate overseas a girl's genitalia).

63A An offence under section 5 of the Domestic Violence, Crime and Victims Act 2004 (causing or allowing the death of a child or vulnerable adult).

64 An offence of –

(a) aiding, abetting, counselling, procuring or inciting the commission of an offence specified in this Part of this Schedule,

(b) conspiring to commit an offence so specified, or

(c) attempting to commit an offence so specified.

65 An attempt to commit murder or a conspiracy to commit murder.

Part 2

Specified Sexual Offences

66 An offence under section 1 of the Sexual Offences Act 1956 (c 69) (rape).

67 An offence under section 2 of that Act (procurement of woman by threats).

68 An offence under section 3 of that Act (procurement of woman by false pretences).

69 An offence under section 4 of that Act (administering drugs to obtain or facilitate intercourse).

70 An offence under section 5 of that Act (intercourse with girl under thirteen).

71 An offence under section 6 of that Act (intercourse with girl under 16).

72 An offence under section 7 of that Act (intercourse with a defective).

73 An offence under section 9 of that Act (procurement of a defective).

74 An offence under section 10 of that Act (incest by a man).

75 An offence under section 11 of that Act (incest by a woman).

76 An offence under section 14 of that Act (indecent assault on a woman).

77 An offence under section 15 of that Act (indecent assault on a man).

78 An offence under section 16 of that Act (assault with intent to commit buggery).

79 An offence under section 17 of that Act (abduction of woman by force or for the sake of her property).

80 An offence under section 19 of that Act (abduction of unmarried girl under eighteen from parent or guardian).

81 An offence under section 20 of that Act (abduction of unmarried girl under sixteen from parent or guardian).

82 An offence under section 21 of that Act (abduction of defective from parent or guardian).

83 An offence under section 22 of that Act (causing prostitution of women).

84 An offence under section 23 of that Act (procuration of girl under twenty-one).

85 An offence under section 24 of that Act (detention of woman in brothel).

86 An offence under section 25 of that Act (permitting girl under thirteen to use premises for intercourse).

87 An offence under section 26 of that Act (permitting girl under sixteen to use premises for intercourse).

88 An offence under section 27 of that Act (permitting defective to use premises for intercourse).

89 An offence under section 28 of that Act (causing or encouraging the prostitution of, intercourse with or indecent assault on girl under sixteen).

90 An offence under section 29 of that Act (causing or encouraging prostitution of defective).

91 An offence under section 32 of that Act (soliciting by men).

92 An offence under section 33 of that Act (keeping a brothel).

93 An offence under section 128 of the Mental Health Act 1959 (c 72) (sexual intercourse with patients).

94 An offence under section 1 of the Indecency with Children Act 1960 (c 33) (indecent conduct towards young child).

95 An offence under section 4 of the Sexual Offences Act 1967 (c 60) (procuring others to commit homosexual acts).

96 An offence under section 5 of that Act (living on earnings of male prostitution).

97 An offence under section 9 of the Theft Act 1968 (c 60) of burglary with intent to commit rape.

98 An offence under section 54 of the Criminal Law Act 1977 (c 45) (inciting girl under sixteen to have incestuous sexual intercourse).

99 An offence under section 1 of the Protection of Children Act 1978 (c 37) (indecent photographs of children).

100 An offence under section 170 of the Customs and Excise Management Act 1979 (c 2) (penalty for fraudulent evasion of duty etc) in relation to goods prohibited to be imported under section 42 of the Customs Consolidation Act 1876 (c 36) (indecent or obscene articles).

101 An offence under section 160 of the Criminal Justice Act 1988 (c 33) (possession of indecent photograph of a child).

102 An offence under section 1 of the Sexual Offences Act 2003 (c 42) (rape).

103 An offence under section 2 of that Act (assault by penetration).

104 An offence under section 3 of that Act (sexual assault).

105 An offence under section 4 of that Act (causing a person to engage in sexual activity without consent).

106 An offence under section 5 of that Act (rape of a child under 13).

107 An offence under section 6 of that Act (assault of a child under 13 by penetration).

108 An offence under section 7 of that Act (sexual assault of a child under 13).

109 An offence under section 8 of that Act (causing or inciting a child under 13 to engage in sexual activity).

110 An offence under section 9 of that Act (sexual activity with a child).

111 An offence under section 10 of that Act (causing or inciting a child to engage in sexual activity).

112 An offence under section 11 of that Act (engaging in sexual activity in the presence of a child).

113 An offence under section 12 of that Act (causing a child to watch a sexual act).

114 An offence under section 13 of that Act (child sex offences committed by children or young persons).

115 An offence under section 14 of that Act (arranging or facilitating commission of a child sex offence).

116 An offence under section 15 of that Act (meeting a child following sexual grooming etc).

117 An offence under section 16 of that Act (abuse of position of trust: sexual activity with a child).

118 An offence under section 17 of that Act (abuse of position of trust: causing or inciting a child to engage in sexual activity).

119 An offence under section 18 of that Act (abuse of position of trust: sexual activity in the presence of a child).

120 An offence under section 19 of that Act (abuse of position of trust: causing a child to watch a sexual act).

121 An offence under section 25 of that Act (sexual activity with a child family member).

122 An offence under section 26 of that Act (inciting a child family member to engage in sexual activity).

123 An offence under section 30 of that Act (sexual activity with a person with a mental disorder impeding choice).

124 An offence under section 31 of that Act (causing or inciting a person with a mental disorder impeding choice to engage in sexual activity).

125 An offence under section 32 of that Act (engaging in sexual activity in the presence of a person with a mental disorder impeding choice).

126 An offence under section 33 of that Act (causing a person with a mental disorder impeding choice to watch a sexual act).

127 An offence under section 34 of that Act (inducement, threat or deception to procure sexual activity with a person with a mental disorder).

128 An offence under section 35 of that Act (causing a person with a mental disorder to engage in or agree to engage in sexual activity by inducement, threat or deception).

129 An offence under section 36 of that Act (engaging in sexual activity in the presence, procured by inducement, threat or deception, of a person with a mental disorder).

130 An offence under section 37 of that Act (causing a person with a mental disorder to watch a sexual act by inducement, threat or deception).

131 An offence under section 38 of that Act (care workers: sexual activity with a person with a mental disorder).

132 An offence under section 39 of that Act (care workers: causing or inciting sexual activity).

133 An offence under section 40 of that Act (care workers: sexual activity in the presence of a person with a mental disorder).

134 An offence under section 41 of that Act (care workers: causing a person with a mental disorder to watch a sexual act).

135 An offence under section 47 of that Act (paying for sexual services of a child).

136 An offence under section 48 of that Act (causing or inciting child prostitution or pornography).

137 An offence under section 49 of that Act (controlling a child prostitute or a child involved in pornography).

138 An offence under section 50 of that Act (arranging or facilitating child prostitution or pornography).
139 An offence under section 52 of that Act (causing or inciting prostitution for gain).
140 An offence under section 53 of that Act (controlling prostitution for gain).
141 An offence under section 57 of that Act (trafficking into the UK for sexual exploitation).
142 An offence under section 58 of that Act (trafficking within the UK for sexual exploitation).
143 An offence under section 59 of that Act (trafficking out of the UK for sexual exploitation).
144 An offence under section 61 of that Act (administering a substance with intent).
145 An offence under section 62 of that Act (committing an offence with intent to commit a sexual offence).
146 An offence under section 63 of that Act (trespass with intent to commit a sexual offence).
147 An offence under section 64 of that Act (sex with an adult relative: penetration).
148 An offence under section 65 of that Act (sex with an adult relative: consenting to penetration).
149 An offence under section 66 of that Act (exposure).
150 An offence under section 67 of that Act (voyeurism).
151 An offence under section 69 of that Act (intercourse with an animal).
152 An offence under section 70 of that Act (sexual penetration of a corpse).
153 An offence of –

(a) aiding, abetting, counselling, procuring or inciting the commission of an offence specified in this Part of this Schedule,
(b) conspiring to commit an offence so specified, or
(c) attempting to commit an offence so specified.

APPENDIX 10

Dangerous offenders: serious specified offences

- Manslaughter.
- Kidnapping.
- False imprisonment.
- An offence under section 4 of the Offences against the Person Act 1861 (c 100) (soliciting murder).
- An offence under section 16 of that Act (threats to kill).
- An offence under section 18 of that Act (wounding with intent to cause grievous bodily harm).
- An offence under section 21 of that Act (attempting to choke, suffocate or strangle in order to commit or assist in committing an indictable offence).
- An offence under section 22 of that Act (using chloroform etc to commit or assist in the committing of any indictable offence).
- An offence under section 23 of that Act (maliciously administering poison etc so as to endanger life or inflict grievous bodily harm).
- An offence under section 28 of that Act (causing bodily injury by explosives).
- An offence under section 29 of that Act (using explosives etc with intent to do grievous bodily harm).
- An offence under section 30 of that Act (placing explosives with intent to do bodily injury).
- An offence under section 32 of that Act (endangering the safety of railway passengers).
- An offence under section 2 of the Explosive Substances Act 1883 (c 3) (causing explosion likely to endanger life or property).
- An offence under section 3 of that Act (attempt to cause explosion, or making or keeping explosive with intent to endanger life or property).
- An offence under section 1 of the Infant Life (Preservation) Act 1929 (c 34) (child destruction).
- An offence under section 1 of the Children and Young Persons Act 1933 (c 12) (cruelty to children).
- An offence under section 1 of the Infanticide Act 1938 (c 36) (infanticide).
- An offence under section 16 of the Firearms Act 1968 (c 27) (possession of firearm with intent to endanger life).
- An offence under section 16A of that Act (possession of firearm with intent to cause fear of violence).
- An offence under section 17(1) of that Act (use of firearm to resist arrest).
- An offence under section 17(2) of that Act (possession of firearm at time of committing or being arrested for offence specified in Schedule 1 to that Act).
- An offence under section 18 of that Act (carrying a firearm with criminal intent).

- An offence under section 8 of the Theft Act 1968 (c 60) (robbery or assault with intent to rob).
- An offence under section 9 of that Act of burglary with intent to –
  - inflict grievous bodily harm on a person, or
  - do unlawful damage to a building or anything in it.
- An offence under section 10 of that Act (aggravated burglary).
- An offence under section 12A of that Act (aggravated vehicle-taking) involving an accident which caused the death of any person.
- An offence of arson under section 1 of the Criminal Damage Act 1971 (c 48).
- An offence under section 1(2) of that Act (destroying or damaging property) other than an offence of arson.
- An offence under section 1 of the Taking of Hostages Act 1982 (c 28) (hostage-taking).
- An offence under section 1 of the Aviation Security Act 1982 (c 36) (hijacking).
- An offence under section 2 of that Act (destroying, damaging or endangering safety of aircraft).
- An offence under section 3 of that Act (other acts endangering or likely to endanger safety of aircraft).
- An offence under section 1 of the Public Order Act 1986 (c 64) (riot).
- An offence under section 134 of the Criminal Justice Act 1988 (c 33) (torture).
- An offence under section 1 of the Road Traffic Act 1988 (c 52) (causing death by dangerous driving).
- An offence under section 3A of that Act (causing death by careless driving when under influence of drink or drugs).
- An offence under section 1 of the Aviation and Maritime Security Act 1990 (c 31) (endangering safety at aerodromes).
- An offence under section 9 of that Act (hijacking of ships).
- An offence under section 10 of that Act (seizing or exercising control of fixed platforms).
- An offence under section 11 of that Act (destroying fixed platforms or endangering their safety).
- An offence under section 12 of that Act (other acts endangering or likely to endanger safe navigation).
- An offence under section 13 of that Act (offences involving threats).
- An offence under Part II of the Channel Tunnel (Security) Order 1994 (SI 1994/570) (offences relating to Channel Tunnel trains and the tunnel system).
- An offence under section 51 or 52 of the International Criminal Court Act 2001 (c 17) (genocide, crimes against humanity, war crimes and related offences), other than one involving murder.
- An offence under section 1 of the Female Genital Mutilation Act 2003 (c 31) (female genital mutilation).
- An offence under section 2 of that Act (assisting a girl to mutilate her own genitalia).
- An offence under section 3 of that Act (assisting a non-UK person to mutilate overseas a girl's genitalia).
- An offence under section 5 of the Domestic Violence, Crime and Victims Act 2004 (causing or allowing the death of a child or vulnerable adult).
- An offence under section 1 of the Sexual Offences Act 1956 (c 69) (rape).
- An offence under section 5 of that Act (intercourse with girl under 13) [not an attempt].

- An offence under section 6 of that Act (intercourse with girl under 16).
- An offence under section 10 of that Act (incest by a man if girl/woman is under 13) [not an attempt].
- An offence under section 14 of that Act (indecent assault on a woman).
- An offence under section 15 of that Act (indecent assault on a man).
- An offence under section 16 of that Act (assault with intent to commit buggery).
- An offence under section 17 of that Act (abduction of woman by force or for the sake of her property).
- An offence under section 25 of that Act (permitting girl under thirteen to use premises for intercourse).
- An offence under section 1 of the Indecency with Children Act 1960 (c 33) (indecent conduct towards young child).
- An offence under section 9 of the Theft Act 1968 (c 60) of burglary with intent to commit rape.
- An offence under section 1 of the Protection of Children Act 1978 (c 37) (indecent photographs of children).
- An offence under section 1 of the Sexual Offences Act 2003 (c 42) (rape).
- An offence under section 2 of that Act (assault by penetration).
- An offence under section 3 of that Act (sexual assault).
- An offence under section 4 of that Act (causing a person to engage in sexual activity without consent).
- An offence under section 5 of that Act (rape of a child under 13).
- An offence under section 6 of that Act (assault of a child under 13 by penetration).
- An offence under section 7 of that Act (sexual assault of a child under 13).
- An offence under section 8 of that Act (causing or inciting a child under 13 to engage in sexual activity).
- An offence under section 9 of that Act (sexual activity with a child).
- An offence under section 10 of that Act (causing or inciting a child to engage in sexual activity).
- An offence under section 11 of that Act (engaging in sexual activity in the presence of a child).
- An offence under section 12 of that Act (causing a child to watch a sexual act).
- An offence under section 14 of that Act (arranging or facilitating commission of a child sex offence).
- An offence under section 15 of that Act (meeting a child following sexual grooming etc).
- An offence under section 25 of that Act (sexual activity with a child family member).
- An offence under section 26 of that Act (inciting a child family member to engage in sexual activity).
- An offence under section 30 of that Act (sexual activity with a person with a mental disorder impeding choice).
- An offence under section 31 of that Act (causing or inciting a person with a mental disorder impeding choice to engage in sexual activity).
- An offence under section 32 of that Act (engaging in sexual activity in the presence of a person with a mental disorder impeding choice).
- An offence under section 33 of that Act (causing a person with a mental disorder impeding choice to watch a sexual act).
- An offence under section 34 of that Act (inducement, threat or deception to procure sexual activity with a person with a mental disorder).
- An offence under section 35 of that Act (causing a person with a mental disorder to engage in or agree to engage in sexual activity by inducement, threat or deception).

- An offence under section 36 of that Act (engaging in sexual activity in the presence, procured by inducement, threat or deception, of a person with a mental disorder).
- An offence under section 37 of that Act (causing a person with a mental disorder to watch a sexual act by inducement, threat or deception).
- An offence under section 38 of that Act (care workers: sexual activity with a person with a mental disorder).
- An offence under section 39 of that Act (care workers: causing or inciting sexual activity).
- An offence under section 47 of that Act (paying for sexual services of a child).
- An offence under section 48 of that Act (causing or inciting child prostitution or pornography).
- An offence under section 49 of that Act (controlling a child prostitute or a child involved in pornography).
- An offence under section 50 of that Act (arranging or facilitating child prostitution or pornography).
- An offence under section 57 of that Act (trafficking into the UK for sexual exploitation).
- An offence under section 58 of that Act (trafficking within the UK for sexual exploitation).
- An offence under section 59 of that Act (trafficking out of the UK for sexual exploitation).
- An offence under section 61 of that Act (administering a substance with intent).
- An offence under section 62 of that Act (committing an offence with intent to commit a sexual offence).
- An offence under section 63 of that Act (trespass with intent to commit a sexual offence).
- An offence of–
  - aiding, abetting, counselling, procurring or inciting the commission of an offence specified in this Appendix,
  - conspiring to commit an offence so specified, or
  - attempting to commit an offence so specified, unless otherwise stated.

Dangerous offenders: Criminal Justice Act 2003, Schedule 15A

OFFENCES SPECIFIED FOR THE PURPOSES OF SECTIONS 225(3A) AND 227(2A)

Part 1

Offences Under the Law of England and Wales

1 Murder.
2 Manslaughter.
3 An offence under section 4 of the Offences against the Person Act 1861 (c 100) (soliciting murder).
4 An offence under section 18 of that Act (wounding with intent to cause grievous bodily harm).
5 An offence under section 1 of the Sexual Offences Act 1956 (c 69) (rape).
6 An offence under section 5 of that Act (intercourse with a girl under 13).
7 An offence under section 16 of the Firearms Act 1968 (c 27) (possession of firearm with intent to endanger life).
8 An offence under section 17(1) of that Act (use of a firearm to resist arrest).
9 An offence under section 18 of that Act (carrying a firearm with criminal intent).
10 An offence of robbery under section 8 of the Theft Act 1968 (c 60) where, at some time during the commission of the offence, the offender had in his possession a firearm or an imitation firearm within the meaning of the Firearms Act 1968.
11 An offence under section 1 of the Sexual Offences Act 2003 (c 42) (rape).
12 An offence under section 2 of that Act (assault by penetration).
13 An offence under section 4 of that Act (causing a person to engage in sexual activity without consent) if the offender was liable on conviction on indictment to imprisonment for life.
14 An offence under section 5 of that Act (rape of a child under 13).
15 An offence under section 6 of that Act (assault of a child under 13 by penetration).
16 An offence under section 8 of that Act (causing or inciting a child under 13 to engage in sexual activity) if the offender was liable on conviction on indictment to imprisonment for life.
17 An offence under section 30 of that Act (sexual activity with a person with a mental disorder impeding choice) if the offender was liable on conviction on indictment to imprisonment for life.
18 An offence under section 31 of that Act (causing or inciting a person with a mental disorder to engage in sexual activity) if the offender was liable on conviction on indictment to imprisonment for life.

19   An offence under section 34 of that Act (inducement, threat or deception to procure sexual activity with a person with a mental disorder) if the offender was liable on conviction on indictment to imprisonment for life.

20   An offence under section 35 of that Act (causing a person with a mental disorder to engage in or agree to engage in sexual activity by inducement etc) if the offender was liable on conviction on indictment to imprisonment for life.

21   An offence under section 47 of that Act (paying for sexual services of a child) if the offender was liable on conviction on indictment to imprisonment for life.

22   An offence under section 62 of that Act (committing an offence with intent to commit a sexual offence) if the offender was liable on conviction on indictment to imprisonment for life.

23   (1) An attempt to commit an offence specified in the preceding paragraphs of this Part of this Schedule ('a listed offence').

       (2) Conspiracy to commit a listed offence.

       (3) Incitement to commit a listed offence.

       (4) An offence under Part 2 of the Serious Crime Act 2007 in relation to which a listed offence is the offence (or one of the offences) which the person intended or believed would be committed.

       (5) Aiding, abetting, counselling or procuring the commission of a listed offence.

Part 2

Offences Under the Law of Scotland

****

Part 3

Offences Under the Law of Northern Ireland

****

Part 4

Offences Under Service Law

51   An offence under section 70 of the Army Act 1955, section 70 of the Air Force Act 1955 or section 42 of the Naval Discipline Act 1957 as respects which the corresponding civil offence (within the meaning of the Act in question) is an offence specified in Part 1 of this Schedule.

52   (1) An offence under section 42 of the Armed Forces Act 2006 as respects which the corresponding offence under the law of England and Wales (within the meaning given by that section) is an offence specified in Part 1 of this Schedule.

(2) Section 48 of the Armed Forces Act 2006 (attempts, conspiracy etc) applies for the purposes of this paragraph as if the reference in subsection (3)(b) of that section to any of the following provisions of that Act were a reference to this paragraph.

Part 5

Interpretation

53 In this Schedule, 'imprisonment for life' includes custody for life and detention for life.

APPENDIX 12

Financial orders: maximum default terms

An amount not exceeding £200	7 days
An amount exceeding £200 but not exceeding £500	14 days
An amount exceeding £500 but not exceeding £1,000	28 days
An amount exceeding £1,000 but not exceeding £2,500	45 days
An amount exceeding £2,500 but not exceeding £5,000	3 months
An amount exceeding £5,000 but not exceeding £10,000	6 months
An amount exceeding £10,000 but not exceeding £20,000	12 months
An amount exceeding £20,000 but not exceeding £50,000	18 months
An amount exceeding £50,000 but not exceeding £100,000	2 years
An amount exceeding £100,000 but not exceeding £250,000	3 years
An amount exceeding £250,000 but not exceeding £1 million	5 years
An amount exceeding £1 million	10 years

APPENDIX 13

Confiscation: Proceeds of Crime Act 2002, Schedule 2

LIFESTYLE OFFENCES: ENGLAND AND WALES

Section 75

Drug trafficking

1   (1)   An offence under any of the following provisions of the Misuse of Drugs Act 1971 (c 38) –

        (a)   section 4(2) or (3) (unlawful production or supply of controlled drugs);
        (b)   section 5(3) (possession of controlled drug with intent to supply);
        (c)   section 8 (permitting certain activities relating to controlled drugs);
        (d)   section 20 (assisting in or inducing the commission outside the UK of an offence punishable under a corresponding law).

    (2)   An offence under any of the following provisions of the Customs and Excise Management Act 1979 (c 2) if it is committed in connection with a prohibition or restriction on importation or exportation which has effect by virtue of section 3 of the Misuse of Drugs Act 1971 –

        (a)   section 50(2) or (3) (improper importation of goods);
        (b)   section 68(2) (exploration of prohibited or restricted goods);
        (c)   section 170 (fraudulent evasion).

    (3)   An offence under either of the following provisions of the Criminal Justice (International Co-operation) Act 1990 (c 5) –

        (a)   section 12 (manufacture or supply of a substance for the time being specified in Schedule 2 to that Act);
        (b)   section 19 (using a ship for illicit traffic in controlled drugs).

Money laundering

2   An offence under either of the following provisions of this Act –

    (a) section 327 (concealing etc criminal property);
    (b) section 328 (assisting another to retain criminal property).

Directing terrorism

3   An offence under section 56 of the Terrorism Act 2000 (c 11) (directing the activities of a terrorist organisation).

People trafficking

4 (1) An offence under section 25, 25A or 25B of the Immigration Act 1971 (c 77) (assisting unlawful immigration etc).

    (2) An offence under any of sections 57 to 59 of the Sexual Offences Act 2003 (trafficking for sexual exploitation).

    (3) An offence under section 4 of the Asylum and Immigration (Treatment of Claimants, etc) Act 2004 (exploitation).

Arms trafficking

5 (1) An offence under either of the following provisions of the Customs and Excise Management Act 1979 if it is committed in connection with a firearm or ammunition –

    (a) section 68(2) (exportation of prohibited goods);
    (b) section 170 (fraudulent evasion).

    (2) An offence under section 3(1) of the Firearms Act 1968 (c 27) (dealing in firearms or ammunition by way of trade or business).

    (3) In this paragraph 'firearm' and 'ammunition' have the same meanings as in section 57 of the Firearms Act 1968 (c 27).

Counterfeiting

6 An offence under any of the following provisions of the Forgery and Counterfeiting Act 1981 (c 45) –

    (a) section 14 (making counterfeit notes or coins);
    (b) section 15 (passing etc counterfeit notes or coins);
    (c) section 16 (having counterfeit notes or coins);
    (d) section 17 (making or possessing materials or equipment for counterfeiting).

Intellectual property

7 (1) An offence under any of the following provisions of the Copyright, Designs and Patents Act 1988 (c 48) –

    (a) section 107(1) (making or dealing in an article which infringes copyright);
    (b) section 107(2) (making or possessing an article designed or adapted for making a copy of a copyright work);
    (c) section 198(1) (making or dealing in an illicit recording);
    (d) section 297A (making or dealing in unauthorised decoders).

    (2) An offence under section 92(1), (2) or (3) of the Trade Marks Act 1994 (c 26) (unauthorised use etc of trade mark).

Prostitution and child sex

8 (1) An offence under section 33 or 34 of the Sexual Offences Act 1956 (keeping or letting premises for use as a brothel).

    (2) An offence under any of the following provisions of the Sexual Offences Act 2003 –

(a)   section 14 (arranging or facilitating commission of a child sex offence);
(b)   section 48 (causing or inciting child prostitution or pornography);
(c)   section 49 (controlling a child prostitute or a child involved in pornography);
(d)   section 50 (arranging or facilitating child prostitution or pornography);
(e)   section 52 (causing or inciting prostitution for gain);
(f)   section 53 (controlling prostitution for gain).

Blackmail

9   An offence under section 21 of the Theft Act 1968 (c 60) (blackmail).
9A   An offence under section 12(1) or (2) of the Gangmasters (Licensing) Act 2004 (acting as a gangmaster other than under the authority of a licence, possession of false documents etc).

Inchoate offences

10   (1)   An offence of attempting, conspiring or inciting the commission of an offence specified in this Schedule.
     (1A)   An offence under section 44 of the Serious Crime Act 2007 of doing an act capable of encouraging or assisting the commission of an offence specified in this Schedule.
     (2)   An offence of aiding, abetting, counselling or procuring the commission of such an offence.

Sexual offences notification and orders: Sexual Offences Act 2003, Schedule 3

SEXUAL OFFENCES FOR PURPOSES OF PART 2

Section 80

England and Wales

1   An offence under section 1 of the Sexual Offences Act 1956 (c 69) (rape).
2   An offence under section 5 of that Act (intercourse with girl under 13).
3   An offence under section 6 of that Act (intercourse with girl under 16), if the offender was 20 or over.
4   An offence under section 10 of that Act (incest by a man), if the victim or (as the case may be) other party was under 18.
5   An offence under section 12 of that Act (buggery) if –

(a)   the offender was 20 or over, and
(b)   the victim or (as the case may be) other party was under 18.

6   An offence under section 13 of that Act (indecency between men) if –

(a)   the offender was 20 or over, and
(b)   the victim or (as the case may be) other party was under 18.

7   An offence under section 14 of that Act (indecent assault on a woman) if –

(a)   the victim or (as the case may be) other party was under 18, or
(b)   the offender, in respect of the offence or finding, is or has been –

(i)   sentenced to imprisonment for a term of at least 30 months; or
(ii)   admitted to a hospital subject to a restriction order.

8   An offence under section 15 of that Act (indecent assault on a man) if –

(a)   the victim or (as the case may be) other party was under 18, or
(b)   the offender, in respect of the offence or finding, is or has been –

(i)   sentenced to imprisonment for a term of at least 30 months; or
(ii)   admitted to a hospital subject to a restriction order.

9   An offence under section 16 of that Act (assault with intent to commit buggery), if the victim or (as the case may be) other party was under 18.
10   An offence under section 28 of that Act (causing or encouraging the prostitution of, intercourse with or indecent assault on girl under 16).
11   An offence under section 1 of the Indecency with Children Act 1960 (c 33) (indecent conduct towards young child).

12 An offence under section 54 of the Criminal Law Act 1977 (c 45) (inciting girl under 16 to have incestuous sexual intercourse).

13 An offence under section 1 of the Protection of Children Act 1978 (c 37) (indecent photographs of children), if the indecent photographs or pseudo-photographs showed persons under 16 and –

(a) the conviction, finding or caution was before the commencement of this Part, or

(b) the offender –

(i) was 18 or over, or

(ii) is sentenced in respect of the offence to imprisonment for a term of at least 12 months.

14 An offence under section 170 of the Customs and Excise Management Act 1979 (c 2) (penalty for fraudulent evasion of duty etc) in relation to goods prohibited to be imported under section 42 of the Customs Consolidation Act 1876 (c 36) (indecent or obscene articles), if the prohibited goods included indecent photographs of persons under 16 and –

(a) the conviction, finding or caution was before the commencement of this Part, or

(b) the offender –

(i) was 18 or over, or

(ii) is sentenced in respect of the offence to imprisonment for a term of at least 12 months.

15 An offence under section 160 of the Criminal Justice Act 1988 (c 33) (possession of indecent photograph of a child), if the indecent photographs or pseudo-photographs showed persons under 16 and –

(a) the conviction, finding or caution was before the commencement of this Part, or

(b) the offender –

(i) was 18 or over, or

(ii) is sentenced in respect of the offence to imprisonment for a term of at least 12 months.

16 An offence under section 3 of the Sexual Offences (Amendment) Act 2000 (c 44) (abuse of position of trust), if the offender was 20 or over.

17 An offence under section 1 or 2 of this Act (rape, assault by penetration).

18 An offence under section 3 of this Act (sexual assault) if –

(a) where the offender was under 18, he is or has been sentenced, in respect of the offence, to imprisonment for a term of at least 12 months;

(b) in any other case –

(i) the victim was under 18, or

(ii) the offender, in respect of the offence or finding, is or has been –

(a) sentenced to a term of imprisonment,

(b) detained in a hospital, or

(c) made the subject of a community sentence of at least 12 months.

19 An offence under any of sections 4 to 6 of this Act (causing sexual activity without consent, rape of a child under 13, assault of a child under 13 by penetration).

20 An offence under section 7 of this Act (sexual assault of a child under 13) if the offender –

    (a) was 18 or over, or
    (b) is or has been sentenced in respect of the offence to imprisonment for a term of at least 12 months.

21 An offence under any of sections 8 to 12 of this Act (causing or inciting a child under 13 to engage in sexual activity, child sex offences committed by adults).

22 An offence under section 13 of this Act (child sex offences committed by children or young persons), if the offender is or has been sentenced, in respect of the offence, to imprisonment for a term of at least 12 months.

23 An offence under section 14 of this Act (arranging or facilitating the commission of a child sex offence) if the offender –

    (a) was 18 or over, or
    (b) is or has been sentenced, in respect of the offence, to imprisonment for a term of at least 12 months.

24 An offence under section 15 of this Act (meeting a child following sexual grooming etc).

25 An offence under any of sections 16 to 19 of this Act (abuse of a position of trust) if the offender, in respect of the offence, is or has been –

    (a) sentenced to a term of imprisonment,
    (b) detained in a hospital, or
    (c) made the subject of a community sentence of at least 12 months.

26 An offence under section 25 or 26 of this Act (familial child sex offences) if the offender –

    (a) was 18 or over, or
    (b) is or has been sentenced in respect of the offence to imprisonment for a term of at least 12 months.

27 An offence under any of sections 30 to 37 of this Act (offences against persons with a mental disorder impeding choice, inducements etc to persons with mental disorder).

28 An offence under any of sections 38 to 41 of this Act (care workers for persons with mental disorder) if –

    (a) where the offender was under 18, he is or has been sentenced in respect of the offence to imprisonment for a term of at least 12 months;
    (b) in any other case, the offender, in respect of the offence or finding, is or has been –

        (i)   sentenced to a term of imprisonment,
        (ii) detained in a hospital, or
        (iii) 'made the subject of a community sentence of at least 12 months.

29 An offence under section 47 of this Act (paying for sexual services of a child) if the victim or (as the case may be) other party was under 16, and the offender –

    (a) was 18 or over, or
    (b) is or has been sentenced in respect of the offence to imprisonment for a term of at least 12 months.

29A An offence under section 48 of this Act (causing or inciting child prostitution or pornography) if the offender –

(a)   was 18 or over, or

(b)   is or has been sentenced in respect of the offence to imprisonment for a term of at least 12 months.

29B   An offence under section 49 of this Act (controlling a child prostitute or a child involved in pornography) if the offender –

(a)   was 18 or over, or

(b)   is or has been sentenced in respect of the offence to imprisonment for a term of at least 12 months.

29C   An offence under section 50 of this Act (arranging or facilitating child prostitution or pornography) if the offender –

(a)   was 18 or over, or

(b)   is or has been sentenced in respect of the offence to imprisonment for a term of at least 12 months.

30   An offence under section 61 of this Act (administering a substance with intent).

31   An offence under section 62 or 63 of this Act (committing an offence or trespassing, with intent to commit a sexual offence) if –

(a)   where the offender was under 18, he is or has been sentenced in respect of the offence to imprisonment for a term of at least 12 months;

(b)   in any other case –

(i)   the intended offence was an offence against a person under 18, or

(ii)   the offender, in respect of the offence or finding, is or has been –

(a)   sentenced to a term of imprisonment,

(b)   detained in a hospital, or

(c)   made the subject of a community sentence of at least 12 months.

32   An offence under section 64 or 65 of this Act (sex with an adult relative) if –

(a)   where the offender was under 18, he is or has been sentenced in respect of the offence to imprisonment for a term of at least 12 months;

(b)   in any other case, the offender, in respect of the offence or finding, is or has been –

(i)   sentenced to a term of imprisonment, or

(ii)   detained in a hospital.

33   An offence under section 66 of this Act (exposure) if –

(a)   where the offender was under 18, he is or has been sentenced in respect of the offence to imprisonment for a term of at least 12 months;

(b)   in any other case –

(i)   the victim was under 18, or

(ii)   the offender, in respect of the offence or finding, is or has been –

(a)   sentenced to a term of imprisonment,

(b)   detained in a hospital, or

(c)   made the subject of a community sentence of at least 12 months.

34   An offence under section 67 of this Act (voyeurism) if –

(a)   where the offender was under 18, he is or has been sentenced in respect of the offence to imprisonment for a term of at least 12 months;

(b)   in any other case –

    (i)   the victim was under 18, or
    (ii)   the offender, in respect of the offence or finding, is or has been –

        (a)   sentenced to a term of imprisonment,
        (b)   detained in a hospital, or
        (c)   made the subject of a community sentence of at least 12 months.

35   An offence under section 69 or 70 of this Act (intercourse with an animal, sexual penetration of a corpse) if –

    (a)   where the offender was under 18, he is or has been sentenced in respect of the offence to imprisonment for a term of at least 12 months;
    (b)   in any other case, the offender, in respect of the offence or finding, is or has been –

        (i)   sentenced to a term of imprisonment, or
        (ii)   detained in a hospital.

35A An offence under section 63 of the Criminal Justice and Immigration Act 2008 (possession of extreme pornographic images) if the offender –

    (a)   was 18 or over, and
    (b)   is sentenced in respect of the offence to imprisonment for a term of at least 2 years.

Scotland

****

Northern Ireland

****

Service offences

93   (1) An offence under –

        (a)   section 70 of the Army Act 1955 (3 & 4 Eliz 2 c 18),
        (b)   section 70 of the Air Force Act 1955 (3 & 4 Eliz 2 c 19), or
        (c)   section 42 of the Naval Discipline Act 1957 (c 53),

      of which the corresponding civil offence (within the meaning of that Act) is an offence listed in any of paragraphs 1 to 35A.
    (2) A reference in any of those paragraphs to being made the subject of a community sentence of at least 12 months is to be read, in relation to an offence under an enactment referred to in sub-paragraph (1), as a reference to being sentenced to a term of service detention of at least 112 days.
    [(3) In sub-paragraph (2), the reference to detention is to detention awarded under section 71(1)(e) of the Army Act 1955 or Air Force Act 1955 or section 43(1)(e) of the Naval Discipline Act 1957.]
[93A(1) An offence under section 42 of the Armed Forces Act 2006 as respects which the corresponding offence under the law of England and Wales (within the meaning given by that section) is an offence listed in any of paragraphs 1 to 35A.

(2) A reference in any of those paragraphs to being made the subject of a community sentence of at least 12 months is to be read, in relation to an offence under that section, as a reference to –

(a) being made the subject of a service community order or overseas community order under the Armed Forces Act 2006 of at least 12 months; or

(b) being sentenced to a term of service detention of at least 112 days.

(3) Section 48 of that Act (attempts, conspiracy, encouragement and assistance and aiding and abetting outside England and Wales) applies for the purposes of this paragraph as if the reference in subsection (3)(b) to any of the following provisions of that Act were a reference to this paragraph.]

General

94 A reference in a preceding paragraph to an offence includes –

(a) a reference to an attempt, conspiracy or incitement to commit that offence, and

(b) except in paragraphs 36 to 43, a reference to aiding, abetting, counselling or procuring the commission of that offence.

94A A reference in a preceding paragraph to an offence ('offence A') includes a reference to an offence under Part 2 of the Serious Crime Act 2007 in relation to which offence A is the offence (or one of the offences) which the person intended or believed would be committed.

95 A reference in a preceding paragraph to a person's age is –

(a) in the case of an indecent photograph, a reference to the person's age when the photograph was taken;

(b) in any other case, a reference to his age at the time of the offence.

96 In this Schedule 'community sentence' has –

(a) in relation to England and Wales, the same meaning as in the Powers of Criminal Courts (Sentencing) Act 2000 (c 6), and

(b) in relation to Northern Ireland, the same meaning as in the Criminal Justice (Northern Ireland) Order 1996 (SI 1996/3160 (NI 24)).

97 For the purposes of paragraphs 14, 44 and 78 –

(a) a person is to be taken to have been under 16 at any time if it appears from the evidence as a whole that he was under that age at that time;

(b) section 7 of the Protection of Children Act 1978 (c 37) (interpretation), subsections (2) to (2C) and (8) of section 52 of the Civic Government (Scotland) Act 1982 (c 45), and Article 2(2) and (3) of the Protection of Children (Northern Ireland) Order 1978 (SI 1978/1047 (NI 17)) (interpretation) (respectively) apply as each provision applies for the purposes of the Act or Order of which it forms part.

98 A determination under paragraph 60 constitutes part of a person's sentence, within the meaning of the Criminal Procedure (Scotland) Act 1995 (c 46), for the purposes of any appeal or review.

Sexual offences notification and orders: Sexual Offences Act 2003, Schedule 5

OTHER OFFENCES FOR PURPOSES OF PART 2

Section 104

England and Wales

1 Murder.
2 Manslaughter.
3 Kidnapping.
4 False imprisonment.
4A Outraging public decency.
5 An offence under section 4 of the Offences against the Person Act 1861 (c 100) (soliciting murder).
6 An offence under section 16 of that Act (threats to kill).
7 An offence under section 18 of that Act (wounding with intent to cause grievous bodily harm).
8 An offence under section 20 of that Act (malicious wounding).
9 An offence under section 21 of that Act (attempting to choke, suffocate or strangle in order to commit or assist in committing an indictable offence).
10 An offence under section 22 of that Act (using chloroform etc to commit or assist in the committing of any indictable offence).
11 An offence under section 23 of that Act (maliciously administering poison etc so as to endanger life or inflict grievous bodily harm).
12 An offence under section 27 of that Act (abandoning children).
13 An offence under section 28 of that Act (causing bodily injury by explosives).
14 An offence under section 29 of that Act (using explosives etc with intent to do grievous bodily harm).
15 An offence under section 30 of that Act (placing explosives with intent to do bodily injury).
16 An offence under section 31 of that Act (setting spring guns etc with intent to do grievous bodily harm).
17 An offence under section 32 of that Act (endangering the safety of railway passengers).
18 An offence under section 35 of that Act (injuring persons by furious driving).
19 An offence under section 37 of that Act (assaulting officer preserving wreck).
20 An offence under section 38 of that Act (assault with intent to resist arrest).
21 An offence under section 47 of that Act (assault occasioning actual bodily harm).
22 An offence under section 2 of the Explosive Substances Act 1883 (c 3) (causing explosion likely to endanger life or property).

23   An offence under section 3 of that Act (attempt to cause explosion, or making or keeping explosive with intent to endanger life or property).

24   An offence under section 1 of the Infant Life (Preservation) Act 1929 (c 34) (child destruction).

25   An offence under section 1 of the Children and Young Persons Act 1933 (c 12) (cruelty to children).

26   An offence under section 1 of the Infanticide Act 1938 (c 36) (infanticide).

27   An offence under section 16 of the Firearms Act 1968 (c 27) (possession of firearm with intent to endanger life).

28   An offence under section 16A of that Act (possession of firearm with intent to cause fear of violence).

29   An offence under section 17(1) of that Act (use of firearm to resist arrest).

30   An offence under section 17(2) of that Act (possession of firearm at time of committing or being arrested for offence specified in Schedule 1 to that Act).

31   An offence under section 18 of that Act (carrying a firearm with criminal intent).

31A An offence under section 1 of the Theft Act 1968 (c 60) (theft).

32   An offence under section 8 of that Act (robbery or assault with intent to rob).

33   An offence under section 9(1)(a) of that Act (burglary with intent to steal, inflict grievous bodily harm or do unlawful damage).

34   An offence under section 10 of that Act (aggravated burglary).

35   An offence under section 12A of that Act (aggravated vehicle-taking) involving an accident which caused the death of any person.

36   An offence of arson under section 1 of the Criminal Damage Act 1971 (c 48).

37   An offence under section 1(2) of that Act (destroying or damaging property) other than an offence of arson.

38   An offence under section 1 of the Taking of Hostages Act 1982 (c 28) (hostage-taking).

39   An offence under section 1 of the Aviation Security Act 1982 (c 36) (hijacking).

40   An offence under section 2 of that Act (destroying, damaging or endangering safety of aircraft).

41   An offence under section 3 of that Act (other acts endangering or likely to endanger safety of aircraft).

42   An offence under section 4 of that Act (offences in relation to certain dangerous articles).

43   An offence under section 127 of the Mental Health Act 1983 (c 20) (ill-treatment of patients).

43A An offence under section 1 of the Child Abduction Act 1984 (c 37) (offence of abduction of child by parent, etc).

43B An offence under section 2 of that Act (offence of abduction of child by other persons).

44   An offence under section 1 of the Prohibition of Female Circumcision Act 1985 (c 38) (prohibition of female circumcision).

45   An offence under section 1 of the Public Order Act 1986 (c 64) (riot).

46   An offence under section 2 of that Act (violent disorder).

47   An offence under section 3 of that Act (affray).

48   An offence under section 134 of the Criminal Justice Act 1988 (c 33) (torture).

49   An offence under section 1 of the Road Traffic Act 1988 (c 52) (causing death by dangerous driving).

50   An offence under section 3A of that Act (causing death by careless driving when under influence of drink or drugs).

51   An offence under section 1 of the Aviation and Maritime Security Act 1990 (c 31) (endangering safety at aerodromes).

52   An offence under section 9 of that Act (hijacking of ships).
53   An offence under section 10 of that Act (seizing or exercising control of fixed platforms).
54   An offence under section 11 of that Act (destroying fixed platforms or endangering their safety).
55   An offence under section 12 of that Act (other acts endangering or likely to endanger safe navigation).
56   An offence under section 13 of that Act (offences involving threats).
56A An offence under section 2 of the Protection from Harassment Act 1997 (c 40) (offence of harassment).
57   An offence under section 4 of that Act (putting people in fear of violence).
58   An offence under section 29 of the Crime and Disorder Act 1998 (c 37) (racially or religiously aggravated assaults).
59   An offence falling within section 31(1)(a) or (b) of that Act (racially or religiously aggravated offences under section 4 or 4A of the Public Order Act 1986 (c 64)).
60   An offence under Part II of the Channel Tunnel (Security) Order 1994 (SI 1994/570) (offences relating to Channel Tunnel trains and the tunnel system).
60A An offence under section 85(3) or (4) of the Postal Services Act 2000 (c 26) (prohibition on sending certain articles by post).
61   An offence under section 51 or 52 of the International Criminal Court Act 2001 (c 17) (genocide, crimes against humanity, war crimes and related offences), other than one involving murder.
61A An offence under section 127(1) of the Communications Act 2003 (c 21) (improper use of public electronic communications network).
62   An offence under section 47 of this Act, where the victim or (as the case may be) other party was 16 or over.
63   An offence under any of sections 51 to 53 or 57 to 59 of this Act.
63A An offence under section 5 of the Domestic Violence, Crime and Victims Act 2004 (causing or allowing the death of a child or vulnerable adult).

Scotland

****

Northern Ireland

****

Service offences

172 An offence under –

(a)   section 70 of the Army Act 1955 (3 & 4 Eliz 2 c 18),
(b)   section 70 of the Air Force Act 1955 (3 & 4 Eliz 2 c 19), or
(c)   section 42 of the Naval Discipline Act 1957 (c 53),

of which the corresponding civil offence (within the meaning of that Act) is an offence under a provision listed in any of paragraphs 1 to 63A.

[172A (1) An offence under section 42 of the Armed Forces Act 2006 as respects which the corresponding offence under the law of England and Wales (within the meaning given by that section) is an offence listed in any of paragraphs 1 to 63A.

(2) Section 48 of that Act (attempts, conspiracy, encouragement and assistance and aiding and abetting outside England and Wales) applies for the purposes of this paragraph as if the reference in subsection (3)(b) to any of the following provisions of that Act were a reference to this paragraph.]

General

173   A reference in a preceding paragraph to an offence includes –

     (a)   a reference to an attempt, conspiracy or incitement to commit that offence, and

     (b)   a reference to aiding, abetting, counselling or procuring the commission of that offence.

173A   A reference in a preceding paragraph to an offence ('offence A') includes a reference to an offence under Part 2 of the Serious Crime Act 2007 in relation to which offence A is the offence (or one of the offences) which the person intended or believed would be committed.

174   A reference in a preceding paragraph to a person's age is a reference to his age at the time of the offence.

APPENDIX 16

Magistrates' Court Sentencing Guidelines

FOREWORD

The Magistrates' Court Sentencing Guidelines have been a settled feature of magistrates' courts for many years. This edition applies to all relevant cases appearing for allocation (mode of trial) or for sentence on or after 4 August 2008 and replaces the guidelines which were effective from 1 January 2004. It also supersedes the part of the Practice Direction covering Mode of Trial Decisions (Part V.51) in relation to offences contained within the guideline.

This is the most extensive guideline produced by the Council and covers most of the offences regularly coming before a magistrates' court which require decisions on allocation or on sentence. The guideline also contains explanatory material that sets out a common approach to more general issues.

For the first time, there is a statutory obligation on every court to have regard to this guideline in a relevant case and to give reasons when imposing a sentence outside the range identified.

This guideline is the result of an intensive and consultative process, which has at all stages benefited from the involvement of key users of the guidelines. The Council is extremely grateful to all who have played a part in developing the guideline and has greatly appreciated the time and thought that has gone into the preparation of responses to each aspect of the consultation.

The Council is also enormously grateful to the Sentencing Advisory Panel and, in particular, to the members of its advisory group, for the extensive consideration they have given, not only to detailed matters of content but also to ensuring a proper balance in the assessment of the seriousness of all the offences involved.

The advisory group has committed a significant amount of time and energy over the past two years to the very detailed work necessary to produce guidelines covering such a wide range of offences and issues. Its members have been Chris Armstrong (Justices' Clerks' Society), Professor Andrew Ashworth (Chairman of the Sentencing Advisory Panel), Cindy Barnett JP (Chairman of the Magistrates' Association), David Brewer (Justices' Clerks' Society), Judge Stephen Day (District Judge (Magistrates' Courts)), Anne Fuller JP (Member of the Sentencing Advisory Panel), David Mallen (Member of the Sentencing Advisory Panel), Judge David Meredith (District Judge (Magistrates' Courts)) and Judge Howard Riddle (District Judge (Magistrates' Courts) and Member of the Sentencing Advisory Panel).

The advice of the Panel, draft guidelines and these definitive guidelines are all available on www.sentencing-guidelines.gov.uk or can be obtained from the

Sentencing Guidelines Secretariat at 4th Floor, 8–10 Great George Street, London SW1P 3AE. The website also contains a summary of the responses to the Council's consultation on the draft guidelines.

Chairman of the Council

May 2008

Contents

Introduction

These guidelines are issued by the Sentencing Guidelines Council and cover offences for which sentence is frequently imposed in a magistrates' court when dealing with adult offenders. They apply to allocation (mode of trial) decisions and to sentences imposed on or after 4 August 2008 and replace the guidelines effective from 1 January 2004.

When dealing with an either way offence for which there is no plea or an indication of a not guilty plea, these guidelines will be relevant to the mode of trial decision and should be consulted at this stage. This is important because, in some cases, the ability to commit an offender to the Crown Court for sentence after trial may be limited. Where an offence is included in these guidelines, the guideline supersedes the equivalent part of the Mode of Trial guidelines in Part V.51 of the Consolidated Criminal Practice Direction.

These guidelines apply to sentencing in a magistrates' court whatever the composition of the court. They apply also to the Crown Court when dealing with appeals against sentences imposed in a magistrates' court and when sentencing for summary only offences. In all other cases, the Crown Court must have regard to any other definitive Council guidelines which are relevant to the offender's case.

Every court is under a statutory obligation to have regard to any relevant Council guideline.[1] **If a court imposes a sentence of a different kind or outside the range indicated in a Council guideline, it is obliged to state its reasons for doing so.**[2]

The guidelines provide greater guidance on both starting points and sentence ranges than the previous edition. They have been expanded to cover additional offences, the explanatory material has been revised and, in respect of offence guidelines, a new format has been adopted to reflect better the sentencing framework established by the Criminal Justice Act 2003. Where appropriate, guidelines issued by the Council or Court of Appeal are incorporated. What is included is necessarily a summary; **the original guideline or Court of Appeal judgment should be consulted for comprehensive guidance**. All guidelines issued by the Council are available at www.sentencing-guidelines.gov.uk or can be obtained from the Sentencing Guidelines Secretariat, 4th Floor, 8–10 Great George Street, London, SW1P 3AE.

---

[1] Criminal Justice Act 2003, s.172(1)
[2] ibid., s.174(2)(a)

User Guide

This user guide explains the key decisions involved in the sentencing process. A step-by-step summary is provided on the pullout card.

1. ASSESS OFFENCE SERIOUSNESS (CULPABILITY AND HARM)

Offence seriousness is the starting point for sentencing under the Criminal Justice Act 2003. The court's assessment of offence seriousness will:

- determine which of the sentencing thresholds has been crossed;
- indicate whether a custodial, community or other sentence is the most appropriate;
- be the key factor in deciding the length of a custodial sentence, the onerousness of requirements to be incorporated in a community sentence and the amount of any fine imposed.

When considering the seriousness of any offence, the court must consider the offender's **culpability** in committing the offence and any **harm** which the offence caused, was intended to cause, or might for[e]seeably have caused.[3] In using these guidelines, this assessment should be approached in two stages:

1. OFFENCE SERIOUSNESS (CULPABILITY AND HARM) A. IDENTIFY THE APPROPRIATE STARTING POINT

The guidelines set out **examples** of the nature of activity which may constitute the offence, progressing from less to more serious conduct, and provide a **starting point** based on a **first time offender** pleading not guilty. The guidelines also specify a sentencing **range** for each example of activity. Refer to pages [317–318] for further guidance on the meaning of the terms 'starting point', 'range' and 'first time offender'.

Sentencers should begin by considering which of the examples of offence activity corresponds most closely to the circumstances of the particular case in order to identify the appropriate **starting point**:

- where the starting point is a fine, this is indicated as band A, B or C. The approach to assessing fines is set out on pages [320–327];
- where the community sentence threshold is passed, the guideline sets out whether the starting point should be a low, medium or high level community order. Refer to pages [331–333] for further guidance;
- where the starting point is a custodial sentence, refer to pages [333–335] for further guidance.

---

[3] Criminal Justice Act 2003, s.143(1)

The Council's definitive guideline *Overarching Principles: Seriousness*, published 16 December 2004, identifies four levels of culpability for sentencing purposes (intention, recklessness, knowledge and negligence). The starting points in the individual offence guidelines assume that culpability is at the highest level applicable to the offence (often, but not always, intention). **Where a lower level of culpability is present, this should be taken into account.**

1. OFFENCE SERIOUSNESS (CULPABILITY AND HARM) B. CONSIDER THE EFFECT OF AGGRAVATING AND MITIGATING FACTORS

Once the starting point has been identified, the court can add to or reduce this to reflect any aggravating or mitigating factors that impact on the **culpability** of the offender and/or **harm** caused by the offence to reach a provisional sentence. Any factors contained in the description of the activity used to reach the starting point must not be counted again.

The **range** is the bracket into which the provisional sentence will normally fall after having regard to factors which aggravate or mitigate the seriousness of the offence.

However:

- the court is not precluded from going outside the range where the facts justify it;
- previous convictions which aggravate the seriousness of the current offence may take the provisional sentence beyond the range, especially where there are significant other aggravating factors present.

In addition, where an offender is being sentenced for multiple offences, the court's assessment of the totality of the offending may result in a sentence above the range indicated for the individual offences, including a sentence of a different type. Refer to pages [318–319] for further guidance.

The guidelines identify aggravating and mitigating factors which may be particularly relevant to each individual offence. These include some factors drawn from the general list of aggravating and mitigating factors in the Council's definitive guideline *Overarching Principles: Seriousness* published 16 December 2004, (reproduced on the pullout card). In each case, sentencers should have regard to the full list, which includes the factors that, by statute, make an offence more serious:

- offence committed while on bail for other offences;
- offence was racially or religiously aggravated;
- offence was motivated by, or demonstrates, hostility based on the victim's sexual orientation (or presumed sexual orientation);
- offence was motivated by, or demonstrates, hostility based on the victim's disability (or presumed disability);
- offender has previous convictions that the court considers can reasonably be treated as aggravating factors having regard to their relevance to the current offence and the time that has elapsed since conviction.

While the lists in the offence guidelines and pullout card aim to identify the most common aggravating and mitigating factors, they are not intended to be exhaustive. Sentencers should always consider whether there are any other factors that make the offence more or less serious.

2. Form a preliminary view of the appropriate sentence, then consider offender mitigation

When the court has reached a provisional sentence based on its assessment of offence seriousness, it should take into account matters of offender mitigation. The Council guideline *Overarching Principles: Seriousness* states that the issue of remorse should be taken into account at this point along with other mitigating features such as admissions to the police in interview.

3. Consider a reduction for a guilty plea

The Council guideline *Reduction in Sentence for a Guilty Plea*, revised 2007, states that the **punitive** elements of the sentence should be reduced to recognise an offender's guilty plea. The reduction has no impact on sentencing decisions in relation to ancillary orders, including disqualification.

The level of the reduction should reflect the stage at which the offender indicated a willingness to admit guilt and will be gauged on a sliding scale, ranging from a **recommended** one third (where the guilty plea was entered at the first reasonable opportunity), reducing to a **recommended** one quarter (where a trial date has been set) and to a **recommended** one tenth (for a guilty plea entered at the 'door of the court' or after the trial has begun). There is a presumption that the recommended reduction will be given unless there are good reasons for a lower amount.

The application of the reduction may affect the type, as well as the severity, of the sentence. It may also take the sentence below the **range** in some cases.

The court must state that it has reduced a sentence to reflect a guilty plea.[4] It should usually indicate what the sentence would have been if there had been no reduction as a result of the plea.

4. Consider ancillary orders, including compensation

Ancillary orders of particular relevance to individual offences are identified in the relevant guidelines; further guidance is set out on pages [339–346].

The court must **always** consider making a compensation order where the offending has resulted in personal injury, loss or damage.[5] The court is required to give reasons if it decides not to make such an order.[6]

5. Decide sentence – Give reasons

Sentencers must state reasons for the sentence passed in **every** case, including for any ancillary orders imposed.[7] It is particularly important to identify any aggravating or mitigating factors, or matters of offender mitigation, that have resulted in a sentence more or less severe than the suggested starting point.

If a court imposes a sentence of a different kind or outside the **range** indicated in the guidelines, it **must state its reasons for doing so**.[8]

The court should also give its reasons for not making an order that has been canvassed before it or that it might have been expected to make.

---

4   Criminal Justice Act 2003, s.174(2)(d)
5   Powers of Criminal Courts (Sentencing) Act 2000, s.130(1)
6   ibid., s.130(3)
7   Criminal Justice Act 2003, s.174(1)
8   ibid., s.174(2)(a)

ALCOHOL SALE OFFENCES

Licensing Act 2003, s.141 (sale of alcohol to drunk person); s.146 (sale of alcohol to children); s.147 (allowing sale of alcohol to children)

Triable only summarily:

Maximum: Level 3 fine (s.141)
             Level 5 fine (ss.146 and 147)

Offence seriousness (culpability and harm)		
A. Identify the appropriate starting point		
Starting points based on first time offender pleading not guilty		
Examples of nature of activity	**Starting point**	**Range**
Sale to a child (i.e. person under 18)/to a drunk person	Band B fine	Band A fine to band C fine

Note: refer to page [323] for approach to fines for offences committed for commercial purposes

Offence seriousness (culpability and harm)	
B. Consider the effect of aggravating and mitigating factors (other than those within examples above)	
Common aggravating and mitigating factors are identified in the pullout card – the following may be particularly relevant but **these lists are not exhaustive**	
Factors indicating higher culpability 1. No attempt made to establish age 2. Spirits/high alcohol level of drink 3. Drunk person highly intoxicated 4. Large quantity of alcohol supplied 5. Sale intended for consumption by group of children/drunk people 6. Offender in senior or management position **Factors indicating greater degree of harm** 1. Younger child/children 2. Drunk person causing distress to others 3. Drunk person aggressive	

Form a preliminary view of the appropriate sentence, then consider offender mitigation
Common factors are identified in the pullout card
Consider a reduction for a guilty plea
Consider ancillary orders, including forfeiture or suspension of personal liquor licence
Refer to pages [339–346] for guidance on available ancillary orders
Decide sentence
Give reasons

Note

Section 23 of the Violent Crime Reduction Act 2006 created a new offence of persistently selling alcohol to children, which came into force on 6 April 2007. This is committed if, on three or more different occasions within a period of three consecutive months, alcohol is unlawfully sold on the same premises to a person under 18. The offence is summary only and the maximum penalty is a £10,000 fine. **Consult your legal adviser for guidance on the approach to sentencing and the court's powers in relation to liquor licences.**

ALCOHOL/TOBACCO, FRAUDULENTLY EVADE DUTY

Customs and Excise Management Act 1979, s.170

Triable either way:

Maximum when tried summarily: Level 5 fine or three times the value of the goods (whichever is greater) and/or 6 months

Maximum when tried on indictment: 7 years

This guideline and accompanying notes reflect the Court of Appeal's decision in *R* v *Czyzewski* [2004] 1 Cr App R (S) 49. Further consideration is being given to the appropriate approach to sentencing for this offence in the context of the Council and Panel's work on fraud offences; this may result in a revised guideline being issued in a future update.

Key factors

(a) In terms of seriousness, the principal factors are the level of duty evaded; the complexity and sophistication of the organisation involved; the function of the offender within the organisation; and the amount of personal profit to the particular offender.

(b) Evidence of professional smuggling will include:

1.   A complex operation with many people involved
2.   Financial accounting or budgets
3.   Obtaining goods from several different sources
4.   Integration of freight movements with commercial organisations
5.   Sophisticated concealment methods such as forged documents or specially adapted vehicles

6. Varying of methods and routes
7. Links with illicit overseas organisations
8. When the amount of goods smuggled is in the order of half a million cigarettes (equates approximately to evasion of £75,000 worth of duty): this is not a precise indication but the value of the goods could be a potential indicator of professional smuggling.

(c) Any customs or excise duty owed is likely to be recovered by the authorities under separate procedures and will not require an order from the sentencing court.

Offence seriousness (culpability and harm)		
A. Identify the appropriate starting point		
Starting points based on first time offender pleading not guilty		
Examples of nature of activity	**Starting point**	**Range**
Duty evaded is £1,000 or less	Band B fine	Band A fine to band C fine Note: a conditional discharge may be appropriate where there is particularly strong mitigation and provided there had been no earlier warning
Duty evaded is more than £1,000 but less than £10,000	Medium level community order	Band C fine to 18 weeks custody Note: the custody threshold is likely to be passed if one or more of the aggravating factors listed opposite is present
Duty evaded is between £10,000 and £50,000	Crown Court	12 weeks custody to Crown Court Note: committal to Crown Court is likely to be appropriate if one or more of the aggravating factors listed opposite is present
Duty evaded exceeds £50,000	Crown Court	Crown Court

Offence seriousness (culpability and harm)

B. Consider the effect of aggravating and mitigating factors (other than those within examples above)

Common aggravating and mitigating factors are identified in the pullout card – the following may be particularly relevant but these lists are not exhaustive

Factors indicating higher culpability	Factors indicating lower culpability
1. Offender played an organisational role	1. Pressure from others to commit offence
2. Offender made repeated importations, particularly in the face of a warning from authorities	2. Minor involvement
3. Offender was a professional smuggler (see opposite)	3. Small personal profit
4. Legitimate business used as a front	
5. Offender abused position of privilege as a customs or police officer, or as an employee, for example, of a security firm, ferry company or port authority	
6. Offender threatened violence to those seeking to enforce the law	
Factors indicating greater degree of harm	
1. Offender dealt in goods with an additional health risk because of possible contamination	
2. Offender used children or vulnerable adults	
3. Offender disposed of goods to under-age purchasers	

Form a preliminary view of the appropriate sentence, then consider offender mitigation

Common factors are identified in the pullout card

Consider a reduction for a guilty plea

Consider ancillary orders, including forfeiture or suspension of personal liquor licence

Refer to pages [339–346] for guidance on available ancillary orders

Consider deprivation of property (including vehicle) and disqualification from driving

Notify licensing authority where licensed premises have been used for sale of smuggled goods

Decide sentence

Give reasons

ANIMAL CRUELTY

Animal Welfare Act 2006, s.4 (unnecessary suffering); s.8 (fighting etc.); s.9 (breach of duty of person responsible for animal to ensure welfare)

Triable only summarily:

Maximum: £20,000 fine and/or 6 months (ss.4 and 8)
             Level 5 fine and/or 6 months (s.9)

Offence seriousness (culpability and harm)

A. Identify the appropriate starting point

Starting points based on first time offender pleading not guilty

Examples of nature of activity	Starting point	Range
One impulsive act causing little or no injury; short term neglect	Band C fine	Band B fine to medium level community order
Several incidents of deliberate ill-treatment/frightening animal(s); medium term neglect	High level community order	Medium level community order to 12 weeks' custody
Attempt to kill/torture; animal baiting/ conducting or permitting cock-fighting etc.; prolonged neglect	18 weeks custody	12 to 26 weeks' custody

---

Offence seriousness (culpability and harm)

B. Consider the effect of aggravating and mitigating factors (other than those within examples above)

Common aggravating and mitigating factors are identified in the pullout card – the following may be particularly relevant but these lists are not exhaustive

Factors indicating higher culpability	Factors indicating lower culpability
1. Offender in position of special responsibility	1. Offender induced by others
2. Adult involves children in offending	2. Ignorance of appropriate care
3. Animal(s) kept for livelihood	3. Offender with limited capability
4. Use of weapon	
5. Offender ignored advice/warnings	
6. Offence committed for commercial gain	
Factors indicating greater degree of harm	
1. Serious injury or death	
2. Several animals affected	

Form a preliminary view of the appropriate sentence, then consider offender mitigation Common factors are identified in the pullout card
Consider a reduction for a guilty plea
Consider ancillary orders, including compensation Refer to pages [339–346] for guidance on available ancillary orders **Consider disqualification from ownership of animal**
Decide sentence **Give reasons**

ARSON (CRIMINAL DAMAGE BY FIRE)

Criminal Damage Act 1971, s.1

Triable either way:

Maximum when tried summarily: Level 5 fine and/or 6 months

Maximum when tried on indictment: Life

Where offence committed in domestic context, refer to page [348] for guidance

Identify dangerous offenders This is a serious offence for the purposes of the public protection provisions in the Criminal Justice Act 2003 – refer to pages [358–359] and consult legal adviser for guidance

Offence seriousness (culpability and harm)

A. Identify the appropriate starting point

Starting points based on first time offender pleading not guilty

Examples of nature of activity	Starting point	Range
Minor damage by fire	High level community order	Medium level community order to 12 weeks custody
Moderate damage by fire	12 weeks custody	6 to 26 weeks custody
Significant damage by fire	Crown Court	Crown Court

Offence seriousness (culpability and harm)
B. Consider the effect of aggravating and mitigating factors (other than those within examples above)
Common aggravating and mitigating factors are identified in the pullout card – the following may be particularly relevant but **these lists are not exhaustive**

Factors indicating higher culpability	Factors indicating lower culpability
1. Revenge attack	1. Damage caused recklessly
Factors indicating greater degree of harm	
1. Damage to emergency equipment	
2. Damage to public amenity	
3. Significant public or private fear caused e.g. in domestic context	

Form a preliminary view of the appropriate sentence, then consider offender mitigation
Common factors are identified in the pullout card
Consider a reduction for a guilty plea
Consider ancillary orders, including compensation
Refer to pages [339–346] for guidance on available ancillary orders
Decide sentence
Give reasons

ANTI-SOCIAL BEHAVIOUR ORDER, BREACH OF – FACTORS TO TAKE INTO CONSIDERATION

This guideline and accompanying notes are taken from the Sentencing Guidelines Council's definitive guideline *Breach of an Anti-Social Behaviour Order*, published 9 December 2008

Key factors

(a) An ASBO may be breached in a very wide range of circumstances and may involve one or more terms not being complied with. The examples given below are intended to illustrate how the scale of the conduct that led to the breach, taken as a whole, might come within the three levels of seriousness:

- **No harm caused or intended** – in the absence of intimidation or the causing of fear of violence, breaches involving being drunk or begging may be at this level, as may prohibited use of public transport or entry into a prohibited area, where there is no evidence that harassment, alarm or distress was caused or intended.
- **Lesser degree of harm intended or likely** – examples may include lesser degrees of threats or intimidation, the use of seriously abusive language, or causing more than minor damage to property.
- **Serious harm caused or intended** – breach at this level of seriousness will involve the use of violence, significant threats or intimidation or the targeting of individuals or groups of people in a manner that leads to a fear of violence.

(b)   The suggested starting points are based on the assumption that the offender had the highest level of culpability.

(c)   In the most serious cases, involving repeat offending and a breach causing serious harassment together with the presence of several aggravating factors, such as the use of violence, a sentence beyond the highest range will be justified.

(d)   When imposing a community order, the court must ensure that the requirements imposed are proportionate to the seriousness of the breach, compatible with each other, and also with the prohibitions of the ASBO if the latter is to remain in force. Even where the threshold for a custodial sentence is crossed, a custodial sentence is not inevitable.

(e)   An offender may be sentenced for more than one offence of breach, which occurred on different days. While consecutive sentences may be imposed in such cases, the overall sentence should reflect the totality principle.

ANTI-SOCIAL BEHAVIOUR ORDER, BREACH OF

Crime and Disorder Act 1988, s.1(10)

Triable either way:

Maximum when tried summarily: Level 5 fine and/or 6 months

Maximum when tried on indictment: 5 years

Note: A conditional discharge is not available as a sentence for this offence

Offence seriousness (culpability and harm)		
A. Identify the appropriate starting point		
Starting points based on first time offender* pleading not guilty		
Examples of nature of activity	**Starting point**	**Range**
Breach where no harassment, alarm or distress was caused or intended	Low level community order	Band B fine to medium level community order
Breach involving a lesser degree of actual or intended harassment, alarm or distress than in the box below, or where such harm would have been likely had the offender not been apprehended	6 weeks custody	Medium level community order to 26 weeks custody
Breach involving serious actual or intended harassment, alarm or distress	26 weeks custody	Custody threshold to Crown Court

Offence seriousness (culpability and harm)	
B. Consider the effect of aggravating and mitigating factors (other than those within examples above)	
Common aggravating and mitigating factors are identified in the pullout card – the following may be particularly relevant but these lists are not exhaustive	
Factors indicating higher culpability	**Factors indicating lower culpability**
1. Offender has a history of disobedience to court orders	1. Breach occurred after a long period of compliance
2. Breach was committed immediately or shortly after the order was made	2. The prohibition(s) breached was not fully understood, especially where an interim order was made without notice
3. Breach was committed subsequent to earlier breach proceedings arising from the same order	
4. Targeting of a person the order was made to protect or a witness in the original proceedings	

Form a preliminary view of the appropriate sentence, then consider offender mitigation
Common factors are identified in the pullout card
Consider a reduction for a guilty plea
Consider ancillary orders, including compensation
Refer to pages [339–346] for guidance on available ancillary orders
Decide sentence
Give reasons

* For the purposes of this guideline a 'first time offender' is one who does not have a previous conviction for breach of an ASBO

ASSAULT OCCASIONING ACTUAL BODILY HARM & RACIALLY OR RELIGIOUSLY AGGRAVATED ASSAULT OCCASIONING ACTUAL BODILY HARM – FACTORS TO TAKE INTO CONSIDERATION

This guideline and accompanying notes are taken from the Sentencing Guidelines Council's definitive guideline *Assault and other offences against the person*, published 20 February 2008

Key factors

(a) Matters of offender mitigation are often highly relevant to sentencing for this offence and may justify a non-custodial sentence, particularly in the case of a first time offender. Such a disposal might also be considered appropriate where there is a guilty plea.

(b) The level of culpability for an offence of ABH is the same as that for an offence of common assault; all that the prosecution must prove is that force was intentionally or recklessly used on another. What distinguishes the two offences is the nature of the injury caused to the victim and this will be the key factor for the CPS to consider when deciding which offence to charge.

(c) The use of a weapon (which for the purposes of this guideline includes traditional items such as an iron bar, baseball bat or knife) or part of the body (such as the head or other body part which may be equipped to inflict harm or greater harm, for example a shod foot) will usually increase the seriousness of an offence:

   (i) In relation to culpability, where a weapon is carried by the offender to the scene with the intention of using it or having it available for use should the opportunity or need arise, high culpability is likely to be indicated.

   (ii) In relation to harm, the type of weapon or part of the body and the way it is used will influence the extent of the effect on the assessment of seriousness. For instance, use of a knife or broken glass raises a high risk of serious injury. Similarly where the offender kicks or stamps on a prone victim, particularly if to a vulnerable part of the body.

(d) Where a weapon is used and the assault is premeditated, that will cause the offence to be in the highest sentencing range. Where that is not the case, possession and/or use of a weapon is likely to increase sentence within the range either through an increase in culpability or an increase in harm.

ASSAULT OCCASIONING ACTUAL BODILY HARM

Offences Against the Person Act 1861, s.47

RACIALLY OR RELIGIOUSLY AGGRAVATED ASSAULT OCCASIONING ACTUAL BODILY HARM

Crime and Disorder Act 1998, s.29

Assault occasioning ABH: triable either way

Maximum when tried summarily: Level 5 fine and/or 6 months

Maximum when tried on indictment: 5 years

Racially or religiously aggravated assault occasioning ABH: triable either way

Maximum when tried summarily: Level 5 fine and/or 6 months

Maximum when tried on indictment: 7 years

Where offence committed in domestic context, refer to page [348] for guidance

---

Identify dangerous offenders

These are specified offences for the purposes of the public protection provisions in the Criminal Justice Act 2003 – refer to page[s 358–359] and consult legal adviser for guidance

---

Offence seriousness (culpability and harm)

A. Identify the appropriate starting point

Starting points based on first time offender pleading not guilty

Examples of nature of activity	Starting point	Range
Other assault resulting in minor, non-permanent injury	High level community order	Medium level community order to 26 weeks custody
Premeditated assault resulting in minor, non-permanent injury	24 weeks custody	12 weeks custody to Crown Court
Premeditated assault either resulting in relatively serious injury or involving the use of a weapon	Crown Court	Crown Court

---

Offence seriousness (culpability and harm)

B. Consider the effect of aggravating and mitigating factors (other than those within examples above)

Common aggravating and mitigating factors are identified in the pullout card – the following may be particularly relevant but these lists are not exhaustive

	Factors indicating lower culpability
	1. Provocation
	2. Unintended injury

Form a preliminary view of the appropriate sentence

If offender charged and convicted of the racially or religiously aggravated offence, increase the sentence to reflect this element

Refer to pages [349–351] for guidance

Consider offender mitigation

Common factors are identified in the pullout card

Consider a reduction for a guilty plea

Consider ancillary orders, including compensation

Refer to pages [339–346] for guidance on available ancillary orders

Decide sentence

Give reasons

189

ASSAULT ON A POLICE CONSTABLE

Police Act 1996, s.89(1)

Triable only summarily:

Maximum: Level 5 fine and/or 6 months

This guideline and accompanying notes are taken from the Sentencing Guidelines Council's definitive guideline *Assault and other offences against the person*, published 20 February 2008

Key factors

(a)   The expectation is that this offence will involve little or no physical harm (it is anticipated that more serious injuries would result in a charge of assault occasioning ABH) and so sentencing will largely be guided by the level of offender culpability. In common with assault with intent to resist arrest, the offence involves an inherent aggravating factor not present in the offence of common assault in that the victim was performing a public service.

(b)   The levels of harm and culpability will be comparable to the offence of assault with intent to resist arrest and the offences are likely to be committed in similar circumstances. However, the maximum penalty for this offence is lower and this has influenced the sentencing ranges proposed.

(c)   Where the offence involves a sustained assault it will generally fall into the highest category of seriousness. Where no injury is occasioned, the appropriate sentence may be at the lower end of the range.

This guideline is based on the assumption that more serious injuries would be charged as ABH

Offence seriousness (culpability and harm)		
A. Identify the appropriate starting point		
Starting points based on first time offender pleading not guilty		
Examples of nature of activity	**Starting point**	**Range**
Assault where no injury caused	Low level community order	Band B fine to medium level community order
Assault (defined as including spitting) resulting in minor, non-permanent injury	High level community order	Band C fine to 18 weeks custody
Sustained assault resulting in minor, non-permanent injury	18 weeks custody	High level community order to 24 weeks' custody

Offence seriousness (culpability and harm)
B. Consider the effect of aggravating and mitigating factors (other than those within examples above)
Common aggravating and mitigating factors are identified in the pullout card – the following may be particularly relevant but these lists are not exhaustive

Factors indicating higher culpability	Factors indicating lower culpability
1. Escape	1. Genuine belief that the arrest was unlawful where this does not found a defence to the charge
2. Head butting, kicking or biting	
3. Picking up an item to use as a weapon, even if not used	

Form a preliminary view of the appropriate sentence, then consider offender mitigation
Common factors are identified in the pullout card
Consider a reduction for a guilty plea
Consider ancillary orders, including compensation
Refer to pages [339–346] for guidance on available ancillary orders
Decide sentence
Give reasons

ASSAULT WITH INTENT TO RESIST ARREST

Offences Against the Person Act 1861, s.38

Triable either way:

Maximum when tried summarily: Level 5 fine and/or 6 months

Maximum when tried on indictment: 2 years

This guideline and accompanying notes are taken from the Sentencing Guidelines Council's definitive guideline *Assault and other offences against the person*, published 20 February 2008

Key factors

(a) The expectation is that this offence will involve little or no physical harm (it is anticipated that more serious injuries would result in a charge of assault occasioning ABH) and so sentencing will largely be guided by the level of offender culpability.

(b) The additional element of intent in this offence relates to the attempt to resist arrest and involves an inherent aggravating factor not present in the offence of common assault in that the victim (whether a police officer or a member of the public carrying out a citizen's arrest) was performing a public service.

(c) If the offender is prosecuted for the offence which gave rise to the arrest, the sentences imposed would normally be consecutive.

This guideline is based on the assumption that more serious injuries would be charged as ABH

Identify dangerous offenders

This is a specified offence for the purposes of the public protection provisions in the Criminal Justice Act 2003 – refer to page[s 358–359] and consult legal adviser for guidance

---

Offence seriousness (culpability and harm)

A. Identify the appropriate starting point

Starting points based on first time offender pleading not guilty

Examples of nature of activity	Starting point	Range
Assault where no injury caused	Low level community order	Band C fine to high level community order
Assault (defined as including spitting) resulting in minor, non-permanent injury	High level community order	Low level community order to 26 weeks custody
Persistent attempt to resist arrest or use of force or threats of force over and above that inherent in the offence	Crown Court	24 weeks custody to Crown Court

---

Offence seriousness (culpability and harm)

B. Consider the effect of aggravating and mitigating factors (other than those within examples above)

Common aggravating and mitigating factors are identified in the pullout card – the following may be particularly relevant but **these lists are not exhaustive**

Factors indicating higher culpability	Factors indicating lower culpability
1. Escape	1. Genuine belief that the arrest was unlawful where this does not found a defence to the charge
2. Head butting, kicking or biting	
3. Picking up an item to use as a weapon, even if not used	

Form a preliminary view of the appropriate sentence, then consider offender mitigation
Common factors are identified in the pullout card
Consider a reduction for a guilty plea
Consider ancillary orders, including compensation
Refer to pages [339–346] for guidance on available ancillary orders
Decide sentence
Give reasons

BAIL, FAILURE TO SURRENDER – FACTORS TO TAKE INTO CONSIDERATION

This guideline and accompanying notes are taken from the Sentencing Guidelines Council's definitive guideline *Fail to Surrender to Bail*, published 29 November 2007

Key factors

(a) Whilst the approach to sentencing should generally be the same whether the offender failed to surrender to a court or to a police station and whether the offence is contrary to ss.6(1) or 6(2), the court must examine all the relevant circumstances.

(b) The following factors may be relevant when assessing the harm caused by the offence:

- Where an offender fails to appear for a first court hearing but attends shortly afterwards, the only harm caused is likely to be the financial cost to the system. Where a case could not have proceeded even if the offender had surrendered to bail, this should be taken into account.

- Where an offender appears for trial on the wrong day but enters a late guilty plea enabling the case to be disposed of to some degree at least, the harm caused by the delay may be offset by the benefits stemming from the change of plea.

- The most serious harm is likely to result when an offender fails to appear for trial, especially if this results in witnesses being sent away. Where it has been possible to conclude proceedings in the absence of the offender, this may be relevant to the assessment of harm caused.

- The level of harm is likely to be assessed as high where an offender fails to appear for sentence and is also seen to be flouting the authority of the court, such as where the avoidance of sentence results in the consequential avoidance of ancillary orders such as disqualification from driving, the payment of compensation or registration as a sex offender. This may increase the level of harm whenever the offender continues to present a risk to public safety.

- Whilst the seriousness of the original offence does not of itself aggravate or mitigate the seriousness of the offence of failing to surrender, the circumstances surrounding the original offence may be relevant in assessing the harm arising from the Bail Act offence.

- The circumstances in which bail to return to a police station is granted are less formal than the grant of court bail and the history of the individual case should be examined. There may be less culpability where bail has been enlarged on a number of occasions and less harm if court proceedings are not significantly delayed.

(c) Where the failure to surrender to custody was 'deliberate':

- at or near the bottom of the sentencing range will be cases where the offender gave no thought at all to the consequences, or other mitigating factors are present, and the degree of delay or interference with the progress of the case was not significant in all the circumstances;

- at or near the top of the range will be cases where aggravating factors 1, 2 or 4 opposite are present if there is also a significant delay and/or interference with the progress of the case.

(d) A previous conviction that is likely to be 'relevant' for the purposes of this offence is one which demonstrates failure to comply with an order of a court.

(e)   Acquittal of the original offence does not automatically mitigate the Bail Act offence.

(f)   The fact that an offender has a disorganised or chaotic lifestyle should not normally be treated as offence mitigation, but may be regarded as offender mitigation depending on the particular facts.

(g)   A misunderstanding which does not amount to a defence may be a mitigating factor whereas a mistake on the part of the offender is his or her own responsibility.

(h)   Where an offender has literacy or language difficulties, these may be mitigation (where they do not amount to a defence) where potential problems were not identified and/or appropriate steps were not taken to mitigate the risk in the circumstances as known at the time that bail was granted.

(i)   An offender's position as the sole or primary carer of dependant relatives may be offender mitigation when it is the reason why the offender failed to surrender to custody.

(j)   The sentence for this offence should usually be in addition to any sentence for the original offence. Where custodial sentences are being imposed for a Bail Act offence and the original offence at the same time, the normal approach should be for the sentences to be consecutive. The length of any custodial sentence imposed must be commensurate with the seriousness of the offence(s).

(k)   If an offence is serious enough to justify the imposition of a community order, a curfew requirement with an electronic monitoring requirement may be particularly appropriate – see pages [331–333].

Bail, failure to surrender

Bail Act 1976, ss.6(1) and 6(2)

Triable either way:

Maximum when tried summarily: Level 5 fine and/or 3 months

Maximum when tried on indictment: 12 months

In certain circumstances, a magistrates' court may commit to the Crown Court for sentence. **Consult your legal adviser for guidance.**

Offence seriousness (culpability and harm)		
A. Identify the appropriate starting point		
Starting points based on first time offender pleading not guilty		
Examples of nature of activity	**Starting point**	**Range**
Surrenders late on day but case proceeds as planned	Band A fine	Band A fine to Band B fine
Negligent or non-deliberate failure to attend causing delay and/or interference with the administration of justice	Band C fine	Band B fine to medium level community order
Deliberate failure to attend causing delay and/or interference with the administration of justice The type and degree of harm actually caused will affect where in the range the case falls – see note (c) opposite	14 days' custody	Low level community order to 10 weeks' custody

<table>
<tr><td colspan="2" align="center">Offence seriousness (culpability and harm)

B. Consider the effect of aggravating and mitigating factors (other than those within examples above)

Common aggravating and mitigating factors are identified in the pullout card – the following may be particularly relevant but these lists are not exhaustive</td></tr>
</table>

Factors indicating higher culpability	**Factors indicating lower culpability**
1. Serious attempts to evade justice	Where not amounting to a defence:
2. Determined attempt seriously to undermine the course of justice	1. Misunderstanding
3. Previous relevant convictions and/or breach of court orders or police bail	2. Failure to comprehend bail significance or requirements
Factor indicating greater degree of harm	3. Caring responsibilities – see note (i) opposite
4. Lengthy absence	**Factor indicating lesser degree of harm**
	4. Prompt voluntary surrender

Form a preliminary view of the appropriate sentence, then consider offender mitigation
Common factors are identified in the pullout card
Consider a reduction for a guilty plea
Decide sentence
Give reasons

In appropriate cases, a magistrates' court may impose one day's detention: Magistrates' Courts Act 1980, s.135

BLADED ARTICLE/OFFENSIVE WEAPON, POSSESSION OF – FACTORS TO TAKE INTO CONSIDERATION

These guidelines and accompanying notes are drawn from the Court of Appeal's decision in *R v. Celaire and Poulton* [2003] 1 Cr App R (S) 116

Key factors

(a) Concurrent sentences may be appropriate if the weapons offence is ancillary to a more serious offence; consecutive sentences may be appropriate if the offences are distinct and independent. **Refer to page[s 318–319] and consult your legal adviser for guidance.**

(b) When assessing offence seriousness, consider the offender's intention, the circumstances of the offence and the nature of the weapon involved.

(c) Some weapons are inherently more dangerous than others but the nature of the weapon is not the primary determinant of offence seriousness. A relatively less dangerous weapon, such as a billiard cue or knuckle-duster, may be used to create fear and such an offence may be at least as serious as one in which a more obviously dangerous weapon, such as a knife or an acid spray, is being carried for self-defence or no actual attempt has been made by the offender to use it.

(d) Nevertheless, the fact that the offender was carrying a weapon which is offensive per se may shed light on his or her intentions.

BLADED ARTICLE/OFFENSIVE WEAPON, POSSESSION OF

Criminal Justice Act 1988, s.139 (bladed article) Prevention of Crime Act 1953, s.1 (offensive weapon)

Triable either way:

Maximum when tried summarily: Level 5 fine and/or 6 months

Maximum when tried on indictment: 4 years

[See additional note at **Appendix 17**]

Offence seriousness (culpability and harm)		
A. Identify the appropriate starting point		
Starting points based on first time offender pleading not guilty		
Examples of nature of activity	**Starting point**	**Range**
Weapon not used to threaten or cause fear	High level community order	Band C fine to 12 weeks custody
Weapon not used to threaten or cause fear but offence committed in dangerous circumstances	6 weeks custody	High level community order to Crown Court
Weapon used to threaten or cause fear and offence committed in dangerous circumstances	Crown Court	Crown Court

Offence seriousness (culpability and harm)	
B. Consider the effect of aggravating and mitigating factors (other than those within examples above)	
Common aggravating and mitigating factors are identified in the pullout card – the following may be particularly relevant but **these lists are not exhaustive**	
Factors indicating higher culpability	**Factors indicating lower culpability**
1. Particularly dangerous weapon	1. Weapon carried only on temporary basis
2. Specifically planned use of weapon to commit violence, threaten violence or intimidate	2. Original possession legitimate e.g. in course of trade or business
3. Offence motivated by hostility towards minority individual or group	
4. Offender under influence of drink or drugs	
5. Offender operating in group or gang	
Factors indicating greater degree of harm	
1. Offence committed at school, hospital or	

other place where vulnerable persons may be present

2. Offence committed on premises where people carrying out public services

3. Offence committed on or outside licensed premises

4. Offence committed on public transport

5. Offence committed at large public gathering, especially where there may be risk of disorder

---

Form a preliminary view of the appropriate sentence, then consider offender mitigation

Common factors are identified in the pullout card

Consider a reduction for a guilty plea

Consider ancillary orders, including compensation

Refer to pages [339–346] for guidance on available ancillary orders

Consider a reduction of property (including weapon)

Decide sentence

Give reasons

BURGLARY IN A DWELLING – FACTORS TO TAKE INTO CONSIDERATION

These guidelines and accompanying notes are drawn from the Court of Appeal's decision in *R* v *McInerney and Keating* [2002] EWCA Crim 3003

Key factors

(a) Even where the custody threshold is passed, consider whether a community order is appropriate (*McInerney and Keating* and refer also to page [160]).

(b) Cases in the Crown Court category may be suitable for a community order (see note (a) above), but should nevertheless be committed to the Crown Court for trial/sentence so that any breach of the order can be sentenced within the powers of that Court.

(c) For attempted burglary or burglary under s.9(1)(a) of the Theft Act 1968, it is the offender's *intention* that will determine which of the three categories opposite the offence falls into, not the fact that nothing was stolen.

(d) Relevant convictions that will aggravate offence seriousness in accordance with s.143(2) of the Criminal Justice Act 2003 may include convictions for both property and violent offences.

BURGLARY IN A DWELLING

Theft Act 1968, s.9

Triable either way:

Maximum when tried summarily: Level 5 fine and/or 6 months

Maximum when tried on indictment: 14 years

[See additional note at **Appendix 18**]

Allocation
Consult legal adviser for guidance

Offence is indictable only and must be sent to the Crown Court if:

(1) The offender has been convicted of two other domestic burglaries committed on separate occasions after 30 November 1999 and one was committed after conviction for the other: Powers of Criminal Courts (Sentencing) Act 2000, s.111;

(2) Any person was subjected to violence or the threat of violence: Magistrates' Courts Act 1980, sch.1

Offence seriousness (culpability and harm)

A. Identify the appropriate starting point

Starting points based on first time offender pleading not guilty

Examples of nature of activity	Starting point	Range
Unforced entry and low value theft with no aggravating features	Medium level community order	Low level community order to 12 weeks custody
Forced entry, goods stolen not high value, no aggravating features	12 weeks custody	High level community order to Crown Court
Goods stolen high value or any aggravating feature present	Crown Court	Crown Court

---

Offence seriousness (culpability and harm)

B. Consider the effect of aggravating and mitigating factors (other than those within examples above)

Common aggravating and mitigating factors are identified in the pullout card – the following may be particularly relevant **but these lists are not exhaustive**

Factors indicating higher culpability	Factors indicating lower culpability
1. Ransacking property	1. Offender played only a minor role in the burglary
2. Professionalism	
3. Victim deliberately targeted e.g. out of spite	2. Offence committed on impulse
4. Housebreaking implements or weapons carried	**Factor indicating lesser degree of harm**
Factors indicating greater degree of harm	1. No damage or disturbance to property
1. Occupier at home or returns home while offender present	
2. Goods stolen of sentimental value	

Form a preliminary view of the appropriate sentence, then consider offender mitigation
Common factors are identified in the pullout card
Consider a reduction for a guilty plea
Consider ancillary orders, including compensation
Refer to pages [339–346] for guidance on available ancillary orders
Consider deprivation of property (including weapon)
Decide sentence
Give reasons

BURGLARY IN A BUILDING OTHER THAN A DWELLING – FACTORS TO TAKE INTO CONSIDERATION

This guideline and accompanying notes are taken from the Sentencing Guidelines Council's definitive guideline *Theft and Burglary in a building other than a dwelling*, published 9 December 2008

Key factors

(a) This guideline is concerned solely with burglary committed in a building other than a dwelling where an offender enters as a trespasser with intent to steal or, having entered as a trespasser, actually goes on to steal.

(b) The starting points and sentencing ranges in this guideline are based on the assumption that the offender was motivated by greed or a desire to live beyond his or her means. To avoid double counting, such a motivation should not be treated as a factor that increases culpability.

(c) The starting point is based on the loss suffered by the victim. Whilst, in general, the greater the loss, the more serious the offence, the monetary value of the loss may not reflect the full extent of the harm caused by the offence. The court should also take into account the impact of the offence on the victim (which may be significantly greater than the monetary value of the loss; this may be particularly important where the value of the loss is high in proportion to the victim's financial circumstances even though relatively low in absolute terms), any harm to persons other than the direct victim, and any harm in the form of public concern or erosion of public confidence.

(d) Offences of this type will be aggravated where the offender targets premises because high value, often easily disposable, property is likely to be found there as this indicates professionalism and organisation in the offending, as well as an intention to derive a high level of gain. Targeting of vulnerable community premises may result in a higher than usual degree of harm due to the inconvenience, distress and expense caused to the victim. Where premises which have been burgled on a prior occasion are targeted, this indicates planning, organisation and professionalism and, therefore, should be regarded as increasing the offender's culpability. Repeat victimisation may also increase the harm caused by the offence in terms of distress, inconvenience and expense to the victim.

(e) The Council has identified the following matters of offender mitigation which may be relevant to this offence:

    (i) *Return of stolen property*
        Whether and the degree to which the return of stolen property constitutes a matter of personal mitigation will depend on an assessment of the

circumstances and, in particular, the voluntariness and timeliness of the return.

(ii) *Impact on sentence of offender's dependency*

Where an offence is motivated by an addiction (often to drugs, alcohol or gambling) this does not mitigate the seriousness of the offence, but a dependency may properly influence the type of sentence imposed. In particular, it may sometimes be appropriate to impose a drug rehabilitation requirement, an alcohol treatment requirement (for dependent drinkers) or an activity or supervision requirement including alcohol specific information, advice and support (for harmful and hazardous drinkers) as part of a community order or a suspended sentence order in an attempt to break the cycle of addiction and offending, even if an immediate custodial sentence would otherwise be warranted.

(iii) *Offender motivated by desperation or need*

The fact that an offence has been committed in desperation or need arising from particular hardship may count as personal mitigation in exceptional circumstances.

BURGLARY IN A BUILDING OTHER THAN A DWELLING

Theft Act 1968, s.9

Triable either way:

Maximum when tried summarily: Level 5 fine and/or 6 months

Maximum when tried on indictment: 10 years

Offence seriousness (culpability and harm)		
A. Identify the appropriate starting point		
Starting points based on first time offender pleading not guilty		
Examples of nature of activity	**Starting point**	**Range**
Burglary involving goods valued at less than £2,000	Medium level community order	Band B fine to 26 weeks custody
Burglary involving goods valued at £2,000 or more but less than £20,000	18 weeks custody	High level community order to Crown Court
Burglary involving goods valued at £20,000 or more	Crown Court	Crown Court

Offence seriousness (culpability and harm)
B. Consider the effect of aggravating and mitigating factors (other than those within examples above)
Common aggravating and mitigating factors are identified in the pullout card – the following may be particularly relevant but **these lists are not exhaustive**

Factors indicating higher culpability	
1. Targeting premises containing property of high value	
2. Targeting vulnerable community premises	
3. Targeting premises which have been burgled on prior occasion(s)	
4. Possession of a weapon (where this is not charged separately)	

Form a preliminary view of the appropriate sentence, then consider offender mitigation
Common factors are identified in the pullout card
Consider a reduction for a guilty plea
Consider ancillary orders, including compensation
Refer to pages [339–346] for guidance on available ancillary orders
Decide sentence
Give reasons

CHILD PROSTITUTION AND PORNOGRAPHY – FACTORS TO TAKE INTO CONSIDERATION

This guideline is taken from the Sentencing Guidelines Council's definitive guideline *Sexual Offences Act 2003*, published 30 April 2007

Key factors

(a) Few cases will be suitable to be dealt with in a magistrates' court for the following reasons:

- The courts should consider making an order confiscating any profits stemming from the offender's criminal lifestyle or forfeiting any possessions (e.g. cameras, computers, property) used in connection with the commission of the offence. Only the Crown Court can make a confiscation order.
- The starting point for the child prostitution and pornography offences will always be a custodial sentence.
- In cases where a number of children are involved, consecutive sentences may be appropriate, leading to cumulative sentences significantly higher than the starting points for individual offences.

(b) In accordance with s.80 and sch.3 of the Sexual Offences Act 2003, automatic notification requirements apply upon conviction to an offender aged 18 or over.

CHILD PROSTITUTION AND PORNOGRAPHY

Sexual Offences Act 2003, s.48 (causing or inciting child prostitution or pornography); s.49 (controlling a child prostitute or a child involved in pornography); s.50 (arranging or facilitating child prostitution or pornography)

Triable either way:

Maximum when tried summarily: Level 5 fine and/or 6 months

Maximum when tried on indictment: 14 years

Identify dangerous offenders

These are serious offences for the purposes of the public protection provisions in the Criminal Justice Act 2003 – refer to page[s 358–359] and consult legal adviser for guidance

---

Offence seriousness (culpability and harm)

A. Identify the appropriate starting point

Starting points based on first time offender pleading not guilty

These offences should normally be dealt with in the Crown Court. However, there may be rare cases of non-penetrative activity involving a victim aged 16 or 17 where the offender's involvement is minimal and not perpetrated for gain in which a custodial sentence within the jurisdiction of a magistrates' court may be appropriate.

Consult your legal adviser for further guidance.

Offence seriousness (culpability and harm)

B. Consider the effect of aggravating and mitigating factors

Common aggravating and mitigating factors are identified in the pullout card – the following may be particularly relevant but **these lists are not exhaustive**

Factors indicating higher culpability	Factors indicating lower culpability
1. Background of threats or intimidation	1. Offender also being controlled in prostitution or pornography and subject to threats or intimidation
2. Large-scale commercial operation	
3. Use of drugs, alcohol or other substance to secure the victim's compliance	
4. Forcing a victim to violate another person	
5. Abduction or detention	
6. Threats to prevent the victim reporting the activity	
7. Threats to disclose victim's activity to friends/relatives	
8. Images distributed to other children or persons known to the victim	
9. Financial or other gain	

Factors indicating greater degree of harm

1. Induced dependency on drugs

2. Victim has been manipulated into physical and emotional dependence on the offender

3. Storing, making available or distributing images in such a way that they can be inadvertently accessed by others

---

Form a preliminary view of the appropriate sentence, then consider offender mitigation

Common factors are identified in the pullout card

Consider a reduction for a guilty plea

Consider ancillary orders, including compensation

Refer to pages [339–346] for guidance on available ancillary orders

Decide sentence

Give reasons

COMMON ASSAULT

Criminal Justice Act 1988, s.39

RACIALLY OR RELIGIOUSLY AGGRAVATED COMMON ASSAULT

Crime and Disorder Act 1998, s.29

Common assault: triable only summarily:

Maximum: Level 5 fine and/or 6 months

Racially or religiously aggravated common assault: triable either way

Maximum when tried summarily: Level 5 fine and/or 6 months

Maximum when tried on indictment: 2 years

Refer to pages [349–351] for further guidance

This guideline and accompanying notes are taken from the Sentencing Guidelines Council's definitive guideline *Assault and other offences against the person*, **published 20 February 2008**

Key factors

(a) Common assault is committed when a defendant intentionally or recklessly causes a victim to apprehend immediate unlawful force, or when such force is used. There is no need for injury to have been sustained or intended. In many cases, however, it is likely that there will be such an injury; indeed, there may be an overlap with the offence of assault occasioning actual bodily harm.

(b) Since there is likely to be a wider range of relevant factors than for other assaults and offences against the person, a different approach to this guideline has been adopted which defines where the sentencing thresholds are crossed by reference to the type and number of aggravating factors.

(c) In accordance with the Sentencing Guidelines Council's definitive guideline *Overarching Principles: Seriousness*, published 16 December 2004, the culpability of an offender is the initial factor in determining the seriousness of an offence. Factors indicating higher culpability are most relevant in terms of the threshold criteria for certain sentences in cases of common assault where no injury may have been inflicted but the victim was put in fear of violence. The list opposite is not intended to be exhaustive.

(d) Where aggravating factors indicating a more than usually serious degree of harm are present, they will influence the determination of the appropriate sentence within the bracket of options available where a particular threshold has been crossed.

(e) It is recognised that not all aggravating factors carry the same weight and that flexibility is required to avoid an over-prescriptive approach to when a threshold is passed. For that reason, the word 'normally' has been used in relation to the point at which the sentencing thresholds are crossed.

Where offence committed in domestic context, refer to page [348] for guidance

---

Identify dangerous offenders

Racially or religiously aggravated common assault is a specified offence for the purposes of the public protection provisions in the Criminal Justice Act 2003 – refer to pages [358–359] and consult legal adviser for guidance

---

Offence seriousness (culpability and harm)

A. Identify the appropriate starting point

Starting points based on first time offender pleading not guilty

Examples of nature of activity	Starting point
Assault where no injury caused	Fine
The community sentence threshold normally is passed where *one* aggravating factor indicating higher culpability is present	Community order
The custody threshold normally is passed where *two or more* aggravating factors indicating higher culpability are present	Custody

Offence seriousness (culpability and harm)

B. Consider the effect of aggravating and mitigating factors (other than those within examples opposite)

Common aggravating and mitigating factors are identified in the pullout card – the following may be particularly relevant but **these lists are not exhaustive**

Factors indicating higher culpability	Factors indicating lower culpability
1. Use of a weapon to frighten or harm victim	1. Provocation
2. Offence was planned or sustained	2. Single push, shove or blow
3. Head-butting, kicking, biting or attempted strangulation	
4. Offence motivated by, or demonstrating, hostility to victim on account of his or her sexual orientation or disability	
5. Offence motivated by hostility towards a minority group, or a member or members of it	
6. Abuse of a position of trust	
7. Offence part of a group action	
Factors indicating greater degree of harm	
1. Injury	
2. Victim is particularly vulnerable or providing a service to the public	
3. Additional degradation of victim	
4. Offence committed in the presence of a child	
5. Forced entry to the victim's home	
6. Offender prevented the victim from seeking or obtaining help	
7. Previous violence or threats to same victim	

Form a preliminary view of the appropriate sentence. If offender charged and convicted of the racially or religiously aggravated offence, increase the sentence to reflect this element

Refer to pages [349–351] for guidance

Consider offender mitigation

Common factors are identified in the pullout card

Consider a reduction for a guilty plea

Consider ancillary orders, including compensation

Refer to pages [339–346] for guidance on available ancillary orders

Decide sentence

Give reasons

COMMUNICATION NETWORK OFFENCES

Communications Act 2003, ss.127(1) and 127(2)

Triable only summarily:

Maximum: Level 5 fine and/or 6 months

Offence seriousness (culpability and harm)

A. Identify the appropriate starting point

Starting points based on first time offender pleading not guilty

Sending grossly offensive, indecent, obscene or menacing messages (s.127(1))

Examples of nature of activity	Starting point	Range
Single offensive, indecent, obscene or menacing call of short duration, having no significant impact on receiver	Band B fine	Band A fine to band C fine
Single call where extreme language used, having only moderate impact on receiver	Medium level community order	Low level community order to high level community order
Single call where extreme language used and substantial distress or fear caused to receiver; OR One of a series of similar calls as described in box above	6 weeks custody	High level community order to 12 weeks custody

Sending false message/persistent use of communications network for purpose of causing annoyance, inconvenience or needless anxiety (s.127(2))

Examples of nature of activity	Starting point	Range
Persistent silent calls over short period to private individual, causing inconvenience or annoyance	Band B fine	Band A fine to band C fine
Single hoax call to public or private organisation resulting in moderate disruption or anxiety	Medium level community order	Low level community order to high level community order
Single hoax call resulting in major disruption or substantial public fear or distress; OR One of a series of similar calls as described in box above	12 weeks custody	High level community order to 18 weeks custody

---

Offence seriousness (culpability and harm)

B. Consider the effect of aggravating and mitigating factors (other than those within examples above)

Common aggravating and mitigating factors are identified in the pullout card

Form a preliminary view of the appropriate sentence, then consider offender mitigation
Common factors are identified in the pullout card
Consider a reduction for a guilty plea
Consider ancillary orders, including compensation
Refer to pages [339–346] for guidance on available ancillary orders
Decide sentence
Give reasons

COMMUNITY ORDER, BREACH OF

Criminal Justice Act 2003, sch.8

These notes are taken from the Sentencing Guidelines Council's definitive guideline *New Sentences: Criminal Justice Act 2003*, **published 16 December 2004**

Options in breach proceedings:

When dealing with breaches of community orders for offences committed after 4 April 2005, the court must either:

- amend the terms of the original order so as to impose more onerous requirements. The court may extend the duration of particular requirements within the order, but it cannot extend the overall length of the original order; or
- revoke the original order and proceed to sentence for the original offence. Where an offender has wilfully and persistently failed to comply with an order made in respect of an offence that is not punishable by imprisonment, the court can impose up to six months' custody.[1]

Approach:

- having decided that a community order is commensurate with the seriousness of the offence, the primary objective when sentencing for breach of requirements is to ensure that those requirements are completed;
- a court sentencing for breach must take account of the extent to which the offender has complied with the requirements of the original order, the reasons for the breach, and the point at which the breach has occurred;
- if increasing the onerousness of requirements, sentencers should take account of the offender's ability to comply and should avoid precipitating further breach by overloading the offender with too many or conflicting requirements;
- there may be cases where the court will need to consider re-sentencing to a differently constructed community order in order to secure compliance with the purposes of the original sentence, perhaps where there has already been partial compliance or where events since the sentence was imposed have shown that a different course of action is likely to be effective;
- where available, custody should be the last resort, reserved for those cases of deliberate and repeated breach where all reasonable efforts to ensure that the offender complies have failed.

---

[1] Criminal Justice Act 2003, sch.8, para. 9(1)(c)

Where the original order was made by the Crown Court, breach proceedings must be commenced in that court unless the order provided that any failure to comply with its requirements may be dealt with in a magistrates' court. **Consult your legal adviser for further guidance when dealing with breach of a community order made in the Crown Court.**

CRIMINAL DAMAGE (OTHER THAN BY FIRE)

Criminal Damage Act 1971, s.1(1)

RACIALLY OR RELIGIOUSLY AGGRAVATED CRIMINAL DAMAGE

Crime and Disorder Act 1998, s.30

Criminal damage: triable only summarily if value involved does not exceed £5,000:

Maximum: Level 4 fine and/or 3 months

Triable either way if value involved exceeds £5,000:

Maximum when tried summarily: Level 5 fine and/or 6 months

Maximum when tried on indictment: 10 years

Racially or religiously aggravated criminal damage: triable either way

Maximum when tried summarily: Level 5 fine and/or 6 months

Maximum when tried on indictment: 14 years

Where offence committed in domestic context, refer to page [348] for guidance

Offence seriousness (culpability and harm)		
A. Identify the appropriate starting point		
Starting points based on first time offender pleading not guilty		
Examples of nature of activity	**Starting point**	**Range**
Minor damage e.g. breaking small window; small amount of graffiti	Band B fine	Conditional discharge to band C fine
Moderate damage e.g. breaking large plate-glass or shop window; widespread graffiti	Low level community order	Band C fine to medium level community order
Significant damage up to £5,000 e.g. damage caused as part of a spree	High level community order	Medium level community order to 12 weeks custody
Damage between £5,000 and £10,000	12 weeks custody	6 to 26 weeks custody
Damage over £10,000	Crown Court	Crown Court

Offence seriousness (culpability and harm)	
B. Consider the effect of aggravating and mitigating factors (other than those within examples above)	
Common aggravating and mitigating factors are identified in the pullout card – the following may be particularly relevant but these lists are not exhaustive	
Factors indicating higher culpability	**Factors indicating lower culpability**
1. Revenge attack	1. Damage caused recklessly
2. Targeting vulnerable victim	2. Provocation
Factors indicating greater degree of harm	
1. Damage to emergency equipment	
2. Damage to public amenity	
3. Significant public or private fear caused e.g. in domestic context	

Form a preliminary view of the appropriate sentence
If offender charged and convicted of the racially or religiously aggravated offence, increase the sentence to reflect this element
Refer to pages [349–351] for guidance
Common factors are identified in the pullout card
Consider a reduction for a guilty plea
Consider ancillary orders, including compensation
Refer to pages [339–346] for guidance on available ancillary orders
Decide sentence
Give reasons

CRUELTY TO A CHILD – FACTORS TO TAKE INTO CONSIDERATION

This guideline and accompanying notes are taken from the Sentencing Guidelines Council's definitive guidelines *Overarching Principles: Assaults on children* and *Cruelty to a child*, published 20 February 2008

Key factors

(a) The same starting point and sentencing range is proposed for offences which might fall into the four categories (assault; ill-treatment or neglect; abandonment; and failure to protect). These are designed to take into account the fact that the victim is particularly vulnerable, assuming an abuse of trust or power and the likelihood of psychological harm, and designed to reflect the seriousness with which society as a whole regards these offences.

(b) As noted above, the starting points have been calculated to reflect the likelihood of psychological harm and this cannot be treated as an aggravating factor. Where there is an especially serious physical or psychological effect on the victim, even if unintended, this should increase sentence.

(c) The normal sentencing starting point for an offence of child cruelty should be a custodial sentence. The length of that sentence will be influenced by the circumstances in which the offence took place.

(d) However, in considering whether a custodial sentence is the most appropriate disposal, the court should take into account any available information concerning the future care of the child.

(e) Where the offender is the sole or primary carer of the victim or other dependants, this potentially should be taken into account for sentencing purposes, regardless of whether the offender is male or female. In such cases, an immediate custodial sentence may not be appropriate.

(f) The most relevant areas of personal mitigation are likely to be:

- Mental illness/depression
- Inability to cope with the pressures of parenthood
- Lack of support
- Sleep deprivation
- Offender dominated by an abusive or stronger partner
- Extreme behavioural difficulties in the child, often coupled with a lack of support
- Inability to secure assistance or support services in spite of every effort having been made by the offender.

Some of the factors identified above, in particular sleep deprivation, lack of support and an inability to cope, could be regarded as an inherent part of caring for children, especially when a child is very young and could be put forward as mitigation by most carers charged with an offence of child cruelty. It follows that, before being accepted as mitigation, there must be evidence that these factors were present to a high degree and had an identifiable and significant impact on the offender's behaviour.

CRUELTY TO A CHILD

Children and Young Persons Act 1933, s.1(1)

Triable either way:

Maximum when tried summarily: Level 5 fine and/or 6 months

Maximum when tried on indictment: 10 years

Identify dangerous offenders

These are serious offences for the purposes of the public protection provisions in the Criminal Justice Act 2003 – refer to page[s 358–359] and consult legal adviser for guidance

---

Offence seriousness (culpability and harm)

A. Identify the appropriate starting point

Starting points based on first time offender pleading not guilty

Examples of nature of activity	Starting point	Range
(i) Short term neglect or ill-treatment	12 weeks custody	Low level community order to 26 weeks custody

(ii) Single incident of short-term abandonment (iii) Failure to protect a child from any of the above		
(i) Assault(s) resulting in injuries consistent with ABH (ii) More than one incident of neglect or ill-treatment (but not amounting to long-term behaviour) (iii) Single incident of long-term abandonment OR regular incidents of short-term abandonment (the longer the period of long-term abandonment or the greater the number of incidents of short-term abandonment, the more serious the offence) (iv) Failure to protect a child from any of the above	Crown Court	26 weeks custody to Crown Court
(i) Series of assaults (ii) Protracted neglect or ill-treatment (iii) Serious cruelty over a period of time (iv) Failure to protect a child from any of the above	Crown Court	Crown Court

---

Offence seriousness (culpability and harm)

B. Consider the effect of aggravating and mitigating factors (other than those within examples above)

Common aggravating and mitigating factors are identified in the pullout card – the following may be particularly relevant but **these lists are not exhaustive**

Factors indicating higher culpability	Factors indicating lower culpability
1. Targeting one particular child from the family 2. Sadistic behaviour 3. Threats to prevent the victim from reporting the offence 4. Deliberate concealment of the victim from the authorities 5. Failure to seek medical help	1. Seeking medical help or bringing the situation to the notice of the authorities

Form a preliminary view of the appropriate sentence, then consider offender mitigation
Common factors are identified in the pullout card
Consider a reduction for a guilty plea
Consider ancillary orders, including compensation
Refer to pages [339–346] for guidance on available ancillary orders
Decide sentence
Give reasons

DRUGS – CLASS A – FAIL TO ATTEND/REMAIN FOR INITIAL ASSESSMENT

Drugs Act 2005, s.12

Triable only summarily:

Maximum: Level 4 fine and/or 3 months

Offence seriousness (culpability and harm)		
A. Identify the appropriate starting point		
Starting points based on first time offender pleading not guilty		
Examples of nature of activity	**Starting point**	**Range**
Failure to attend at the appointed place and time	Medium level community order	Band C fine to high level community order

Offence seriousness (culpability and harm)	
B. Consider the effect of aggravating and mitigating factors (other than those within examples above)	
Common aggravating and mitigating factors are identified in the pullout card – the following may be particularly relevant but **these lists are not exhaustive**	
Factors indicating higher culpability	**Factors indicating lower culpability**
1. Threats or abuse to assessor or other staff	1. Offender turns up but at wrong place or time or fails to remain for duration of appointment
	2. Subsequent voluntary contact to rearrange appointment

Form a preliminary view of the appropriate sentence, then consider offender mitigation
Common factors are identified in the pullout card
Consider a reduction for a guilty plea
Consider ancillary orders
Refer to pages [339–346] for guidance on available ancillary orders
Decide sentence
Give reasons

DRUGS – CLASS A – FAIL/REFUSE TO PROVIDE A SAMPLE

Police and Criminal Evidence Act 1984, s.63B

Triable only summarily:

Maximum: Level 4 fine and/or 3 months

Offence seriousness (culpability and harm)		
A. Identify the appropriate starting point		
Starting points based on first time offender pleading not guilty		
Examples of nature of activity	**Starting point**	**Range**
Refusal to provide sample without good cause when required by police officer	Medium level community order	Band C fine to high level community order

Offence seriousness (culpability and harm)	
B. Consider the effect of aggravating and mitigating factors (other than those within examples above)	
Common aggravating and mitigating factors are identified in the pullout card – the following may be particularly relevant but **these lists are not exhaustive**	
Factors indicating higher culpability	**Factors indicating lower culpability**
1. Threats or abuse to staff	1. Subsequent voluntary contact with drug workers 2. Subsequent compliance with testing on arrest/charge

Form a preliminary view of the appropriate sentence, then consider offender mitigation
Common factors are identified in the pullout card
Consider a reduction for a guilty plea
Consider ancillary orders
Refer to pages [339–346] for guidance on available ancillary orders
Decide sentence
Give reasons

DRUGS – CLASS A – POSSESSION

Misuse of Drugs Act 1971, s.5(2)

Triable either way:

Maximum when tried summarily: Level 5 fine and/or 6 months

Maximum when tried on indictment: 7 years

<table>
<tr><td colspan="3">Offence seriousness (culpability and harm)
A. Identify the appropriate starting point
Starting points based on first time offender pleading not guilty</td></tr>
<tr><td>Examples of nature of activity</td><td>Starting point</td><td>Range</td></tr>
<tr><td>Possession of a very small quantity of the drug e.g. one small wrap or tablet</td><td>Band C fine</td><td>Band B fine to medium level community order</td></tr>
<tr><td>More than a very small quantity of the drug e.g. up to six wraps or tablets</td><td>Medium level community order</td><td>Low level community order to high level community order</td></tr>
<tr><td>Larger amounts</td><td>High level community order</td><td>Medium level community order to Crown Court</td></tr>
<tr><td>Possession of drug in prison – whether by prisoner or another</td><td>Crown Court</td><td>Crown Court</td></tr>
</table>

<table>
<tr><td colspan="2">Offence seriousness (culpability and harm)
B. Consider the effect of aggravating and mitigating factors (other than those within examples above)
Common aggravating and mitigating factors are identified in the pullout card – the following may be particularly relevant but these lists are not exhaustive</td></tr>
<tr><td>Factors indicating higher culpability
1. Offender exercising or acting in position of special responsibility

Factor indicating greater degree of harm
1. Possession of drug in a public place or school</td><td></td></tr>
</table>

<table>
<tr><td>Form a preliminary view of the appropriate sentence, then consider offender mitigation
Common factors are identified in the pullout card</td></tr>
<tr><td>Consider a reduction for a guilty plea</td></tr>
<tr><td>Consider ancillary orders
Refer to pages [339–346] for guidance on available ancillary orders</td></tr>
<tr><td>Decide sentence
Give reasons</td></tr>
</table>

DRUGS – CLASS A – PRODUCE, SUPPLY, POSSESS WITH INTENT TO SUPPLY

Misuse of Drugs Act 1971, ss.4(2), 4(3), 5(3)

Triable either way:

Maximum when tried summarily: Level 5 fine and/or 6 months

Maximum when tried on indictment: Life

Offence seriousness (culpability and harm)
A. Identify the appropriate starting point
Starting points based on first time offender pleading not guilty
These offences should normally be dealt with in the Crown Court. However, there may be very rare cases involving non-commercial supply (e.g. between equals) of a very small amount (e.g. one small wrap or tablet) in which a custodial sentence within the jurisdiction of a magistrates' court may be appropriate.

DRUGS – CLASS B AND C – POSSESSION

Misuse of Drugs Act 1971, s.5(2)

Triable either way:

Maximum when tried summarily: Level 4 fine and/or 3 months (class B); level 3 fine and/or 3 months (class C)

Maximum when tried on indictment: 5 years (class B); 2 years (class C)

Offence seriousness (culpability and harm)		
A. Identify the appropriate starting point		
Starting points based on first time offender pleading not guilty		
Examples of nature of activity	**Starting point**	**Range**
Possession of a small amount of class B drug for personal use	Band B fine	Band A fine to low level community order
Possession of large amount of class B drug for personal use	Band C fine	Band B fine to 12 weeks custody

Offence seriousness (culpability and harm)
B. Consider the effect of aggravating and mitigating factors (other than those within examples above)
Common aggravating and mitigating factors are identified in the pullout card – the following may be particularly relevant but these lists are not exhaustive

Factors indicating higher culpability	Factors indicating lower culpability
1. Offender exercising or acting in position of special responsibility	1. Possession of Class C rather than Class B drug
Factor indicating greater degree of harm	2. Evidence that use was to help cope with a medical condition
1. Possession of drugs in a public place or school	

Form a preliminary view of the appropriate sentence, then consider offender mitigation
Common factors are identified in the pullout card
Consider a reduction for a guilty plea
Consider ancillary orders, including compensation
Refer to pages [339–346] for guidance on available ancillary orders
Decide sentence
Give reasons

DRUGS – CLASS B AND C – SUPPLY, POSSESS WITH INTENT TO SUPPLY

Misuse of Drugs Act 1971, ss.4(3) and 5(3)

Triable either way:

Maximum when tried summarily: Level 5 fine and/or 6 months (class B); level 4 fine and/or 3 months (class C)

Maximum when tried on indictment: 14 years (class B and class C)

Offence seriousness (culpability and harm)		
A. Identify the appropriate starting point		
Starting points based on first time offender pleading not guilty		
Examples of nature of activity	**Starting point**	**Range**
Sharing minimal quantity between equals on a non-commercial basis e.g. a reefer	Band C fine	Band B fine to low level community order
Small scale retail supply to consumer	High level community order (class C)	Low level community order to 6 weeks custody (class C)
	6 weeks custody (class B)	Medium level community order to 26 weeks custody (class B)
Any other supply, including small scale supply in prison – whether by prisoner or another	Crown Court	Crown Court

---

Offence seriousness (culpability and harm)

B. Consider the effect of aggravating and mitigating factors (other than those within examples above)

Common aggravating and mitigating factors are identified in the pullout card – the following may be particularly relevant but these lists are not exhaustive

Factors indicating higher culpability	
1. Offender exercising or acting in position of special responsibility	
Factors indicating greater degree of harm	
1. Supply to vulnerable persons including children	
2. Offence committed on/in vicinity of school premises	
(Note: supply on or in the vicinity of school premises is a statutory aggravating factor: Misuse of Drugs Act 1971, s.4A. Consult your legal adviser for guidance.)	

Form a preliminary view of the appropriate sentence, then consider offender mitigation

Common factors are identified in the pullout card

Consider a reduction for a guilty plea

Consider ancillary orders, including forfeiture and destruction of drug and forfeiture or suspension of personal liquor licence

Refer to pages [339–346] for guidance on available ancillary orders

Decide sentence

Give reasons

DRUGS – CULTIVATION OF CANNABIS

Misuse of Drugs Act 1971, s.6(2)

Triable either way:

Maximum when tried summarily: Level 5 fine and/or 6 months

Maximum when tried on indictment: 14 years

Offence seriousness (culpability and harm)		
A. Identify the appropriate starting point		
Starting points based on first time offender pleading not guilty		
Examples of nature of activity	**Starting point**	**Range**
Very small scale cultivation for personal use only i.e. one or two plants	Band C fine	Band B fine to low level community order
Small scale cultivation for personal use and non-commercial supply to small circle of friends	High level community order	Medium level community order to 12 weeks custody
Commercial cultivation	Crown Court	Crown Court

Offence seriousness (culpability and harm)	
B. Consider the effect of aggravating and mitigating factors (other than those within examples above)	
Common aggravating and mitigating factors are identified in the pullout card – the following may be particularly relevant but **these lists are not exhaustive**	
Factors indicating higher culpability	**Factors indicating lower culpability**
1. Use of sophisticated growing system	1. Evidence drug used to help with a medical condition
2. Use of sophisticated system of concealment	2. Original planting carried out by others
3. Persistent use/cultivation of cannabis	
Factor indicating greater degree of harm	
1. Involvement of vulnerable/young persons	

Form a preliminary view of the appropriate sentence, then consider offender mitigation
Common factors are identified in the pullout card
Consider a reduction for a guilty plea
Consider ancillary orders, including forfeiture and destruction of drug
Refer to pages [339–346] for guidance on available ancillary orders
Decide sentence
Give reasons

DRUNK AND DISORDERLY IN A PUBLIC PLACE

Criminal Justice Act 1967, s.91

Triable only summarily:

Maximum: Level 3 fine

Offence seriousness (culpability and harm)		
A. Identify the appropriate starting point		
Starting points based on first time offender pleading not guilty		
Examples of nature of activity	**Starting point**	**Range**
Shouting, causing disturbance for some minutes	Band A fine	Conditional discharge to band B fine
Substantial disturbance caused	Band B fine	Band A fine to band C fine

Offence seriousness (culpability and harm)
B. Consider the effect of aggravating and mitigating factors (other than those within examples above)
Common aggravating and mitigating factors are identified in the pullout card – the following may be particularly relevant but **these lists are not exhaustive**

Factors indicating higher culpability	**Factors indicating lower culpability**
1. Offensive words or behaviour involved	1. Minor and non-threatening
2. Lengthy incident	2. Stopped as soon as police arrived
3. Group action	
Factors indicating greater degree of harm	
1. Offence committed at school, hospital or other place where vulnerable persons may be present	
2. Offence committed on public transport	
3. Victim providing public service	

Form a preliminary view of the appropriate sentence, then consider offender mitigation
Common factors are identified in the pullout card
Consider a reduction for a guilty plea
Consider ancillary orders, including compensation and football banning order (where appropriate)
Refer to pages [339–346] for guidance on available ancillary orders
Decide sentence
Give reasons

ELECTRICITY, ABSTRACT/USE WITHOUT AUTHORITY – FACTORS TO TAKE INTO CONSIDERATION

Key factors

(a) The starting points and sentencing ranges in this guideline are based on the assumption that the offender was motivated by greed or a desire to live beyond his or her means. To avoid double counting, such a motivation should not be treated as a factor that increases culpability.

(b) When assessing the harm caused by this offence, the starting point should be the loss suffered by the victim. In general, the greater the loss, the more serious the offence. However, the monetary value of the loss may not reflect the full extent of the harm caused by the offence. The court should also take into account the impact of the offence on the victim, any harm to persons other than the direct victim, and any harm in the form of public alarm or erosion of public confidence.

(c) The following matters of offender mitigation may be relevant to this offence:

(i) *Offender motivated by desperation or need*
The fact that an offence has been committed in desperation or need arising from particular hardship may count as offender mitigation in exceptional circumstances.

(ii) *Voluntary restitution*
Whether and the degree to which payment for stolen electricity constitutes a matter of offender mitigation will depend on an assessment of the circumstances and, in particular, the voluntariness and timeliness of the payment.

(iii) *Impact on sentence of offender's dependency*
Many offenders convicted of acquisitive crimes are motivated by an addiction, often to drugs, alcohol or gambling. This does not mitigate the seriousness of the offence, but an offender's dependency may properly influence the type of sentence imposed. In particular, it may sometimes be appropriate to impose a drug rehabilitation requirement or an alcohol treatment requirement as part of a community order or a suspended sentence order in an attempt to break the cycle of addiction and offending, even if an immediate custodial sentence would otherwise be warranted.[1]

ELECTRICITY, ABSTRACT/USE WITHOUT AUTHORITY

Theft Act 1968, s.13

Triable either way:

Maximum when tried summarily: Level 5 fine and/or 6 months

Maximum when tried on indictment: 5 years

---

[1] See para.2 on p.163. The Court of Appeal gave guidance on the approach to making drug treatment and testing orders, which also applies to imposing a drug rehabilitation requirement in *Attorney General's Reference No. 64 of 2003 (Boujettif and Harrison)* [2003] EWCA Crim 3514 and *Woods and Collins* [2005] EWCA Crim 2065 summarised in the *Sentencing Guidelines Council Guideline Judgments Case Compendium* (section (A) Generic Sentencing Principles) available at: www.sentencing-guidelines.gov.uk

Offence seriousness (culpability and harm)		
A. Identify the appropriate starting point		
Starting points based on first time offender pleading not guilty		
Examples of nature of activity	Starting point	Range
Where the offence results in substantial commercial gain, a custodial sentence may be appropriate		
Offence involving evidence of planning and indication that the offending was intended to be continuing, such as using a device to interfere with the electricity meter or re-wiring to by-pass the meter	Medium level community order	Band A fine to high level community order

Offence seriousness (culpability and harm)	
B. Consider the effect of aggravating and mitigating factors (other than those within examples above)	
Common aggravating and mitigating factors are identified in the pullout card – the following may be particularly relevant but **these lists are not exhaustive**	
Factors indicating greater degree of harm	
1. Risk of danger caused to property and/or life	

Form a preliminary view of the appropriate sentence, then consider offender mitigation
Common factors are identified in the pullout card – see also note (c) opposite
Consider a reduction for a guilty plea
Consider ancillary orders, including compensation
Refer to pages [339–346] for guidance on available ancillary orders
Decide sentence
Give reasons

EXPLOITATION OF PROSTITUTION

Sexual Offences Act 2003, s.52 (causing or inciting prostitution for gain); s.53 (controlling prostitution for gain)

Triable either way:

Maximum when tried summarily: Level 5 fine or 6 months

Maximum when tried on indictment: 7 years

This guideline is taken from the Sentencing Guidelines Council's definitive guideline *Sexual Offences Act 2003*, published 30 April 2007

Identify dangerous offenders

These are specified offences for the purposes of the public protection provisions in the Criminal Justice Act 2003 – refer to page[s 358–359] and consult legal adviser for guidance

---

Offence seriousness (culpability and harm)

A. Identify the appropriate starting point

Starting points based on first time offender pleading not guilty

Examples of nature of activity	Starting point	Range
No evidence victim was physically coerced or corrupted, and the involvement of the offender was minimal	Medium level community order	Band C fine to high level community order
No coercion or corruption but the offender is closely involved in the victim's prostitution	Crown Court	26 weeks custody to Crown Court
Evidence of physical and/or mental coercion	Crown Court	Crown Court

---

Offence seriousness (culpability and harm)

B. Consider the effect of aggravating and mitigating factors (other than those within examples above)

Common aggravating and mitigating factors are identified in the pullout card – the following may be particularly relevant but **these lists are not exhaustive**

Factors indicating higher culpability	Factors indicating lower culpability
1. Background of threats, intimidation or coercion 2. Large-scale commercial operation 3. Substantial gain (in the region of £5,000 and up) 4. Use of drugs, alcohol or other substance to secure the victim's compliance 5. Abduction or detention 6. Threats to prevent the victim reporting the activity 7. Threats to disclose victim's activity to friends/relatives **Factor indicating greater degree of harm** 1. Induced dependency on drugs	1. Offender also being controlled in prostitution and subject to threats or intimidation

Form a preliminary view of the appropriate sentence, then consider offender mitigation
Common factors are identified in the pullout card
Consider a reduction for a guilty plea
Consider ancillary orders, including compensation
Refer to pages [339–346] for guidance on available ancillary orders
Decide sentence
Give reasons

Note

Where an offender has profited from his or her involvement in the prostitution of others, the court should consider making a confiscation order approximately equivalent to the profits enjoyed. Such an order may be made only in the Crown Court.

EXPOSURE

Sexual Offences Act 2003, s.66

Triable either way:

Maximum when tried summarily: Level 5 fine or 6 months

Maximum when tried on indictment: 2 years

This guideline is taken from the Sentencing Guidelines Council's definitive guideline *Sexual Offences Act 2003*, published 30 April 2007

Key factors

(a) This offence is committed where an offender intentionally exposes his or her genitals and intends that someone will see them and be caused alarm or distress. It is gender neutral, covering exposure of male or female genitalia to a male or female witness.

(b) The Sentencing Guidelines Council guideline provides that, when dealing with a repeat offender, the starting point should be 12 weeks custody with a range of 4 to 26 weeks custody. The presence of aggravating factors may suggest that a sentence above the range is appropriate and that the case should be committed to the Crown Court.

(c) In accordance with s.80 and sch.3 of the Sexual Offences Act 2003, automatic notification requirements apply upon conviction to an offender aged 18 or over where:

(1) the victim was under 18; or

(2) a term of imprisonment or a community sentence of at least 12 months is imposed.

(d) This guideline may be relevant by way of analogy to conduct charged as the common law offence of outraging public decency; the offence is triable either way and has a maximum penalty of a level 5 fine and/or 6 months imprisonment when tried summarily.

223

Identify dangerous offenders
This is a specified offence for the purposes of the public protection provisions in the Criminal Justice Act 2003 – refer to page[s 358–359] and consult legal adviser for guidance

Offence seriousness (culpability and harm)

A. Identify the appropriate starting point

Starting points based on first time offender pleading not guilty

Examples of nature of activity	Starting point	Range
Basic offence as defined in the Act, assuming no aggravating or mitigating factors	Low level community order	Band B fine to medium level community order
Offence with an aggravating factor	Medium level community order	Low level community order to high level community order
Two or more aggravating factors	12 weeks custody	6 weeks custody to Crown Court

Offence seriousness (culpability and harm)

B. Consider the effect of aggravating and mitigating factors (other than those within examples above)

Common aggravating and mitigating factors are identified in the pullout card – the following may be particularly relevant but **these lists are not exhaustive**

Factors indicating higher culpability 1. Threats to prevent the victim reporting an offence 2. Intimidating behaviour/threats of violence **Factor indicating greater degree of harm** 1. Victim is a child	

Form a preliminary view of the appropriate sentence, then consider offender mitigation
Common factors are identified in the pullout card
Consider a reduction for a guilty plea
Consider ancillary orders, including compensation
Refer to pages [339–346] for guidance on available ancillary orders
Decide sentence
Give reasons

FALSE ACCOUNTING

Theft Act 1968, s.17

Triable either way:

Maximum when tried summarily: Level 5 fine and/or 6 months

Maximum when tried on indictment: 7 years

Awaiting SGC guideline

FIREARM, CARRYING IN PUBLIC PLACE

Firearms Act 1968, s.19

Triable either way (but triable only summarily if the firearm is an air weapon):

Maximum when tried summarily: Level 5 fine and/or 6 months

Maximum when tried on indictment: 7 years (12 months for imitation firearms)

Offence seriousness (culpability and harm)		
A. Identify the appropriate starting point		
Starting points based on first time offender pleading not guilty		
Examples of nature of activity	**Starting point**	**Range**
Carrying an unloaded air weapon	Low level community order	Band B fine to medium level community order
Carrying loaded air weapon/imitation firearm/unloaded shot gun without ammunition	High level community order	Medium level community order to 26 weeks custody (air weapon) Medium level community order to Crown Court (imitation firearm, unloaded shot gun)
Carrying loaded shot gun/carrying shot gun or any other firearm together with ammunition for it	Crown Court	Crown Court

225

Offence seriousness (culpability and harm)
B. Consider the effect of aggravating and mitigating factors (other than those within examples above)
Common aggravating and mitigating factors are identified in the pullout card – the following may be particularly relevant but **these lists are not exhaustive**

Factors indicating higher culpability	**Factors indicating lower culpability**
1. Brandishing the firearm	1. Firearm not in sight
2. Carrying firearm in a busy place	2. No intention to use firearm
3. Planned illegal use	3. Firearm to be used for lawful purpose (not amounting to a defence)
Factors indicating greater degree of harm	
1. Person or people put in fear	
2. Offender participating in violent incident	

Form a preliminary view of the appropriate sentence, then consider offender mitigation
Common factors are identified in the pullout card
Consider a reduction for a guilty plea
Consider ancillary orders, including compensation, forfeiture or suspension of personal liquor licence and football banning order (where appropriate)
Refer to pages [339–346] for guidance on available ancillary orders
Decide sentence
Give reasons

FOOTBALL RELATED OFFENCES

Sporting Events (Control of Alcohol etc.) Act 1985: s.2(1) (possession of alcohol whilst entering or trying to enter ground); s.2(2) (being drunk in, or whilst trying to enter, ground)

Football Offences Act 1991: s.2 (throwing missile); s.3 (indecent or racist chanting); s.4 (going onto prohibited areas)

Criminal Justice and Public Order Act 1994: s.166 (unauthorised sale or attempted sale of tickets)

Triable only summarily:

Maximum: Level 2 fine (being drunk in ground)
Level 3 fine (throwing missile; indecent or racist chanting; going onto prohibited areas)
Level 5 fine (unauthorised sale of tickets)
Level 3 fine and/or 3 months (possession of alcohol)

Offence seriousness (culpability and harm)

A. Identify the appropriate starting point

Starting points based on first time offender pleading not guilty

Examples of nature of activity	Starting point	Range
Being drunk in, or whilst trying to enter, ground	Band A fine	Conditional discharge to band B fine
Going onto playing or other prohibited area; Unauthorised sale or attempted sale of tickets	Band B fine	Band A fine to band C fine
Throwing missile; Indecent or racist chanting	Band C fine	Band C fine
Possession of alcohol whilst entering or trying to enter ground	Band C fine	Band B fine to high level community order

Offence seriousness (culpability and harm)

B. Consider the effect of aggravating and mitigating factors (other than those within examples above)

Common aggravating and mitigating factors are identified in the pullout card – the following may be particularly relevant but **these lists are not exhaustive**

Factors indicating higher culpability

1. Commercial ticket operation; potential high cash value; counterfeit tickets

2. Inciting others to misbehave

3. Possession of large quantity of alcohol

4. Offensive language or behaviour (where not an element of the offence)

Factors indicating greater degree of harm

1. Missile likely to cause serious injury e.g. coin, glass, bottle, stone

Form a preliminary view of the appropriate sentence, then consider offender mitigation

Common factors are identified in the pullout card

Consider a reduction for a guilty plea

Consider ancillary orders, including compensation and football banning order

Refer to pages [339–346] for guidance on available ancillary orders

Decide sentence

Give reasons

GOING EQUIPPED, FOR THEFT

Theft Act 1968, s.25

Triable either way:

Maximum when tried summarily: Level 5 fine and/or 6 months

Maximum when tried on indictment: 3 years

May disqualify if offence committed with reference to theft or taking of motor vehicles (no points available)

Offence seriousness (culpability and harm)		
A. Identify the appropriate starting point		
Starting points based on first time offender pleading not guilty		
Examples of nature of activity	**Starting point**	**Range**
Possession of items for theft from shop or of vehicle	Medium level community order	Band C fine to high level community order
Possession of items for burglary, robbery	High level community order	Medium level community order to Crown Court

Offence seriousness (culpability and harm)	
B. Consider the effect of aggravating and mitigating factors (other than those within examples above)	
Common aggravating and mitigating factors are identified in the pullout card – the following may be particularly relevant but **these lists are not exhaustive**	
Factors indicating higher culpability 1. Circumstances suggest offender equipped for particularly serious offence 2. Items to conceal identity	

Form a preliminary view of the appropriate sentence, then consider offender mitigation
Common factors are identified in the pullout card
Consider a reduction for a guilty plea
Consider ancillary orders
Refer to pages [339–346] for guidance on available ancillary orders
Consider disqualification from driving and deprivation of property
Decide sentence
Give reasons

GRIEVOUS BODILY HARM/UNLAWFUL WOUNDING & RACIALLY OR RELIGIOUSLY AGGRAVATED GRIEVOUS BODILY HARM/UNLAWFUL WOUNDING – FACTORS TO TAKE INTO CONSIDERATION

This guideline and accompanying notes are taken from the Sentencing Guidelines Council's definitive guideline *Assault and other offences against the person*, published 20 February 2008

Key factors

(a) Matters of offender mitigation are often highly relevant to sentencing for this offence and may justify a non-custodial sentence, particularly in the case of a first time offender. Such a disposal might also be considered appropriate where there is a guilty plea.

(b) Offences contrary to s.20 and s.47 carry the same maximum penalty of 5 years imprisonment. However, the definitions of the offences make it clear that the degree of harm in a s.20 offence will be more serious. The CPS Charging Standard provides that more minor injuries should be charged under s.47. Where the offence ought to be sentenced as an assault occasioning actual bodily harm, that guideline should be used.

(c) The use of a weapon (which for the purposes of this guideline includes traditional items such as an iron bar, baseball bat or knife) or part of the body (such as the head or other body part which may be equipped to inflict harm or greater harm for example a shod foot) will usually increase the seriousness of an offence:

   (i) In relation to culpability, where a weapon is carried by the offender to the scene with the intention of using it or having it available for use should the opportunity or need arise, high culpability is likely to be indicated.

   (ii) In relation to harm, the type of weapon or part of the body and the way it is used will influence the extent of the effect on the assessment of seriousness. For instance, use of a knife or broken glass raises a high risk of serious injury. Similarly where the offender kicks or stamps on a prone victim, particularly if to a vulnerable part of the body.

(d) Relative seriousness of this offence is based on whether or not the assault was premeditated and on the degree of harm that resulted. Use of a weapon will cause the offence to be in a higher sentencing range than where a weapon is not used.

GRIEVOUS BODILY HARM/UNLAWFUL WOUNDING

Offences Against the Person Act 1861, s.20

RACIALLY OR RELIGIOUSLY AGGRAVATED GRIEVOUS BODILY HARM/UNLAWFUL WOUNDING

Crime and Disorder Act 1998, s.29

Inflicting GBH/unlawful wounding: triable either way

Maximum when tried summarily: Level 5 fine and/or 6 months

Maximum when tried on indictment: 5 years

Racially or religiously aggravated GBH/unlawful wounding: triable either way

Maximum when tried summarily: Level 5 fine and/or 6 months

Maximum when tried on indictment: 7 years

Where offence committed in domestic context, refer to page [348] for guidance

Identify dangerous offenders
These are specified offences for the purposes of the public protection provisions in the Criminal Justice Act 2003 – refer to page[s 358–359] and consult legal adviser for guidance

Offence seriousness (culpability and harm)		
A. Identify the appropriate starting point		
Starting points based on first time offender pleading not guilty		
Examples of nature of activity	**Starting point**	**Range**
Other assault where no weapon has been used	24 weeks custody	High level community order to Crown Court
Premeditated assault where no weapon has been used	Crown Court	24 weeks custody to Crown Court
Premeditated assault where a weapon has been used **or** Other assault where particularly grave injury results or a weapon has been used	Crown Court	Crown Court

Offence seriousness (culpability and harm)	
B. Consider the effect of aggravating and mitigating factors (other than those within examples above)	
Common aggravating and mitigating factors are identified in the pullout card – the following may be particularly relevant but **these lists are not exhaustive**	
	Factors indicating lower culpability
	1. Provocation

Form a preliminary view of the appropriate sentence
If offender charged and convicted of the racially or religiously aggravated offence, increase the sentence to reflect this element
Refer to page[s 349–351] for guidance
Consider offender mitigation
Common factors are identified in the pullout card
Consider a reduction for a guilty plea
Consider ancillary orders, including compensation
Refer to pages [339–346] for guidance on available ancillary orders
Decide sentence
Give reasons

HANDLING STOLEN GOODS

Theft Act 1968, s.22

Triable either way:

Maximum when tried summarily: Level 5 fine and/or 6 months

Maximum when tried on indictment: 14 years

These guidelines are drawn from the Court of Appeal's decision in *R* v *Webbe and others* [2001] EWCA Crim 1217

Offence seriousness (culpability and harm)		
A. Identify the appropriate starting point		
Starting points based on first time offender pleading not guilty		
Examples of nature of activity	**Starting point**	**Range**
Property worth £1,000 or less acquired for offender's own use	Band B fine	Band B fine to low level community order
Property worth £1,000 or less acquired for re-sale; or	Medium level community order	Low level community order to 12 weeks custody
Property worth more than £1,000 acquired for offender's own use; or Presence of at least one aggravating factor listed below – regardless of value		Note: the custody threshold is likely to be passed if the offender has a record of dishonesty offences
Sophisticated offending; or Presence of at least two aggravating factors listed below	12 weeks custody	6 weeks custody to Crown Court

231

Offence committed in context of a business; or Offender acts as organiser/distributor of proceeds of crime; or Offender makes self available to other criminals as willing to handle the proceeds of thefts or burglaries; or Offending highly organised, professional; or Particularly serious original offence, such as armed robbery	Crown Court	Crown Court

---

Offence seriousness (culpability and harm)

B. Consider the effect of aggravating and mitigating factors (other than those within examples above)

Common aggravating and mitigating factors are identified in the pullout card – the following may be particularly relevant but **these lists are not exhaustive**

Factors indicating higher culpability	**Factors indicating lower culpability**
1. Closeness of offender to primary offence. Closeness may be geographical, arising from presence at or near the primary offence when it was committed, or temporal, where the handler instigated or encouraged the primary offence beforehand, or, soon after, provided a safe haven or route for disposal 2. High level of profit made or expected by offender **Factors indicating greater degree of harm** 1. Seriousness of the primary offence, including domestic burglary 2. High value of goods to victim, including sentimental value 3. Threats of violence or abuse of power by offender over others, such as an adult commissioning criminal activity by children, or a drug dealer pressurising addicts to steal in order to pay for their habit	1. Little or no benefit to offender 2. Voluntary restitution to victim **Factor indicating lower degree of harm** 1. Low value of goods

Form a preliminary view of the appropriate sentence, then consider offender mitigation
Common factors are identified in the pullout card
Consider a reduction for a guilty plea
Consider ancillary orders, including restitution and compensation
Refer to pages [339–346] for guidance on available ancillary orders
Consider deprivation of property
Decide sentence
Give reasons

HARASSMENT – PUTTING PEOPLE IN FEAR OF VIOLENCE

Protection from Harassment Act 1997, s.4

RACIALLY OR RELIGIOUSLY AGGRAVATED HARASSMENT – PUTTING PEOPLE IN FEAR OF VIOLENCE

Crime and Disorder Act 1998, s.32

Harassment: triable either way

Maximum when tried summarily: Level 5 fine and/or 6 months

Maximum when tried on indictment: 5 years

Racially or religiously aggravated harassment: triable either way

Maximum when tried summarily: Level 5 fine and/or 6 months

Maximum when tried on indictment: 7 years

Where offence committed in domestic context, refer to page [348] for guidance

Identify dangerous offenders
This is a specified offence for the purposes of the public protection provisions in the Criminal Justice Act 2003 – refer to page[s 358–359] and consult legal adviser for guidance

Offence seriousness (culpability and harm)		
A. Identify the appropriate starting point		
Starting points based on first time offender pleading not guilty		
Examples of nature of activity	**Starting point**	**Range**
A pattern of two or more incidents of unwanted contact	6 weeks custody	High level community order to 18 weeks custody
Deliberate threats, persistent action over a longer period; or Intention to cause fear of violence	18 weeks custody	12 weeks custody to Crown Court
Sexual threats, vulnerable person targeted	Crown Court	Crown Court

233

Offence seriousness (culpability and harm)

B. Consider the effect of aggravating and mitigating factors (other than those within examples above)

Common aggravating and mitigating factors are identified in the pullout card – the following may be particularly relevant but **these lists are not exhaustive**

Factors indicating higher culpability	**Factors indicating lower culpability**
1. Planning	1. Limited understanding of effect on victim
2. Offender ignores obvious distress	2. Initial provocation
3. Visits in person to victim's home or workplace	
4. Offender involves others	
5. Using contact arrangements with a child to instigate offence	
Factors indicating greater degree of harm	
1. Victim needs medical help/counselling	
2. Physical violence used	
3. Victim aware that offender has history of using violence	
4. Grossly violent or offensive material sent	
5. Children frightened	
6. Evidence that victim changed lifestyle to avoid contact	

Form a preliminary view of the appropriate sentence
If offender charged and convicted of the racially or religiously aggravated offence, increase the sentence to reflect this element
Refer to pages [349–351] for guidance
Consider offender mitigation
Common factors are identified in the pullout card
Consider a reduction for a guilty plea
Consider making a restraining order
Consider ancillary orders, including compensation
Refer to pages [339–346] for guidance on available ancillary orders
Decide sentence
Give reasons

HARASSMENT (WITHOUT VIOLENCE)

Protection from Harassment Act 1997, s.2

RACIALLY OR RELIGIOUSLY AGGRAVATED HARASSMENT (NON VIOLENT)
Crime and Disorder Act 1998, s.32

Harassment: triable only summarily

Maximum: Level 5 fine and/or 6 months

Racially or religiously aggravated harassment: triable either way

Maximum when tried summarily: Level 5 fine and/or 6 months

Maximum when tried on indictment: 2 years

Where offence committed in domestic context, refer to page [348] for guidance

<table>
<tr><td colspan="3">Offence seriousness (culpability and harm)
A. Identify the appropriate starting point
Starting points based on first time offender pleading not guilty</td></tr>
<tr><th>Examples of nature of activity</th><th>Starting point</th><th>Range</th></tr>
<tr><td>Small number of incidents</td><td>Medium level community order</td><td>Band C fine to high level community order</td></tr>
<tr><td>Constant contact at night, trying to come into workplace or home, involving others</td><td>6 weeks custody</td><td>Medium level community order to 12 weeks custody</td></tr>
<tr><td>Threatening violence, taking personal photographs, sending offensive material</td><td>18 weeks custody</td><td>12 to 26 weeks custody</td></tr>
</table>

<table>
<tr><td colspan="2">Offence seriousness (culpability and harm)
B. Consider the effect of aggravating and mitigating factors (other than those within examples above)
Common aggravating and mitigating factors are identified in the pullout card – the following may be particularly relevant but these lists are not exhaustive</td></tr>
<tr><td>Factors indicating higher culpability
1. Planning
2. Offender ignores obvious distress
3. Offender involves others
4. Using contact arrangements with a child to instigate offence

Factors indicating greater degree of harm
1. Victim needs medical help/counselling
2. Action over long period
3. Children frightened
4. Use or distribution of photographs</td><td>Factors indicating lower culpability
1. Limited understanding of effect on victim
2. Initial provocation</td></tr>
</table>

Form a preliminary view of the appropriate sentence. If offender charged and convicted of the racially or religiously aggravated offence, increase the sentence to reflect this element Refer to pages [349–351] for guidance
Consider offender mitigation Common factors are identified in the pullout card
Consider a reduction for a guilty plea
Consider making a restraining order **Consider ancillary orders, including compensation** Refer to pages [339–346] for guidance on available ancillary orders
Decide sentence **Give reasons**

IDENTITY DOCUMENTS – POSSESS FALSE/ANOTHER'S/IMPROPERLY OBTAINED

Identity Cards Act 2006, s.25(5) (possession of a false identity document (as defined in s.26 – includes a passport))

Triable either way:

Maximum when tried summarily: Level 5 fine and/or 6 months

Maximum when tried on indictment: 2 years (s.25(5))

Note: possession of a false identity document with the intention of using it is an indictable-only offence (Identity Cards Act 2006, s.25(1)). The maximum penalty is 10 years imprisonment.

Offence seriousness (culpability and harm)		
A. Identify the appropriate starting point		
Starting points based on first time offender pleading not guilty		
Examples of nature of activity	**Starting point**	**Range**
Single document possessed	Medium level community order	Band C fine to high level community order
Small number of documents, no evidence of dealing	12 weeks custody	6 weeks custody to Crown Court
Considerable number of documents possessed, evidence of involvement in larger operation	Crown Court	Crown Court

Offence seriousness (culpability and harm)
B. Consider the effect of aggravating and mitigating factors (other than those within examples above)
Common aggravating and mitigating factors are identified in the pullout card – the following may be particularly relevant but these lists are not exhaustive

Factors indicating higher culpability	Factors indicating lower culpability
1. Clear knowledge that documents false	1. Genuine mistake or ignorance
2. Number of documents possessed (where not in offence descriptions above)	
Factors indicating greater degree of harm	
1. Group activity	
2. Potential impact of use (where not in offence descriptions above)	

Form a preliminary view of the appropriate sentence, then consider offender mitigation
Common factors are identified in the pullout card
Consider a reduction for a guilty plea
Decide sentence
Give reasons

INCOME TAX EVASION

Finance Act 2000, s.144

Triable either way:

Maximum when tried summarily: Level 5 fine and/or 6 months

Maximum when tried on indictment: 7 years

Awaiting SGC guideline

INDECENT PHOTOGRAPHS OF CHILDREN

Protection of Children Act 1978, s.1; Criminal Justice Act 1988, s.160

Triable either way:

Maximum when tried summarily: Level 5 fine or 6 months

Maximum when tried on indictment: 5 years for possession; otherwise 10 years

This guideline is taken from the Sentencing Guidelines Council's definitive guideline *Sexual Offences Act 2003*, **published 30 April 2007**

Key factors:

(a) The levels of seriousness (in ascending order) for sentencing for offences involving pornographic images are:

Level 1   Images depicting erotic posing with no sexual activity
Level 2   Non-penetrative sexual activity between children, or solo masturbation by a child
Level 3   Non-penetrative sexual activity between adults and children
Level 4   Penetrative sexual activity involving a child or children, or both children and adults
Level 5   Sadism or penetration of, or by, an animal.

(b)   Pseudo-photographs generally should be treated less seriously than real photographs.
(c)   Starting points should be higher where the subject of the indecent photograph(s) is a child under 13.
(d)   In accordance with section 80 and schedule 3 of the Sexual Offences Act 2003, automatic notification requirements apply upon conviction to an offender aged 18 or over where the offence involved photographs of children aged under 16.

Offence seriousness (culpability and harm)		
A. Identify the appropriate starting point		
Starting points based on first time offender pleading not guilty		
Examples of nature of activity	**Starting point**	**Range**
Possession of a large amount of level 1 material and/or no more than a small amount of level 2, and the material is for personal use and has not been distributed or shown to others	Medium level community order	Band C fine to high level community order
Offender in possession of a large amount of material at level 2 or a small amount at level 3	12 weeks custody	4 to 26 weeks custody
Offender has shown or distributed material at level 1 on a limited scale		
Offender has exchanged images at level 1 or 2 with other collectors, but with no element of financial gain		
Possession of a large quantity of level 3 material for personal use	26 weeks custody	4 weeks custody to Crown Court
Possession of a small number of images at level 4 or 5		
Large number of level 2 images shown or distributed		
Small number of level 3 images shown or distributed		
Possession of a large quantity of level 4 or 5 material for personal use only	Crown Court	26 weeks custody to Crown Court
Large number of level 3 images shown or distributed		
Offender traded material at levels 1–3		
Level 4 or 5 images shown or distributed		
Offender involved in the production of material of any level	Crown Court	Crown Court

---

Offence seriousness (culpability and harm)

B. Consider the effect of aggravating and mitigating factors (other than those within examples above)

Common aggravating and mitigating factors are identified in the pullout card – the following may be particularly relevant but **these lists are not exhaustive**

Factors indicating higher culpability	**Factors indicating lower culpability**
1. Collection is systematically stored or organised, indicating a sophisticated approach to trading or a high level of personal interest	1. A few images held solely for personal use
	2. Images viewed but not stored
2. Use of drugs, alcohol or other substance to facilitate the offence of making or taking	3. A few images held solely for personal use and it is established that the subject is aged 16 or 17 and that he or she was consenting
3. Background of intimidation or coercion	
4. Threats to prevent victim reporting the activity	
5. Threats to disclose victim's activity to friends/relatives	
6. Financial or other gain	
Factors indicating greater degree of harm	
1. Images shown or distributed to others, especially children	
2. Images stored, made available or distributed in such a way that they can be inadvertently accessed by others	

Form a preliminary view of the appropriate sentence, then consider offender mitigation

Common factors are identified in the pullout card

Consider a reduction for a guilty plea

Consider ancillary orders, including compensation and deprivation of property used to commit the offence

Refer to pages [339–346] for guidance on available ancillary orders

Decide sentence

Give reasons

KEEPING A BROTHEL USED FOR PROSTITUTION

Sexual Offences Act 2003, s.55

Triable either way:

Maximum when tried summarily: Level 5 fine and/or 6 months

Maximum when tried on indictment: 7 years

This guideline is taken from the Sentencing Guidelines Council's definitive guideline *Sexual Offences Act 2003*, **published 30 April 2007**

Offence seriousness (culpability and harm)		
A. Identify the appropriate starting point		
Starting points based on first time offender pleading not guilty		
Examples of nature of activity	**Starting point**	**Range**
Involvement of the offender was minimal	Medium level community order	Band C fine to high level community order
Offender is the keeper of the brothel and is personally involved in its management	Crown Court	26 weeks to Crown Court
Offender is the keeper of a brothel and has made substantial profits in the region of £5,000 and upwards	Crown Court	Crown Court

Offence seriousness (culpability and harm)	
B. Consider the effect of aggravating and mitigating factors (other than those within examples above)	
Common aggravating and mitigating factors are identified in the pullout card – the following may be particularly relevant but **these lists are not exhaustive**	
Factors indicating higher culpability	**Factors indicating lower culpability**
1. Background of threats, intimidation or coercion 2. Large-scale commercial operation 3. Personal involvement in the prostitution of others 4. Abduction or detention 5. Financial or other gain	1. Using employment as a route out of prostitution and not actively involved in exploitation 2. Coercion by third party

Form a preliminary view of the appropriate sentence, then consider offender mitigation
Common factors are identified in the pullout card
Consider a reduction for a guilty plea
Consider ancillary orders, including compensation
Refer to pages [339–346] for guidance on available ancillary orders
Decide sentence
Give reasons

Note

Where an offender has profited from his or her involvement in the prostitution of others, the courts should always consider making a confiscation order approximately equivalent to the profits enjoyed. Such an order may be made only in the Crown Court.

MAKING OFF WITHOUT PAYMENT – FACTORS TO TAKE INTO CONSIDERATION

Key factors

(a) The starting points and sentencing ranges in this guideline are based on the assumption that the offender was motivated by greed or a desire to live beyond his or her means. To avoid double counting, such a motivation should not be treated as a factor that increases culpability.

(b) When assessing the harm caused by this offence, the starting point should be the loss suffered by the victim. In general, the greater the loss, the more serious the offence. However, the monetary value of the loss may not reflect the full extent of the harm caused by the offence. The court should also take into account the impact of the offence on the victim, any harm to persons other than the direct victim, and any harm in the form of public alarm or erosion of public confidence.

(c) The following matters of offender mitigation may be relevant to this offence:

(i) *Offender motivated by desperation or need*
The fact that an offence has been committed in desperation or need arising from particular hardship may count as offender mitigation in exceptional circumstances.

(ii) *Voluntary return of stolen property*
Whether and the degree to which the return of stolen property constitutes a matter of offender mitigation will depend on an assessment of the circumstances and, in particular, the voluntariness and timeliness of the return.

(iii) *Impact on sentence of offender's dependency*
Many offenders convicted of acquisitive crimes are motivated by an addiction, often to drugs, alcohol or gambling. This does not mitigate the seriousness of the offence, but an offender's dependency may properly influence the type of sentence imposed. In particular, it may sometimes be appropriate to impose a drug rehabilitation requirement or an alcohol treatment requirement as part of a community order or a suspended sentence order in an attempt to break the cycle of addiction and offending, even if an immediate custodial sentence would otherwise be warranted.[1]

MAKING OFF WITHOUT PAYMENT

Theft Act 1978, s.3

Triable either way:

Maximum when tried summarily: Level 5 fine and/or 6 months

Maximum when tried on indictment: 2 years

---

[1] See para.2 on p.163. The Court of Appeal gave guidance on the approach to making drug treatment and testing orders, which also applies to imposing a drug rehabilitation requirement in *Attorney General's Reference No. 64 of 2003 (Boujettif and Harrison)* [2003] EWCA Crim 2514 and *Woods and Collins* [2005] EWCA Crim 2065 summarised in the Sentencing Guidelines Council Guideline *Judgments Case Compendium* (section (A) Generic Sentencing Principles) available at: www.sentencing-guidelines.gov.uk

Offence seriousness (culpability and harm)		
A. Identify the appropriate starting point		
Starting points based on first time offender pleading not guilty		
Examples of nature of activity	**Starting point**	**Range**
Single offence committed by an offender acting alone with evidence of little or no planning, goods or services worth less than £200	Band C fine	Band A fine to high level community order
Offence displaying one or more of the following: – offender acting in unison with others – evidence of planning – offence part of a 'spree' – intimidation of victim – goods or services worth £200 or more	Medium level community order	Low level community order to 12 weeks' custody

Offence seriousness (culpability and harm)
B. Consider the effect of aggravating and mitigating factors (other than those within examples above)
Common aggravating and mitigating factors are identified in the pullout card

Form a preliminary view of the appropriate sentence, then consider offender mitigation
Common factors are identified in the pullout card – see also note (c) opposite
Consider a reduction for a guilty plea
Consider ancillary orders, including compensation
Refer to pages [339–346] for guidance on available ancillary orders
Decide sentence
Give reasons

OBSTRUCT/RESIST A POLICE CONSTABLE IN EXECUTION OF DUTY

Police Act 1996, s.89(2)

Triable only summarily:

Maximum: Level 3 fine and/or one month

Offence seriousness (culpability and harm)		
A. Identify the appropriate starting point		
Starting points based on first time offender pleading not guilty		
Examples of nature of activity	**Starting point**	**Range**
Failure to move when required to do so	Band A fine	Conditional discharge to band B fine
Attempt to prevent arrest or other lawful police action; or giving false details	Band B fine	Band A fine to band C fine
Several people attempting to prevent arrest or other lawful police action	Low level community order	Band C fine to medium level community order

Offence seriousness (culpability and harm)	
B. Consider the effect of aggravating and mitigating factors (other than those within examples above)	
Common aggravating and mitigating factors are identified in the pullout card – the following may be particularly relevant but **these lists are not exhaustive**	
Factors indicating higher culpability	**Factors indicating lower culpability**
1. Premeditated action	1. Genuine mistake or misjudgement
2. Aggressive words/threats	2. Brief incident
3. Aggressive group action	

Form a preliminary view of the appropriate sentence, then consider offender mitigation
Common factors are identified in the pullout card
Consider a reduction for a guilty plea
Consider ancillary orders
Refer to pages [339–346] for guidance on available ancillary orders
Decide sentence
Give reasons

OBTAINING SERVICES DISHONESTLY

Fraud Act 2006, s.11

Triable either way:

Maximum when tried summarily: Level 5 fine and/or 6 months

Maximum when tried on indictment: 5 years

Awaiting SGC Guideline

PROTECTIVE ORDER, BREACH OF – FACTORS TO TAKE INTO CONSIDERATION

This guideline and accompanying notes are taken from the Sentencing Guidelines Council's definitive guideline *Breach of a Protective Order*, published 7 December 2006

Aims of sentencing

(a) The main aim of sentencing for breach of a protective order (which would have been imposed to protect a victim from future harm) should be to achieve future compliance with that order.

(b) The court will need to assess the level of risk posed by the offender. Willingness to undergo treatment or accept help may influence sentence.

Key factors

(i) The nature of the conduct that caused the breach of the order. In particular, whether the contact was direct or indirect, although it is important to recognise that indirect contact is capable of causing significant harm or anxiety.

(ii) **There may be exceptional cases where the nature of the breach is particularly serious but has not been dealt with by a separate offence being charged. In these cases the risk posed by the offender and the nature of the breach will be particularly significant in determining the response.**

(iii) The nature of the original conduct or offence is relevant in so far as it allows a judgement to be made on the level of harm caused to the victim by the breach, and the extent to which that harm was intended.

(iv) The sentence following a breach is for the breach alone and must avoid punishing the offender again for the offence or conduct as a result of which the order was made.

(v) It is likely that all breaches of protective orders will pass the threshold for a community sentence. Custody is the starting point where violence is used. Non-violent conduct may also cross the custody threshold where a high degree of harm or anxiety has been caused.

(vi) Where an order was made in civil proceedings, its purpose may have been to cause the subject of the order to modify behaviour rather than to imply that the conduct was especially serious. If so, it is likely to be disproportionate to impose a custodial sentence if the breach of the order did not involve threats or violence.

(vii) In some cases where a breach might result in a short custodial sentence but the court is satisfied that the offender genuinely intends to reform his or her behaviour and there is a real prospect of rehabilitation, the court may consider it appropriate to impose a sentence that will allow this. This may mean imposing a suspended sentence order or a community order (where appropriate with a requirement to attend an accredited domestic violence programme).

PROTECTIVE ORDER, BREACH OF

Protection from Harassment Act 1997, s.5(5) (breach of restraining order)

Family Law Act 1996, s.42A (breach of non-molestation order)

Triable either way:

Maximum when tried summarily: Level 5 fine and/or 6 months

Maximum when tried on indictment: 5 years

Where the conduct is particularly serious, it would normally be charged as a separate offence. These starting points are based on the premise that the activity has either been prosecuted separately as an offence or is not of a character sufficient to justify prosecution of it as an offence in its own right.

Where offence committed in domestic context, refer to page [348] for guidance

<table>
<tr><td colspan="3" align="center">Offence seriousness (culpability and harm)

A. Identify the appropriate starting point

Starting points based on first time offender pleading not guilty</td></tr>
<tr><td>Examples of nature of activity</td><td>Starting point</td><td>Range</td></tr>
<tr><td>Single breach involving no/minimal direct contact</td><td>Low level community order</td><td>Band C fine to medium level community order</td></tr>
<tr><td>More than one breach involving no/minimal contact or some direct contact</td><td>Medium level community order</td><td>Low level community order to high level community order</td></tr>
<tr><td>Single breach involving some violence and/or significant physical or psychological harm to the victim</td><td>18 weeks custody</td><td>13 to 26 weeks custody</td></tr>
<tr><td>More than one breach involving some violence and/or significant physical or psychological harm to the victim</td><td>Crown Court</td><td>26 weeks custody to Crown Court</td></tr>
<tr><td>Breach (whether one or more) involving significant physical violence and significant physical or psychological harm to the victim</td><td>Crown Court</td><td>Crown Court</td></tr>
</table>

<table>
<tr><td colspan="2" align="center">Offence seriousness (culpability and harm)

B. Consider the effect of aggravating and mitigating factors (other than those within examples above)

Common aggravating and mitigating factors are identified in the pullout card – the following may be particularly relevant but these lists are not exhaustive</td></tr>
<tr><td>Factors indicating higher culpability</td><td>Factors indicating lower culpability</td></tr>
<tr><td>1. Proven history of violence or threats by the offender

2. Using contact arrangements with a child to instigate offence

3. Offence is a further breach, following earlier breach proceedings

4. Offender has history of disobedience to court orders

5. Breach committed immediately or shortly after order made</td><td>1. Breach occurred after long period of compliance

2. Victim initiated contact</td></tr>
</table>

Factors indicating greater degree of harm

1. Victim is particularly vulnerable

2. Impact on children

3. Victim is forced to leave home

Form a preliminary view of the appropriate sentence, then consider offender mitigation

Common factors are identified in the pullout card

Consider a reduction for a guilty plea

Consider ancillary orders

Refer to pages [339–346] for guidance on available ancillary orders

Decide sentence

Give reasons

PUBLIC ORDER ACT, S.2 – VIOLENT DISORDER

Public Order Act 1986, s.2

Triable either way:

Maximum when tried summarily: Level 5 fine and/or 6 months

Maximum when tried on indictment: 5 years

Identify dangerous offenders

This is a specified offence for the purposes of the public protection provisions in the Criminal Justice Act 2003 – refer to pages [358–359] and consult legal adviser for guidance

---

Offence seriousness (culpability and harm)

A. Identify the appropriate starting point

Starting points based on first time offender pleading not guilty

These offences should normally be dealt with in the Crown Court. However, there may be rare cases involving minor violence or threats of violence leading to no or minor injury, with few people involved and no weapon or missiles, in which a custodial sentence within the jurisdiction of a magistrates' court may be appropriate.

PUBLIC ORDER ACT, S.3 – AFFRAY

Public Order Act 1986, s.3

Triable either way:

Maximum when tried summarily: Level 5 fine and/or 6 months

Maximum when tried on indictment: 3 years

Identify dangerous offenders

This is a specified offence for the purposes of the public protection provisions in the Criminal Justice Act 2003 – refer to page[s 358–359] and consult legal adviser for guidance

---

Offence seriousness (culpability and harm)

A. Identify the appropriate starting point

Starting points based on first time offender pleading not guilty

Examples of nature of activity	Starting point	Range
Brief offence involving low-level violence, no substantial fear created	Low level community order	Band C fine to medium level community order
Degree of fighting or violence that causes substantial fear	High level community order	Medium level community order to 12 weeks custody
Fight involving a weapon/throwing objects, or conduct causing risk of serious injury	18 weeks custody	12 weeks custody to Crown Court

---

Offence seriousness (culpability and harm)

B. Consider the effect of aggravating and mitigating factors (other than those within examples above)

Common aggravating and mitigating factors are identified in the pullout card – the following may be particularly relevant but **these lists are not exhaustive**

Factors indicating higher culpability	Factors indicating lower culpability
1. Group action	1. Did not start the trouble
2. Threats	2. Provocation
3. Lengthy incident	3. Stopped as soon as police arrived
Factors indicating greater degree of harm	
1. Vulnerable person(s) present	
2. Injuries caused	
3. Damage to property	

Form a preliminary view of the appropriate sentence, then consider offender mitigation

Common factors are identified in the pullout card

Consider a reduction for a guilty plea

Consider ancillary orders, including compensation and football banning order (where appropriate)

Refer to pages [339–346] for guidance on available ancillary orders

Decide sentence

Give reasons

PUBLIC ORDER ACT, S.4 – THREATENING BEHAVIOUR – FEAR OR PROVOCATION OF VIOLENCE

Public Order Act 1986, s.4

RACIALLY OR RELIGIOUSLY AGGRAVATED THREATENING BEHAVIOUR

Crime and Disorder Act 1998, s.31

Threatening behaviour: triable only summarily

Maximum: Level 5 fine and/or 6 months

Racially or religiously aggravated threatening behaviour: triable either way

Maximum when tried summarily: Level 5 fine and/or 6 months

Maximum when tried on indictment: 2 years

Where offence committed in domestic context, refer to page [348] for guidance

Offence seriousness (culpability and harm)		
A. Identify the appropriate starting point		
Starting points based on first time offender pleading not guilty		
Examples of nature of activity	**Starting point**	**Range**
Fear or threat of low level immediate unlawful violence such as push, shove or spit	Low level community order	Band B fine to medium level community order
Fear or threat of medium level immediate unlawful violence such as punch	High level community order	Low level community order to 12 weeks custody
Fear or threat of high level immediate unlawful violence such as use of weapon; missile thrown; gang involvement	12 weeks custody	6 to 26 weeks custody

Offence seriousness (culpability and harm)	
B. Consider the effect of aggravating and mitigating factors (other than those within examples above)	
Common aggravating and mitigating factors are identified in the pullout card – the following may be particularly relevant but **these lists are not exhaustive**	
Factors indicating higher culpability	**Factors indicating lower culpability**
1. Planning	1. Impulsive action
2. Offender deliberately isolates victim	2. Short duration
3. Group action	3. Provocation
4. Threat directed at victim because of job	
5. History of antagonism towards victim	

Factors indicating greater degree of harm

1. Offence committed at school, hospital or other place where vulnerable persons may be present

2. Offence committed on enclosed premises such as public transport

3. Vulnerable victim(s)

4. Victim needs medical help/counselling

Form a preliminary view of the appropriate sentence.

If offender charged and convicted of the racially or religiously aggravated offence, increase the sentence to reflect this element

Refer to pages [349–351] for guidance

Consider offender mitigation

Common factors are identified in the pullout card

Consider a reduction for a guilty plea

Consider ancillary orders, including compensation and football banning order (where appropriate)

Refer to pages [339–346] for guidance on available ancillary orders

Decide sentence

Give reasons

PUBLIC ORDER ACT, S.4A – DISORDERLY BEHAVIOUR WITH INTENT TO CAUSE HARASSMENT, ALARM OR DISTRESS

Public Order Act 1986, s.4A

RACIALLY OR RELIGIOUSLY AGGRAVATED DISORDERLY BEHAVIOUR WITH INTENT TO CAUSE HARASSMENT, ALARM OR DISTRESS

Crime and Disorder Act 1998, s.31

Disorderly behaviour with intent to cause harassment, alarm or distress: triable only summarily

Maximum: Level 5 fine and/or 6 months

Racially or religiously aggravated disorderly behaviour with intent to cause harassment etc.: triable either way

Maximum when tried summarily: Level 5 fine and/or 6 months

Maximum when tried on indictment: 2 years

Offence seriousness (culpability and harm)		
A. Identify the appropriate starting point		
Starting points based on first time offender pleading not guilty		
Examples of nature of activity	**Starting point**	**Range**
Threats, abuse or insults made more than once but on same occasion against the same person e.g. while following down the street	Band C fine	Band B fine to low level community order
Group action or deliberately planned action against targeted victim	Medium level community order	Low level community order to 12 weeks custody
Weapon brandished or used or threats against vulnerable victim – course of conduct over longer period	12 weeks custody	High level community order to 26 weeks custody

Offence seriousness (culpability and harm)	
B. Consider the effect of aggravating and mitigating factors (other than those within examples above)	
Common aggravating and mitigating factors are identified in the pullout card – the following may be particularly relevant but **these lists are not exhaustive**	
Factors indicating higher culpability	**Factors indicating lower culpability**
1. High degree of planning	1. Very short period
2. Offender deliberately isolates victim	2. Provocation
Factors indicating greater degree of harm	
1. Offence committed in vicinity of victim's home	
2. Large number of people in vicinity	
3. Actual or potential escalation into violence	
4. Particularly serious impact on victim	

Form a preliminary view of the appropriate sentence.
If offender charged and convicted of the racially or religiously aggravated offence, increase the sentence to reflect this element
Refer to pages [349–351] for guidance
Consider offender mitigation
Common factors are identified in the pullout card
Consider a reduction for a guilty plea
Consider ancillary orders, including compensation and football banning order (where appropriate)
Refer to pages [339–346] for guidance on available ancillary orders
Decide sentence
Give reasons

PUBLIC ORDER ACT, S.5 – DISORDERLY BEHAVIOUR (HARASSMENT, ALARM OR DISTRESS)

Public Order Act 1986, s.5

RACIALLY OR RELIGIOUSLY AGGRAVATED DISORDERLY BEHAVIOUR

Crime and Disorder Act 1998, s.31

Disorderly behaviour: triable only summarily

Maximum: Level 3 fine

Racially or religiously aggravated disorderly behaviour: triable only summarily

Maximum: Level 4 fine

Offence seriousness (culpability and harm)		
A. Identify the appropriate starting point		
Starting points based on first time offender pleading not guilty		
Examples of nature of activity	**Starting point**	**Range**
Shouting, causing disturbance for some minutes	Band A fine	Conditional discharge to band B fine
Substantial disturbance caused	Band B fine	Band A fine to band C fine

251

Offence seriousness (culpability and harm)
B. Consider the effect of aggravating and mitigating factors (other than those within examples above)
Common aggravating and mitigating factors are identified in the pullout card – the following may be particularly relevant but **these lists are not exhaustive**

Factors indicating higher culpability	Factors indicating lower culpability
1. Group action	1. Stopped as soon as police arrived
2. Lengthy incident	2. Brief/minor incident
Factors indicating greater degree of harm	3. Provocation
1. Vulnerable person(s) present	
2. Offence committed at school, hospital or other place where vulnerable persons may be present	
3. Victim providing public service	

Form a preliminary view of the appropriate sentence. If offender charged and convicted of the racially or religiously aggravated offence, increase the sentence to reflect this element
Refer to pages [349–351] for guidance
Consider offender mitigation
Common factors are identified in the pullout card
Consider a reduction for a guilty plea
Consider ancillary orders, including compensation and football banning order (where appropriate)
Refer to pages [339–346] for guidance on available ancillary orders
Decide sentence
Give reasons

RAILWAY FARE EVASION

Regulation of Railways Act 1889, s.5(3) (travelling on railway without paying fare, with intent to avoid payment); s.5(1) (failing to produce ticket)

Triable only summarily:

Maximum: Level 3 fine or 3 months (s.5(3)); level 2 fine (s.5(1))

Offence seriousness (culpability and harm)

A. Identify the appropriate starting point

Starting points based on first time offender pleading not guilty

Examples of nature of activity	Starting point	Range
Failing to produce ticket or pay fare on request	Band A fine	Conditional discharge to band B fine
Travelling on railway without having paid the fare or knowingly and wilfully travelling beyond the distance paid for, with intent to avoid payment	Band B fine	Band A fine to band C fine

Offence seriousness (culpability and harm)

B. Consider the effect of aggravating and mitigating factors (other than those within examples above)

Common aggravating and mitigating factors are identified in the pullout card – the following may be particularly relevant but **these lists are not exhaustive**

Factors indicating higher culpability 1. Offensive or intimidating language or behaviour towards railway staff **Factor indicating greater degree of harm** 1. High level of loss caused or intended to be caused	

Form a preliminary view of the appropriate sentence, then consider offender mitigation

Common factors are identified in the pullout card

Consider a reduction for a guilty plea

Consider ancillary orders, including compensation

Refer to pages [339–346] for guidance on available ancillary orders

Decide sentence

Give reasons

School non-attendance

Education Act 1996, s.444(1) (parent fails to secure regular attendance at school of registered pupil); s.444(1A) (parent knowingly fails to secure regular attendance at school of registered pupil)

Triable only summarily

Maximum: Level 3 fine (s.444(1)); level 4 fine and/or 3 months (s.444(1A))

Offence seriousness (culpability and harm)		
A. Identify the appropriate starting point		
Starting points based on first time offender pleading not guilty		
Examples of nature of activity	**Starting point**	**Range**
Short period following previous good attendance (s.444(1))	Band A fine	Conditional discharge to band A fine
Erratic attendance for long period (s.444(1))	Band B fine	Band B fine to Band C fine
Colluding in and condoning non-attendance or deliberately instigating non-attendance (s.444(1A))	Medium level community order	Low level community order to high level community order

Offence seriousness (culpability and harm)
B. Consider the effect of aggravating and mitigating factors (other than those within examples above)
Common aggravating and mitigating factors are identified in the pullout card – the following may be particularly relevant but **these lists are not exhaustive**

Factors indicating higher culpability	**Factors indicating lower culpability**
1. Parental collusion (s.444(1) only)	1. Parent unaware of child's whereabouts
2. Lack of parental effort to ensure attendance (s.444(1) only)	2. Parent tried to ensure attendance
3. Threats to teachers and/or officials	3. Parent concerned by child's allegations of bullying/unable to get school to address bullying
4. Refusal to co-operate with school and/or officials	
Factors indicating greater degree of harm	
1. More than one child	
2. Harmful effect on other children in family	

Form a preliminary view of the appropriate sentence, then consider offender mitigation
Common factors are identified in the pullout card
Consider a reduction for a guilty plea
Consider ancillary orders, including parenting order
Refer to pages [339–346] for guidance on available ancillary orders
Decide sentence
Give reasons

SEX OFFENDERS REGISTER – FAIL TO COMPLY WITH NOTIFICATION REQUIRE-
MENTS

Sexual Offences Act 2003, s.91(1)(a) (fail to comply with notification requirements); s.91(1)(b) (supply false information)

Triable either way:

Maximum when tried summarily: Level 5 fine and/or 6 months

Maximum when tried on indictment: 5 years

<table>
<tr><td colspan="3" align="center">Offence seriousness (culpability and harm)

A. Identify the appropriate starting point

Starting points based on first time offender (see note below) pleading not guilty</td></tr>
<tr><td>Examples of nature of activity</td><td>Starting point</td><td>Range</td></tr>
<tr><td>Negligent or inadvertent failure to comply with requirements</td><td>Medium level community order</td><td>Band C fine to high level community order</td></tr>
<tr><td>Deliberate failure to comply with requirements OR

Supply of information known to be false</td><td>6 weeks custody</td><td>High level community order to 26 weeks custody</td></tr>
<tr><td>Conduct as described in box above AND

Long period of non-compliance OR

Attempts to avoid detection</td><td>18 weeks custody</td><td>6 weeks custody to Crown Court</td></tr>
</table>

<table>
<tr><td colspan="2" align="center">Offence seriousness (culpability and harm)

B. Consider the effect of aggravating and mitigating factors (other than those within examples above)

Common aggravating and mitigating factors are identified in the pullout card – the following may be particularly relevant but these lists are not exhaustive</td></tr>
<tr><td>Factors indicating higher culpability
1. Long period of non-compliance (where not in the examples above)
Factor indicating greater degree of harm
1. Alarm or distress caused to victim
2. Particularly serious original offence</td><td>Factors indicating lower culpability
1. Genuine misunderstanding</td></tr>
</table>

<table>
<tr><td align="center">Form a preliminary view of the appropriate sentence, then consider offender mitigation
Common factors are identified in the pullout card</td></tr>
<tr><td align="center">Consider a reduction for a guilty plea</td></tr>
<tr><td align="center">Consider ancillary orders
Refer to pages [339–346] for guidance on available ancillary orders</td></tr>
<tr><td align="center">Decide sentence
Give reasons</td></tr>
</table>

Note

An offender convicted of this offence will always have at least one relevant previous conviction for the offence that resulted in the notification requirements being imposed. The starting points and ranges take this into account; any other previous convictions should be considered in the usual way – see pages [178] and [317].

SEXUAL ACTIVITY IN A PUBLIC LAVATORY

Sexual Offences Act 2003, s.71

Triable only summarily

Maximum: Level 5 fine and/or 6 months

This guideline and accompanying notes are taken from the Sentencing Guidelines Council's definitive guideline *Sexual Offences Act 2003*, published 30 April 2007

Key factors

(a) This offence is committed where an offender intentionally engages in sexual activity in a public lavatory. It was introduced to give adults and children the freedom to use public lavatories for the purpose for which they are designed, without the fear of being an unwilling witness to overtly sexual behaviour of a kind that most people would not expect to be conducted in public. It is primarily a public order offence rather than a sexual offence.

(b) When dealing with a repeat offender, the starting point should be a low level community order with a range of Band C fine to medium level community order. The presence of aggravating factors may suggest that a sentence above the range is appropriate.

(c) This guideline may be relevant by way of analogy to conduct charged as the common law offence of outraging public decency; the offence is triable either way and has a maximum penalty of a level 5 fine and/or 6 months imprisonment when tried summarily.

Offence seriousness (culpability and harm)		
A. Identify the appropriate starting point		
Starting points based on first time offender pleading not guilty		
Examples of nature of activity	**Starting point**	**Range**
Basic offence as defined in the Act, assuming no aggravating or mitigating factors	Band C fine	Band C fine
Offence with aggravating factors	Low level community order	Band C fine to medium level community order

Offence seriousness (culpability and harm)
B. Consider the effect of aggravating and mitigating factors (other than those within examples above)
Common aggravating and mitigating factors are identified in the pullout card – the following may be particularly relevant but **these lists are not exhaustive**

Factors indicating higher culpability	
1. Intimidating behaviour/threats of violence to member(s) of the public	
2. Blatant behaviour	

Form a preliminary view of the appropriate sentence, then consider offender mitigation
Common factors are identified in the pullout card
Consider a reduction for a guilty plea
Consider ancillary orders, including compensation
Refer to pages [339–346] for guidance on available ancillary orders
Decide sentence
Give reasons

SEXUAL ASSAULT

Sexual Offences Act 2003, ss.3 and 7 (sexual assault of child under 13)

Triable either way:

Maximum when tried summarily: Level 5 fine and/or 6 months

Maximum when tried on indictment: 10 years (s.3), 14 years (s.7)

This guideline is taken from the Sentencing Guidelines Council's definitive guideline *Sexual Offences Act 2003*, published 30 April 2007

Identify dangerous offenders
These are serious offences for the purposes of the public protection provisions in the Criminal Justice Act 2003 – refer to page[s 358–359] and consult legal adviser for guidance

Offence seriousness (culpability and harm)		
A. Identify the appropriate starting point		
Starting points based on first time offender pleading not guilty		
Examples of nature of activity	**Starting point**	**Range**
Contact between part of offender's body (other than the genitalia) with part of the victim's body (other than the genitalia)	26 weeks custody if the victim is under 13	4 weeks custody to Crown Court
	Medium level community order if the victim is aged 13 or over	Band C fine to 6 weeks custody
Contact between naked genitalia of offender and another part of victim's body	Crown Court if the victim is under 13	Crown Court
Contact with naked genitalia of victim by offender using part of his or her body other than the genitalia, or an object	Crown Court if the victim is aged 13 or over	26 weeks custody to Crown Court
Contact between either the clothed genitalia of offender and naked genitalia of victim or naked genitalia of offender and clothed genitalia of victim		
Contact between naked genitalia of offender and naked genitalia, face or mouth of the victim	Crown Court	Crown Court

Offence seriousness (culpability and harm)	
B. Consider the effect of aggravating and mitigating factors (other than those within examples above)	
Common aggravating and mitigating factors are identified in the pullout card – the following may be particularly relevant but **these lists are not exhaustive**	
Factors indicating higher culpability	**Factors indicating lower culpability**
1. Background of intimidation or coercion	1. Youth and immaturity of the offender
2. Use of drugs, alcohol or other substance to facilitate the offence	2. Minimal or fleeting contact
3. Threats to prevent the victim reporting the incident	*Where the victim is aged 16 or over*
4. Abduction or detention	3. Victim engaged in consensual activity with the offender on the same occasion and immediately before the offence
5. Offender aware that he or she is suffering from a sexually transmitted infection	
6. Prolonged activity or contact	

Factors indicating greater degree of harm	Where the victim is under 16
1. Offender ejaculated or caused victim to ejaculate 2. Physical harm caused	4. Sexual activity between two children (one of whom is the offender) was mutually agreed and experimental

Form a preliminary view of the appropriate sentence, then consider offender mitigation Common factors are identified in the pullout card
Consider a reduction for a guilty plea
Consider ancillary orders, including compensation Refer to pages [339–346] for guidance on available ancillary orders
Decide sentence
Give reasons

Note

(a) In accordance with section 80 and schedule 3 of the Sexual Offences Act 2003, automatic notification requirements apply upon conviction to an offender aged 18 or over where:

(1) the victim was under 18; or

(2) a term of imprisonment or a community sentence of at least 12 months is imposed.

SOCIAL SECURITY BENEFIT, FALSE STATEMENT/REPRESENTATION TO OBTAIN

Social Security Administration Act 1992, s.111A (dishonestly makes false statement/ representation); s.112 (makes statement/ representation known to be false)

S.111A offence: triable either way

Maximum when tried summarily: Level 5 fine and/or 6 months

Maximum when tried on indictment: 7 years

S.112 offence: triable only summarily

Maximum: Level 5 fine and/or 3 months

This guideline reflects the Court of Appeal's decisions in *R v. Stewart* [1987] 2 All ER 383 and *R v. Graham and Whatley* [2004] EWCA Crim 2755. Further consideration is being given to the appropriate approach to sentencing for this offence in the context of the Council and Panel's work on fraud offences; this may result in a revised guideline being issued in a future update.

Offence seriousness (culpability and harm)

A. Identify the appropriate starting point

Starting points based on first time offender pleading not guilty

Examples of nature of activity	Starting point	Range
Claim fraudulent from the start, up to £5,000 obtained (s.111A or 112)	Medium level community order	Band B fine to high level community order
Claim fraudulent from the start, more than £5,000 but less than £20,000 obtained	12 weeks custody	Medium level community order to Crown Court
Claim fraudulent from the start, large-scale, professional offending	Crown Court	Crown Court

---

Offence seriousness (culpability and harm)

B. Consider the effect of aggravating and mitigating factors (other than those within examples above)

Common aggravating and mitigating factors are identified in the pullout card – the following may be particularly relevant but **these lists are not exhaustive**

Factors indicating higher culpability	Factors indicating lower culpability
1. Offending carried out over a long period	1. Pressurised by others
2. Offender acting in unison with one or more others	2. Claim initially legitimate
3. Planning	**Factor indicating lesser degree of harm**
4. Offender motivated by greed or desire to live beyond his/her means	1. Voluntary repayment of amounts overpaid
5. False identities or other personal details used	
6. False or forged documents used	
7. Official documents altered or falsified	

Form a preliminary view of the appropriate sentence, then consider offender mitigation

Common factors are identified in the pullout card

Consider a reduction for a guilty plea

Consider ancillary orders, including compensation

Refer to pages [339–346] for guidance on available ancillary orders

Decide sentence

Give reasons

Note

A maximum of £5,000 compensation may be imposed for each offence of which the offender has been convicted. The above guidelines have been drafted on the assumption that, in most cases, the Department for Work and Pensions will take separate steps to recover the overpayment.

TAX CREDIT FRAUD

Tax Credits Act 2002, s.35

Triable either way:

Maximum when tried summarily: Level 5 fine and/or 6 months

Maximum when tried on indictment: 7 years

Awaiting SGC guideline

TAXI TOUTING/SOLICITING FOR HIRE

Criminal Justice and Public Order Act 1994, s.167

Triable only summarily:

Maximum: Level 4 fine

Offence seriousness (culpability and harm)		
A. Identify the appropriate starting point		
Starting points based on first time offender pleading not guilty		
Examples of nature of activity	**Starting point**	**Range**
Licensed taxi-driver touting for trade (i.e. making approach rather than waiting for a person to initiate hiring)	Band A fine	Conditional discharge to band A fine and consider disqualification 1–3 months
PHV licence held but touting for trade rather than being booked through an operator; an accomplice to touting	Band B fine	Band A fine to band C fine and consider disqualification 3–6 months
No PHV licence held	Band C fine	Band B fine to Band C fine and disqualification 6–12 months

Note: refer to page [323] for approach to fines for offences committed for commercial purposes

Offence seriousness (culpability and harm)
B. Consider the effect of aggravating and mitigating factors (other than those within examples above)
Common aggravating and mitigating factors are identified in the pullout card – the following may be particularly relevant but **these lists are not exhaustive**

Factors indicating higher culpability	Factors indicating lower culpability
1. Commercial business/large scale operation	1. Providing a service when no licensed taxi available
2. No insurance/invalid insurance	
3. No driving licence and/or no MOT	
4. Vehicle not roadworthy	
Factors indicating greater degree of harm	
1. Deliberately diverting trade from taxi rank	
2. PHV licence had been refused/offender ineligible for licence	

Form a preliminary view of the appropriate sentence, then consider offender mitigation
Common factors are identified in the pullout card
Consider a reduction for a guilty plea
Consider ancillary orders
Refer to pages [339–346] for guidance on available ancillary orders
Consider disqualification from driving and deprivation of property
Decide sentence
Give reasons

THEFT – GENERAL PRINCIPLES

1. The guideline *Theft and Burglary in a building other than a dwelling*, published by the Sentencing Guidelines Council 9 December 2008 covers four forms of theft. However, the principles relating to the assessment of seriousness in the guideline are of general application and are likely to be of assistance where a court is sentencing for a form of theft not covered by a specific guideline. These are summarised below for ease of reference.

Assessing seriousness

(i) Culpability and harm

2. As it is an essential element of the offence of theft that the offender acted dishonestly, an offender convicted of theft will have a high level of culpability. Even so, the precise level of culpability will vary according to factors such as the offender's motivation, whether the offence was planned or spontaneous and whether the offender was in a position of trust. An offence will be aggravated where there is evidence of planning.

3. When assessing the harm caused by a theft offence, the starting point is normally based on the loss suffered by the victim. Whilst, in general, the greater the loss, the more serious the offence, the monetary value of the loss may not reflect the full extent of the harm caused by the offence. The court should also take into account the impact of the offence on the victim (which may be significantly greater than the monetary value of the loss; this may be particularly important where the value of the loss is high in proportion to the victim's financial circumstances even though relatively low in absolute terms), any harm to persons other than the direct victim, and any harm in the form of public concern or erosion of public confidence.

(ii) Aggravating and mitigating factors

4. The most common factors that are likely to aggravate an offence of theft are:

    factors indicating higher culpability: planning of an offence, offenders operating in groups or gangs, and deliberate targeting of vulnerable victims
    factors indicating a more than usually serious degree of harm: victim is particularly vulnerable, high level of gain from the offence, and high value (including sentimental value) of property to the victim or substantial consequential loss

(iii) Offender mitigation

5. The Council has identified the following matters of offender mitigation that might apply to offences of theft:

    (a) *Return of stolen property* – depending on the circumstances and in particular, the voluntariness and timeliness of the return.
    (b) *Impact on sentence of offender's dependency* – where an offence is motivated by an addiction (often to drugs, alcohol or gambling) this does not mitigate the seriousness of the offence, but a dependency may properly influence the type of sentence imposed. In particular, it may sometimes be appropriate to impose a drug rehabilitation requirement, an alcohol treatment requirement (for dependent drinkers) or an activity or supervision requirement including alcohol specific information, advice and support (for harmful and hazardous drinkers) as part of a community order or a suspended sentence order in an attempt to break the cycle of addiction and offending, even if an immediate custodial sentence would otherwise be warranted.
    (c) *Offender motivated by desperation or need* – the fact that an offence has been committed in desperation or need arising from particular hardship may count as offender mitigation in **exceptional circumstances**.

THEFT – BREACH OF TRUST – FACTORS TO TAKE INTO CONSIDERATION

This guideline and accompanying notes are taken from the Sentencing Guidelines Council's definitive guideline *Theft and Burglary in a building other than a dwelling*, published 9 December 2008

Key factors

(a) When assessing the harm caused by this offence, the starting point should be the loss suffered by the victim. In general, the greater the loss, the more serious the offence. However, the monetary value of the loss may not reflect the full extent of the harm caused by the offence. The court should also take into account the

263

impact of the offence on the victim (which may be significant and disproportionate to the value of the loss having regard to their financial circumstances),
any harm to persons other than the direct victim, and any harm in the form of
public concern or erosion of public confidence.

(b) In general terms, the seriousness of the offence will increase in line with the level
of trust breached. The extent to which the nature and degree of trust placed in
an offender should be regarded as increasing seriousness will depend on a careful
assessment of the circumstances of each individual case, including the type and
terms of the relationship between the offender and victim.

(c) The concept of breach of trust for the purposes of the offence of theft includes
employer/employee relationships and those between a professional adviser and
client. It also extends to relationships in which a person is in a position of
authority in relation to the victim or would be expected to have a duty to protect
the interests of the victim, such as medical, social or care workers. The targeting
of a vulnerable victim by an offender through a relationship or position of trust
will indicate a higher level of culpability.

(d) The Council has identified the following matters of offender mitigation which
may be relevant to this offence:

(i) *Return of stolen property*
Whether and the degree to which the return of stolen property constitutes
a matter of offender mitigation will depend on an assessment of the
circumstances and, in particular, the voluntariness and timeliness of the
return.

(ii) *Impact on sentence of offender's dependency*
Where an offence is motivated by an addiction (often to drugs, alcohol or
gambling) this does not mitigate the seriousness of the offence, but a
dependency may properly influence the type of sentence imposed. In
particular, it may sometimes be appropriate to impose a drug rehabilitation
requirement, an alcohol treatment requirement (for dependent drinkers) or
an activity or supervision requirement including alcohol specific information, advice and support (for harmful and hazardous drinkers) as part of a
community order or a suspended sentence order in an attempt to break the
cycle of addiction and offending, even if an immediate custodial sentence
would otherwise be warranted.

(iii) *Offender motivated by desperation or need*
The fact that an offence has been committed in desperation or need arising
from particular hardship may count as offender mitigation in **exceptional
circumstances**.

(iv) *Inappropriate degree of trust or responsibility*
The fact that an offender succumbed to temptation having been placed in a
position of trust or given responsibility to an inappropriate degree may be
regarded as offender mitigation.

(v) *Voluntary cessation of offending*
The fact that an offender voluntarily ceased offending before being discov-
ered does not reduce the seriousness of the offence. However, if the claim
to have stopped offending is genuine, it may constitute offender mitigation,
particularly if it is evidence of remorse.

(vi) *Reporting an undiscovered offence*
Where an offender brings the offending to the attention of his or her
employer or the authorities, this may be treated as offender mitigation.

(f) In many cases of theft in breach of trust, termination of an offender's employment will be a natural consequence of committing the offence. Other than in the most exceptional of circumstances, loss of employment and any consequential hardship should *not* constitute offender mitigation.

(g) Where a court is satisfied that a custodial sentence is appropriate for an offence of theft in breach of trust, consideration should be given to whether that sentence can be suspended in accordance with the criteria in the Council guideline *New Sentences: Criminal Justice Act 2003*. A suspended sentence may be particularly appropriate where this would allow for reparation to be made either to the victim or to the community at large.

THEFT – BREACH OF TRUST

Theft Act 1968, s.1

Triable either way:

Maximum when tried summarily: Level 5 fine and/or 6 months

Maximum when tried on indictment: 7 years

Offence seriousness (culpability and harm)		
A. Identify the appropriate starting point		
Starting points based on first time offender pleading not guilty		
Examples of nature of activity	**Starting point**	**Range**
Theft of less than £2,000	Medium level community order	Band B fine to 26 weeks custody
Theft of £2,000 or more but less than £20,000 OR Theft of less than £2,000 in breach of a high degree of trust	18 weeks custody	High level community order to Crown Court
Theft of £20,000 or more OR Theft of £2,000 or more in breach of a high degree of trust	Crown Court	Crown Court

Offence seriousness (culpability and harm)	
B. Consider the effect of aggravating and mitigating factors (other than those within examples above)	
Common aggravating and mitigating factors are identified in the pullout card – the following may be particularly relevant but **these lists are not exhaustive**	
Factors indicating higher culpability	
1. Long course of offending	
2. Suspicion deliberately thrown on others	
3. Offender motivated by intention to cause harm or out of revenge	

Form a preliminary view of the appropriate sentence, then consider offender mitigation
Common factors are identified in the pullout card – see also note (d) opposite
Consider a reduction for a guilty plea
Consider ancillary orders, including compensation
Refer to pages [339–346] for guidance on available ancillary orders
Decide sentence
Give reasons

THEFT – DWELLING – FACTORS TO TAKE INTO CONSIDERATION

This guideline and accompanying notes are taken from the Sentencing Guidelines Council's definitive guideline *Theft and Burglary in a building other than a dwelling*, published 9 December 2008

Key factors

(a) The category of theft in a dwelling covers the situation where a theft is committed by an offender who is present in a dwelling with the authority of the owner or occupier. Examples include thefts by lodgers or visitors to the victim's residence, such as friends, relatives or salespeople. Such offences involve a violation of the privacy of the victim's home and constitute an abuse of the victim's trust. Where an offender enters a dwelling as a trespasser in order to commit theft, his or her conduct will generally constitute the more serious offence of burglary; **this guideline does not apply where the offender has been convicted of burglary – see pages [197–199] for guidance**.

(b) The starting points and sentencing ranges in this guideline are based on the assumption that the offender was motivated by greed or a desire to live beyond his or her means. To avoid double counting, such a motivation should not be treated as a factor that increases culpability.

(c) For the purpose of this guideline, a 'vulnerable victim' is a person targeted by the offender because it is anticipated that he or she is unlikely or unable to resist the theft. The exploitation of a vulnerable victim indicates a high level of culpability and will influence the category of seriousness into which the offence falls.

(d) The guideline is based on the assumption that most thefts in a dwelling do not involve property of high monetary value or of high value to the victim. Where the property stolen is of high monetary value or of high value (including sentimental value) to the victim, the appropriate sentence may be beyond the range into which the offence otherwise would fall. For the purpose of this form of theft property worth more than £2,000 should generally be regarded as being of 'high monetary value', although this will depend on an assessment of all the circumstances of the particular case.

(e) A sentence beyond the range into which the offence otherwise would fall may also be appropriate where the effect on the victim is particularly severe or where substantial consequential loss results (such as where the theft of equipment causes serious disruption to the victim's life or business).

(f) The Council has identified the following matters of offender mitigation which may be relevant to this offence:

(i) *Return of stolen property*

Whether and the degree to which the return of stolen property constitutes a matter of offender mitigation will depend on an assessment of the circumstances and, in particular, the voluntariness and timeliness of the return.

(ii) *Impact on sentence of offender's dependency*

Where an offence is motivated by an addiction (often to drugs, alcohol or gambling) this does not mitigate the seriousness of the offence, but a dependency may properly influence the type of sentence imposed. In particular, it may sometimes be appropriate to impose a drug rehabilitation requirement, an alcohol treatment requirement (for dependent drinkers) or an activity or supervision requirement including alcohol specific information, advice and support (for harmful and hazardous drinkers) as part of a community order or a suspended sentence order in an attempt to break the cycle of addiction and offending, even if an immediate custodial sentence would otherwise be warranted.

(iii) *Offender motivated by desperation or need*

The fact that an offence has been committed in desperation or need arising from particular hardship may count as offender mitigation in **exceptional circumstances**.

THEFT – DWELLING

Theft Act 1968, s.1

Triable either way:

Maximum when tried summarily: Level 5 fine and/or 6 months

Maximum when tried on indictment: 7 years

Offence seriousness (culpability and harm)		
A. Identify the appropriate starting point		
Starting points based on first time offender pleading not guilty		
Examples of nature of activity	**Starting point**	**Range**
Where the effect on the victim is particularly severe, the stolen property is of high value (as defined in note (d) opposite), or substantial consequential loss results, a sentence higher than the range into which the offence otherwise would fall may be appropriate		
Theft in a dwelling not involving vulnerable victim	Medium level community order	Band B fine to 18 weeks custody
Theft from a vulnerable victim (as defined in note (c) opposite)	18 weeks custody	High level community order to Crown Court
Theft from a vulnerable victim (as defined in note (c) opposite) involving intimidation or the use or threat of force (falling short of robbery) or the use of deception	Crown Court	Crown Court

<table>
<tr><td colspan="2" align="center">**Offence seriousness (culpability and harm)**

B. Consider the effect of aggravating and mitigating factors (other than those within examples above)

Common aggravating and mitigating factors are identified in the pullout card – the following may be particularly relevant but **these lists are not exhaustive**</td></tr>
<tr><td>

Factors indicating higher culpability

1. Offender motivated by intention to cause harm or out of revenge

Factors indicating greater degree of harm

1. Intimidation or face-to-face confrontation with victim [except where this raises the offence into a higher sentencing range]

2. Use of force, or threat of force, against victim (not amounting to robbery) [except where this raises the offence into a higher sentencing range]

3. Use of deception [except where this raises the offence into a higher sentencing range]

4. Offender takes steps to prevent the victim from reporting the crime or seeking help

</td><td></td></tr>
</table>

Form a preliminary view of the appropriate sentence, then consider offender mitigation Common factors are identified in the pullout card – see also note (f) opposite
Consider a reduction for a guilty plea
Consider ancillary orders, including compensation Refer to pages [339–346] for guidance on available ancillary orders
Decide sentence **Give reasons**

THEFT – PERSON – FACTORS TO TAKE INTO CONSIDERATION

This guideline and accompanying notes are taken from the Sentencing Guidelines Council's definitive guideline *Theft and Burglary in a building other than a dwelling*, published 9 December 2008

Key factors

(a) Theft from the person may encompass conduct such as 'pick-pocketing', where the victim is unaware that the property is being stolen, as well as the snatching of handbags, wallets, jewellery and mobile telephones from the victim's possession or from the vicinity of the victim. The offence constitutes an invasion of the victim's privacy and may cause the victim to experience distress, fear and inconvenience either during or after the event. While in some cases the conduct may be similar, **this guideline does not apply where the offender has been convicted of robbery; sentencers should instead refer to the Council guideline on robbery.**

(b)   The starting points and sentencing ranges in this guideline are based on the assumption that the offender was motivated by greed or a desire to live beyond his or her means. To avoid double counting, such a motivation should not be treated as a factor that increases culpability.

(c)   For the purpose of this guideline, a 'vulnerable victim' is a person targeted by the offender because it is anticipated that he or she is unlikely or unable to resist the theft. Young or elderly persons, or those with disabilities may fall into this category. The exploitation of a vulnerable victim indicates a high level of culpability and will influence the category of seriousness into which the offence falls.

(d)   Offences of this type will be aggravated where there is evidence of planning, such as where tourists are targeted because of their unfamiliarity with an area and a perception that they will not be available to give evidence.

(e)   The guideline is based on the assumption that most thefts from the person do not involve property of high monetary value or of high value to the victim. Where the stolen property is of high monetary value or of high value (including sentimental value) to the victim, the appropriate sentence may be beyond the range into which the offence otherwise would fall. For the purposes of this form of theft, 'high monetary value' is defined as more than £2,000.

(f)   A sentence beyond the range into which the offence otherwise would fall may also be appropriate where the effect on the victim is particularly severe or where substantial consequential loss results (such as where the theft of equipment causes serious disruption to the victim's life or business).

(g)   The Council has identified the following matters of offender mitigation which may be relevant to this offence:

   (i)   *Return of stolen property*
         Whether and the degree to which the return of stolen property constitutes a matter of offender mitigation will depend on an assessment of the circumstances and, in particular, the voluntariness and timeliness of the return.

   (ii) *Impact on sentence of offender's dependency*
         Where an offence is motivated by an addiction (often to drugs, alcohol or gambling) this does not mitigate the seriousness of the offence, but a dependency may properly influence the type of sentence imposed. In particular, it may sometimes be appropriate to impose a drug rehabilitation requirement, an alcohol treatment requirement (for dependent drinkers) or an activity or supervision requirement including alcohol specific information, advice and support (for harmful and hazardous drinkers) as part of a community order or a suspended sentence order in an attempt to break the cycle of addiction and offending, even if an immediate custodial sentence would otherwise be warranted.

   (iii) *Offender motivated by desperation or need*
         The fact that an offence has been committed in desperation or need arising from particular hardship may count as offender mitigation in **exceptional circumstances.**

THEFT – PERSON

Theft Act 1968, s.1

Triable either way:

Maximum when tried summarily: Level 5 fine and/or 6 months

Maximum when tried on indictment: 7 years

Offence seriousness (culpability and harm)

A. Identify the appropriate starting point

Starting points based on first time offender pleading not guilty

Examples of nature of activity	Starting point	Range
Where the effect on the victim is particularly severe, the stolen property is of high value (as defined in note (f) opposite), or substantial consequential loss results, a sentence higher than the range into which the offence otherwise would fall may be appropriate		
Theft from the person not involving vulnerable victim	Medium level community order	Band B fine to 18 weeks custody
Theft from a vulnerable victim (as defined in note (c) opposite)	18 weeks custody	High level community order to Crown Court
Theft involving the use or threat of force (falling short of robbery) against a vulnerable victim (as defined in note (c) opposite)	Crown Court	Crown Court

Offence seriousness (culpability and harm)

B. Consider the effect of aggravating and mitigating factors (other than those within examples above)

Common aggravating and mitigating factors are identified in the pullout card – the following may be particularly relevant but **these lists are not exhaustive**

Factors indicating higher culpability

1. Offender motivated by intention to cause harm or out of revenge

Factors indicating greater degree of harm

1. Intimidation or face-to-face confrontation with victim [except where this raises the offence into a higher sentencing range]

2. Use of force, or threat of force, against victim (not amounting to robbery) [except where this raises the offence into a higher sentencing range]

3. High level of inconvenience caused to victim, e.g. replacing house keys, credit cards etc

Form a preliminary view of the appropriate sentence, then consider offender mitigation Common factors are identified in the pullout card – see also note (g) opposite
Consider a reduction for a guilty plea
Consider ancillary orders, including compensation Refer to pages [339–346] for guidance on available ancillary orders
Decide sentence **Give reasons**

THEFT – SHOP – FACTORS TO TAKE INTO CONSIDERATION

This guideline and accompanying notes are taken from the Sentencing Guidelines Council's definitive guideline *Theft and Burglary in a building other than a dwelling*, published 9 December 2008

Key factors

(a) The circumstances of this offence can vary significantly. At the least serious end of the scale are thefts involving low value goods, no (or little) planning and no violence or damage; a non-custodial sentence will usually be appropriate for a first time offender. At the higher end of the spectrum are thefts involving organised gangs or groups or the threat or use of force and a custodial starting point will usually be appropriate.

(b) The starting points and sentencing ranges in this guideline are based on the assumption that the offender was motivated by greed or a desire to live beyond his or her means. To avoid double counting, such a motivation should not be treated as a factor that increases culpability.

(c) When assessing the level of harm, the circumstances of the retailer are a proper consideration; a greater level of harm may be caused where the theft is against a small retailer.

(d) Retailers may suffer additional loss as a result of this type of offending such as the cost of preventative security measures, higher insurance premiums and time spent by staff dealing with the prosecution of offenders. However, the seriousness of an individual case must be judged on its own dimension of harm and culpability and the sentence on an individual offender should not be increased to reflect the harm caused to retailers in general by the totality of this type of offending.

(e) Any recent previous convictions for theft and dishonesty offences will need to be taken into account in sentencing. Where an offender demonstrates a level of 'persistent' or 'seriously persistent' offending, the community and custody thresholds may be crossed even though the other characteristics of the offence would otherwise warrant a lesser sentence.

(f) The list of aggravating and mitigating factors on the pullout card identifies high value as an aggravating factor in property offences. In cases of theft from a shop, theft of high value goods may be associated with other aggravating factors such as the degree of planning, professionalism and/or operating in a group, and care will need to be taken to avoid double counting. Deliberately targeting high value goods will always make an offence more serious.

(g) The Council has identified the following matters of offender mitigation which may be relevant to this offence:

271

(i) *Return of stolen property*
Whether and the degree to which the return of stolen property constitutes a matter of offender mitigation will depend on an assessment of the circumstances and, in particular, the voluntariness and timeliness of the return.

(ii) *Impact on sentence of offender's dependency*
Where an offence is motivated by an addiction (often to drugs, alcohol or gambling) this does not mitigate the seriousness of the offence, but a dependency may properly influence the type of sentence imposed. In particular, it may sometimes be appropriate to impose a drug rehabilitation requirement, an alcohol treatment requirement (for dependent drinkers) or an activity or supervision requirement including alcohol specific information, advice and support (for harmful and hazardous drinkers) as part of a community order or a suspended sentence order in an attempt to break the cycle of addiction and offending, even if an immediate custodial sentence would otherwise be warranted.

(iii) *Offender motivated by desperation or need*
The fact that an offence has been committed in desperation or need arising from particular hardship may count as offender mitigation in **exceptional circumstances**.

THEFT – SHOP

Theft Act 1968, s.1

Triable either way:

Maximum when tried summarily: Level 5 fine and/or 6 months

Maximum when tried on indictment: 7 years

Offence seriousness (culpability and harm)		
A. Identify the appropriate starting point		
Starting points based on first time offender pleading not guilty		
Examples of nature of activity	**Starting point**	**Range**
Little or no planning or sophistication **and** Goods stolen of low value	Band B fine	Conditional discharge to low level community order
Low level intimidation or threats **or** Some planning e.g. a session of stealing on the same day or going equipped **or** Some related damage	Low level community order	Band B fine to medium level community order
Significant intimidation or threats **or** Use of force resulting in slight injury **or** Very high level of planning **or** Significant related damage	6 weeks custody	High level community order to Crown Court
Organised gang/group **and** Intimidation or the use or threat of force (short of robbery)	Crown Court	Crown Court

---

Offence seriousness (culpability and harm)

B. Consider the effect of aggravating and mitigating factors (other than those within examples above)

Common aggravating and mitigating factors are identified in the pullout card – the following may be particularly relevant but **these lists are not exhaustive**

Factors indicating higher culpability	
1. Child accompanying offender is involved or aware of theft	
2. Offender is subject to a banning order that includes the store targeted	
3. Offender motivated by intention to cause harm or out of revenge	
4. Professional offending	
Factors indicating greater degree of harm	
1. Victim particularly vulnerable (e.g. small independent shop)	
2. Offender targeted high value goods	

Form a preliminary view of the appropriate sentence, then consider offender mitigation

Common factors are identified in the pullout card – see also note (g) opposite

Consider a reduction for a guilty plea

Consider ancillary orders, including compensation

Refer to pages [339–346] for guidance on available ancillary orders

Decide sentence

Give reasons

THREATS TO KILL

Offences Against the Person Act 1861, s.16

Triable either way:

Maximum when tried summarily: Level 5 fine and/or 6 months

Maximum when tried on indictment: 10 years

Where offence committed in domestic context, refer to page [348] for guidance

---

Identify dangerous offenders

This is a serious offence for the purposes of the public protection provisions in the Criminal Justice Act 2003 – refer to page[s 358–359] and consult legal adviser for guidance

---

Offence seriousness (culpability and harm)

A. Identify the appropriate starting point

Starting points based on first time offender pleading not guilty

Examples of nature of activity	Starting point	Range
One threat uttered in the heat of the moment, no more than fleeting impact on victim	Medium level community order	Low level community order to high level community order
Single calculated threat or victim fears that threat will be carried out	12 weeks custody	6 to 26 weeks custody
Repeated threats or visible weapon	Crown Court	Crown Court

Offence seriousness (culpability and harm)

B. Consider the effect of aggravating and mitigating factors (other than those within examples above)

Common aggravating and mitigating factors are identified in the pullout card – the following may be particularly relevant but **these lists are not exhaustive**

Factors indicating higher culpability	Factors indicating lower culpability
1. Planning	1. Provocation
2. Offender deliberately isolates victim	
3. Group action	
4. Threat directed at victim because of job	
5. History of antagonism towards victim	
Factors indicating greater degree of harm	
1. Vulnerable victim	
2. Victim needs medical help/counselling	

Form a preliminary view of the appropriate sentence, then consider offender mitigation

Common factors are identified in the pullout card

Consider a reduction for a guilty plea

Consider ancillary orders, including compensation and football banning order (where appropriate)

Refer to pages [339–346] for guidance on available ancillary orders

Decide sentence

Give reasons

TRADE MARK, UNAUTHORISED USE OF ETC.

Trade Marks Act 1994, s.92

Triable either way:

Maximum when tried summarily: Level 5 fine and/or 6 months

Maximum when tried on indictment: 10 years

Offence seriousness (culpability and harm)		
A. Identify the appropriate starting point		
Starting points based on first time offender pleading not guilty		
Examples of nature of activity	**Starting point**	**Range**
Small number of counterfeit items	Band C fine	Band B fine to low level community order
Larger number of counterfeit items but no involvement in wider operation	Medium level community order, plus fine*	Low level community order to 12 weeks custody, plus fine*
High number of counterfeit items or involvement in wider operation e.g. manufacture or distribution	12 weeks custody	6 weeks custody to Crown Court
Central role in large-scale operation	Crown Court	Crown Court

* This may be an offence for which it is appropriate to combine a fine with a community order. Consult your legal adviser for further guidance.

Offence seriousness (culpability and harm)	
B. Consider the effect of aggravating and mitigating factors (other than those within examples above)	
Common aggravating and mitigating factors are identified in the pullout card – the following may be particularly relevant but **these lists are not exhaustive**	
Factors indicating higher culpability	**Factors indicating lower culpability**
1. High degree of professionalism	1. Mistake or ignorance about provenance of goods
2. High level of profit	
Factor indicating greater degree of harm	
1. Purchasers at risk of harm e.g. from counterfeit drugs	

Form a preliminary view of the appropriate sentence, then consider offender mitigation   Common factors are identified in the pullout card
Consider a reduction for a guilty plea
Consider ancillary orders   Refer to pages [339–346] for guidance on available ancillary orders
Decide sentence   **Give reasons**

TV LICENCE PAYMENT EVASION

Communications Act 2003, s.363

Triable only summarily:

Maximum: Level 3 fine

Offence seriousness (culpability and harm)		
A. Identify the appropriate starting point		
Starting points based on first time offender pleading not guilty		
Examples of nature of activity	**Starting point**	**Range**
Up to 6 months unlicensed use	Band A fine	Band A fine
Over 6 months unlicensed use	Band B Fine	Band A fine to band B fine

Offence seriousness (culpability and harm)
B. Consider the effect of aggravating and mitigating factors (other than those within examples above)
Common aggravating and mitigating factors are identified in the pullout card – the following may be particularly relevant but these lists are not exhaustive

	Factors indicating lower culpability
	1. Accidental oversight or belief licence held
	2. Confusion of responsibility
	3. Licence immediately obtained

Form a preliminary view of the appropriate sentence, then consider offender mitigation
Common factors are identified in the pullout card
Consider a reduction for a guilty plea
Consider ancillary orders
Refer to pages [339–346] for guidance on available ancillary orders
Decide sentence
Give reasons

VAT EVASION

Value Added Tax Act 1994, s.72

Triable either way:

Maximum when tried summarily: Level 5 fine and/or 6 months

Maximum when tried on indictment: 7 years

Awaiting SGC guideline

VEHICLE INTERFERENCE

Criminal Attempts Act 1981, s.9

Triable only summarily:

Maximum: Level 4 fine and/or 3 months

Offence seriousness (culpability and harm)		
A. Identify the appropriate starting point		
Starting points based on first time offender pleading not guilty		
Examples of nature of activity	**Starting point**	**Range**
Trying door handles; no entry gained to vehicle; no damage caused	Band C fine	Band A fine to low level community order
Entering vehicle, little or no damage caused	Medium level community order	Band C fine to high level community order
Entering vehicle, with damage caused	High level community order	Medium level community order to 12 weeks custody

277

Offence seriousness (culpability and harm)
B. Consider the effect of aggravating and mitigating factors (other than those within examples above)
Common aggravating and mitigating factors are identified in the pullout card – the following may be particularly relevant but **these lists are not exhaustive**

Factors indicating higher culpability	
1. Targeting vehicle in dark/isolated location	
Factors indicating greater degree of harm	
1. Emergency services vehicle	
2. Disabled driver's vehicle	
3. Part of series	

Form a preliminary view of the appropriate sentence, then consider offender mitigation
Common factors are identified in the pullout card
Consider a reduction for a guilty plea
Consider ancillary orders, including compensation
Refer to pages [339–346] for guidance on available ancillary orders
Consider disqualification from driving
Decide sentence
Give reasons

VEHICLE LICENCE/REGISTRATION FRAUD

Vehicle Excise and Registration Act 1994, s.44

Triable either way:

Maximum when tried summarily: Level 5 fine

Maximum when tried on indictment: 2 years

Offence seriousness (culpability and harm)		
A. Identify the appropriate starting point		
Starting points based on first time offender pleading not guilty		
Examples of nature of activity	**Starting point**	**Range**
Use of unaltered licence from another vehicle	Band B fine	Band B fine
Forged licence bought for own use, or forged/altered for own use	Band C fine	Band C fine
Use of number plates from another vehicle; or Licence/number plates forged or altered for sale to another	High level community order (in Crown Court)	Medium level community order to Crown Court (Note: community order and custody available only in Crown Court)

Offence seriousness (culpability and harm)

B. Consider the effect of aggravating and mitigating factors (other than those within examples above)

Common aggravating and mitigating factors are identified in the pullout card – the following may be particularly relevant but **these lists are not exhaustive**

Factors indicating higher culpability	Factors indicating lower culpability
1. LGV, PSV, taxi etc.	1. Licence/registration mark from another vehicle owned by defendant
2. Long-term fraudulent use	
Factors indicating greater degree of harm	2. Short-term use
1. High financial gain	
2. Innocent victim deceived	
3. Legitimate owner inconvenienced	

Form a preliminary view of the appropriate sentence, then consider offender mitigation

Common factors are identified in the pullout card

Consider a reduction for a guilty plea

Consider ancillary orders

Refer to pages [339–346] for guidance on available ancillary orders

Consider disqualification from driving and deprivation of property (including vehicle)

Decide sentence

Give reasons

VEHICLE TAKING, WITHOUT CONSENT

Theft Act 1968, s.12

Triable only summarily:

Maximum: Level 5 fine and/or 6 months

May disqualify (no points available)

Offence seriousness (culpability and harm)

A. Identify the appropriate starting point

Starting points based on first time offender pleading not guilty

Examples of nature of activity	Starting point	Range
Exceeding authorised use of e.g. employer's or relative's vehicle; retention of hire car beyond return date	Low level community order	Band B fine to medium level community order
As above with damage caused to lock/ignition; OR Stranger's vehicle involved but no damage caused	Medium level community order	Low level community order to high level community order

Taking vehicle from private premises; OR Causing damage to e.g. lock/ignition of stranger's vehicle	High level community order	Medium level community order to 26 weeks custody

---

Offence seriousness (culpability and harm)

B. Consider the effect of aggravating and mitigating factors (other than those within examples above)

Common aggravating and mitigating factors are identified in the pullout card – the following may be particularly relevant but **these lists are not exhaustive**

Factors indicating higher culpability	**Factors indicating lower culpability**
1. Vehicle later burnt	1. Misunderstanding with owner
2. Vehicle belonging to elderly/disabled person	**Factor indicating lesser degree of harm**
3. Emergency services vehicle	1. Offender voluntarily returned vehicle to owner
4. Medium to large goods vehicle	
5. Passengers carried	

Form a preliminary view of the appropriate sentence, then consider offender mitigation

Common factors are identified in the pullout card

Consider a reduction for a guilty plea

Consider ancillary orders

Refer to pages [339–346] for guidance on available ancillary orders

Consider disqualification from driving

Decide sentence

Give reasons

VEHICLE TAKING (AGGRAVATED)

Damage caused to property other than the vehicle in accident or damage caused to the vehicle

Theft Act 1968, ss.12A(2)(c) and (d)

Triable either way (triable only summarily if damage under £5,000):

Maximum when tried summarily: Level 5 fine and/or 6 months

Maximum when tried on indictment: 2 years

- Must endorse and disqualify for at least 12 months
- Must disqualify for **at least** 2 years if offender has had two or more disqualifications for periods of 56 days or more in preceding 3 years – **refer to page [355] and consult your legal adviser for further guidance**

If there is a delay in sentencing after conviction, consider interim disqualification

<table>
<tr><td colspan="3">
Offence seriousness (culpability and harm)
A. Identify the appropriate starting point
Starting points based on first time offender pleading not guilty
</td></tr>
<tr>
<td>Examples of nature of activity</td>
<td>Starting point</td>
<td>Range</td>
</tr>
<tr>
<td>Exceeding authorised use of e.g. employer's or relative's vehicle; retention of hire car beyond return date; minor damage to taken vehicle</td>
<td>Medium level community order</td>
<td>Low level community order to high level community order</td>
</tr>
<tr>
<td>Greater damage to taken vehicle and/or moderate damage to another vehicle and/or property</td>
<td>High level community order</td>
<td>Medium level community order to 12 weeks custody</td>
</tr>
<tr>
<td>Vehicle taken as part of burglary or from private premises; severe damage</td>
<td>18 weeks custody</td>
<td>12 to 26 weeks custody (Crown Court if damage over £5,000)</td>
</tr>
</table>

<table>
<tr><td colspan="2">
Offence seriousness (culpability and harm)
B. Consider the effect of aggravating and mitigating factors (other than those within examples above)
Common aggravating and mitigating factors are identified in the pullout card – the following may be particularly relevant but these lists are not exhaustive
</td></tr>
<tr>
<td>
Factors indicating higher culpability
1. Vehicle deliberately damaged/destroyed
2. Offender under influence of alcohol/drugs
Factors indicating greater degree of harm
1. Passenger(s) carried
2. Vehicle belonging to elderly or disabled person
3. Emergency services vehicle
4. Medium to large goods vehicle
5. Damage caused in moving traffic accident
</td>
<td>
Factors indicating lower culpability
1. Misunderstanding with owner
2. Damage resulting from actions of another (where this does not provide a defence)
</td>
</tr>
</table>

<table>
<tr><td>
Form a preliminary view of the appropriate sentence, then consider offender mitigation
Common factors are identified in the pullout card
</td></tr>
<tr><td> Consider a reduction for a guilty plea </td></tr>
<tr><td>
Consider ancillary orders, including compensation
Refer to pages [339–346] for guidance on available ancillary orders
</td></tr>
<tr><td>
Decide sentence
Give reasons
</td></tr>
</table>

Vehicle taking (aggravated)

Dangerous driving or accident causing injury

Theft Act 1968, ss.12A(2)(a) and (b)

Triable either way:

Maximum when tried summarily: Level 5 fine and/or 6 months

Maximum when tried on indictment: 2 years; 14 years if accident caused death

- Must endorse and disqualify for at least 12 months
- Must disqualify for **at least** 2 years if offender has had two or more disqualifications for periods of 56 days or more in preceding 3 years – **refer to page [355] and consult your legal adviser for further guidance**

If there is a delay in sentencing after conviction, consider interim disqualification

Offence seriousness (culpability and harm)		
A. Identify the appropriate starting point		
Starting points based on first time offender pleading not guilty		
Examples of nature of activity	**Starting point**	**Range**
Taken vehicle involved in single incident of bad driving where little or no damage or risk of personal injury	High level community order	Medium level community order to 12 weeks custody
Taken vehicle involved in incident(s) involving excessive speed or showing off, especially on busy roads or in built-up area	18 weeks custody	12 to 26 weeks custody
Taken vehicle involved in prolonged bad driving involving deliberate disregard for safety of others	Crown Court	Crown Court

Offence seriousness (culpability and harm)	
B. Consider the effect of aggravating and mitigating factors (other than those within examples above)	
Common aggravating and mitigating factors are identified in the pullout card – the following may be particularly relevant but **these lists are not exhaustive**	
Factors indicating higher culpability	**Factors indicating greater degree of harm**
1. Disregarding warnings of others	1. Injury to others
2. Evidence of alcohol or drugs	2. Damage to other vehicles or property
3. Carrying out other tasks while driving	
4. Carrying passengers or heavy load	
5. Tiredness	
6. Trying to avoid arrest	
7. Aggressive driving, such as driving much too close to vehicle in front, inappropriate attempts to overtake, or cutting in after overtaking	

Form a preliminary view of the appropriate sentence, then consider offender mitigation
Common factors are identified in the pullout card
Consider a reduction for a guilty plea
Consider ordering disqualification until appropriate driving test passed
Consider ancillary orders, including compensation
Refer to pages [339–346] for guidance on available ancillary orders
Decide sentence
Give reasons

VOYEURISM – FACTORS TO TAKE INTO CONSIDERATION

This guideline is taken from the Sentencing Guidelines Council's definitive guideline *Sexual Offences Act 2003*, published 30 April 2007

Key factors

(a) This offence is committed where, for the purpose of obtaining sexual gratification, an offender observes a person doing a private act and knows that the other person does not consent to being observed. It may be committed in a number of ways such as by direct observation on the part of the offender, by recording someone doing a private act with the intention that the recorded image will be viewed by the offender or another person, or by installing equipment or constructing or adapting a structure with the intention of enabling the offender or another person to observe a private act. For the purposes of this offence, 'private act' means an act carried out in a place which, in the circumstances, would reasonably be expected to provide privacy and: the person's genitals, buttocks or breasts are exposed or covered only in underwear; or the person is using a lavatory; or the person is doing a sexual act that is not of a kind ordinarily done in public.

(b) In accordance with section 80 and schedule 3 of the Sexual Offences Act 2003, automatic notification requirements apply upon conviction to an offender aged 18 or over where:

(1) the victim was under 18; or
(2) a term of imprisonment or a community sentence of at least 12 months is imposed.

VOYEURISM

Sexual Offences Act 2003, s.67

Triable either way:

Maximum when tried summarily: Level 5 fine and/or 6 months

Maximum when tried on indictment: 2 years

Identify dangerous offenders
This is a specified offence for the purposes of the public protection provisions in the Criminal Justice Act 2003 – refer to page[s 358–359] and consult legal adviser for guidance

Offence seriousness (culpability and harm)		
A. Identify the appropriate starting point		
Starting points based on first time offender pleading not guilty		
Examples of nature of activity	**Starting point**	**Range**
Basic offence as defined in the Act, assuming no aggravating or mitigating factors, e.g. the offender spies through a hole he or she has made in a changing room wall	Low level community order	Band B fine to high level community order
Offence with aggravating factors such as recording sexual activity and showing it to others	26 weeks custody	4 weeks custody to Crown Court
Offence with serious aggravating factors such as recording sexual activity and placing it on a website or circulating it for commercial gain	Crown Court	26 weeks to Crown Court

Offence seriousness (culpability and harm)

B. Consider the effect of aggravating and mitigating factors (other than those within examples above)

Common aggravating and mitigating factors are identified in the pullout card – the following may be particularly relevant but **these lists are not exhaustive**

Factors indicating higher culpability 1. Threats to prevent the victim reporting an offence 2. Recording activity and circulating pictures/videos 3. Circulating pictures or videos for commercial gain – particularly if victim is vulnerable e.g. a child or a person with a mental or physical disorder **Factor indicating greater degree of harm** 1. Distress to victim e.g. where the pictures/videos are circulated to people known to the victim	

Form a preliminary view of the appropriate sentence, then consider offender mitigation
Common factors are identified in the pullout card
Consider a reduction for a guilty plea
Consider ancillary orders, including compensation
Refer to page[s 339–346] for guidance on available ancillary orders
Decide sentence
Give reasons

WITNESS INTIMIDATION

Criminal Justice and Public Order Act 1994, s.51

Triable either way:

Maximum when tried summarily: 6 months or level 5 fine

Maximum when tried on indictment: 5 years

Where offence committed in domestic context, refer to page [348] for guidance

Offence seriousness (culpability and harm)		
A. Identify the appropriate starting point		
Starting points based on first time offender pleading not guilty		
Examples of nature of activity	**Starting point**	**Range**
Sudden outburst in chance encounter	6 weeks custody	Medium level community order to 18 weeks custody
Conduct amounting to a threat; staring at, approaching or following witnesses; talking about the case; trying to alter or stop evidence	18 weeks custody	12 weeks custody to Crown Court
Threats of violence to witnesses and/or their families; deliberately seeking out witnesses	Crown Court	Crown Court

Offence seriousness (culpability and harm)	
B. Consider the effect of aggravating and mitigating factors (other than those within examples above)	
Common aggravating and mitigating factors are identified in the pullout card – the following may be particularly relevant but **these lists are not exhaustive**	
Factors indicating higher culpability	
1. Breach of bail conditions	
2. Offender involves others	
Factors indicating greater degree of harm	
1. Detrimental impact on administration of justice	
2. Contact made at or in vicinity of victim's home	

Form a preliminary view of the appropriate sentence, then consider offender mitigation Common factors are identified in the pullout card
Consider a reduction for a guilty plea
Consider ancillary orders, including compensation Refer to pages [339–346] for guidance on available ancillary orders
Decide sentence **Give reasons**

CARELESS DRIVING (DRIVE WITHOUT DUE CARE AND ATTENTION)

Road Traffic Act 1988, s.3

Triable only summarily:

Maximum: Level 5 fine

Must endorse and may disqualify. If no disqualification, impose 3–9 points

Offence seriousness (culpability and harm)

A. Identify the appropriate starting point

Starting points based on first time offender pleading not guilty

Examples of nature of activity	Starting point	Range
Momentary lapse of concentration or misjudgement at low speed	Band A fine	Band A fine 3–4 points
Loss of control due to speed, mishandling or insufficient attention to road conditions, or carelessly turning right across on-coming traffic	Band B fine	Band B fine 5–6 points
Overtaking manoeuvre at speed resulting in collision of vehicles, or driving bordering on the dangerous	Band C fine	Band C fine Consider disqualification OR 7–9 points

Offence seriousness (culpability and harm)

B. Consider the effect of aggravating and mitigating factors (other than those within examples above)

Common aggravating and mitigating factors are identified in the pullout card – the following may be particularly relevant but **these lists are not exhaustive**

Factors indicating higher culpability	Factors indicating lower culpability
1. Excessive speed	1. Minor risk
2. Carrying out other tasks while driving	2. Inexperience of driver
3. Carrying passengers or heavy load	3. Sudden change in road or weather conditions
4. Tiredness	

Factors indicating greater degree of harm 1. Injury to others 2. Damage to other vehicles or property 3. High level of traffic or pedestrians in vicinity 4. Location e.g. near school when children are likely to be present	

Form a preliminary view of the appropriate sentence, then consider offender mitigation Common factors are identified in the pullout card
Consider a reduction for a guilty plea
Consider ordering disqualification until appropriate driving test passed
Consider ancillary orders, including compensation Refer to page[s 339–346] for guidance on available ancillary orders
Decide sentence **Give reasons**

CAUSING DEATH BY CARELESS OR INCONSIDERATE DRIVING – FACTORS TO TAKE INTO CONSIDERATION

This guideline and accompanying notes are taken from the Sentencing Guidelines Council's definitive guideline *Causing Death by Driving*, published 15 July 2008

Key factors

(a) It is unavoidable that some cases will be on the borderline between *dangerous* and *careless* driving, or may involve a number of factors that significantly increase the seriousness of an offence. As a result, the guideline for this offence identifies three levels of seriousness, the range for the highest of which overlaps with ranges for the lower levels of seriousness for *causing death by dangerous driving*.

(b) The three levels of seriousness are defined by the degree of carelessness involved in the standard of driving:

- the most serious level for this offence is where the offender's driving fell *not that far short of dangerous*;
- the least serious group of offences relates to those cases where the level of culpability is low – for example in a case involving an offender who misjudges the speed of another vehicle, or turns without seeing an oncoming vehicle because of restricted visibility;
- other cases will fall into the intermediate level.

(c) Where the level of carelessness is low and there are no aggravating factors, even the fact that death was caused is not sufficient to justify a prison sentence.

(d) A fine is unlikely to be an appropriate sentence for this offence; where a non-custodial sentence is considered appropriate, this should be a community order. The nature of the requirements will be determined by the purpose[1] identified by the court as of primary importance. Requirements most likely to be relevant

---

[1] Criminal Justice Act 2003, s.142(1)

include unpaid work requirement, activity requirement, programme requirement and curfew requirement.

(e) Offender mitigation particularly relevant to this offence includes conduct after the offence such as where the offender gave direct, positive, assistance at the scene of a collision to victim(s). It may also include remorse – whilst it can be expected that anyone who has caused a death by driving would be remorseful, this cannot undermine its importance for sentencing purposes. It is for the court to determine whether an expression of remorse is genuine.

(f) Where an offender has a good driving record, this is not a factor that automatically should be treated as mitigation, especially now that the presence of previous convictions is a statutory aggravating factor. However, any evidence to show that an offender has previously been an exemplary driver, for example having driven an ambulance, police vehicle, bus, taxi or similar vehicle conscientiously and without incident for many years, is a fact that the courts may well wish to take into account by way of offender mitigation. This is likely to have even greater effect where the driver is driving on public duty (for example, on ambulance, fire services or police duties) and was responding to an emergency.

(g) Disqualification of the offender from driving and endorsement of the offender's driving licence are mandatory, and the offence carries between 3 and 11 penalty points when the court finds special reasons for not imposing disqualification. There is a discretionary power[2] to order an extended driving test/re-test where a person is convicted of this offence.

Causing death by careless or inconsiderate driving

Road Traffic Act 1988, s.2B

Triable either way:

Maximum when tried summarily: Level 5 fine and/or 6 months

Maximum when tried on indictment: 5 years

Offence seriousness (culpability and harm)		
A. Identify the appropriate starting point		
Starting points based on first time offender pleading not guilty		
Examples of nature of activity	**Starting point**	**Range**
Careless or inconsiderate driving arising from momentary inattention with no aggravating factors	Medium level community order	Low level community order to high level community order
Other cases of careless or inconsiderate driving	Crown Court	High level community order to Crown Court
Careless or inconsiderate driving falling not far short of dangerous driving	Crown Court	Crown Court

---

[2]   Road Traffic Offenders Act 1988, s.36(4)

Offence seriousness (culpability and harm)

B. Consider the effect of aggravating and mitigating factors (other than those within examples above)

Common aggravating and mitigating factors are identified in the pullout card – the following may be particularly relevant but **these lists are not exhaustive**

Factors indicating higher culpability	Factors indicating lower culpability
1. Other offences committed at the same time, such as driving other than in accordance with the terms of a valid licence; driving while disqualified; driving without insurance; taking a vehicle without consent; driving a stolen vehicle	1. Offender seriously injured in the collision
	2. The victim was a close friend or relative
2. Previous convictions for motoring offences, particularly offences that involve bad driving	3. The actions of the victim or a third party contributed to the commission of the offence
3. Irresponsible behaviour, such as failing to stop or falsely claiming that one of the victims was responsible for the collision	4. The offender's lack of driving experience contributed significantly to the likelihood of a collision occurring and/or death resulting
Factors indicating greater degree of harm	5. The driving was in response to a proven and genuine emergency falling short of a defence
1. More than one person was killed as a result of the offence	
2. Serious injury to one or more persons in addition to the death(s)	

Form a preliminary view of the appropriate sentence, then consider offender mitigation

Common factors are identified in the pullout card

Consider a reduction for a guilty plea

Consider ancillary orders, including disqualification and deprivation of property

Refer to pages [339–346] for guidance on available ancillary orders

Decide sentence

Give reasons

CAUSING DEATH BY DRIVING: UNLICENSED, DISQUALIFIED OR UNINSURED DRIVERS – FACTORS TO TAKE INTO CONSIDERATION

This guideline and accompanying notes are taken from the Sentencing Guidelines Council's definitive guideline *Causing Death by Driving*, published 15 July 2008

Key factors

(a)   Culpability arises from the offender driving a vehicle on a road or other public place when, by law, not allowed to do so; the offence does not involve any fault in the standard of driving.

(b)　Since driving whilst disqualified is more culpable than driving whilst unlicensed or uninsured, a higher starting point is proposed when the offender was disqualified from driving at the time of the offence.

(c)　Being uninsured, unlicensed or disqualified are the only determinants of seriousness for this offence, as there are no factors relating to the standard of driving. The list of aggravating factors identified is slightly different as the emphasis is on the decision to drive by an offender who is not permitted by law to do so.

(d)　A fine is unlikely to be an appropriate sentence for this offence; where a non-custodial sentence is considered appropriate, this should be a community order.

(e)　Where the *decision to drive was brought about by a genuine and proven emergency*, that may mitigate offence seriousness and so it is included as an additional mitigating factor.

(f)　An additional mitigating factor covers those situations where an offender genuinely believed that there was valid insurance or a valid licence.

(g)　Offender mitigation particularly relevant to this offence includes conduct after the offence such as where the offender gave direct, positive, assistance at the scene of a collision to victim(s). It may also include remorse – whilst it can be expected that anyone who has caused a death by driving would be remorseful, this cannot undermine its importance for sentencing purposes. It is for the court to determine whether an expression of remorse is genuine.

(h)　Where an offender has a good driving record, this is not a factor that automatically should be treated as mitigation, especially now that the presence of previous convictions is a statutory aggravating factor. However, any evidence to show that an offender has previously been an exemplary driver, for example having driven an ambulance, police vehicle, bus, taxi or similar vehicle conscientiously and without incident for many years, is a fact that the courts may well wish to take into account by way of offender mitigation. This is likely to have even greater effect where the driver is driving on public duty (for example, on ambulance, fire services or police duties) and was responding to an emergency.

(i)　Disqualification of the offender from driving and endorsement of the offender's driving licence are mandatory, and the offence carries between 3 and 11 penalty points when the court finds special reasons for not imposing disqualification. There is a discretionary power[1] to order an extended driving test/re-test where a person is convicted of this offence.

CAUSING DEATH BY DRIVING: UNLICENSED, DISQUALIFIED OR UNINSURED DRIVERS

Road Traffic Act 1988, s.3ZB

Triable either way:

Maximum when tried summarily: Level 5 fine and/or 6 months

Maximum when tried on indictment: 2 years

---

[1]　Road Traffic Offenders Act 1988, s.36(4)

Offence seriousness (culpability and harm)		
A. Identify the appropriate starting point		
Starting points based on first time offender pleading not guilty		
Examples of nature of activity	**Starting point**	**Range**
The offender was unlicensed or uninsured – no aggravating factors	Medium level community order	Low level community order to high level community order
The offender was unlicensed or uninsured plus at least 1 aggravating factor from the list below	26 weeks custody	High level community order to Crown Court
The offender was disqualified from driving OR The offender was unlicensed or uninsured plus 2 or more aggravating factors from the list below	Crown Court	Crown Court

Factors indicating higher culpability	Factors indicating lower culpability
1. Previous convictions for motoring offences, whether involving bad driving or involving an offence of the same kind that forms part of the present conviction (i.e. unlicensed, disqualified or uninsured driving) 2. Irresponsible behaviour such as failing to stop or falsely claiming that someone else was driving **Factors indicating greater degree of harm** 1. More than one person was killed as a result of the offence 2. Serious injury to one or more persons in addition to the death(s)	1. The decision to drive was brought about by a proven and genuine emergency falling short of a defence 2. The offender genuinely believed that he or she was insured or licensed to drive 3. The offender was seriously injured as a result of the collision 4. The victim was a close friend or relative

Form a preliminary view of the appropriate sentence, then consider offender mitigation
Common factors are identified in the pullout card
Consider a reduction for a guilty plea
Consider ancillary orders, including disqualification and deprivation of property
Refer to pages [339–346] for guidance on available ancillary orders
Decide sentence **Give reasons**

DANGEROUS DRIVING

Road Traffic Act 1988, s.2

Triable either way:

Maximum when tried summarily: Level 5 fine and/or 6 months

Maximum when tried on indictment: 2 years

- Must endorse and disqualify for at least 12 months. Must order extended re-test
- Must disqualify for **at least** 2 years if offender has had two or more disqualifications for periods of 56 days or more in preceding 3 years – **refer to page [355] and consult your legal adviser for further guidance**

If there is a delay in sentencing after conviction, consider interim disqualification

Offence seriousness (culpability and harm)		
A. Identify the appropriate starting point		
Starting points based on first time offender pleading not guilty		
Examples of nature of activity	**Starting point**	**Range**
Single incident where little or no damage or risk of personal injury	Medium level community order	Low level community order to high level community order
		Disqualify 12–15 months
Incident(s) involving excessive speed or showing off, especially on busy roads or in built-up area; OR	12 weeks custody	High level community order to 26 weeks custody
Single incident where little or no damage or risk of personal injury but offender was disqualified driver		Disqualify 15–24 months
Prolonged bad driving involving deliberate disregard for safety of others; OR Incident(s) involving excessive speed or showing off, especially on busy roads or in built-up area, by disqualified driver; OR Driving as described in box above while being pursued by police	Crown Court	Crown Court

Offence seriousness (culpability and harm)

B. Consider the effect of aggravating and mitigating factors (other than those within examples above)

Common aggravating and mitigating factors are identified in the pullout card – the following may be particularly relevant but **these lists are not exhaustive**

Factors indicating higher culpability	**Factors indicating lower culpability**
1. Disregarding warnings of others	1. Genuine emergency
2. Evidence of alcohol or drugs	2. Speed not excessive
3. Carrying out other tasks while driving	3. Offence due to inexperience rather than irresponsibility of driver
4. Carrying passengers or heavy load	
5. Tiredness	
6. Aggressive driving, such as driving much too close to vehicle in front, racing, inappropriate attempts to overtake, or cutting in after overtaking	
7. Driving when knowingly suffering from a medical condition which significantly impairs the offender's driving skills	
8. Driving a poorly maintained or dangerously loaded vehicle, especially where motivated by commercial concerns	
Factors indicating greater degree of harm	
1. Injury to others	
2. Damage to other vehicles or property	

Form a preliminary view of the appropriate sentence, then consider offender mitigation

Common factors are identified in the pullout card

Consider a reduction for a guilty plea

Consider ancillary orders, including compensation and deprivation of property

Refer to pages [339–346] for guidance on available ancillary orders

Decide sentence

Give reasons

DRIVE WHILST DISQUALIFIED

Road Traffic Act 1988, s.103

Triable only summarily:

Maximum: Level 5 fine and/or 6 months

Must endorse and may disqualify. If no disqualification, impose 6 points

Offence seriousness (culpability and harm)		
A. Identify the appropriate starting point		
Starting points based on first time offender pleading not guilty		
Examples of nature of activity	**Starting point**	**Range**
Full period expired but retest not taken	Low level community order	Band C fine to medium level community order 6 points or disqualify for 3–6 months
Lengthy period of ban already served	High level community order	Medium level community order to 12 weeks custody Lengthen disqualification for 6–12 months beyond expiry of current ban
Recently imposed ban	12 weeks custody	High level community order to 26 weeks custody Lengthen disqualification for 12–18 months beyond expiry of current ban

Offence seriousness (culpability and harm)	
B. Consider the effect of aggravating and mitigating factors (other than those within examples above)	
Common aggravating and mitigating factors are identified in the pullout card – the following may be particularly relevant but **these lists are not exhaustive**	
Factors indicating higher culpability	**Factors indicating lower culpability**
1. Never passed test 2. Planned long-term evasion 3. Vehicle obtained during ban 4. Driving for remuneration **Factors indicating greater degree of harm** 1. Distance driven 2. Evidence of associated bad driving 3. Offender caused accident	1. Defendant not present when disqualification imposed and genuine reason why unaware of ban 2. Genuine emergency established

Form a preliminary view of the appropriate sentence, then consider offender mitigation
Common factors are identified in the pullout card
Consider a reduction for a guilty plea
Consider ancillary orders, including deprivation of property
Refer to pages [339–346] for guidance on available ancillary orders
Decide sentence
Give reasons

Note

An offender convicted of this offence will always have at least one relevant previous conviction for the offence that resulted in disqualification. The starting points and ranges take this into account; any other previous convictions should be considered in the usual way – see pages [178 and 317].

EXCESS ALCOHOL (DRIVE/ATTEMPT TO DRIVE)

Road Traffic Act 1988, s.5(1)(a)

Triable only summarily:

Maximum: Level 5 fine and/or 6 months

- Must endorse and disqualify for at least 12 months
- Must disqualify for **at least** 2 years if offender has had two or more disqualifications for periods of 56 days or more in preceding 3 years – **refer to page [355] and consult your legal adviser for further guidance**
- Must disqualify for **at least** 3 years if offender has been convicted of a relevant offence in preceding 10 years – **refer to page [356] and consult your legal adviser for further guidance**

If there is a delay in sentencing after conviction, consider interim disqualification

Note: the final column below provides guidance regarding the length of disqualification that may be appropriate in cases to which the 3 year minimum applies. The period to be imposed in any individual case will depend on an assessment of all the relevant circumstances, including the length of time since the earlier ban was imposed and the gravity of the current offence.

Offence seriousness (culpability and harm)						
A. Identify the appropriate starting point						
Starting points based on first time offender pleading not guilty						
Level of alcohol			Starting point	Range	Disqualification	Disqual. 2nd offence in 10 years – see note above
Breath (mg)	Blood (ml)	Urine (ml)				
36–59	81–137	108–183	Band C fine	Band C fine	12–16 months	36–40 months
60–89	138–206	184–274	Band C fine	Band C fine	17–22 months	36–46 months
90–119	207–275	275–366	Medium level community order	Low level community order to high level community order	23–28 months	36–52 months
120–150 and above	276–345 and above	367–459 and above	12 weeks custody	High level community order to 26 weeks custody	29–36 months	36–60 months

Offence seriousness (culpability and harm)
B. Consider the effect of aggravating and mitigating factors (other than those within examples above)
Common aggravating and mitigating factors are identified in the pullout card – the following may be particularly relevant but **these lists are not exhaustive**

Factors indicating higher culpability	Factors indicating lower culpability
1. LGV, HGV, PSV etc.	1. Genuine emergency established *
2. Poor road or weather conditions	2. Spiked drinks *
3. Carrying passengers	3. Very short distance driven *
4. Driving for hire or reward	* even where not amounting to special reasons
5. Evidence of unacceptable standard of driving	
Factors indicating greater degree of harm	
1. Involved in accident	
2. Location e.g. near school	
3. High level of traffic or pedestrians in the vicinity	

Form a preliminary view of the appropriate sentence, then consider offender mitigation Common factors are identified in the pullout card
Consider a reduction for a guilty plea
Consider offering drink/drive rehabilitation course
Consider ancillary orders, including forfeiture or suspension of personal liquor licence Refer to pages [339–346] for guidance on available ancillary orders
Decide sentence **Give reasons**

EXCESS ALCOHOL (IN CHARGE)

Road Traffic Act 1988, s.5(1)(b)

Triable only summarily:

Maximum: Level 4 fine and/or 3 months

Must endorse and may disqualify. If no disqualification, impose 10 points

Offence seriousness (culpability and harm)				
A. Identify the appropriate starting point				
Starting points based on first time offender pleading not guilty				
Level of alcohol			**Starting point**	**Range**
Breath (mg)	**Blood (ml)**	**Urine (ml)**		
36–59	81–137	108–183	Band B fine	Band B fine
				10 points
60–89	138–206	184–274	Band B fine	Band B fine
				10 points OR consider disqualification
90–119	207–275	275–366	Band C fine	Band C fine to medium level community order
				Consider disqualification up to 6 months OR 10 points
120–150 and above	276–345 and above	367–459 and above	Medium level community order	Low level community order to 6 weeks custody Disqualify 6–12 months

297

Offence seriousness (culpability and harm)
B. Consider the effect of aggravating and mitigating factors (other than those within examples above)
Common aggravating and mitigating factors are identified in the pullout card – the following may be particularly relevant but **these lists are not exhaustive**

Factors indicating higher culpability	Factors indicating lower culpability
1. LGV, HGV, PSV etc.	1. Low likelihood of driving
2. Ability to drive seriously impaired	
3. High likelihood of driving	
4. Driving for hire or reward	

Form a preliminary view of the appropriate sentence, then consider offender mitigation
Common factors are identified in the pullout card
Consider a reduction for a guilty plea
Consider ancillary orders, including forfeiture or suspension of personal liquor licence
Refer to pages [339–346] for guidance on available ancillary orders
Decide sentence
Give reasons

FAIL TO STOP/REPORT ROAD ACCIDENT

Road Traffic Act 1988, s.170(4)

Triable only summarily:

Maximum: Level 5 fine and/or 6 months

Must endorse and may disqualify. If no disqualification, impose 5–10 points

Offence seriousness (culpability and harm)		
A. Identify the appropriate starting point		
Starting points based on first time offender pleading not guilty		
Examples of nature of activity	**Starting point**	**Range**
Minor damage/injury or stopped at scene but failed to exchange particulars or report	Band B fine	Band B fine 5–6 points
Moderate damage/injury or failed to stop and failed to report	Band C fine	Band C fine 7–8 points Consider disqualification
Serious damage/injury and/or evidence of bad driving	High level community order	Band C fine to 26 weeks custody Disqualify 6–12 months OR 9–10 points

---

Offence seriousness (culpability and harm)

B. Consider the effect of aggravating and mitigating factors (other than those within examples above)

Common aggravating and mitigating factors are identified in the pullout card – the following may be particularly relevant but **these lists are not exhaustive**

Factors indicating higher culpability	Factors indicating lower culpability
1. Evidence of drink or drugs/evasion of test	1. Believed identity known
2. Knowledge/suspicion that personal injury caused (where not an element of the offence)	2. Genuine fear of retribution
	3. Subsequently reported
3. Leaving injured party at scene	
4. Giving false details	

Form a preliminary view of the appropriate sentence, then consider offender mitigation

Common factors are identified in the pullout card

Consider a reduction for a guilty plea

Consider ancillary orders, including compensation

Refer to pages [339–346] for guidance on available ancillary orders

Decide sentence

Give reasons

FAIL TO PROVIDE SPECIMEN FOR ANALYSIS (DRIVE/ATTEMPT TO DRIVE)

Road Traffic Act 1988, s.7(6)

Triable only summarily:

Maximum: Level 5 fine and/or 6 months

- Must endorse and disqualify for at least 12 months
- Must disqualify for **at least** 2 years if offender has had two or more disqualifications for periods of 56 days or more in preceding 3 years – **refer to page [355] and consult your legal adviser for further guidance**
- Must disqualify for at least 3 years if offender has been convicted of a relevant offence in preceding 10 years – **refer to page [356] and consult your legal adviser for further guidance**

If there is a delay in sentencing after conviction, consider interim disqualification

Note: the final column below provides guidance regarding the length of disqualification that may be appropriate in cases to which the 3 year minimum applies. The period to be imposed in any individual case will depend on an assessment of all the relevant circumstances, including the length of time since the earlier ban was imposed and the gravity of the current offence.

Offence seriousness (culpability and harm)

A. Identify the appropriate starting point

Starting points based on first time offender pleading not guilty

Examples of nature of activity	Starting point	Range	Disqualification	Disqual. 2nd offence in 10 years
Defendant refused test when had honestly held but unreasonable excuse	Band C fine	Band C fine	12–16 months	36–40 months
Deliberate refusal or deliberate failure	Low level community order	Band C fine to high level community order	17–28 months	36–52 months
Deliberate refusal or deliberate failure where evidence of serious impairment	12 weeks custody	High level community order to 26 weeks custody	29–36 months	36–60 months

Offence seriousness (culpability and harm)

B. Consider the effect of aggravating and mitigating factors (other than those within examples above)

Common aggravating and mitigating factors are identified in the pullout card – the following may be particularly relevant but **these lists are not exhaustive**

Factors indicating higher culpability	Factors indicating lower culpability
1. Evidence of unacceptable standard of driving	1. Genuine but unsuccessful attempt to provide specimen
2. LGV, HGV, PSV etc.	
3. Obvious state of intoxication	
4. Driving for hire or reward	
Factor indicating greater degree of harm	
1. Involved in accident	

Form a preliminary view of the appropriate sentence, then consider offender mitigation

Common factors are identified in the pullout card

Consider a reduction for a guilty plea

Consider offering drink/drive rehabilitation course; consider ancillary orders

Refer to pages [339–346] for guidance on available ancillary orders

Decide sentence

Give reasons

FAIL TO PROVIDE SPECIMEN FOR ANALYSIS (IN CHARGE)

Road Traffic Act 1988, s.7(6)

Triable only summarily:

Maximum: Level 4 fine and/or 3 months

Must endorse and may disqualify. If no disqualification, impose 10 points

Offence seriousness (culpability and harm)		
A. Identify the appropriate starting point		
Starting points based on first time offender pleading not guilty		
Examples of nature of activity	**Starting point**	**Range**
Defendant refused test when had honestly held but unreasonable excuse	Band B fine	Band B fine 10 points
Deliberate refusal or deliberate failure	Band C fine	Band C fine to medium level community order Consider disqualification OR 10 points
Deliberate refusal or deliberate failure where evidence of serious impairment	Medium level community order	Low level community order to 6 weeks' custody Disqualify 6–12 months

Offence seriousness (culpability and harm)	
B. Consider the effect of aggravating and mitigating factors (other than those within examples above)	
Common aggravating and mitigating factors are identified in the pullout card – the following may be particularly relevant but **these lists are not exhaustive**	
Factors indicating higher culpability	**Factors indicating lower culpability**
1. Obvious state of intoxication	1. Genuine but unsuccessful attempt to provide specimen
2. LGV, HGV, PSV etc.	2. Low likelihood of driving
3. High likelihood of driving	
4. Driving for hire or reward	

Form a preliminary view of the appropriate sentence, then consider offender mitigation
Common factors are identified in the pullout card
Consider a reduction for a guilty plea
Consider ancillary orders, including compensation
Refer to pages [339–346] for guidance on available ancillary orders
Decide sentence
Give reasons

No insurance

Road Traffic Act 1988, s.143

Triable only summarily:

Maximum: Level 5 fine

Must endorse and may disqualify. If no disqualification, impose 6–8 points – see notes below.

Offence seriousness (culpability and harm)		
A. Identify the appropriate starting point		
Starting points based on first time offender pleading not guilty		
Examples of nature of activity	**Starting point**	**Range**
Using a motor vehicle on a road or other public place without insurance	Band C fine	Band C fine 6 points–12 months disqualification – see notes below

Offence seriousness (culpability and harm)
B. Consider the effect of aggravating and mitigating factors (other than those within examples above)
Common aggravating and mitigating factors are identified in the pullout card – the following may be particularly relevant but **these lists are not exhaustive**

Factors indicating higher culpability	**Factors indicating lower culpability**
1. Never passed test	1. Responsibility for providing insurance rests with another
2. Gave false details	2. Genuine misunderstanding
3. Driving LGV, HGV, PSV etc.	3. Recent failure to renew or failure to transfer vehicle details where insurance was in existence
4. Driving for hire or reward	
5. Evidence of sustained uninsured use	4. Vehicle not being driven
Factor indicating greater degree of harm	
1. Involved in accident	
2. Accident resulting in injury	

Form a preliminary view of the appropriate sentence, then consider offender mitigation
Common factors are identified in the pullout card
Consider a reduction for a guilty plea
Consider ancillary orders
Refer to pages [339–346] for guidance on available ancillary orders
Decide sentence
Give reasons

Notes

Consider range from 7 points–2 months disqualification where vehicle was being driven and no evidence that the offender has held insurance.

Consider disqualification of 6–12 months if evidence of sustained uninsured use and/or involvement in accident.

SPEEDING

Road Traffic Regulation Act 1984, s.89(10)

Triable only summarily:

Maximum: Level 3 fine (level 4 if motorway)

Must endorse and may disqualify. If no disqualification, impose 3–6 points

Offence seriousness (culpability and harm)			
A. Identify the appropriate starting point			
Starting points based on first time offender pleading not guilty			
Speed limit (mph)	**Recorded speed (mph)**		
20	21–30	31–40	41–50
30	31–40	41–50	51–60
40	41–55	56–65	66–75
50	51–65	66–75	76–85
60	61–80	81–90	91–100
70	71–90	91–100	101–110
Starting point	**Band A fine**	**Band B fine**	**Band B fine**
Range	**Band A fine**	**Band B fine**	**Band B fine**
Points/disqualification	3 points	4–6 points OR Disqualify 7–28 days	Disqualify 7–56 days OR 6 points

Offence seriousness (culpability and harm)	
B. Consider the effect of aggravating and mitigating factors (other than those within examples above)	
Common aggravating and mitigating factors are identified in the pullout card – the following may be particularly relevant but **these lists are not exhaustive**	
Factors indicating higher culpability	**Factors indicating lower culpability**
1. Poor road or weather conditions	1. Genuine emergency established
2. LGV, HGV, PSV etc.	
3. Towing caravan/trailer	
4. Carrying passengers or heavy load	
5. Driving for hire or reward	
6. Evidence of unacceptable standard of driving over and above speed	

Factors indicating greater degree of harm	
1. Location e.g. near school	
2. High level of traffic or pedestrians in the vicinity	

Form a preliminary view of the appropriate sentence, then consider offender mitigation
Common factors are identified in the pullout card
Consider a reduction for a guilty plea
Consider ancillary orders
Refer to pages [339–346] for guidance on available ancillary orders
Decide sentence
Give reasons

UNFIT THROUGH DRINK OR DRUGS (DRIVE/ATTEMPT TO DRIVE)

Road Traffic Act 1988, s.4(1)

Triable only summarily:

Maximum: Level 5 fine and/or 6 months

- Must endorse and disqualify for at least 12 months
- Must disqualify for **at least** 2 years if offender has had two or more disqualifications for periods of 56 days or more in preceding 3 years – **refer to page [355] and consult your legal adviser for further guidance**
- Must disqualify for **at least** 3 years if offender has been convicted of a relevant offence in preceding 10 years – **refer to page [356] and consult your legal adviser for further guidance**

If there is a delay in sentencing after conviction, consider interim disqualification

Note: the final column below provides guidance regarding the length of disqualification that may be appropriate in cases to which the 3 year minimum applies. The period to be imposed in any individual case will depend on an assessment of all the relevant circumstances, including the length of time since the earlier ban was imposed and the gravity of the current offence.

Offence seriousness (culpability and harm)

A. Identify the appropriate starting point

Starting points based on first time offender pleading not guilty

Examples of nature of activity	Starting point	Range	Disqualification	Disqual. 2nd offence in 10 years
Evidence of moderate level of impairment and no aggravating factors	Band C fine	Band C fine	12–16 months	36–40 months
Evidence of moderate level of impairment and presence of one or more aggravating factors listed below	Band C fine	Band C fine	17–22 months	36–46 months
Evidence of high level of impairment and no aggravating factors	Medium level community order	Low level community order to high level community order	23–28 months	36–52 months
Evidence of high level of impairment and presence of one or more aggravating factors listed below	12 weeks custody	High level community order to 26 weeks custody	29–36 months	36–60 months

Offence seriousness (culpability and harm)

B. Consider the effect of aggravating and mitigating factors (other than those within examples above)

Common aggravating and mitigating factors are identified in the pullout card – the following may be particularly relevant but **these lists are not exhaustive**

Factors indicating higher culpability	Factors indicating lower culpability
1. LGV, HGV, PSV etc.	1. Genuine emergency established *
2. Poor road or weather conditions	2. Spiked drinks *
3. Carrying passengers	3. Very short distance driven *
4. Driving for hire or reward	* even where not amounting to special reasons
5. Evidence of unacceptable standard of driving	
Factors indicating greater degree of harm	
1. Involved in accident	
2. Location e.g. near school	
3. High level of traffic or pedestrians in the vicinity	

Form a preliminary view of the appropriate sentence, then consider offender mitigation
Common factors are identified in the pullout card
Consider a reduction for a guilty plea
Consider offering drink/drive rehabilitation course
Consider ancillary orders
Refer to pages [339–346] for guidance on available ancillary orders
Decide sentence
Give reasons

UNFIT THROUGH DRINK OR DRUGS (IN CHARGE)

Road Traffic Act 1988, s.4(2)

Triable only summarily:

Maximum: Level 4 fine and/or 3 months

Must endorse and may disqualify. If no disqualification, impose 10 points

Offence seriousness (culpability and harm)		
A. Identify the appropriate starting point		
Starting points based on first time offender pleading not guilty		
Examples of nature of activity	**Starting point**	**Range**
Evidence of moderate level of impairment and no aggravating factors	Band B fine	Band B fine 10 points
Evidence of moderate level of impairment and presence of one or more aggravating factors listed below	Band B fine	Band B fine 10 points or consider disqualification
Evidence of high level of impairment and no aggravating factors	Band C fine	Band C fine to medium level community order 10 points or consider disqualification
Evidence of high level of impairment and presence of one or more aggravating factors listed below	High level community order	Medium level community order to 12 weeks custody Consider disqualification OR 10 points

<table>
<tr><td colspan="2" align="center">Offence seriousness (culpability and harm)
B. Consider the effect of aggravating and mitigating factors (other than those within examples above)
Common aggravating and mitigating factors are identified in the pullout card – the following may be particularly relevant but these lists are not exhaustive</td></tr>
<tr><td>Factors indicating higher culpability

1. LGV, HGV, PSV etc.

2. High likelihood of driving

3. Driving for hire or reward</td><td>Factors indicating lower culpability

1. Low likelihood of driving</td></tr>
</table>

Form a preliminary view of the appropriate sentence, then consider offender mitigation Common factors are identified in the pullout card
Consider a reduction for a guilty plea
Consider ancillary orders Refer to pages [339–346] for guidance on available ancillary orders
Decide sentence **Give reasons**

OFFENCES APPROPRIATE FOR IMPOSITION OF FINE OR DISCHARGE

Part 1: Offences concerning the driver

Offence	Maximum	Points	Starting point	Special considerations
Fail to co-operate with preliminary (roadside) breath test	L3	4	B	
Fail to give information of driver's identity as required	L3	6	C	For limited companies, endorsement is not available; a fine is the only available penalty
Fail to produce insurance certificate	L4	–	A	Fine per offence, not per document
Fail to produce test certificate	L3	–	A	
Drive otherwise than in accordance with licence (where could be covered)	L3	–	A	
Drive otherwise than in accordance with licence	L3	3–6	A	Aggravating factor if no licence ever held

Part 2: Offences concerning the vehicle

* The guidelines for some of the offences below differentiate between three types of offender when the offence is committed in the course of business: driver, owner-driver and owner-company. **For owner-driver, the starting point is the same as for driver; however, the court should consider an uplift of at least 25%.**

Offence	Maximum	Points	Starting point	Special considerations
No excise licence	L3 or 5 times annual duty, whichever is greater	–	A (1–3 months unpaid) B (4–6 months unpaid) C (7–12 months unpaid)	Add duty lost
Fail to notify change of ownership to DVLA	L3	–	A	If offence committed in course of business: A (driver) A* (owner-driver) B (owner-company)
No test certificate	L3	–	A	If offence committed in course of business: A (driver) A* (owner-driver) B (owner-company)
Brakes defective	L4	3	B	If offence committed in course of business: B (driver) B* (owner-driver) C (owner-company) L5 if goods vehicle – see Part 5 below
Steering defective	L4	3	B	If offence committed in course of business: B (driver) B* (owner-driver) C (owner-company) L5 if goods vehicle – see Part 5 below
Tyres defective	L4	3	B	If offence committed in course of business: B (driver) B* (owner-driver) C (owner-company) L5 if goods vehicle – see Part 5 below Penalty per tyre

Condition of vehicle/accessories/equipment involving danger of injury (Road Traffic Act 1988, s.40A)	L4	3	B	Must disqualify for at least 6 months if offender has one or more previous convictions for same offence within three years If offence committed in course of business: B (driver) B* (owner-driver) C (owner-company) L5 if goods vehicle – see Part 5 below
Exhaust defective	L3	–	A	If offence committed in course of business: A (driver) A* (owner-driver) B (owner-company)
Lights defective	L3	–	A	If offence committed in course of business: A (driver) A* (owner-driver) B (owner-company)

Part 3: Offences concerning use of vehicle

* The guidelines for some of the offences below differentiate between three types of offender when the offence is committed in the course of business: driver, owner-driver and owner-company. **For owner-driver, the starting point is the same as for driver; however, the court should consider an uplift of at least 25%.**

Offence	Maximum	Points	Starting point	Special considerations
Weight, position or distribution of load or manner in which load secured involving danger of injury (Road Traffic Act 1988, s.40A)	L4	3	B	Must disqualify for at least 6 months if offender has one or more previous convictions for same offence within three years If offence committed in course of business: A (driver) A* (owner-driver) B (owner-company) L5 if goods vehicle – see Part 5 below

Offence	Maximum	Points	Starting point	Special considerations
Number of passengers or way carried involving danger of injury (Road Traffic Act 1988, s.40A)	L4	3	B	If offence committed in course of business: A (driver) A* (owner-driver) B (owner-company) L5 if goods vehicle – see Part 5 below
Position or manner in which load secured (not involving danger) (Road Traffic Act 1988, s.42)	L3	–	A	L4 if goods vehicle – see Part 5 below
Overloading/exceeding axle weight	L5	–	A	Starting point caters for cases where the overload is up to and including 10%. Thereafter, 10% should be added to the penalty for each additional 1% of overload Penalty per axle If offence committed in course of business: A (driver) A* (owner-driver) B (owner-company) If goods vehicle – see art 5 below
Dangerous parking	L3	3	A	
Pelican/zebra crossing contravention	L3	3	A	
Fail to comply with traffic sign (e.g. red traffic light, stop sign, double white lines, no entry sign)	L3	3	A	
Fail to comply with traffic sign (e.g. give way sign, keep left sign, temporary signs)	L3	–	A	
Fail to comply with police constable directing traffic	L3	3	A	
Fail to stop when required by police constable	L5 (mechanically propelled vehicle) L3 (cycle)	–	B	

Use of mobile telephone	L3	3	A	
Seat belt offences	L2 (adult or child in front) L2 (child in rear)	–	A	
Fail to use appropriate child car seat	L2	–	A	

Part 4: Motorway offences

Offence	Maximum	Points	Starting point	Special considerations
Drive in reverse or wrong way on slip road	L4	3	B	
Drive in reverse or wrong way on motorway	L4	3	C	
Drive off carriageway (central reservation or hard shoulder)	L4	3	B	
Make U turn	L4	3	C	
Learner driver or excluded vehicle	L4	3	B	
Stop on hard shoulder	L4	–	A	
Vehicle in prohibited lane	L4	3	A	
Walk on motorway, slip road or hard shoulder	L4	–	A	

Part 5: Offences re buses/goods vehicles over 3.5 tonnes (GVW)

* The guidelines for these offences differentiate between three types of offender: driver; owner-driver; and owner-company. **For owner-driver, the starting point is the same as for driver; however, the court should consider an uplift of at least 25%.**

** In all cases, take safety, damage to roads and commercial gain into account. Refer to page [323] for approach to fines for 'commercially motivated' offences.

311

Offence	Maximum	Points	Starting point	Special considerations
No goods vehicle plating certificate	L3	–	A (driver) A* (owner-driver) B (owner-company)	
No goods vehicle test certificate	L4	–	B (driver) B* (owner-driver) C (owner-company)	
Brakes defective	L5	3	B (driver) B* (owner-driver) C (owner-company)	
Steering defective	L5	3	B (driver) B* (owner-driver) C (owner-company)	
Tyres defective	L5	3	B (driver) B* (owner-driver) C (owner-company)	Penalty per tyre
Exhaust emission	L4	–	B (driver) B* (owner-driver) C (owner-company)	
Condition of vehicle/ accessories/equipment involving danger of injury (Road Traffic Act 1988, s.40A)	L5	3	B (driver) B* (owner-driver) C (owner-company)	Must disqualify for at least 6 months if offender has one or more previous convictions for same offence within three years
Number of passengers or way carried involving danger of injury (Road Traffic Act 1988, s.40A)	L5	3	B (driver) B* (owner-driver) C (owner-company)	Must disqualify for at least 6 months if offender has one or more previous convictions for same offence within three years
Weight, position or distribution of load or manner in which load secured involving danger of injury (Road Traffic Act 1988, s.40A)	L5	3	B (driver) B* (owner-driver) C (owner-company)	Must disqualify for at least 6 months if offender has one or more previous convictions for same offence within three years
Position or manner in which load secured (not involving danger) (Road Traffic Act 1988, s.42)	L4	–	B (driver) B* (owner-driver) C (owner-company)	

Overloading/ exceeding axle weight	L5	–	B (driver) B* (owner-driver) C (owner-company)	Starting points cater for cases where the overload is up to and including 10%. Thereafter, 10% should be added to the penalty for each additional 1% of overload Penalty per axle
No operators licence	L4	–	B (driver) B* (owner-driver) C (owner-company)	
Speed limiter not used or incorrectly calibrated	L4	–	B (driver) B* (owner-driver) C (owner-company)	
Tachograph not used/not working	L5	–	B (driver) B* (owner-driver) C (owner-company)	
Exceed permitted driving time/periods of duty	L4	–	B (driver) B* (owner-driver) C (owner-company)	
Fail to keep/return written record sheets	L4	–	B (driver) B* (owner-driver) C (owner-company)	
Falsify or alter records with intent to deceive	L5/2 years	–	B (driver) B* (owner-driver) C (owner-company)	Either way offence

Explanatory material – detailed list of contents

315

Explanatory Material

MEANING OF 'RANGE', 'STARTING POINT' AND 'FIRST TIME OFFENDER'

As in previous editions, and consistent with other Sentencing Guidelines Council guidelines, these guidelines are for a **first time offender** convicted after a trial. They provide a **starting point** based on an assessment of the seriousness of the offence and a **range** within which the sentence will normally fall in most cases.

A clear, consistent understanding of each of these terms is essential and the Council and the Sentencing Advisory Panel have agreed the meanings set out in paragraphs 1(a)–(d) below.

They are explained in a format that follows the structured approach to the sentencing decision which identifies first those aspects that affect the assessment of the seriousness of the offence, then those aspects that form part of personal mitigation and, finally, any reduction for a guilty plea.

In practice, the boundaries between these stages will not always be as clear cut but the underlying principles will remain the same.

In accordance with section 174 of the Criminal Justice Act 2003, a court is obliged to *'state in open court, in ordinary language and in general terms, its reasons for deciding on the sentence passed'*.

In particular, *'where guidelines indicate that a sentence of a particular kind, or within a particular range, would normally be appropriate and the sentence is of a different kind, or is outside that range'* the court must give its reasons for imposing a sentence of a different kind or outside the range.

Assessing the seriousness of the offence

1. a) These guidelines apply to an offence that can be committed in a variety of circumstances with different levels of seriousness. They apply to a **first time offender** who has been convicted after a trial.[1] Within the guidelines, a **first time offender** is a person who does not have a conviction which, by virtue of section 143(2) of the Criminal Justice Act 2003, must be treated as an aggravating factor.

    b) As an aid to consistency of approach, a guideline will describe a number of types of activity falling within the broad definition of the offence. These are set out in a column headed 'examples of nature of activity'.

    c) The expected approach is for a court to identify the description that most nearly matches the particular facts of the offence for which sentence is

---

[1] This means any case in which there is no guilty plea including, e.g., where an offender is convicted in absence after evidence has been heard

being imposed. This will identify a **starting point** from which the sentencer can depart to reflect aggravating or mitigating factors affecting the seriousness of the offence (beyond those contained in the description itself) to reach a **provisional sentence**.

d) The range is the bracket into which the **provisional sentence** will normally fall after having regard to factors which aggravate or mitigate the seriousness of the *offence*. The particular circumstances may, however, make it appropriate that the **provisional sentence** falls outside the **range**.

2. Where the offender has previous convictions which aggravate the seriousness of the current offence, that may take the **provisional sentence** beyond the **range** given particularly where there are significant other aggravating factors present.

Offender Mitigation

3. Once the **provisional sentence** has been identified (by reference to the factors affecting the seriousness of the **offence**), the court will take into account any relevant factors of **offender** mitigation. Again, this may take the provisional sentence outside the range.

Reduction for guilty plea

4. Where there has been a guilty plea, any reduction attributable to that plea will be applied to the sentence at this stage. This reduction may take the sentence below the **range** provided.

FINE BAND STARTING POINTS AND RANGES

In these guidelines, where the starting point or range for an offence is or includes a fine, it is expressed as one of three fine bands (A, B or C). As detailed on page [320] below, each fine band has both a starting point and a range.

On some offence guidelines, both the starting point and the range are expressed as a single fine band; see for example careless driving on pages [286–287] where the starting point and range for the first level of offence activity are 'band A fine'. This means that the starting point will be the starting point for fine band A (50% of the offender's relevant weekly income) and the range will be the range for fine band A (25–75% of relevant weekly income). On other guidelines, the range encompasses more than one fine band; see for example drunk and disorderly in a public place on page [218–219] where the starting point for the second level of offence activity is 'band B fine' and the range is 'band A fine to band C fine'. This means that the starting point will be the starting point for fine band B (100% of relevant weekly income) and the range will be the lowest point of the range for fine band A to the highest point of the range for fine band C (25%-175% of relevant weekly income).

SENTENCING FOR MULTIPLE OFFENCES

The starting points and ranges indicated in the individual offence guidelines assume that the offender is being sentenced for a single offence. Where an offender is being sentenced for multiple offences, the overall sentence must be just and appropriate having regard to the totality of the offending; the court should not simply aggregate the sentences considered suitable for the individual offences. The court's assessment of the totality of the offending may result in an overall sentence above the range indicated for the individual offences, including a sentence of a different type.[1]

While concurrent sentences are generally to be preferred where the offences arose out of a single incident, consecutive sentences may be desirable in some circumstances. **Consult your legal adviser for further guidance.**

OFFENCES NOT INCLUDED IN THE GUIDELINES

A number of offences are currently under consideration by the Council and will be included in the MCSG by way of an update when agreed. In the interim, the relevant guideline from the previous version of the MCSG has been included for ease of reference – **these do not constitute formal guidelines issued by the Council.**

Where there is no guideline for an offence, it may assist in determining sentence to consider the starting points and ranges indicated for offences that are of a similar level of seriousness.

When sentencing for the breach of any order for which there is not a specific guideline, the primary objective will be to ensure compliance. Reference to existing guidelines in respect of breaches of orders may provide a helpful point of comparison (see in particular page [207] (breach of community order) and page [244] (breach of protective order)).

Consult your legal adviser for further guidance.

---

[1] When considering whether the threshold for a community or custodial sentence is passed, ss.148(1) and 152(2) of the Criminal Justice Act 2003 confirm that the court may have regard to the combination of the offence and one or more offences associated with it

Approach to the assessment of fines

INTRODUCTION

1. The amount of a fine must reflect the **seriousness** of the offence.[1]
2. The court must also take into account the **financial circumstances** of the offender; this applies whether it has the effect of increasing or reducing the fine.[2] Normally a fine should be of an amount that is capable of being paid within 12 months.
3. The aim is for the fine to have an equal impact on offenders with different financial circumstances; it should be a hardship but should not force the offender below a reasonable 'subsistence' level.
4. The guidance below aims to establish a clear, consistent and principled approach to the assessment of fines that will apply fairly in the majority of cases. However, it is impossible to anticipate every situation that may be encountered and in each case the court will need to exercise its judgement to ensure that the fine properly reflects the **seriousness of the offence** and takes into account the **financial circumstances** of the offender.

FINE BANDS

5. For the purpose of the offence guidelines, a fine is based on one of three bands (A, B or C).[3] The selection of the relevant fine band, and the position of the individual offence within that band, is determined by the **seriousness** of the offence.

	Starting point	Range
Fine Band A	50% of relevant weekly income	25 – 75% of relevant weekly income
Fine Band B	100% of relevant weekly income	75 – 125% of relevant weekly income
Fine Band C	150% of relevant weekly income	125 – 175% of relevant weekly income

6. For an explanation of the meaning of starting point and range, both generally and in relation to fines, see pages [317–318].

---

[1] Criminal Justice Act 2003, s.164(2)
[2] ibid., ss.164(1) and 164(4)
[3] As detailed in paras.36–38 below, two further bands are provided which apply where the offence has passed the threshold for a community order (Band D) or a custodial sentence (Band E) but the court decides that it need not impose such a sentence and that a financial penalty is appropriate

DEFINITION OF RELEVANT WEEKLY INCOME

7. The **seriousness** of an offence determines the choice of fine band and the position of the offence within the range for that band. The offender's **financial circumstances** are taken into account by expressing that position as a proportion of the offender's **relevant weekly income**.
8. Where an offender is in receipt of income from employment or is self-employed **and** that income is more than £100 per week after deduction of tax and national insurance (or equivalent where the offender is self-employed), the actual income is the **relevant weekly income**.
9. Where an offender's only source of income is state benefit (including where there is relatively low additional income as permitted by the benefit regulations) or the offender is in receipt of income from employment or is self-employed but the amount of income after deduction of tax and national insurance is £100 or less, the **relevant weekly income is deemed to be £100**. Additional information about the basis for this approach is set out on page [327].
10. In calculating relevant weekly income, no account should be taken of tax credits, housing benefit, child benefit or similar.

No reliable information

11. Where an offender has failed to provide information, or the court is not satisfied that it has been given sufficient reliable information, it is entitled to make such determination as it thinks fit regarding the financial circumstances of the offender.[4] Any determination should be clearly stated on the court records for use in any subsequent variation or enforcement proceedings. In such cases, a record should also be made of the applicable fine band and the court's assessment of the position of the offence within that band based on the seriousness of the offence.
12. Where there is no information on which a determination can be made, the court should proceed on the basis of an **assumed relevant weekly income of £350**. This is derived from national median pretax earnings; a gross figure is used as, in the absence of financial information from the offender, it is not possible to calculate appropriate deductions.[5]
13. Where there is some information that tends to suggest a significantly lower or higher income than the recommended £350 default sum, the court should make a determination based on that information.
14. A court is empowered to remit a fine in whole or part if the offender subsequently provides information as to means.[6] The assessment of offence seriousness and, therefore, the appropriate fine band and the position of the offence within that band is not affected by the provision of this information.

ASSESSMENT OF FINANCIAL CIRCUMSTANCES

15. While the initial consideration for the assessment of a fine is the offender's relevant weekly income, the court is required to take account of the offender's **financial circumstances** more broadly. Guidance on important parts of this assessment is set out below.

---

[4] Criminal Justice Act 2003, s.164(5)
[5] For 2004–05, the median pre-tax income of all tax payers was £315 per week: HMRC Survey of Personal Incomes. This figure has been increased to take account of inflation
[6] Criminal Justice Act 2003, s.165(2)

16. An offender's financial circumstances may have the effect of increasing or reducing the amount of the fine; however, they are **not** relevant to the assessment of offence seriousness. They should be considered separately from the selection of the appropriate fine band and the court's assessment of the position of the offence within the range for that band.

Out of the ordinary expenses

17. In deciding the proportions of relevant weekly income that are the starting points and ranges for each fine band, account has been taken of reasonable living expenses. Accordingly, no further allowance should normally be made for these. In addition, no allowance should normally be made where the offender has dependants.

18. Outgoings will be relevant to the amount of the fine only where the expenditure is **out of the ordinary** and **substantially** reduces the ability to pay a financial penalty so that the requirement to pay a fine based on the standard approach would lead to **undue** hardship.

Unusually low outgoings

19. Where the offender's living expenses are substantially **lower** than would normally be expected, it may be appropriate to adjust the amount of the fine to reflect this. This may apply, for example, where an offender does not make any financial contribution towards his or her living costs.

Savings

20. Where an offender has savings these will not normally be relevant to the assessment of the amount of a fine although they may influence the decision on time to pay.

21. However, where an offender has little or no income but has substantial savings, the court may consider it appropriate to adjust the amount of the fine to reflect this.

Household has more than one source of income

22. Where the household of which the offender is a part has more than one source of income, the fine should normally be based on the income of the offender alone.

23. However, where the offender's part of the income is very small (or the offender is wholly dependent on the income of another), the court may have regard to the extent of the household's income and assets which will be available to meet any fine imposed on the offender.[7]

Potential earning capacity

24. Where there is reason to believe that an offender's potential earning capacity is greater than his or her current income, the court may wish to adjust the amount of the fine to reflect this.[8] This may apply, for example, where an unemployed

---

[7] *R* v *Engen* [2004] EWCA Crim 1536 (CA)
[8] *R* v *Little* (unreported) 14 April 1976 (CA)

offender states an expectation to gain paid employment within a short time. The basis for the calculation of fine should be recorded in order to ensure that there is a clear record for use in variation or enforcement proceedings.

High income offenders

25. Where the offender is in receipt of very high income, a fine based on a proportion of relevant weekly income may be disproportionately high when compared with the seriousness of the offence. In such cases, the court should adjust the fine to an appropriate level; as a general indication, in most cases the fine for a first time offender pleading not guilty should not exceed 75% of the maximum fine.

OFFENCE COMMITTED FOR 'COMMERCIAL' PURPOSES

26. Some offences are committed with the intention of gaining a significant commercial benefit. These often occur where, in order to carry out an activity lawfully, a person has to comply with certain processes which may be expensive. They include, for example, 'taxi-touting' (where unauthorised persons seek to operate as taxi drivers) and 'fly-tipping' (where the cost of lawful disposal is considerable).
27. In some of these cases, a fine based on the standard approach set out above may not reflect the level of financial gain achieved or sought through the offending. Accordingly:

    a.   where the offender has generated income or avoided expenditure to a level that can be calculated or estimated, the court may wish to consider that amount when determining the financial penalty;

    b.   where it is not possible to calculate or estimate that amount, the court may wish to draw on information from the enforcing authorities about the general costs of operating within the law.

REDUCTION FOR A GUILTY PLEA

28. Where a guilty plea has been entered, the amount of the fine should be reduced by the appropriate proportion. See page [178] of the user guide for guidance.

OTHER CONSIDERATIONS

Maximum fines

29. A fine must not exceed the statutory limit. Where this is expressed in terms of a 'level', the maxima are:

Level 1	£200
Level 2	£500
Level 3	£1,000
Level 4	£2,500
Level 5	£5,000

Victims surcharge

30. Whenever a court imposes a fine in respect of an offence committed after 1 April 2007, it *must* order the offender to pay a surcharge of £15.[9]
31. Where the offender is of adequate means, the court must not reduce the fine to allow for imposition of the surcharge. Where the offender does not have sufficient means to pay the total financial penalty considered appropriate by the court, the order of priority is compensation, surcharge, fine, costs.
32. Further guidance is set out in *Guidance on Victims Surcharge* issued by the Justices' Clerks' Society and Magistrates' Association (30 March 2007).

Costs

33. See page [346] for guidance on the approach to costs. Where the offender does not have sufficient means to pay the total financial penalty considered appropriate by the court, the order of priority is compensation, surcharge, fine, costs.

Multiple offences

34. Where an offender is to be fined for two or more offences that arose out of the same incident, it will often be appropriate to impose on the most serious offence a fine which reflects the totality of the offending where this can be achieved within the maximum penalty for that offence. 'No separate penalty' should be imposed for the other offences.
35. Where compensation is being ordered, that will need to be attributed to the relevant offence as will any necessary ancillary orders.

Fine Bands D and E

36. Two further fine bands are provided to assist a court in calculating a fine where the offence and general circumstances would otherwise warrant a community order (band D) or a custodial sentence (band E) but the court has decided that it need not impose such a sentence and that a financial penalty is appropriate. See pages [331] and [333] for further guidance.
37. The following starting points and ranges apply:

	Starting point	**Range**
Fine Band D	250% of relevant weekly income	200–300% of relevant weekly income
Fine Band E	400% of relevant weekly income	300–500% of relevant weekly income

38. In cases where these fine bands apply, it may be appropriate for the fine to be of an amount that is larger than can be repaid within 12 months. See paragraph 43 below.

---

[9] Criminal Justice Act 2003, ss.161A and 161B

Imposition of fines with custodial sentences

39. A fine and a custodial sentence may be imposed for the same offence although there will be few circumstances in which this is appropriate, particularly where the custodial sentence is to be served immediately. One example might be where an offender has profited financially from an offence but there is no obvious victim to whom compensation can be awarded. Combining these sentences is most likely to be appropriate only where the custodial sentence is short and/or the offender clearly has, or will have, the means to pay.

40. Care must be taken to ensure that the overall sentence is proportionate to the seriousness of the offence and that better off offenders are not able to 'buy themselves out of custody'.

Consult your legal adviser in any case in which you are considering combining a fine with a custodial sentence.

Payment

41. A fine is payable in full on the day on which it is imposed. The offender should always be asked for immediate payment when present in court and some payment on the day should be required wherever possible.

42. Where that is not possible, the court may, in certain circumstances, require the offender to be detained. More commonly, a court will allow payments to be made over a period set by the court:

a. if periodic payments are allowed, the fine should normally be payable within a maximum of 12 months. However, it may be unrealistic to expect those on very low incomes to maintain payments for as long as a year;

b. compensation should normally be payable within 12 months. However, in exceptional circumstances it may be appropriate to allow it to be paid over a period of up to 3 years.

43. Where fine bands D and E apply (see paragraphs 36–38 above), it may be appropriate for the fine to be of an amount that is larger than can be repaid within 12 months. In such cases, the fine should normally be payable within a maximum of 18 months (band D) or 2 years (band E).

44. It is generally recognised that the maximum weekly payment by a person in receipt of state benefit should rarely exceed £5.

45. When allowing payment by instalments by an offender in receipt of earned income, the following approach may be useful. If the offender has dependants or larger than usual commitments, the weekly payment is likely to be decreased.

Net weekly income	Starting point for weekly payment
£60	£5
£120	£10
£200	£25
£250	£30
£300	£50
£400	£80

46. The payment terms must be included in any collection order made in respect of the amount imposed; see pages [328–331]

[PULLOUT CARD]

ASSESSMENT OF FINES: SENTENCING STRUCTURE

1. Decide that a fine is appropriate
2. Offence seriousness **A. Identify the appropriate fine band**
• In the offence guidelines, the starting point for a fine is identified as fine band A, B or C • Each fine band provides a **starting point** and a **range** related to the **seriousness** of the offence expressed as a proportion of the offender's **relevant weekly income** – see paragraph 5 on page [320]
2. Offence seriousness **B. Consider the effect of aggravating and mitigating factors**
• **Move up or down from the starting point** to reflect aggravating or mitigating factors that affect the **seriousness** of the offence – this will usually be within the indicated **range** for the fine band but the court is not precluded from going outside the range where the facts justify it – see pages [317–319]
3. Consider offender mitigation
• The court may consider it appropriate to make a further adjustment to the starting point in light of any matters of offender mitigation – see page [178] of the user guide
4. Form a view of the position of the offence within the range for the fine band then take into account the offender's financial circumstances
• Require the offender to provide a statement of financial circumstances. Obtain further information through questioning if necessary. Failure to provide the information when required is an offence • The provision of financial information does not affect the seriousness of the offence or, therefore, the position of the offence within the range for the applicable fine band • The initial consideration for the assessment of the fine is the offender's **relevant weekly income** – see paragraphs 7–10 on page [321] • However, the court must take account of the offender's financial circumstances more broadly. These may have the effect of **increasing or reducing** the amount of the fine – see paragraphs 15–25 on pages [321–323] • Where the court has **insufficient information** to make a proper determination of the offender's financial circumstances, it may make such determination as it thinks fit – see paragraphs 11–14 on page [321]
5. Consider a reduction for a guilty plea
• Reduce the fine by the appropriate proportion – see page [178] of the user guide
6. Consider ancillary orders, including compensation
• Consider compensation in every case where the offending has resulted in personal injury, loss or damage – give reasons if order not made – see pages [335–339]. Compensation takes priority over a fine where there are insufficient resources to pay both • See pages [339–346] for guidance on available ancillary orders

---

7. Decide sentence

Give reasons

- **The resulting fine must reflect the seriousness of the offence and must take into account the offender's financial circumstances**

- Consider the proposed total financial penalty, including compensation, victims surcharge and costs. Where there are insufficient resources to pay the total amount, the order of priority is compensation, surcharge, fine, costs

- Give reasons for the sentence passed, including any ancillary orders

- State if the sentence has been reduced to reflect a guilty plea; indicate what the sentence would otherwise have been

- Explain if the sentence is of a different kind or outside the range indicated in the guidelines

- Expect immediate payment. If payment by instalments allowed, the court must make a collection order unless this would be impracticable or inappropriate – see pages [328–331]

ADDITIONAL INFORMATION: APPROACH TO OFFENDERS ON LOW INCOME

1. An offender whose primary source of income is state benefit will generally receive a base level of benefit (e.g. job seekers' allowance, a relevant disability benefit or income support) and may also be eligible for supplementary benefits depending on his or her individual circumstances (such as child tax credits, housing benefit, council tax benefit and similar).

2. If relevant weekly income were defined as the amount of benefit received, this would usually result in higher fines being imposed on offenders with a higher level of need; in most circumstances that would not properly balance the seriousness of the offence with the financial circumstances of the offender. While it might be possible to exclude from the calculation any allowance above the basic entitlement of a single person, that could be complicated and time consuming.

3. Similar issues can arise where an offender is in receipt of a low earned income since this may trigger eligibility for means related benefits such as working tax credits and housing benefit depending on the particular circumstances. It will not always be possible to determine with any confidence whether such a person's financial circumstances are significantly different from those of a person whose primary source of income is state benefit.

4. For these reasons, a simpler and fairer approach to cases involving offenders in receipt of low income (whether primarily earned or as a result of benefit) is to identify an amount that is deemed to represent the offender's relevant weekly income.

5. While a precise calculation is neither possible nor desirable, it is considered that an amount that is approximately half-way between the base rate for job seekers' allowance and the net weekly income of an adult earning the minimum wage for 30 hours per week represents a starting point that is both realistic and appropriate; **this is currently £100**.[1] The calculation is based on a 30 hour working week

---

[1] With effect from 1 October 2007, the minimum wage is £5.52 per hour for an adult aged 22 or over. Based on a 30 hour week, this equates to approximately £149.14 after deductions for tax and national insurance. To ensure equivalence of approach, the level of job seekers' allowance for a single person aged 22 has been used for the purpose of calculating the mid point; this is currently £46.85

in recognition of the fact that many of those on minimum wage do not work a full 37 hour week and that lower minimum wage rates apply to younger people.

6. It is expected that this figure will remain in use until 31 March 2011. Future revisions of the guideline will update the amount in accordance with current benefit and minimum wage levels.

ENFORCEMENT OF FINES

1. The Courts Act 2003 created a new fines collection scheme which provides for greater administrative enforcement of fines. The main features are set out below. **Consult your legal adviser for further guidance**.

Attachment of earnings orders/applications for benefit deductions

2. Unless it would be impracticable or inappropriate to do so, the court must make an attachment of earnings order (AEO) or application for benefit deductions (ABD) whenever:

    *   compensation is imposed;[1] or
    *   the court concludes that the offender is an existing defaulter and that the existing default cannot be disregarded.[2]

3. In other cases, the court may make an AEO or ABD with the offender's consent.[3]

Collection orders

4. The court must make a collection order in every case in which a fine or compensation order is imposed unless this would be impracticable or inappropriate.[4] The collection order must state:

    *   the amount of the sum due, including the amount of any fine, compensation order or other sum;
    *   whether the court considers the offender to be an existing defaulter;
    *   whether an AEO or ABD has been made and information about the effect of the order;
    *   if the court has not made an AEO or ABD, the payment terms;
    *   if an AEO or ABD has been made, the reserve terms (i.e. the payment terms that will apply if the AEO or ABD fails). It will often be appropriate to set a reserve term of payment in full within 14 days.

5. If an offender defaults on a collection order and is not already subject to an AEO or ABD, a fines officer must make an AEO or ABD.[5] Where this would be impracticable or inappropriate, or where the offender is already subject to an AEO or ABD, a fines officer must either:[6]

    *   issue a 'further steps' notice advising that the officer intends to take any of the enforcement action listed below; or
    *   refer the case to a magistrates' court.

---

[1] Courts Act 2003, sch.5, para.7A
[2] ibid., para.8
[3] ibid., para.9
[4] ibid., para.12
[5] ibid., para.26
[6] ibid., para.37

6. The following enforcement action is available to a fines officer:[7]

- making an AEO or ABD;
- issuing a distress warrant;
- registering the sum in the register of judgments and orders;
- making a clamping order. A magistrates' court may order the sale of the vehicle if the sum remains unpaid one month after the vehicle was clamped;[8]
- taking enforcement proceedings in the High Court or county court.

7. Where a fines officer refers the case to a magistrates' court, the court may:[9]

- vary the payment terms or reserve terms;
- take any of the enforcement steps available to fines officers listed above;
- where the court is satisfied that the default is due to wilful refusal or culpable neglect, increase the fine by up to 50 per cent;[10]
- discharge the collection order and exercise any of the court's standard fine enforcement powers.

8. The case may also be referred to a magistrates' court if an offender appeals against a 'further steps' notice issued by a fines officer.[11]

Standard fine enforcement powers

9. These powers are normally available if:

- a collection order is not made; or
- a case is referred to a magistrates' court by a fines officer; or
- an offender appeals against a 'further steps' notice issued by a fines officer.

Remission of fine

10. The court can remit a fine 'if it thinks it just to do so having regard to a change of circumstances since the date of conviction'.[12] This requirement may be satisfied where:

- the defaulter's means have changed since the fine was imposed;
- arrears have accumulated by the imposition of additional fines to a level which makes repayment of the total amount within a reasonable time unlikely;
- the defaulter is serving a term of imprisonment; remission may be more practical than lodging concurrent warrants of imprisonment.

11. There is no power to remit excise penalties (which include fines and back duty for using an untaxed vehicle).

12. Compensation and costs cannot be remitted but, where payment is unlikely or impractical due to the defaulter's means or circumstances, the sum may be discharged or reduced. Victims and claimants should be consulted and given an opportunity to attend the hearing.

---

[7] ibid., para.38
[8] Courts Act 2003, sch.5, para.41
[9] ibid., para.39
[10] ibid., para.42A
[11] ibid., para.37
[12] Magistrates' Courts Act 1980, s.85

13. The court is also empowered to remit a fine that was imposed in the absence of information about the offender's means.[13]

Imprisonment in default of payment

14. A court may issue a warrant of commitment if the defaulter is already serving a custodial sentence.[14]

15. If a means inquiry establishes that the defaulter has the ability to pay immediately, and the offence was punishable by imprisonment, the court can commit him or her to prison.[15]

16. Otherwise, the court may issue a warrant of commitment only if there has been a means inquiry and the court:[16]

- is satisfied that the default is due to wilful refusal or culpable neglect; and
- has considered or tried all other methods of enforcing payment and concluded that they are inappropriate or unsuccessful.

17. The other methods that the court is required to have considered or tried are:

- money payment supervision order;[17]
- application for deductions from benefit;
- attachment of earnings order;
- distress warrant;
- taking enforcement proceedings in the High Court or county court
- if the offender is aged under 25, an attendance centre order (where available).[18]

18. The period of commitment should be the shortest which is likely to succeed in obtaining payment; the periods prescribed in schedule 4 of the Magistrates' Courts Act 1980 (set out below) should be regarded as maxima rather than the norm. The period of imprisonment may be suspended on condition that regular payments are made. Where such payments are not made, the defaulter should be brought back before the court for consideration of whether the period of imprisonment should be implemented.

Maximum periods of imprisonment in default of payment	
Amount not exceeding £200	7 days
Amount exceeding £200 but not exceeding £500	14 days
Amount exceeding £500 but not exceeding £1,000	28 days
Amount exceeding £1,000 but not exceeding £2,500	45 days
Amount exceeding £2,500 but not exceeding £5,000	3 months
Amount exceeding £5,000 but not exceeding £10,000	6 months
Amount exceeding £10,000	12 months

---

[13] Criminal Justice Act 2003, s.165
[14] Magistrates' Courts Act 1980, s.82(3)
[15] Magistrates' Courts Act 1980, s.82(4)(a)
[16] ibid., s.82(4)(b)
[17] ibid., s.88
[18] Powers of Criminal Courts (Sentencing) Act 2000, s.60

Detention in the precincts of the court or at a police station

19. The court may order that an offender be detained for a specified period ending no later than 8pm on the day on which the order is made:[19] this is available both as a sentence in its own right and as an order in respect of unpaid fines where it can be used as an alternative to remission. No means inquiry is required.

Warrant for detention in police station overnight

20. The court may issue a warrant for the overnight detention of a defaulter in a police station.[20] The defaulter must be released at 8am the following day, or the same day if arrested after midnight.

Discharge of fines by unpaid work (being piloted in specified areas until 31 March 2009)

21. Schedule 6 of the Courts Act 2003 empowers the court to order that an offender discharge a fine by performing work for a specified number of hours. This is not a community order; it is an enforcement provision that may be invoked following a court's decision on the information before it that a fine was an appropriate sentence for the offence.

22. The order can be made only where other means of enforcing the sum are likely to be impractical or inappropriate. The offender must be suitable for unpaid work and consent to the order. The number of hours is determined by dividing the sum due by the 'prescribed hourly sum' (currently £6 per hour).

COMMUNITY ORDERS

1. Community orders have the effect of restricting the offender's liberty while providing punishment in the community, rehabilitation for the offender, and/or ensuring that the offender engages in reparative activities. They are available in respect of all offences, including those for which the maximum penalty is a fine.

2. A community order must not be imposed unless the offence is 'serious enough to warrant such a sentence'.[1] For detailed guidance regarding this threshold and the approach to community orders, sentencers should refer to the Sentencing Guidelines Council's definitive guideline *New Sentences: Criminal Justice Act 2003*, published 16 December 2004, and the National Standards for the Probation Service. The Council guideline emphasises that:

   • sentencers must consider all available disposals at the time of sentence; even where the threshold for a community sentence has been passed, a fine or discharge may be an appropriate penalty;

   • where an offender is being sentenced for a non-imprisonable offence, great care is needed in assessing whether a community sentence is appropriate since failure to comply could result in a custodial sentence (see page [207]).[2]

3. Community orders consist of one or more of the following requirements:

---

[19] Magistrates' Courts Act 1980, s.135
[20] ibid., s.136
[1] Criminal Justice Act 2003, s.148
[2] The power to make a community order for a non-imprisonable offence will be removed by provisions in the Criminal Justice and Immigration Act 2008 when in force

- unpaid work requirement;
- activity requirement;
- programme requirement;
- prohibited activity requirement;
- curfew requirement;
- exclusion requirement;
- residence requirement;
- mental health treatment requirement;
- drug rehabilitation requirement;
- alcohol treatment requirement;
- supervision requirement;
- in a case where the offender is aged under 25, attendance centre requirement (where available).

Low	Medium	High
Offences only just cross community order threshold, where the seriousness of the offence or the nature of the offender's record means that a discharge or fine is inappropriate	Offences that obviously fall within the community order band	Offences only just fall below the custody threshold or the custody threshold is crossed but a community order is more appropriate in the circumstances
In general, only one requirement will be appropriate and the length may be curtailed if additional requirements are necessary		More intensive sentences which combine two or more requirements may be appropriate
Suitable requirements might include: • 40–80 hours unpaid work • Curfew requirement within the lowest range (e.g. up to 12 hours per day for a few weeks) • Exclusion requirement, without electronic monitoring, for a few months • Prohibited activity requirement • Attendance centre requirement (where available)	Suitable requirements might include: • Greater number of hours of unpaid work (e.g. 80–150 hours) • Curfew requirement within the middle range (e.g. up to 12 hours for 2–3 months) • Exclusion requirement lasting in the region of 6 months • Prohibited activity requirement	Suitable requirements might include: • 150–300 hours unpaid work • Activity requirement up to the maximum of 60 days • Curfew requirement up to 12 hours per day for 4–6 months • Exclusion order lasting in the region of 12 months

4. The court must ensure that the restriction on the offender's liberty is commensurate with the seriousness of the offence and that the requirements are the most suitable for the offender.[3] Where two or more requirements are included, they must be compatible with each other.[4]

5.   The Council guideline provides that the seriousness of the offence should be the *initial* factor in determining which requirements to include in a community order. It establishes three sentencing ranges within the community order band based on offence seriousness (low, medium and high), and identifies non-exhaustive examples of requirements that might be appropriate in each. These are set out below. The examples focus on punishment in the community; other requirements of a rehabilitative nature may be more appropriate in some cases.

6.   The particular requirements imposed within the range must be suitable for the individual offender and will be influenced by a wide range of factors including the stated purpose(s) of the sentence, the risk of re-offending, the ability of the offender to comply, and the availability of the requirements in the local area. Sentencers must ensure that the sentence strikes the right balance between proportionality and suitability. The resulting restriction on liberty must be a proportionate response to the offence that was committed.

7.   In many cases, a pre-sentence report will be pivotal in helping the court decide whether to impose a community order and, if so, whether particular requirements or combinations of requirements are suitable for an individual offender. Whenever the court reaches the provisional view that a community order may be appropriate, it should usually request a pre-sentence report. It will be helpful to indicate the court's preliminary opinion as to which of the three sentencing ranges is relevant and the purpose(s) of sentencing that the package of requirements is expected to fulfil. Ideally this should be provided to the Probation Service in written form, with a copy retained on the court file for the benefit of the sentencing bench.

Electronic monitoring

8.   Subject to limited exceptions, the court must impose an electronic monitoring requirement where it makes a community order with a curfew or exclusion requirement, and may do so in all other cases.[5] Electronic monitoring should be used with the primary purpose of promoting and monitoring compliance with other requirements, in circumstances where the punishment of the offender and/or the need to safeguard the public and prevent re-offending are the most important concerns.

Breach of Community Order

9.   **Refer to page [207] above for guidance on the approach to sentencing for breaches of community orders.**

CUSTODIAL SENTENCES

1.   A custodial sentence must not be imposed unless the offence 'was so serious that neither a fine alone nor a community sentence can be justified for the offence'.[1] Guidance regarding this threshold and the approach to the imposition of

---

[3]   Criminal Justice Act 2003, ss.148(2)(a) and 148(2)(b)
[4]   ibid., s.177(6)
[5]   Criminal Justice Act 2003, ss.177(3) and 177(4)
[1]   Criminal Justice Act 2003, s.152(2)

custodial sentences is set out in the Sentencing Guidelines Council's definitive guideline *Overarching Principles: Seriousness*, published 16 December 2004.

2. The guideline emphasises that:

- the clear intention of the threshold test is to reserve prison as a punishment for the most serious offences;
- passing the custody threshold does not mean that a custodial sentence should be deemed inevitable; custody can still be avoided in light of offender mitigation or where there is a suitable intervention in the community which provides sufficient restriction (by way of punishment) while addressing the rehabilitation of the offender to prevent future crime. However, where the offence would otherwise appear to warrant a term of imprisonment within the Crown Court's jurisdiction, it is for the Crown Court to make that judgement;
- the approach to the imposition of a custodial sentence should be as follows:

  (a) Has the custody threshold been passed?

  (b) If so, is it unavoidable that a custodial sentence be imposed?

  (c) If so, can that sentence be suspended? (Sentencers should be clear that they would have imposed a custodial sentence if the power to suspend had not been available.)

  (d) If not, impose a sentence which takes immediate effect for the shortest term commensurate with the seriousness of the offence.[2]

Suspended sentences

3. If the court imposes a term of imprisonment between 14 days and six months,[3] it may suspend the sentence for between 6 months and 2 years (the 'operational period').[4] Where the court imposes two or more sentences to be served consecutively, the power to suspend the sentence is not available in relation to any of them unless the aggregate of the terms does not exceed six months.[5]

4. When the court suspends a sentence, it must impose one or more requirements for the offender to undertake in the community. The requirements are identical to those available for community orders.

5. If the offender fails to comply with a community requirement or commits a further offence, the court must *either* activate the suspended sentence in full or in part *or* amend the order so as to:[6]

   a) extend the period during which the offender is subject to community requirements;

   b) make the community requirements more onerous; or

   c) extend the operational period.

6. There are many similarities between suspended sentences and community orders: requirements can be imposed on the offender and the court can respond to breach by sending him or her to custody. The crucial difference is that a

---

[2] ibid., s.153(2)

[3] When implemented, provisions in the Criminal Justice and Immigration Act 2008 will restrict the use of this power in magistrates' courts

[4] Criminal Justice Act 2003, s.189(1)

[5] ibid., s.189(2) as amended by art.2(2)(b) of the Criminal Justice Act 2003 (Sentencing) (Transitory Provisions) Order 2005

[6] ibid., sch.12, para.8

suspended sentence is a prison sentence; **it may be imposed only where the court is satisfied both that the custodial threshold has been passed and that it is not appropriate to impose a community order, fine or other non-custodial sentence.**

7. A further difference is the approach to any breach; when sentencing for breach of a community order, the primary objective is to ensure that the requirements of the order are complied with. When responding to breach of a suspended sentence, the statutory presumption is that the custodial sentence will be activated.[7]

8. Detailed guidance regarding suspended sentences and the appropriate response to breaches is set out in the Sentencing Guidelines Council's definitive guideline New Sentences: Criminal Justice Act 2003, published 16 December 2004. The guideline emphasises that:

- **a custodial sentence that is suspended should be for the same term that would have applied if the sentence was to be served immediately;**
- the time for which a sentence is suspended should reflect the length of the sentence; up to 12 months might normally be appropriate for a suspended sentence of up to 6 months;
- the imposition of a custodial sentence is both punishment and a deterrent; to ensure that the overall terms of the sentence are commensurate with offence seriousness, requirements imposed as part of the sentence should generally be less onerous than if a community order had been imposed;
- a court wishing to impose onerous or intensive requirements should reconsider whether a community sentence might be more appropriate (refer to pages [331–333]);
- where an offender has breached a suspended sentence, there is a presumption that the suspended prison term will be activated in full or in part. Relevant considerations will include the extent to which (if any) the offender complied with the requirements, and the circumstances of the breach.

9. When the court imposes a suspended sentence, it may also order that the sentence be reviewed periodically at a review hearing.[8]

COMPENSATION

1. The court *must* consider making a compensation order in any case where personal injury, loss or damage has resulted from the offence.[1] It can either be a sentence in its own right or an ancillary order. The court must give reasons if it decides not to order compensation.

2. Up to £5,000 compensation may be imposed in respect of each offence of which the offender has been convicted.[2] Compensation may also be ordered in respect of offences taken into consideration. The total amount of compensation must not exceed the maximum available for the offence(s) of which the offender has been convicted so that, e.g., where an offender has been convicted of two offences, the maximum amount of compensation able to be awarded is £10,000 regardless of the number of offences taken into consideration.

---

[7] Criminal Justice Act 2003, sch.12, para.8(3)
[8] ibid., s.191
[1] Powers of Criminal Courts (Sentencing) Act 2000, s.130
[2] ibid., s.131(1)

3. Where the personal injury, loss or damage arises from a road accident, a compensation order may be made only if there is a conviction for an offence under the Theft Act 1968, or the offender is uninsured and the Motor Insurers' Bureau will not cover the loss.[3] Compensation paid by the Motor Insurers' Bureau is subject to an excess of £300.

4. Subject to consideration of the victim's views (see paragraph 6 below), the court must order compensation wherever possible and should not have regard to the availability of other sources such as civil litigation or the Criminal Injuries Compensation Scheme. Any amount paid by an offender under a compensation order will generally be deducted from a subsequent civil award or payment under the Scheme to avoid double compensation.[4]

5. Compensation may be ordered for such amount as the court considers appropriate having regard to any evidence and any representations made by the offender or prosecutor.[5] The court must also take into account the offender's means (see also paragraphs 11–13 below).[6]

6. Compensation should benefit, not inflict further harm on, the victim. Any financial recompense from the offender may cause distress. A victim may or may not want compensation from the offender and assumptions should not be made either way. The victim's views are properly obtained through sensitive discussion by the police or witness care unit, when it can be explained that the offender's ability to pay will ultimately determine whether, and how much, compensation is ordered and whether the compensation will be paid in one lump sum or by instalments. If the victim does not want compensation, this should be made known to the court and respected.

7. In cases where it is difficult to ascertain the full amount of the loss suffered by the victim, consideration should be given to making a compensation order for an amount representing the agreed or likely loss. Where relevant information is not immediately available, it may be appropriate to grant an adjournment for it to be obtained.

8. The court should consider two types of loss:

    -   financial loss sustained as a result of the offence such as the cost of repairing damage or, in case of injury, any loss of earnings or medical expenses;
    -   pain and suffering caused by the injury (including terror, shock or distress) and any loss of facility. This should be assessed in light of all factors that appear to the court to be relevant, including any medical evidence, the victim's age and personal circumstances.

9. The tables below suggest starting points for compensating physical and mental injuries commonly encountered in a magistrates' court. They have been developed to be consistent with the approach in the Criminal Injuries Compensation Authority tariff (revised 2001), available at: www.cica.gov.uk

---

[3] ibid., s.130(6)
[4] The minimum amount payable under the Criminal Injuries Compensation Scheme is £1,000
[5] Powers of Criminal Courts (Sentencing) Act 2000, s.130(4)
[6] ibid., s.130(11)

Physical injury

Type of injury	Description	Starting point
Graze	Depending on size	Up to £75
Bruise	Depending on size	Up to £100
Cut: no permanent scar	Depending on size and whether stitched	£100–500
Black eye		£125
Eye	Blurred or double vision lasting up to 6 weeks	Up to £1,000
	Blurred or double vision lasting for 6 to 13 weeks	£1,000
	Blurred or double vision lasting for more than 13 weeks (recovery expected)	£1,750
Brain	Concussion lasting one week	£1,500
Nose	Undisplaced fracture of nasal bone	£1,000
	Displaced fracture requiring manipulation	£2,000
	Deviated nasal septum requiring septoplasty	£2,000
Loss of non-front tooth	Depending on cosmetic effect	£1,250
Loss of front tooth		£1,750
Facial scar	Minor disfigurement (permanent)	£1,500
Arm	Fractured humerus, radius, ulna (substantial recovery)	£3,300
Shoulder	Dislocated (substantial recovery)	£1,750
Wrist	Dislocated/fractured – including scaphoid fracture (substantial recovery)	£3,300
	Fractured – colles type (substantial recovery)	£4,400
Sprained wrist, ankle	Disabling for up to 6 weeks	Up to £1,000
	Disabling for 6 to 13 weeks	£1,000
	Disabling for more than 13 weeks	£2,500
Finger	Fractured finger other than index finger (substantial recovery)	£1,000
	Fractured index finger (substantial recovery)	£1,750
	Fractured thumb (substantial recovery)	£2,000
Leg	Fractured fibula (substantial recovery)	£2,500
	Fractured femur, tibia (substantial recovery)	£3,800
Abdomen	Injury requiring laparotomy	£3,800

Mental injury

Description	Starting point
Temporary mental anxiety (including terror, shock, distress), not medically verified	Up to £1,000
Disabling mental anxiety, lasting more than 6 weeks, medically verified*	£1,000
Disabling mental illness, lasting up to 28 weeks, confirmed by psychiatric diagnosis*	£2,500

* In this context, 'disabling' means a person's functioning is significantly impaired in some important aspect of his or her life, such as impaired work or school performance or significant adverse effects on social relationships.

10. The following table, which is also based on the Criminal Injuries Compensation Authority tariff, sets out suggested starting points for compensating physical and sexual abuse. It will be rare for cases involving this type of harm to be dealt with in a magistrates' court and it will be important to **consult your legal adviser for guidance in these situations**.

Physical and sexual abuse

Type of abuse	Description	Starting point
Physical abuse of adult	Intermittent physical assaults resulting in accumulation of healed wounds, burns or scalds, but with no appreciable disfigurement	£2,000
Physical abuse of child	Isolated or intermittent assault(s) resulting in weals, hair pulled from scalp etc.	£1,000
	Intermittent physical assaults resulting in accumulation of healed wounds, burns or scalds, but with no appreciable disfigurement	£2,000
Sexual abuse of adult	Non-penetrative indecent physical acts over clothing	£1,000
	Non-penetrative indecent act(s) under clothing	£2,000
Sexual abuse of child (under 18)	Non-penetrative indecent physical act(s) over clothing	£1,000
	Non-penetrative frequent assaults over clothing or non-penetrative indecent act under clothing	£2,000
	Repetitive indecent acts under clothing	£3,300

11. Once the court has formed a preliminary view of the appropriate level of compensation, it must have regard to the means of the offender so far as they are known. Where the offender has little money, the order may have to be scaled down or additional time allowed to pay; the court may allow compensation to be paid over a period of up to three years in appropriate cases.

12. The fact that a custodial sentence is imposed does not, in itself, make it inappropriate to order compensation; however, it may be relevant to whether the offender has the means to satisfy the order.

13. Where the court considers that it would be appropriate to impose a fine and a compensation order but the offender has insufficient means to pay both, priority should be given to compensation. Compensation also takes priority over the victim surcharge where the offender's means are an issue.

Ancillary orders

1. There are several ancillary orders available in a magistrates' court which should be considered in appropriate cases. Annex A lists the offences in respect of which certain orders are available. The individual offence guidelines above also identify ancillary orders particularly likely to be relevant to the offence. **In all cases, consult your legal adviser regarding available orders and their specific requirements and effects.**

2. Ancillary orders should be taken into account when assessing whether the overall penalty is commensurate with offence seriousness.

Anti-social behaviour orders

- The court may make an anti-social behaviour order (ASBO) in respect of any person convicted of an offence.[1]
- Before making an order, the court must find that the offender acted in an anti-social manner, i.e in a manner likely to cause harassment, alarm or distress.
- The court must also consider that the order is necessary to protect the public from further anti-social acts by the offender.
- The order must have effect for at least two years. If the offender is sentenced to custody, the provisions of the order may be suspended until release.
- An ASBO may include only prohibitions; there is no power to impose positive obligations.
- **The following is a summary of principles and other considerations relevant to the making of an ASBO in relation to adults and youths taken from the Sentencing Guidelines Council's definitive guideline** *Breach of an Anti-Social Behaviour Order*:

  (1) Proceedings for the imposition of an ASBO are civil in nature, so that hearsay evidence is admissible, but a court must be satisfied to a criminal standard that the individual has acted in the anti-social manner alleged.

  (2) The test of 'necessity' requires the exercise of judgement or evaluation; it does not require proof beyond reasonable doubt that the order is "necessary".

  (3) It is particularly important that the findings of fact giving rise to the making of the order are recorded by the court.

  (4) As the ASBO is a preventative order it is unlawful to use it as a punishment; so, when sentencing an offender, a court must not allow itself to be diverted into making an ASBO as an alternative or additional sanction.

---

[1] Crime and Disorder Act 1998, s.1C

(5) The police have powers to arrest an individual for any criminal offence, and the court should not impose an order which prohibits the subject from committing an offence if it will not add significantly to the existing powers of the police to protect others from anti-social behaviour by the subject. An order must not prohibit a criminal offence merely to increase the sentence range available for that offence.

(6) The terms of the order made must be precise and capable of being understood by the subject. Where the subject is aged under 18, it is important for both the subject and the parent or guardian to confirm their understanding of the order and its terms. The prohibitions must be enforceable in the sense that they should allow a breach to be readily identified and capable of being proved.

(7) An order should not impose a 'standard list' of prohibitions, but should identify and prohibit the particular type of anti-social behaviour that gives rise to the necessity of an ASBO. Each separate prohibition must be necessary to protect persons from anti-social behaviour by the subject, and each order must be specifically fashioned to deal with the individual concerned.

(8) The order must be proportionate to the legitimate aim pursued and commensurate with the risk guarded against. The court should avoid making compliance very difficult through the imposition of numerous prohibitions, and those that will cause great disruption to the subject should be considered with particular care. It is advisable to make an order for a specific period; when considering the duration of an order imposed on a youth, the potential for the subject to mature may be a relevant factor.

(9) Not all prohibitions set out in an ASBO have to run for the full term of the ASBO itself. The test must always be what is necessary to deal with the particular anti-social behaviour of the offender and what is proportionate in the circumstances. At least one of the prohibitions must last for the duration of the order but not all are required to last for the 2 years that is the minimum length of an order. The court can vary the terms of an order at any time upon application by the subject (or the applicant in the case of an order made upon application).

(10) When making an order upon conviction, the court has the power to suspend its terms until the offender has been released from a custodial sentence. However, where a custodial sentence of 12 months or more is imposed and the offender is liable to be released on licence and thus subject to recall, an order will not generally be necessary. There might be cases where geographical restraints could supplement licence conditions.

(11) Other considerations:

    (i) Where an ASBO is imposed on a subject aged 10–17, the court must consider whether a **Parenting order** would be desirable in the interests of preventing repetition of the antisocial behaviour.[2] Such an order *must* be made where the offender is aged under 16 and the condition is met, but is discretionary where the offender is aged 16 or 17.

---

[2] Crime and Disorder Act 1998, s.8. The Anti-social Behaviour Act 2003 [ASBA] now provides for a court to impose stand-alone Parenting Orders, if it is satisfied that the child has engaged in criminal or anti-social behaviour. The ASBA also provides for certain agencies to enter into Parenting Contracts which, as an alternative to legal action, have much in common with the non-statutory Acceptable Behaviour Contracts

(ii)   Where a magistrates' court imposes a stand-alone ASBO, it must also consider whether an **Individual support order** (ISO) would be desirable to tackle the underlying causes of the behaviour.[3]

(iii)   In the case of an adult, the court may make an **Intervention order** if the underlying causes of the anti-social behaviour are drug-related and appropriate treatment is available.[4]

(12)   Interim orders:

Where a decision to impose an order (either upon application or conviction) is pending, the court may make an interim order if it considers it just to do so.[5] The court must balance the seriousness of the behaviour and the urgency with which it is necessary to take steps to control it, with the likely impact of an interim order upon the potential subject.[6]

- Further guidance is set out in *A Guide for the Judiciary (third edition)* January 2007 (supplement January 2008) published by the Judicial Studies Board.[7] Refer also to *Anti-Social Behaviour Orders – A Guide to Law and Procedure in the Magistrates' Court* published by the Justices' Clerks' Society.[8]

Binding over orders

- The court has the power to bind an individual over to keep the peace.[5]
- The order is designed to prevent future misconduct and requires the individual to promise to pay a specified sum if the terms of the order are breached. Exercise of the power does not depend upon conviction.
- Guidance on the making of binding over orders is set out in part III.31 of the Consolidated Criminal Practice Direction, as amended in March 2007. Key principles include:

(1)   before imposing the order, the court must be satisfied beyond reasonable doubt that a breach of the peace involving violence or an imminent threat of violence has occurred, or that there is a real risk of violence in the future. The court should hear evidence and the parties before making any order;

(2)   the court should state its reasons for making the order;

(3)   the order should identify the specific conduct or activity from which the individual must refrain, the length of the order and the amount of the recognisance;

(4)   the length of the order should be proportionate to the harm sought to be avoided and should not generally exceed 12 months;

(5)   when fixing the amount of the recognisance, the court should have regard to the individual's financial resources.

---

3   ibid., s.1AA
4   ibid., s.1G
5   ibid., s.1D
6   *Leeds Magistrates' Court, ex parte Kenny; Secretary of State for Constitutional Affairs and another, ex parte M* [2004] EWCA Civ 312
7   www.jsboard.co.uk
8   www.jc-society.com/File/ASBO_updated_GPG_May_2006.pdf
5   Justices of the Peace Act 1361, Magistrates Court Act 1980, s.115

Confiscation orders

- Confiscation orders under the Proceeds of Crime Act 2002 may only be made by the Crown Court.
- An offender convicted of an offence in a magistrates' court must be committed to the Crown Court where this is requested by the prosecution with a view to a confiscation order being considered.[6]
- If the committal is made in respect of an either way offence, the court must state whether it would have committed the offender to the Crown Court for sentencing had the issue of a confiscation order not arisen.

Deprivation orders

- The court has the power to deprive an offender of property used for the purpose of committing or facilitating the commission of an offence, whether or not it deals with the offender in any other way.[7]
- Before making the order, the court must have regard to the value of the property and the likely financial and other effects on the offender.
- Without limiting the circumstances in which the court may exercise the power, a vehicle is deemed to have been used for the purpose of committing the offence where the offence is punishable by imprisonment and consists of:

  (1)   driving, attempting to drive, or being in charge of a motor vehicle;
  (2)   failing to provide a specimen; or
  (3)   failing to stop and/or report an accident.[8]

Deprivation of ownership of animal

- Where an offender is convicted of one of the following offences under the Animal Welfare Act 2006, the court may make an order depriving him or her of ownership of the animal and for its disposal:[9]

  (1)   causing unnecessary suffering (s.4);
  (2)   mutilation (s.5);
  (3)   docking of dogs' tails (ss.6(1) and 6(2));
  (4)   fighting etc. (s.8);
  (5)   breach of duty to ensure welfare (s.9);
  (6)   breach of disqualification order (s.36(9)).

- The court is required to give reasons if it decides not to make such an order.
- Deprivation of ownership may be ordered instead of or in addition to dealing with the offender in any other way.

Disqualification from ownership of animals

- Where an offender is convicted of one of the following offences under the Animal Welfare Act 2006, the court may disqualify him or her from owning or keeping animals, dealing in animals, and/or transporting animals:[10]

---

[6]   Proceeds of Crime Act 2002, s.70
[7]   Powers of Criminal Courts (Sentencing) Act 2000, s.143
[8]   ibid., ss.143(6) and 143(7)
[9]   Animal Welfare Act 2006, s.33
[10] ibid., s.34

(1)   causing unnecessary suffering (s.4);
(2)   mutilation (s.5);
(3)   docking of dogs' tails (ss.6(1) and 6(2));
(4)   administration of poisons etc. (s.7);
(5)   fighting etc. (s.8);
(6)   breach of duty to ensure welfare (s.9);
(7)   breach of licensing or registration requirements (s.13(6));
(8)   breach of disqualification order (s.36(9)).

- The court is required to give reasons if it decides not to make such an order.
- The court may specify a period during which an offender may not apply for termination of the order under section 43 of the Animal Welfare Act 2006; if no period is specified, an offender may not apply for termination of the order until one year after the order was made.
- Disqualification may be imposed instead of or in addition to dealing with the offender in any other way.

Disqualification orders

- The court may disqualify any person convicted of an offence from driving for such period as it thinks fit.[11] This may be instead of or in addition to dealing with the offender in any other way.
- The section does not require the offence to be connected to the use of a vehicle. The Court of Appeal has held that the power is available as part of the overall punitive element of a sentence, and the only restrictions on the exercise of the power are those in the statutory provision.[12]

Disqualification of company directors

- The Company Directors Disqualification Act 1986 empowers the court to disqualify an offender from being a director or taking part in the promotion, formation or management of a company for up to five years.
- An order may be made in two situations:

(1)   where an offender has been convicted of an indictable offence in connection with the promotion, formation, management, liquidation or striking off of a company;[13] or
(2)   where an offender has been convicted of an offence involving a failure to file documents with, or give notice to, the registrar of companies. If the offence is triable only summarily, disqualification can be ordered only where the offender has been the subject of three default orders or convictions in the preceding five years.[14]

Drinking banning orders (when in force)

- Where an offender is convicted of an offence which was committed while under the influence of alcohol, the court must consider whether a drinking banning order is necessary for the purpose of protecting others from further criminal or disorderly

---

[11] Powers of Criminal Courts (Sentencing) Act 2000, s.146
[12] *R v. Sofekun* [2008] EWCA Crim 2035
[13] Company Directors Disqualification Act 1988, s.2
[14] ibid., s.5

conduct by the offender while he or she is under the influence of alcohol.[15] If the court decides not to make such an order, it must state its reasons.

- A drinking banning order may impose any prohibition on the offender which is necessary for the purpose identified above, and must include such prohibition as the court considers necessary on the offender's entering licensed premises.[16]
- The court must specify the duration of the order, which must be between two months and two years.[17]
- The court may direct that the order will cease to have effect before the end of the specified period if the offender completes an approved course;[18] consult your legal adviser for guidance on this provision. The court is required to give reasons if it does not include such a direction in the order.

Exclusion orders

- The court may make an exclusion order where an offender has been convicted of an offence committed on licensed premises involving the use or threat of violence.
- The order prohibits the offender from entering **specified** licensed premises without the consent of the licensee.[19]
- The term of the order must be between three months and two years.
- Note that the provisions regarding exclusion orders will be repealed when the power to impose drinking banning orders is brought into force.

Football banning orders

- The court must make a football banning order where an offender has been convicted of a relevant offence and it is satisfied that there are reasonable grounds to believe that making a banning order would help to prevent violence or disorder.[20] If the court is not so satisfied, it must state that fact and give its reasons.
- Relevant offences are those set out in schedule 1 of the Football Spectators Act 1989; see Annex A.
- The order requires the offender to report to a police station within five days, may require the offender to surrender his or her passport, and may impose requirements on the offender in relation to any regulated football matches.
- Where the order is imposed in addition to a sentence of immediate imprisonment, the term of the order must be between six and ten years. In other cases, the term of the order must be between three and five years.

Forfeiture and destruction of drugs

- Where an offender is convicted of an offence under the Misuse of Drugs Act 1971, the court may order forfeiture and destruction of anything shown to the satisfaction of the court to relate to the offence.[21]

---

[15] Violent Crime Reduction Act 2006, s.6
[16] ibid., s.1
[17] ibid., s.2
[18] ibid., ss.2(3)–(8)
[19] Licensed Premises (Exclusion of Certain Persons) Act 1980, s.1
[20] Football Spectators Act 1989, s.14A
[21] Misuse of Drugs Act 1971, s.27(1)

Forfeiture and destruction of goods bearing unauthorised trade mark

- Where the court is satisfied that an offence under section 92 of the Trade Marks Act 1994 has been committed, it must (on the application of a person who has come into possession of the goods in connection with the investigation or prosecution of the offence) order forfeiture of the goods.[22]
- If it considers it appropriate, instead of ordering destruction of the goods, the court may direct that they be released to a specified person on condition that the offending sign is erased, removed or obliterated.

Forfeiture or suspension of liquor licence

- Where an offender who holds a personal licence to supply alcohol is charged with a 'relevant offence', he or she is required to produce the licence to the court, or inform the court of its existence, no later than his or her first appearance.
- 'Relevant offences' are listed in schedule 4 of the Licensing Act 2003; see Annex A.
- Where the offender is convicted, the court may order forfeiture of the licence or suspend it for up to six months.[23] When deciding whether to order forfeiture or suspension, the court may take account of the offender's previous convictions for 'relevant offences'.[24]
- Whether or not forfeiture or suspension is ordered, the court is required to notify the licensing authority of the offender's conviction and the sentence imposed.

Parenting orders

- The court may make a parenting order where an offender has been convicted of an offence under section 444 of the Education Act 1996 (failing to secure regular attendance at school) and the court is satisfied that the order would be desirable in the interests of preventing the commission of any further offence under that section.[25]
- The order may impose such requirements that the court considers desirable in the interests of preventing the commission of a further offence under section 444.
- A requirement to attend a counselling or guidance programme may be included only if the offender has been the subject of a parenting order on a previous occasion.
- The term of the order must not exceed 12 months.

Restitution orders

- Where goods have been stolen and an offender is convicted of any offence with reference to theft of those goods, the court may make a restitution order.[26]
- The court may:

  (1)   order anyone in possession or control of the stolen goods to restore them to the victim;

  (2)   on the application of the victim, order that goods directly or indirectly representing the stolen goods (as being the proceeds of any disposal or realisation of the stolen goods) be transferred to the victim; or

---

[22]   Trade Marks Act 1994, s.97
[23]   Licensing Act 2003, s.129(2)
[24]   ibid., s.129(3)
[25]   Crime and Disorder Act 1998, s.8
[26]   Powers of Criminal Courts (Sentencing) Act 2000, s.148

(3)   order that a sum not exceeding the value of the stolen goods be paid to the victim out of any money taken out of the offender's possession on his or her apprehension.

Restraining orders

- Where an offender is convicted of harassment or conduct causing fear of violence, the court may make a restraining order.[27]
- The order may prohibit the offender from doing anything for the purpose of protecting the victim of the offence, or any other person mentioned in the order, from further conduct which amounts to harassment or will cause a fear of violence.[28]
- The order may have effect for a specified period or until further order.[29]
- When in force, section 5A of the Protection from Harassment Act 1997 will enable the court to make a restraining order in respect of an offender who has been acquitted of an offence if the court considers that it is necessary to protect a person from harassment. **Consult your legal adviser for guidance**.

Sexual offences prevention orders

- The court may make a sexual offences prevention order where it deals with an offender in respect of an offence listed in schedules 3 or 5 of the Sexual Offences Act 2003; see Annex A.[30]
- The court must be satisfied that the order is necessary to protect others from 'serious sexual harm' from the offender; the prohibitions in the order must also be necessary for this purpose.
- 'Serious sexual harm' means serious physical or psychological harm caused by the offender committing an offence listed in schedule 3 of the Sexual Offences Act 2003.
- The order may include only negative prohibitions; there is no power to impose positive obligations.
- The order must have effect for at least five years.

COSTS

1.   Where an offender is convicted of an offence, the court has discretion to make such order as to costs as it considers just and reasonable.[1]
2.   The Court of Appeal has given the following guidance:[2]

- an order for costs should never exceed the sum which, having regard to the offender's means and any other financial order imposed, he or she is able to pay and which it is reasonable to order him or her to pay;
- an order for costs should never exceed the sum which the prosecutor actually and reasonably incurred;
- the purpose of the order is to compensate the prosecutor. Where the conduct of the defence has put the prosecutor to avoidable expense, the

---

[27] Protection from Harassment Act 1997, s.5
[28] ibid., s.5(2)
[29] ibid., s.5(3)
[30] Sexual Offences Act 2003, s.104
[1] Prosecution of Offences Act 1985, s.18
[2] *R v. Northallerton Magistrates' Court, ex parte Dove* [2000] 1 Cr App R (S) 136 (CA)

offender may be ordered to pay some or all of that sum to the prosecutor but the offender must not be punished for exercising the right to defend himself or herself;

- the costs ordered to be paid should not be grossly disproportionate to any fine imposed for the offence. This principle was affirmed in *BPS Advertising Limited* v. *London Borough of Barnet*[3] in which the Court held that, while there is no question of an arithmetical relationship, the question of costs should be viewed in the context of the maximum penalty considered by Parliament to be appropriate for the seriousness of the offence;
- if the combined total of the proposed fine and the costs sought by the prosecutor exceeds the sum which the offender could reasonably be ordered to pay, the costs order should be reduced rather than the fine;
- it is for the offender to provide details of his or her financial position so as to enable the court to assess what he or she can reasonably afford to pay. If the offender fails to do so, the court is entitled to draw reasonable inferences as to means from all the circumstances of the case;
- if the court proposes to make any financial order against the offender, it must give him or her fair opportunity to adduce any relevant financial information and to make appropriate submissions.

3. A costs award may cover the costs of investigation as well as prosecution. However, where the investigation was carried out as part of a council officer's routine duties, for which he or she would have been paid in the normal way, this is a relevant factor to be taken into account when deciding the appropriate amount of any costs order.[4]

4. Where the court wishes to impose costs in addition to a fine, compensation and/or the victim's' surcharge but the offender has insufficient resources to pay the total amount, the order of priority is:

i) compensation;
ii) victim's' surcharge;
iii) fine;
iv) costs.

DEFERRED SENTENCES

1. The court is empowered to defer passing sentence for up to six months.[1] The court may impose any conditions during the period of deferment that it considers appropriate. These could be specific requirements as set out in the provisions for community sentences, or requirements that are drawn more widely. The purpose of deferment is to enable the court to have regard to the offender's conduct after conviction or any change in his or her circumstances, including the extent to which the offender has complied with any requirements imposed by the court.

2. Three conditions must be satisfied before sentence can be deferred:

- the offender must consent;
- the offender must undertake to comply with requirements imposed by the court; and
- the court must be satisfied that deferment is in the interests of justice.

---

[3] [2006] EWCA 3335 (Admin) QBD
[4] ibid.
[1] Powers of Criminal Courts (Sentencing) Act 2000, s.1 as amended by Criminal Justice Act 2003, s.278 and sch.23, para.1

3. Guidance regarding deferred sentences is set out in the Sentencing Guidelines Council's definitive guideline *New Sentences: Criminal Justice Act 2003*, published 16 December 2004. The guideline emphasises that:

    *   deferred sentences will be appropriate in very limited circumstances;
    *   deferred sentences are likely to be relevant predominantly in a small group of cases close to either the community or custodial sentence threshold where, should the offender be prepared to adapt his behaviour in a way clearly specified by the sentencer, the court may be prepared to impose a lesser sentence;
    *   sentencers should impose specific and measurable conditions that do not involve a serious restriction on liberty;
    *   the court should give a clear indication of the type of sentence it would have imposed if it had decided not to defer;
    *   the court should also ensure that the offender understands the consequences of failure to comply with the court's wishes during the deferment period.

4. If the offender fails to comply with any requirement imposed in connection with the deferment, or commits another offence, he or she can be brought back to court before the end of the deferment period and the court can proceed to sentence.

OFFENCES COMMITTED IN A DOMESTIC CONTEXT

1. **When sentencing an offence committed in a domestic context, refer to the Sentencing Guidelines Council's definitive guideline *Overarching Principles: Domestic Violence*, published 7 December 2006.** The guideline emphasises that:

    *   as a starting point for sentence, offences committed in a domestic context should be regarded as no less serious than offences committed in a non-domestic context;
    *   many offences of violence in a domestic context are dealt with in a magistrates' court as an offence of common assault or assault occasioning actual bodily harm because the injuries sustained are relatively minor. Offences involving serious violence will warrant a custodial sentence in the majority of cases;
    *   a number of aggravating factors may commonly arise by virtue of the offence being committed in a domestic context (see list below);
    *   since domestic violence takes place within the context of a current or past relationship, the history of the relationship will often be relevant in assessing the gravity of the offence. A court is entitled to take into account anything occurring within the relationship as a whole, which may reveal relevant aggravating or mitigating factors;
    *   in respect of an offence of violence in a domestic context, an offender's good character in relation to conduct outside the home should generally be of no relevance where there is a proven pattern of behaviour;
    *   assertions that the offence has been provoked by conduct of the victim need to be treated with great care, both in determining whether they have a factual basis and in considering whether the circumstances of the alleged conduct amounts to provocation sufficient to mitigate the seriousness of the offence;
    *   where the custody threshold is only just crossed, so that if a custodial sentence is imposed it will be a short sentence, the court will wish to consider

whether the better option is a suspended sentence order or a community order, including in either case a requirement to attend an accredited domestic violence programme. Such an option will only be appropriate where the court is satisfied that the offender genuinely intends to reform his or her behaviour and that there is a real prospect of rehabilitation being successful. Such a situation is unlikely to arise where there has been a pattern of abuse.

Refer to paragraphs 4.1 to 4.4 of the Council guideline for guidance regarding the relevance of the victim's wishes to sentence.

Aggravating factors

2. The following aggravating factors may be of particular relevance to offences committed in a domestic context and should be read alongside the general factors set out on the pullout card:

Factors indicating higher culpability

1. Abuse of trust and abuse of power
2. Using contact arrangements with a child to instigate an offence
3. Proven history of violence or threats by the offender in a domestic setting
4. History of disobedience to court orders

Factors indicating a greater degree of harm

1. Victim is particularly vulnerable
2. Impact on children

AGGRAVATION RELATED TO RACE, RELIGION, DISABILITY OR SEXUAL ORIENTATION

Racial or religious aggravation – statutory provisions

1. Sections 29 to 32 of the Crime and Disorder Act 1998 create specific racially or religiously aggravated offences, which have higher maximum penalties than the non-aggravated versions of those offences. The individual offence guidelines indicate whether there is a specifically aggravated form of the offence.
2. An offence is racially or religiously aggravated for the purposes of sections 29–32 of the Act if the offender demonstrates hostility towards the victim based on his or her membership (or presumed membership) of a racial or religious group, or if the offence is racially or religiously motivated.[1]
3. For all other offences, section 145 of the Criminal Justice Act 2003 provides that the court must regard racial or religious aggravation as an aggravating factor.
4. The court should not treat an offence as racially or religiously aggravated for the purposes of section 145 where a racially or religiously aggravated form of the offence was charged but resulted in an acquittal.[2] The court should not normally treat an offence as racially or religiously aggravated if a racially or religiously aggravated form of the offence was available but was not charged.[3] Consult your legal adviser for further guidance in these situations.

---

[1] Crime and Disorder Act 1988, s.28
[2] Refer to *R* v *McGillivray* [2005] EWCA Crim 604 (CA)
[3] Refer to *R* v *O'Callaghan* [2005] EWCA Crim 317 (CA)

Aggravation related to disability or sexual orientation – statutory provisions

5. Under section 146 of the Criminal Justice Act 2003, the court must treat as an aggravating factor the fact that:

- an offender demonstrated hostility towards the victim based on his or her sexual orientation or disability (or presumed sexual orientation or disability); or
- the offence was motivated by hostility towards persons who are of a particular sexual orientation or who have a particular disability.

Approach to sentencing

6. A court should not conclude that offending involved aggravation related to race, religion, disability or sexual orientation without first putting the offender on notice and allowing him or her to challenge the allegation.

7. When sentencing any offence where such aggravation is found to be present, the following approach should be followed. **This applies both to the specific racially or religiously aggravated offences under the Crime and Disorder Act 1998 and to offences which are regarded as aggravated under section 145 or 146 of the Criminal Justice Act 2003:**[4]

- sentencers should first determine the appropriate sentence, leaving aside the element of aggravation related to race, religion, disability or sexual orientation but taking into account all other aggravating or mitigating factors;
- the sentence should then be increased to take account of the aggravation related to race, religion, disability or sexual orientation;
- the increase may mean that a more onerous penalty of the same type is appropriate, or that the threshold for a more severe type of sentence is passed;
- the sentencer must state in open court that the offence was aggravated by reason of race, religion, disability or sexual orientation;
- the sentencer should state what the sentence would have been without that element of aggravation.

8. The extent to which the sentence is increased will depend on the seriousness of the aggravation. The following factors could be taken as indicating a high level of aggravation:

Offender's intention

- The element of aggravation based on race, religion, disability or sexual orientation was planned
- The offence was part of a pattern of offending by the offender
- The offender was a member of, or was associated with, a group promoting hostility based on race, religion, disability or sexual orientation
- The incident was deliberately set up to be offensive or humiliating to the victim or to the group of which the victim is a member

---

[4] Refer to *R* v *Kelly and Donnelly* [2001] EWCA Crim 170 in which the Court considered the approach to sentencing in cases involving racial or religious aggravation

Impact on the victim or others

- The offence was committed in the victim's home
- The victim was providing a service to the public
- The timing or location of the offence was calculated to maximise the harm or distress it caused
- The expressions of hostility were repeated or prolonged
- The offence caused fear and distress throughout a local community or more widely
- The offence caused particular distress to the victim and/or the victim's family.

9. At the lower end of the scale, the aggravation may be regarded as less serious if:

- It was limited in scope or duration
- The offence was not motivated by hostility on the basis of race, religion, disability or sexual orientation, and the element of hostility or abuse was minor or incidental

10. In these guidelines, the specific racially or religiously aggravated offences under the Crime and Disorder Act 1998 are addressed on the same page as the 'basic offence'; the starting points and ranges indicated on the guideline relate to the 'basic' (i.e. non-aggravated) offence. The increase for the element of racial or religious aggravation may result in a sentence above the range; **this will not constitute a departure from the guideline for which reasons must be given.**

ENVIRONMENTAL/HEALTH AND SAFETY OFFENCES

1. The main environmental protection offences are:

Summary of offence	Legislation	Maximum penalty
Depositing, recovering or disposing of waste without a site licence/permit or in breach of its conditions (covers fly-tipping)	Environmental Protection Act 1990, s.33	On summary conviction: £50,000 fine and/or 6 months imprisonment On indictment: unlimited fine and/or 5 years imprisonment
Polluting or solid waste matter entering controlled waters	Water Resources Act 1991, s.85	On summary conviction: £20,000 fine and/or 3 months imprisonment On indictment: unlimited fine and/or 2 years imprisonment
Failure to comply with the waste 'duty of care' (often associated with fly-tipping)	Environmental Protection Act 1990, s.34	On summary conviction: £5,000 fine On indictment: unlimited fine
Fishing with a rod and line without a licence	Salmon and Freshwater Fisheries Act 1975, s.27(a)	On summary conviction: level 4 fine

Summary of offence	Legislation	Maximum penalty
Failure to hold a permit for an activity (e.g. a landfill site) or failure to comply with condition of a permit	Pollution Prevention and Control Regulations 2000, regs. 9(1), 32(1)(a) and (b)	On summary conviction: £20,000 fine
	Environmental Permitting (England and Wales) Regulations 2007, regs. 12, 38(1)(a) and 38(1)(b)	On indictment: unlimited fine
Failure to comply with requirements associated with producing, transporting and managing hazardous wastes	Hazardous Waste Regulations (England and Wales) 2005, regs. 65 and 68	**Offences under reg. 65 in connection with regs. 21–22, 24–26, 34, 35–44, 46 and schedule 7, 53, 54 and 55:** On summary conviction: level 5 fine **Other offences under regs. 65 or 68:** On summary conviction: fine not exceeding statutory maximum On indictment: unlimited fine and/or 2 years imprisonment

2.   The main health and safety offences are:

Offence	Legislation	Maximum penalty
Failing to comply with an improvement or prohibition notice, or a court remedy order	Health and Safety at Work etc Act 1974, ss.33(1)(g) and 33(1)(o)	On summary conviction: £20,000 fine and/or 6 months imprisonment On indictment: unlimited fine and/or 2 years imprisonment
Breaching general duties in Health and Safety at Work Act ss.2 to 6	Health and Safety at Work etc Act 1974, s.33(1)(a)	On summary conviction: £20,000 fine On indictment: unlimited fine
Breaching health and safety regulations or licensing conditions	Health and Safety at Work etc Act 1974, s.33(1)(c)	On summary conviction: £5,000 fine On indictment: unlimited fine Where the offence involves contravention of a licence, maximum penalty On indictment: 2 years imprisonment

3. **It is important to consult your legal adviser in these cases. The Court of Appeal gave guidance on health and safety sentencing in *R* v. *Howe*[1] and *R* v. *Balfour Beatty Infrastructure Services Ltd.*[2] These principles are relevant also to sentencing for environmental offences. In addition, refer to the environmental offences training materials on the Magistrates' Association website www.magistrates-association.org.uk**

4. Offences under these Acts are serious, especially where the maximum penalty in a magistrates' court is £20,000 or above. Imprisonment is available for some offences. Particular care needs to be taken when considering whether to accept jurisdiction or to commit a case to the Crown Court, especially when the defendant is a large company (see paragraph 11 below).

Offence seriousness

5. Sentencers should assess offence seriousness following the approach set out in the Sentencing Guidelines Council's definitive guideline *Overarching Principles: Seriousness*, published 16 December 2004.

6. In some cases, much more or much less harm may result than could have been reasonably anticipated. In these circumstances, the Council guideline states that the offender's culpability should be the initial factor in assessing the seriousness of the offence.

7. The following factors may be particularly relevant to all environmental/health and safety offences, **but these lists are not exhaustive**:

Factors which may indicate higher than usual culpability:

*   Offence deliberate or reckless breach of law rather than result of carelessness
*   Action or lack of action prompted by financial motives (profit or cost-saving), for example by neglecting to take preventative measures or avoiding payment for relevant licence
*   Regular or continuing breach, not isolated lapse
*   Failure to respond to advice, cautions or warning from regulatory authority
*   Ignoring concerns raised by employees or others
*   Offender has committed previous offences of a similar nature
*   Offender exhibited obstructive or dismissive attitude to authorities
*   Offender carrying out operations without an appropriate licence

Factors which may indicate greater than usual degree of harm:

*   Death or serious injury or ill-health resulted from or risked by offence
*   High degree of damage resulting from offence (but lack of actual damage does not render the offence merely technical; it is still serious if there is risk)
*   Considerable potential for harm to workers or public
*   Animal health or flora affected
*   Extensive clean-up operation or other remedial steps required
*   Other lawful activities interfered with
*   In respect of offences of fly-tipping, tipping dangerous or offensive waste; tipping near housing, children's play areas, schools, livestock or environmentally sensitive sites; any escape of waste to streams or atmosphere

---

[1] [1999] 2 Cr App R (S) 37 (CA)
[2] [2006] EWCA Crim 1586 (CA)

Factors which may indicate lower than usual culpability:

- Offender played a relatively minor role or had little personal responsibility
- Genuine and reasonable lack of awareness or understanding of specific regulations
- Isolated lapse

Matters of offender mitigation may include

- Offender's prompt reporting of offence and ready co-operation with regulatory authority
- Offender took steps to remedy the problem as soon as possible
- Good previous record

8. In the case of *Friskies Petcare (UK) Limited*[3] it was recommended that the HSE should set out in writing the facts of the case and the aggravating features, and the defence should do likewise with the mitigating features, so as to assist the court in coming to the proper basis for sentence after a guilty plea. Where the plea is entered on an agreed basis, that should be set out in writing for the court.

The level of fine

9. A fine should be the starting point for sentencing both companies and individuals for these offences. Sentencers should determine the appropriate level of fine in accordance with the Criminal Justice Act 2003, which requires offence seriousness and the financial circumstances of the offender to be taken into account.

10. For both individual and corporate offenders, the level of fine should reflect the extent to which the offender fell below the required standard. The sentence should also take account of any economic gain from the offence; it should not be cheaper to offend than to take the appropriate precautions.

11. The following factors will be relevant when sentencing corporate offenders:

- the fine must be substantial enough to have a real economic impact which, together with the bad publicity arising from prosecution, will bring home to both management and shareholders the need to improve regulatory compliance;
- appropriate fines for large companies might be beyond the summary fines limit. In such circumstances the case should be dealt with in the Crown Court. Where larger companies are dealt with in a magistrates' court, the court should look to a starting point near the maximum fine level and then consider aggravating and mitigating factors;
- care should be taken to ensure that fines imposed on smaller companies are not beyond their capability to pay. The court might not wish the fine to result in the company not being able to pay for improved procedures or to cause the company to go out of business. Where necessary, the payment of fines could be spread over a longer period than the usual 12 months;
- there is no single measure of ability to pay in respect of corporate offenders; turnover, profitability and liquidity should all be considered. It is not usual for an expert accountant to be available in summary cases;
- if a company does not produce its accounts, the court can assume that the company can pay whatever fine the court imposes.

---

[3] [2000] EWCA Crim 95

12. When sentencing public authorities, the court may have regard to the fact that a very substantial financial penalty may inhibit the performance of the public function that the body was set up to fulfil. This is not to suggest that public bodies are subject to a lesser standard of duty or care in safety and environmental matters, but it is proper for the court to take into account all the facts of the case, including how any financial penalty will be paid.[4]

Other sentencing options

13. A discharge will rarely be appropriate in these cases.
14. Compensation must be considered if there is a specific victim who has suffered injury, loss or damage. Under s.33B of the Environmental Protection Act 1990, a magistrates' court's power to impose compensation for clean-up costs is not limited to £5,000. Refer to pages [335–339] for further guidance on the approach to compensation.
15. Under section 42(1) of the Health and Safety at Work etc. Act 1974, the court may impose a remedial order in addition to or instead of imposing any punishment on the offender. Where the offence involves the acquisition or possession of an explosive article or substance, section 42(4) enables the court to order forfeiture of the explosive.
16. Where the offender is a director or senior manager of a company, the court may be able to exercise its power of disqualification under the Company Directors Disqualification Act 1986 (see page [343]). **Consult your legal adviser for further guidance regarding the exercise of these powers.**

Costs

17. The prosecution will normally claim the costs of investigation and presentation. These may be substantial and can incorporate time and activity expended on containing and making the area safe. The relevant principles are set out on page [346] above.

ROAD TRAFFIC OFFENCES
Disqualification

Obligatory disqualification

1. Some offences carry obligatory disqualification for a minimum of 12 months.[1] The minimum period is automatically increased where there have been certain previous convictions and disqualifications.
2. An offender must be disqualified for **at least two years** if he or she has been disqualified two or more times for a period of at least 56 days in the three years preceding the commission of the offence.[2] The following disqualifications are to be disregarded for the purposes of this provision:

   - interim disqualification;
   - disqualification where vehicle used for the purpose of crime;

---

[4] *R* v. *Southampton University Hospital NHS Trust* [2006] EWCA Crim 2971 (CA)
[1] Road Traffic Offenders Act 1988, s.34
[2] ibid., s.34(4)

- disqualification for stealing or taking a vehicle or going equipped to steal or take a vehicle.

3. An offender must be disqualified for **at least three years** if he or she is convicted of one of the following offences *and* has within the ten years preceding the commission of the offence been convicted of any of these offences:[3]

   - causing death by careless driving when under the influence of drink or drugs;
   - driving or attempting to drive while unfit;
   - driving or attempting to drive with excess alcohol;
   - failing to provide a specimen (drive/attempting to drive).

4. The individual offence guidelines above indicate whether disqualification is mandatory for the offence and the applicable minimum period. **Consult your legal adviser for further guidance.**

5. The period of disqualification may be reduced or avoided if there are special reasons.[4] These must relate to the offence; circumstances peculiar to the offender cannot constitute special reasons.[5] The Court of Appeal has established that, to constitute a special reason, a matter must:[6]

   - be a mitigating or extenuating circumstance;
   - not amount in law to a defence to the charge;
   - be directly connected with the commission of the offence;
   - be one which the court ought properly to take into consideration when imposing sentence.

6. **Consult your legal adviser for further guidance on special reasons applications.**

'Totting up' disqualification

7. Disqualification for a **minimum** of six months must be ordered if an offender incurs 12 penalty points or more within a three-year period.[7] The minimum period may be automatically increased if the offender has been disqualified within the preceding three years. Totting up disqualifications, unlike other disqualifications, erase all penalty points.

8. The period of a totting up disqualification can be reduced or avoided for exceptional hardship or other mitigating circumstances. No account is to be taken of hardship that is not exceptional hardship or circumstances alleged to make the offence not serious. Any circumstances taken into account in the preceding three years to reduce or avoid a totting disqualification must be disregarded.[8]

9. **Consult your legal adviser for further guidance on exceptional hardship applications.**

Discretionary disqualification

10. Whenever an offender is convicted of an endorsable offence or of taking a vehicle without consent, the court has a discretionary power to disqualify instead of imposing penalty points. The individual offence guidelines above indi-

---

3   Road Traffic Offenders Act 1988, s.34(3)
4   ibid., s.34(1)
5   *Whittal* v. *Kirby* [1946] 2 All ER 552 (CA)
6   *R* v. *Wickens* (1958) 42 Cr App R 436 (CA)
7   Road Traffic Offenders Act 1988, s.35
8   ibid.

cate whether the offence is endorsable and the number or range of penalty points it carries.

11. The number of variable points or the period of disqualification should reflect the seriousness of the offence. Some of the individual offence guidelines above include penalty points and/or periods of disqualification in the sentence starting points and ranges; however, the court is not precluded from sentencing outside the range where the facts justify it. Where a disqualification is for less than 56 days, there are some differences in effect compared with disqualification for a longer period; in particular, the licence will automatically come back into effect at the end of the disqualification period (instead of requiring application by the driver) and the disqualification is not taken into account for the purpose of increasing subsequent obligatory periods of disqualification.[9]

12. In some cases in which the court is considering discretionary disqualification, the offender may already have sufficient penalty points on his or her licence that he or she would be liable to a 'totting up' disqualification if further points were imposed. In these circumstances, the court should impose penalty points rather than discretionary disqualification so that the minimum totting up disqualification period applies (see paragraph 7 above).

Disqualification until a test is passed

13. Where an offender is convicted of dangerous driving, the court must order disqualification until an extended driving test is passed.

14. The court has discretion to disqualify until a test is passed where an offender is convicted of any endorsable offence.[10] Where disqualification is obligatory, the extended test applies. In other cases, it will be the ordinary test.

15. An offender disqualified as a 'totter' under the penalty points provisions may also be ordered to retake a driving test; in this case, the extended test applies.

16. The discretion to order a re-test is likely to be exercised where there is evidence of inexperience, incompetence or infirmity, or the disqualification period is lengthy (that is, the offender is going to be 'off the road' for a considerable time).

Reduced period of disqualification for completion of rehabilitation course

17. Where an offender is disqualified for 12 months or more in respect of an alcohol-related driving offence, the court may order that the period of disqualification will be reduced if the offender satisfactorily completes an approved rehabilitation course.[11]

18. Before offering an offender the opportunity to attend a course, the court must be satisfied that an approved course is available and must inform the offender of the effect of the order, the fees that the offender is required to pay, and when he or she must pay them.

19. The court should also explain that the offender may be required to satisfy the Secretary of State that he or she does not have a drink problem and is fit to drive before the offender's licence will be returned at the end of the disqualification period.[12]

[9]   ibid., ss.34(4), 35(2), 37(1A)
[10] ibid., s.36(4)
[11] Road Traffic Offenders Act 1988, s.34A
[12] Road Traffic Act 1988, s.94 and Motor Vehicles (Driving Licences) Regulations 1999, reg.74
[13] Magistrates' Courts Act 1980, s.11(4)

20. In general, a court should consider offering the opportunity to attend a course to all offenders convicted of a relevant offence for the first time. The court should be willing to consider offering an offender the opportunity to attend a second course where it considers there are good reasons. It will not usually be appropriate to give an offender the opportunity to attend a third course.

21. The reduction must be at least three months but cannot be more than one quarter of the total period of disqualification:

- a period of 12 months' disqualification must be reduced to nine months;
- in other cases, a reduction of one week should be made for every month of the disqualification so that, for example, a disqualification of 24 months will be reduced by 24 weeks.

22. When it makes the order, the court must specify a date for completion of the course which is at least two months before the end of the reduced period of disqualification.

Disqualification in the offender's absence

23. A court is able to disqualify an offender in absence provided that he or she has been given adequate notice of the hearing and that disqualification is to be considered.[13] It is recommended, however, that the court should avoid exercising this power wherever possible unless it is sure that the offender is aware of the hearing and the likely imposition of disqualification. This is because an offender who is disqualified in absence commits an offence by driving from the time the order is made, even if he or she has not yet received notification of it, and, as a result of the disqualification, is likely to be uninsured in relation to any injury or damage caused.

New drivers

24. Drivers who incur six points or more during the two-year probationary period after passing the driving test will have their licence revoked automatically by the Secretary of State; they will be able to drive only after application for a provisional licence pending the passing of a further test.[14]

25. An offender liable for an endorsement which will cause the licence to be revoked under the new drivers' provisions may ask the court to disqualify rather than impose points. This will avoid the requirement to take a further test. Generally, this would be inappropriate since it would circumvent the clear intention of Parliament.

DANGEROUS OFFENDERS

1. The Criminal Justice Act 2003 established a new regime for dealing with dangerous offenders. The provisions apply where an offender is convicted of a specified violent or sexual offence. They have been substantially amended by the Criminal Justice and Immigration Act 2008.

2. Specified offences are listed in schedule 15 to the Act and include affray, assault occasioning actual bodily harm, putting people in fear of violence, sexual assault and violent disorder. The individual offence guidelines above indicate whether the offence is specified under the Act. A specified offence which (in the case

---

[14] Road Traffic (New Drivers) Act 1995

of a person aged 18 years or over) is punishable with a maximum of life imprisonment or imprisonment for 10 years or more is defined as a 'serious offence'.

3. Where an offender is convicted of a specified offence that is not a 'serious offence', the court may impose an extended sentence of imprisonment.[1]

4. Where an offender is convicted of a specified offence that is a 'serious offence', the court may impose a life sentence or imprisonment for public protection.[2]

5. All these sentences may be imposed only in the Crown Court and only if the court is satisfied that there is a significant risk of serious harm from the offender committing a further specified offence. Even in such circumstances, a court has a discretion whether or not to impose a sentence under the dangerous offender provisions.

6. A significant change has been the requirement that (except where the offender has a previous conviction for one of the offences listed in schedule 15A to the 2003 Act)[3] a sentence under these provisions may be imposed only if the equivalent determinate sentence would have been at least 4 years.

7. Accordingly, it is very unlikely that a magistrates' court will need to consider these provisions specifically since an offence likely to result in a sentence of 4 years or more will be committed for trial or sentence under other provisions.

8. **Consult your legal adviser for further guidance.**

Inserted July 2008

INFORMAL WARNINGS, CANNABIS WARNINGS AND SIMPLE CAUTIONS

1. There are several alternatives to formal charges available to police, including informal warnings, cannabis warnings and simple cautions.

2. A cannabis warning may be given where the offender is found in possession of a small amount of cannabis consistent with personal use and the offender admits the elements of the offence.

3. A simple caution may be issued where there is evidence that the offender has committed an offence, the offender admits to the offence, and the offender agrees to being given the caution.

4. When sentencing an offender who has received a warning or simple caution on a previous occasion:

   • the warning or simple caution is not a previous conviction and, therefore, is not a statutory aggravating factor;

   • the earlier warning or simple caution does not increase the seriousness of the current offence.

CONDITIONAL CAUTIONS

1. The Criminal Justice Act 2003 empowers the Crown Prosecution Service to issue a conditional caution, which requires an offender to comply with rehabilitative and/or reparative conditions, as an alternative to prosecution. Before the caution can be given, the offender must admit the offence and consent to the conditions.

---

[1] Criminal Justice Act 2003, s.227 (as amended)
[2] ibid., s.225 (as amended)
[3] As inserted by Schedule 5 to the Criminal Justice and Immigration Act 2008

Approach to sentencing for offence for which offender was cautioned but failed to comply with conditions

2. If the offender fails, without reasonable cause, to comply with the conditional caution, he or she may be prosecuted for the original offence. When sentencing in such a case:

    -   the offender's non-compliance with the conditional caution does not increase the seriousness of the original offence and must not be regarded as an aggravating factor;
    -   the offender's non-compliance may be relevant to selection of the type of sentence. For example, it may indicate that it is inappropriate to include certain requirements as part of a community order. The circumstances of the offender's failure to satisfy the conditions, and any partial compliance, will be relevant to this assessment.

Approach to sentencing for later offence where offender has had a previous conditional caution

3. When sentencing an offender who has received a conditional caution in respect of an earlier offence:

    -   a conditional caution is not a previous conviction and, therefore, is not a statutory aggravating factor;
    -   the earlier conditional caution does not increase the level of seriousness of the current offence;
    -   nevertheless, the offender's response to the caution may properly influence the court's assessment of the offender's suitability for a particular sentence, so long as it remains within the limits established by the seriousness of the current offence.

PENALTY NOTICES – FIXED PENALTY NOTICES AND PENALTY NOTICES FOR DISORDER

1. Penalty notices may be issued as an alternative to prosecution in respect of a range of offences. Unlike conditional cautions, an admission of guilt is not a prerequisite to issuing a penalty notice.
2. An offender who is issued with a penalty notice may nevertheless be prosecuted for the offence if he or she:

    -   asks to be tried for the offence;
    -   fails to pay the penalty within the period stipulated in the notice and the prosecutor decides to proceed with charges.[1]

Approach to sentencing for offence for which penalty notice was available

3. When sentencing in cases in which a penalty notice was available:

---

[1] In some cases of non-payment, the penalty is automatically registered and enforceable as a fine without need for recourse to the courts. This procedure applies to penalty notices for disorder and fixed penalty notices issued in respect of certain road traffic offences but not to fixed penalty notices issued for most other criminal offences

- the fact that the offender did not take advantage of the penalty (whether that was by requesting a hearing or failing to pay within the specified time-frame) does not increase the seriousness of the offence and must not be regarded as an aggravating factor. The appropriate sentence must be determined in accordance with the sentencing principles set out above (including the amount of any fine, which must take an offender's financial circumstances into account), disregarding the availability of the penalty;
- where a penalty notice was not offered or taken up for reasons unconnected with the offence itself, such as administrative difficulties, the starting point should be a fine equivalent to the amount of the penalty and no order of costs should be imposed. The offender should not be disadvantaged by the unavailability of the penalty notice in these circumstances. A list of offences for which penalty notices are available, and the amount of the penalty, is set out in Annex B.

Approach to sentencing for later offence where offender has had previous penalty notices

4. The fact that an offender has previously been issued with a penalty notice does not increase the seriousness of the current offence and must not be regarded as an aggravating factor. It may, however, properly influence the court's assessment of the offender's suitability for a particular sentence, so long as it remains within the limits established by the seriousness of the current offence.

PRE-SENTENCE REPORTS

1. The purpose of a pre-sentence report ('PSR') is to provide information to help the court decide on the most suitable sentence. In relation to an offender aged 18 or over, unless the court considers a report to be unnecessary, it is required to request a report before deciding:

- that the community or custody threshold is passed;
- what is the shortest term of a custodial sentence that is commensurate with the seriousness of the offence;
- whether the restrictions on liberty within a community order are commensurate with the seriousness of the offence; and
- whether the requirements are suitable for the offender.[1]

2. A report should not normally be requested where the court considers that it is appropriate to impose a fine.
3. A report may be oral or written.
4. Written reports may be either:

Fast delivery reports ('FDR')

- Completed without a full OASys assessment.
- Where community orders are being considered, generally appropriate for low or medium seriousness cases and may be appropriate in some high seriousness cases.
- Should normally be available within 24 hours.

---

[1] Criminal Justice Act 2003, ss.156(3) and 156(4)

Standard delivery reports ('SDR')

- Based on a full OASys assessment.
- Generally appropriate where a custodial sentence is being considered, although in some straightforward cases a fast delivery PSR may be sufficient.
- Where community orders are being considered, generally appropriate for high seriousness cases.
- Should normally be available within 15 working days; 10 working days if the offender is in custody.

Probation staff are able to determine the most appropriate type of report based on the circumstances of the case and the requirements of the court.

5. Every report should contain:[2]

- basic facts about the offender and the sources used to prepare the report;
- an offence analysis;
- an assessment of the offender;
- an assessment of the risk of harm to the public and the likelihood of re-offending;
- a sentencing proposal.

VICTIM PERSONAL STATEMENTS

1. Victim personal statements give victims a formal opportunity to say how a crime has affected them. Where the victim has chosen to make such a statement, a court should consider and take it into account prior to passing sentence.

2. The Consolidated Criminal Practice Direction (as amended March 2007) emphasises that:

- evidence of the effects of an offence on the victim must be in the form of a witness statement under section 9 of the Criminal Justice Act 1967 or an expert's report;
- the statement must be served on the defence prior to sentence;
- except where inferences can properly be drawn from the nature of or circumstances surrounding the offence, the court must not make assumptions unsupported by evidence about the effects of an offence on the victim;
- the court must pass what it judges to be the appropriate sentence having regard to the circumstances of the offence and the offender, taking into account, so far as the court considers it appropriate, the consequences to the victim;
- the opinions of the victim or the victim's close relatives as to what the sentence should be are not relevant.

3. For cases involving sexual offences, see also page [336] regarding the relevance of the victim's views to any compensation order that may be imposed.

ANNEX A: AVAILABILITY OF ANCILLARY ORDERS

The lists below identify offences covered in the MCSG for which particular ancillary orders are available. **In all cases, consult your legal adviser regarding available orders and their specific requirements and effects.**

---

[2]   Probation Bench Handbook (2005)

Football banning orders – Football Spectators Act 1989, s.14A

Available on conviction of a 'relevant offence', listed in schedule 1 of the Football Spectators Act 1989.

These include:

- possession of alcohol or being drunk while entering/trying to enter ground – Sporting Events (Control of Alcohol etc) Act 1985, s.2;
- disorderly behaviour – Public Order Act 1986, s.5 – committed:

  (a)   during a period relevant to a football match (see below) at any premises while the offender was at, or was entering or leaving or trying to enter or leave, the premises;

  (b)   on a journey to or from a football match and the court makes a declaration that the offence related to football matches; or

  (c)   during a period relevant to a football match (see below) and the court makes a declaration that the offence related to that match;

- any offence involving the use or threat of violence towards another person committed:

  (a)   during a period relevant to a football match (see below) at any premises while the offender was at, or was entering or leaving or trying to enter or leave, the premises;

  (b)   on a journey to or from a football match and the court makes a declaration that the offence related to football matches; or

  (c)   during a period relevant to a football match (see below) and the court makes a declaration that the offence related to that match;

- any offence involving the use or threat of violence towards property committed:

  (a)   during a period relevant to a football match (see below) at any premises while the offender was at, or was entering or leaving or trying to enter or leave, the premises;

  (b)   on a journey to or from a football match and the court makes a declaration that the offence related to football matches; or

  (c)   during a period relevant to a football match (see below) and the court makes a declaration that the offence related to that match;

- any offence involving the use, carrying or possession of an offensive weapon or firearm committed:

  (a)   during a period relevant to a football match (see below) at any premises while the offender was at, or was entering or leaving or trying to enter or leave, the premises;

  (b)   on a journey to or from a football match and the court makes a declaration that the offence related to football matches; or

  (c)   during a period relevant to a football match (see below) and the court makes a declaration that the offence related to that match;

- drunk and disorderly – Criminal Justice Act 1967, s.91(1) – committed on a journey to or from a football match and the court makes a declaration that the offence related to football matches;
- driving/attempting to drive when unfit through drink or drugs – Road Traffic Act 1988, s.4 – committed on a journey to or from a football match and the court makes a declaration that the offence related to football matches;

- in charge of a vehicle when unfit through drink or drugs – Road Traffic Act 1988, s.4 – committed on a journey to or from a football match and the court makes a declaration that the offence related to football matches;
- driving/attempting to drive with excess alcohol – Road Traffic Act 1988, s.5 – committed on a journey to or from a football match and the court makes a declaration that the offence related to football matches;
- in charge of a vehicle with excess alcohol – Road Traffic Act 1988, s.5 – committed on a journey to or from a football match and the court makes a declaration that the offence related to football matches;
- any offence under the Football (Offences) Act 1991;
- unauthorised sale of tickets – Criminal Justice and Public Order Act 1994, s.166.

The following periods are 'relevant' to a football match:

(a) the period beginning:

    (i)   two hours before the start of the match; or
    (ii) two hours before the time at which it is advertised to start; or
    (iii) with the time at which spectators are first admitted to the premises,
    whichever is the earliest, and ending one hour after the end of the match;

(b) where a match advertised to start at a particular time on a particular day is post-poned to a later day, or does not take place, the period in the advertised day beginning two hours before and ending one hour after that time.

Forfeiture or suspension of personal liquor licence – Licensing Act 2003, s.129

Available on conviction of a 'relevant offence', listed in schedule 4 of the Licensing Act 2003.

    These include:

- an offence under the Licensing Act 2003;
- an offence under the Firearms Act 1968;
- theft – Theft Act 1968, s.1;
- burglary – Theft Act 1968, s.9;
- abstracting electricity – Theft Act 1968, s.13;
- handling stolen goods – Theft Act 1968, s.22;
- going equipped for theft – Theft Act 1968, s.25;
- production of a controlled drug – Misuse of Drugs Act 1971, s.4(2);
- supply of a controlled drug – Misuse of Drugs Act 1971, s.4(3);
- possession of a controlled drug with intent to supply – Misuse of Drugs Act 1971, s.5(3);
- evasion of duty – Customs and Excise Management Act 1979, s.170 (excluding s.170(1)(a));
- driving/attempting to drive when unfit through drink or drugs – Road Traffic Act 1988, s.4;
- in charge of a vehicle when unfit through drink or drugs – Road Traffic Act 1988, s.4;
- driving/attempting to drive with excess alcohol – Road Traffic Act 1988, s.5;
- in charge of a vehicle with excess alcohol – Road Traffic Act 1988, s.5;
- unauthorised use of trade mark where the goods in question are or include alcohol – Trade Marks Act 1994, ss.92(1) and 92(2);
- sexual assault – Sexual Offences Act 2003, s.3;
- exploitation of prostitution – Sexual Offences Act 2003, ss.52 and 53;
- exposure – Sexual Offences Act 2003, s.66;

- voyeurism – Sexual Offences Act 2003, s.67;
- a violent offence, being any offence which leads, or is intended or likely to lead, to death or to physical injury.

Sexual offences prevention orders

Available in respect of an offence listed in schedule 3 or 5 of the Sexual Offences Act 2003. These include:

- sexual assault – Sexual Offences Act 2003, s.3 – provided that:

  (a)   where the offender was under 18, he or she has been sentenced to at least 12 months' imprisonment;

  (b)   in any other case:

    (i)   the victim was under 18; or
    (ii)   the offender has been sentenced to a term of imprisonment, detained in a hospital, or made the subject of a community sentence of at least 12 months;

- exposure – Sexual Offences Act 2003, s.66 – provided that:

  (a)   where the offender was under 18, he or she has been sentenced to at least 12 months' imprisonment;

  (b)   in any other case:

    (i)   the victim was under 18; or
    (ii)   the offender has been sentenced to a term of imprisonment, detained in a hospital, or made the subject of a community sentence of at least 12 months;

- voyeurism – Sexual Offences Act 2003, s.67 – provided that:

  (a)   where the offender was under 18, he or she has been sentenced to at least 12 months' imprisonment;

  (b)   in any other case:

    (i)   the victim was under 18; or
    (ii)   the offender has been sentenced to a term of imprisonment, detained in a hospital, or made the subject of a community sentence of at least 12 months;

- threats to kill – Offences against the Person Act 1861, s.16;
- wounding/causing grievous bodily harm – Offences against the Person Act 1861, s.20;
- assault with intent to resist arrest – Offences against the Person Act 1861, s.38;
- assault occasioning actual bodily harm – Offences against the Person Act 1861, s.47;
- burglary with intent to inflict grievous bodily harm or to do unlawful damage to a building/anything within it – Theft Act 1968, s.9;
- arson – Criminal Damage Act 1971, s.1;
- violent disorder – Public Order Act 1986, s.2;
- affray – Public Order Act 1986, s.3;
- harassment – conduct causing fear of violence – Protection from Harassment Act 1994, s.4;
- racially or religiously aggravated wounding/causing grievous bodily harm – Crime and Disorder Act 1998, s.29;

- racially or religiously aggravated assault occasioning actual bodily harm – Crime and Disorder Act 1998, s.29;
- racially or religiously aggravated common assault – Crime and Disorder Act 1998, s.29;
- racially or religiously aggravated threatening behaviour – Crime and Disorder Act 1998, s.31(1)(a);
- racially or religiously aggravated disorderly behaviour with intent to cause harassment, alarm or distress – Crime and Disorder Act 1998, s.31(1)(b);
- exploitation of prostitution – Sexual Offences Act 2003, ss.52 and 53.

ANNEX B: OFFENCES FOR WHICH PENALTY NOTICES ARE AVAILABLE

The tables below list the offences covered in the MCSG for which penalty notices are available and the amount of the penalty. **Consult your legal adviser for further guidance.**

Penalty notices for disorder

Offence	Legislation	Amount
Criminal damage (where damage under £500 in value, and not normally where damage over £300)	Criminal Damage Act 1971, s.1	£80
Disorderly behaviour	Public Order Act 1986, s.5	£80
Drunk and disorderly	Criminal Justice Act 1967, s.91	£80
Sale of alcohol to drunk person on relevant premises (not including off-licenses)	Licensing Act 2003, s.141	£80
Sale of alcohol to person under 18 (staff only; licensees should be subject of a summons)	Licensing Act 2003, s.146	£80
Theft from a shop (where goods under £200 in value, and not normally where goods over £100)	Theft Act 1968, s.1	£80

Fixed penalty notices

Offence	Legislation	Amount	Penalty points
Brakes, steering or tyres defective	Road Traffic Act 1988, s.41A	£60	3
Breach of other construction and use requirements	Road Traffic Act 1988, s.42	£60	3
Driving other than in accordance with licence	Road Traffic Act 1988, s.87(1)	£60	3
Failing to comply with police officer signal	Road Traffic Act 1988, s.35	£30	3
Failing to comply with traffic sign	Road Traffic Act 1988, s.36	£60	3

Failing to supply details of driver's identity	Road Traffic Act 1988, s.172	£120	6
No insurance	Road Traffic Act 1988, s.143	£200	6
No test certificate	Road Traffic Act 1988, s.47	£30	–
Overloading/exceeding axle weight	Road Traffic Act 1988, s.41B	£30	–
Pelican/zebra crossing contravention	Road Traffic Regulation Act 1984, s.25(5)	£60	3
Railway fare evasion (where penalty notice scheme in operation by train operator)	Railways (Penalty Fares) Regulations 1994	£20 or twice the full single fare to next stop, whichever is greater	–
Seat belt offences	Road Traffic Act 1988, s.14	£30	–
School non-attendance	Education Act 1996, s.444(1)	£50 if paid within 28 days; £100 if paid within 42 days	–
Speeding	Road Traffic Regulation Act 1984, s.89(1)	£60	3
Using hand-held mobile phone while driving	Road Traffic Act 1988, s.41D	£60	3
Using vehicle in dangerous condition	Road Traffic Act 1988, s.40A	£60	3

367

SENTENCING STRUCTURE

> **1. Offence seriousness (culpability and harm)**
> **A. Identify the appropriate starting point**

- Consider which of the examples of offence activity corresponds most closely to the circumstances of the case to identify the appropriate **starting point**.
- Starting points are based on a **first time offender pleading not guilty**.
- Refer to the following where starting point is, or range includes, a:

  (i)   fine – pages [320–327];
  (ii) community order – pages [331–333];
  (iii) custodial sentence – pages [333–335].

- Refer to pages [317–318] for the meaning of the terms 'starting point', 'range' and 'first time offender'.

> **1. Offence seriousness (culpability and harm)**
> **B. Consider the effect of aggravating and mitigating factors**

- Move up or down from the starting point to reflect aggravating or mitigating factors that affect the seriousness of the offence to reach a provisional sentence.
- Common aggravating and mitigating factors are set out overleaf; relevant factors are also identified in the individual offence guidelines. **These lists are not exhaustive.**
- Do not double-count any aggravating or mitigating factors in the description of the activity used to reach the starting point.
- The **range** is the bracket into which the provisional sentence will normally fall but the court is not precluded from going outside the range where the facts justify it.
- Previous convictions which aggravate the seriousness of the current offence may take the provisional sentence beyond the range, especially if there are significant other aggravating factors present.

> **2. Form a preliminary view of the appropriate sentence, then consider offender mitigation**

- Matters of offender mitigation may include remorse and admissions to police in interview.

> **3. Consider a reduction for a guilty plea**

- Apply the sliding scale reduction for a guilty plea to punitive elements of the sentence – refer to page [178].
- Application of the reduction may take the sentence below the range in some cases.

> **4. Consider ancillary orders, including compensation**

- Refer to pages [339–346] and Annex A for guidance on available ancillary orders.
- Consider compensation in every case where the offending has resulted in personal injury, loss or damage – give reasons if order not made – see pages [335–339].

> **5. Decide sentence**
> **Give reasons**

- Review the total sentence to ensure that it is proportionate to the offending behaviour and properly balanced.
- Give reasons for the sentence passed, including any ancillary orders.
- State if the sentence has been reduced to reflect a guilty plea; indicate what the sentence would otherwise have been.
- Explain if the sentence is of a different kind or outside the range indicated in the guidelines.

LIST OF AGGRAVATING AND MITIGATING FACTORS – TAKEN FROM SENTENCING GUIDELINES COUNCIL GUIDELINE *OVERARCHING PRINCIPLES: SERIOUSNESS*

Aggravating factors

Factors indicating higher culpability:

- Offence committed whilst on bail for other offences
- Failure to respond to previous sentences
- Offence was racially or religiously aggravated
- Offence motivated by, or demonstrating, hostility to the victim based on his or her sexual orientation (or presumed sexual orientation)
- Offence motivated by, or demonstrating, hostility based on the victim's disability (or presumed disability)
- Previous conviction(s), particularly where a pattern of repeat offending is disclosed
- Planning of an offence
- An intention to commit more serious harm than actually resulted from the offence
- Offenders operating in groups or gangs
- 'Professional' offending
- Commission of the offence for financial gain (where this is not inherent in the offence itself)
- High level of profit from the offence
- An attempt to conceal or dispose of evidence
- Failure to respond to warnings or concerns expressed by others about the offender's behaviour
- Offence committed whilst on licence
- Offence motivated by hostility towards a minority group, or a member or members of it
- Deliberate targeting of vulnerable victim(s)
- Commission of an offence while under the influence of alcohol or drugs
- Use of a weapon to frighten or injure victim
- Deliberate and gratuitous violence or damage to property, over and above what is needed to carry out the offence
- Abuse of power
- Abuse of a position of trust

Factors indicating a more than usually serious degree of harm:

- Multiple victims
- An especially serious physical or psychological effect on the victim, even if unintended
- A sustained assault or repeated assaults on the same victim
- Victim is particularly vulnerable
- Location of the offence (for example, in an isolated place)
- Offence is committed against those working in the public sector or providing a service to the public
- Presence of others e.g. relatives, especially children or partner of the victim
- Additional degradation of the victim (e.g. taking photographs of a victim as part of a sexual offence)
- In property offences, high value (including sentimental value) of property to the victim, or substantial consequential loss (e.g. where the theft of equipment causes serious disruption to a victim's life or business)

Mitigating factors

Factors indicating lower culpability:

- A greater degree of provocation than normally expected
- Mental illness or disability
- Youth or age, where it affects the responsibility of the individual defendant
- The fact that the offender played only a minor role in the offence

Offender mitigation

- Genuine remorse
- Admissions to police in interview
- Ready co-operation with authorities

Offence guidelines – alphabetical index

Offence guidelines – group index

378

Additional note to knife crime guideline

SENTENCING FOR POSSESSION OF A WEAPON – KNIFE CRIME

A guideline is provided on pages 32–33 of the Magistrates' Court Sentencing Guidelines for sentencing offenders found in possession of a bladed article or offensive weapon. Significant attention has been paid to this guideline ahead of it coming into effect as a result of the current focus of the press/media on violent crimes involving knives.

The purpose of this note is to set out the effect of the guideline (which is not limited to the possession of knives) and of the Court of Appeal decision in *Povey*.[1]

1. The guideline has been strengthened from the previous Court of Appeal guideline *Celaire and Poulton*[2] and is likely to result in many more offences (committed by adult offenders) crossing the custody threshold.

2. In *Povey*, attention was drawn to the recent escalation in offences of this kind and the importance, for the time being, of courts focussing on the purposes of sentencing of reduction of crime (including its reduction by deterrence) and the protection of the public.

3. In *Povey*, the Court of Appeal recommended that the Magistrates' Court Sentencing Guidelines guideline should normally be applied at the most severe end of the appropriate range to reflect current prevalence concerns. This will be likely to lead to more cases being sentenced in the Crown Court.

4. When the current concerns have been overcome, courts will be notified that the approach should return to the guideline as published.

5. The guideline provides three categories of seriousness:

   - level 1 is for the situation where a person has a weapon or bladed article, is not in a 'dangerous circumstance' and the weapon or bladed article is not used to threaten or to cause fear; in those circumstances:

     - applying *Povey*, where the offensive weapon is a knife the starting point would be close to 12 weeks' custody for a first time adult offender who has pleaded not guilty;
     - in relation to an offensive weapon other than a knife, the starting point for a first time adult offender who has pleaded not guilty is a high level community order.

   - level 2 is for the situation where a weapon is in the possession of the offender in 'dangerous circumstances' but is not used to threaten or to cause fear; in those circumstances:

---

[1] [2008] EWCA Crim 1261
[2] [2003] 1 Cr.App.R.(S) 116

– applying *Povey*, where the offensive weapon is a knife the starting point for a first time adult offender who has pleaded not guilty is committal to the Crown Court and, therefore, a custodial sentence in excess of 6 months;

– in relation to an offensive weapon other than a knife, the starting point for a first time adult offender who has pleaded not guilty is a custodial sentence of 6 weeks.

- level 3 is for the situation where a weapon is used in dangerous circumstances to threaten or cause fear; in those circumstances, both the starting point and range for a first time adult offender who has pleaded not guilty are for sentencing in the Crown Court and, therefore, in excess of 6 months custody.

'Dangerous circumstances' has not been judicially defined but was used in the previous Court of Appeal guideline judgment in *Celaire and Poulton*. In relation to a knife, a circumstance is likely to be dangerous if there is a real possibility that it could be used.

Additional note to burglary in a dwelling guideline

In the Magistrates' Court Sentencing Guidelines, pages 34/35 provide a summary of the effect of the Court of Appeal guideline judgment in *McInerney* and *Keating* as it applies both to mode of trial (allocation) and to sentencing decisions in a magistrates' court. In the light of experience and pending any fuller consideration by the Sentencing Guidelines Council, that judgment has been reviewed and clarified by the Court of Appeal in *R.* v. *Saw and others* [2009] EWCA Crim 1.

The purpose of this note is to clarify the effect of the decision on the application of this part of the Magistrates' Court Sentencing Guidelines.

APPROACH TO SENTENCING – KEY POINTS

1. The aim of the judgment is to achieve consistency of approach, clearly recognising the seriousness of this offence – not only is it an offence against property but it is also an offence against the person. Particular focus is required on the impact of the offence on those living in the burgled house; sentences should reflect the level of harmful consequences even when not intended by the offender.
2. The sentence must reflect the criminality of the offender. Previous convictions and the record of an offender are of more significance than in the case of some other crimes. Burglary of a dwelling should be treated as more serious when committed by an offender with previous convictions for relevant dishonesty than an identical offence committed by a first offender.
3. The judgment states that it does not add anything to the Magistrates' Court Sentencing Guidelines, emphasising the importance of addressing the aggravating and mitigating factors referred to in the judgment. The Magistrates' Court Sentencing Guidelines currently provide for committal to the Crown Court where an aggravating feature is present and sentence within the powers of the Crown Court is included within the range in some other circumstances.
4. A non-exhaustive list of aggravating and mitigating features commonly encountered in burglary is provided in the judgment; this is more extensive than the list in the Magistrates' Court Sentencing Guidelines derived from *McInerney* and *Keating*. They are summarised at the end of this note. The importance of the aggravating features derives from the *increase in the impact* of the offence that results from them, or from the *increase in the culpability* of the offender that they demonstrate, or from a combination of the two.

THE GUIDELINE – CATEGORIES OF SERIOUSNESS

The Magistrates' Court Sentencing Guidelines set out three categories of offence seriousness:

Category 1 – Offences likely to be able to be sentenced within the jurisdiction of a magistrates' court (when committed by a first time offender) are those where the entry to the premises was unforced, the property stolen of low value and there were *no* aggravating features; the starting point is a community sentence. In determining whether an aggravating feature was present, the court should refer to the list set out in *Saw and others*.

Category 2 – Where the entry was forced, the goods were not of high value, and there were *no* aggravating features, the sentencing range commences within the jurisdiction of a magistrates' court but ends within the jurisdiction of the Crown Court; the starting point is 12 weeks custody. In determining whether an aggravating feature was present, the court should refer to the list set out in *Saw and others*.

Although *Saw and others* requires particular focus on the impact of the offence on the victim, it confirms that a low level burglary with minimal loss and minimal damage and without raised culpability or raised impact, committed by a first time offender, may be dealt with by way of a community order rather than an immediate custodial penalty.

Category 3 – An offence would be expected to be committed to the Crown Court where the goods stolen were of high value or any aggravating feature was present.

Saw and others provides that the court must address the overall criminality of the offender (in the light of previous convictions) and the impact of the offence on the victim(s):

- where there is *limited raised culpability and/or impact*, it is likely that the sentence will be within a general range of 9 to 18 months custody; a shorter sentence (including the making of a community order) may be appropriate where it is established that the offender played a subsidiary role or was exploited by other offenders;
- where there is *seriously raised culpability and/or serious impact*, the starting point should be a custodial sentence in excess of 18 months; a community order should be considered only in the most extreme and exceptional circumstances.

As noted on page 34 of the Magistrates' Court Sentencing Guidelines, where a case otherwise appropriate for sentence in the Crown Court is, on its own particular facts likely to attract a community order, it should nonetheless be sentenced in the Crown Court so that any sanction for non-compliance can be imposed with the powers of that court rather than within the more limited powers of a magistrates' court.

AGGRAVATING AND MITIGATING FEATURES (NOT EXHAUSTIVE)

Aggravating features:

- the use or threat of force on or against the victim (NB: this would make the offence triable on indictment only),
- trauma to the victim beyond that normally associated with this type of offence,
- pre-meditation and professional planning or organisation, such as by offenders working in groups or when housebreaking implements are carried
- vandalism of the premises burgled,
- deliberate targeting of any vulnerable victim,

- deliberate targeting of any victim,
- the presence of the occupier whether at night or during the day,
- high economic or sentimental value of the property stolen or damaged, offence committed on bail or shortly after imposition of a non-custodial sentence,
- two or more burglaries of homes rather than a single offence,
- the offender's previous convictions.

Mitigating features:

- nothing, or only property of very low value is taken,
- offender played a minor part in the burglary, and treated by others in group as if he were on the fringes exploited by others
- offence committed on impulse
- age and state of health (mental and physical)
- good character
- evidence of genuine regret and remorse
- ready co-operation with the police
- positive response to previous sentences

Consult your legal adviser for guidance

Index